T0281041

Lecture Notes in Computer Science 14710

Founding Editors

Gerhard Goos
Juris Hartmanis

Editorial Board Members

The series Lecture Notes in Computer Science (LNCS), including its subseries Lecture Notes in Artificial Intelligence (LNAI) and Lecture Notes in Bioinformatics (LNBI), has established itself as a medium for the publication of new developments in computer science and information technology research, teaching, and education.

LNCS enjoys close cooperation with the computer science R & D community, the series counts many renowned academics among its volume editors and paper authors, and collaborates with prestigious societies. Its mission is to serve this international community by providing an invaluable service, mainly focused on the publication of conference and workshop proceedings and postproceedings. LNCS commenced publication in 1973.

Vincent G. Duffy

Editor

Digital Human Modeling and Applications in Health, Safety, Ergonomics and Risk Management

15th International Conference, DHM 2024
Held as Part of the 26th HCI International Conference, HCII 2024
Washington, DC, USA, June 29 – July 4, 2024
Proceedings, Part II

 Springer

Editor
Vincent G. Duffy
Purdue University
West Lafayette, IN, USA

ISSN 0302-9743   ISSN 1611-3349 (electronic)
Lecture Notes in Computer Science
ISBN 978-3-031-61062-2   ISBN 978-3-031-61063-9 (eBook)
https://doi.org/10.1007/978-3-031-61063-9

This Springer imprint is published by the registered company Springer Nature Switzerland AG
The registered company address is: Gewerbestrasse 11, 6330 Cham, Switzerland

If disposing of this product, please recycle the paper.

Foreword

This year we celebrate 40 years since the establishment of the HCI International (HCII) Conference, which has been a hub for presenting groundbreaking research and novel ideas and collaboration for people from all over the world.

The HCII conference was founded in 1984 by Prof. Gavriel Salvendy (Purdue University, USA, Tsinghua University, P.R. China, and University of Central Florida, USA) and the first event of the series, "1st USA-Japan Conference on Human-Computer Interaction", was held in Honolulu, Hawaii, USA, 18–20 August. Since then, HCI International is held jointly with several Thematic Areas and Affiliated Conferences, with each one under the auspices of a distinguished international Program Board and under one management and one registration. Twenty-six HCI International Conferences have been organized so far (every two years until 2013, and annually thereafter).

Over the years, this conference has served as a platform for scholars, researchers, industry experts and students to exchange ideas, connect, and address challenges in the ever-evolving HCI field. Throughout these 40 years, the conference has evolved itself, adapting to new technologies and emerging trends, while staying committed to its core mission of advancing knowledge and driving change.

As we celebrate this milestone anniversary, we reflect on the contributions of its founding members and appreciate the commitment of its current and past Affiliated Conference Program Board Chairs and members. We are also thankful to all past conference attendees who have shaped this community into what it is today.

The 26th International Conference on Human-Computer Interaction, HCI International 2024 (HCII 2024), was held as a 'hybrid' event at the Washington Hilton Hotel, Washington, DC, USA, during 29 June – 4 July 2024. It incorporated the 21 thematic areas and affiliated conferences listed below.

A total of 5108 individuals from academia, research institutes, industry, and government agencies from 85 countries submitted contributions, and 1271 papers and 309 posters were included in the volumes of the proceedings that were published just before the start of the conference, these are listed below. The contributions thoroughly cover the entire field of human-computer interaction, addressing major advances in knowledge and effective use of computers in a variety of application areas. These papers provide academics, researchers, engineers, scientists, practitioners and students with state-of-the-art information on the most recent advances in HCI.

The HCI International (HCII) conference also offers the option of presenting 'Late Breaking Work', and this applies both for papers and posters, with corresponding volumes of proceedings that will be published after the conference. Full papers will be included in the 'HCII 2024 - Late Breaking Papers' volumes of the proceedings to be published in the Springer LNCS series, while 'Poster Extended Abstracts' will be included as short research papers in the 'HCII 2024 - Late Breaking Posters' volumes to be published in the Springer CCIS series.

I would like to thank the Program Board Chairs and the members of the Program Boards of all thematic areas and affiliated conferences for their contribution towards the high scientific quality and overall success of the HCI International 2024 conference. Their manifold support in terms of paper reviewing (single-blind review process, with a minimum of two reviews per submission), session organization and their willingness to act as goodwill ambassadors for the conference is most highly appreciated.

This conference would not have been possible without the continuous and unwavering support and advice of Gavriel Salvendy, founder, General Chair Emeritus, and Scientific Advisor. For his outstanding efforts, I would like to express my sincere appreciation to Abbas Moallem, Communications Chair and Editor of HCI International News.

July 2024   Constantine Stephanidis

HCI International 2024 Thematic Areas and Affiliated Conferences

- HCI: Human-Computer Interaction Thematic Area
- HIMI: Human Interface and the Management of Information Thematic Area
- EPCE: 21st International Conference on Engineering Psychology and Cognitive Ergonomics
- AC: 18th International Conference on Augmented Cognition
- UAHCI: 18th International Conference on Universal Access in Human-Computer Interaction
- CCD: 16th International Conference on Cross-Cultural Design
- SCSM: 16th International Conference on Social Computing and Social Media
- VAMR: 16th International Conference on Virtual, Augmented and Mixed Reality
- DHM: 15th International Conference on Digital Human Modeling & Applications in Health, Safety, Ergonomics & Risk Management
- DUXU: 13th International Conference on Design, User Experience and Usability
- C&C: 12th International Conference on Culture and Computing
- DAPI: 12th International Conference on Distributed, Ambient and Pervasive Interactions
- HCIBGO: 11th International Conference on HCI in Business, Government and Organizations
- LCT: 11th International Conference on Learning and Collaboration Technologies
- ITAP: 10th International Conference on Human Aspects of IT for the Aged Population
- AIS: 6th International Conference on Adaptive Instructional Systems
- HCI-CPT: 6th International Conference on HCI for Cybersecurity, Privacy and Trust
- HCI-Games: 6th International Conference on HCI in Games
- MobiTAS: 6th International Conference on HCI in Mobility, Transport and Automotive Systems
- AI-HCI: 5th International Conference on Artificial Intelligence in HCI
- MOBILE: 5th International Conference on Human-Centered Design, Operation and Evaluation of Mobile Communications

List of Conference Proceedings Volumes Appearing Before the Conference

1. LNCS 14684, Human-Computer Interaction: Part I, edited by Masaaki Kurosu and Ayako Hashizume
2. LNCS 14685, Human-Computer Interaction: Part II, edited by Masaaki Kurosu and Ayako Hashizume
3. LNCS 14686, Human-Computer Interaction: Part III, edited by Masaaki Kurosu and Ayako Hashizume
4. LNCS 14687, Human-Computer Interaction: Part IV, edited by Masaaki Kurosu and Ayako Hashizume
5. LNCS 14688, Human-Computer Interaction: Part V, edited by Masaaki Kurosu and Ayako Hashizume
6. LNCS 14689, Human Interface and the Management of Information: Part I, edited by Hirohiko Mori and Yumi Asahi
7. LNCS 14690, Human Interface and the Management of Information: Part II, edited by Hirohiko Mori and Yumi Asahi
8. LNCS 14691, Human Interface and the Management of Information: Part III, edited by Hirohiko Mori and Yumi Asahi
9. LNAI 14692, Engineering Psychology and Cognitive Ergonomics: Part I, edited by Don Harris and Wen-Chin Li
10. LNAI 14693, Engineering Psychology and Cognitive Ergonomics: Part II, edited by Don Harris and Wen-Chin Li
11. LNAI 14694, Augmented Cognition, Part I, edited by Dylan D. Schmorrow and Cali M. Fidopiastis
12. LNAI 14695, Augmented Cognition, Part II, edited by Dylan D. Schmorrow and Cali M. Fidopiastis
13. LNCS 14696, Universal Access in Human-Computer Interaction: Part I, edited by Margherita Antona and Constantine Stephanidis
14. LNCS 14697, Universal Access in Human-Computer Interaction: Part II, edited by Margherita Antona and Constantine Stephanidis
15. LNCS 14698, Universal Access in Human-Computer Interaction: Part III, edited by Margherita Antona and Constantine Stephanidis
16. LNCS 14699, Cross-Cultural Design: Part I, edited by Pei-Luen Patrick Rau
17. LNCS 14700, Cross-Cultural Design: Part II, edited by Pei-Luen Patrick Rau
18. LNCS 14701, Cross-Cultural Design: Part III, edited by Pei-Luen Patrick Rau
19. LNCS 14702, Cross-Cultural Design: Part IV, edited by Pei-Luen Patrick Rau
20. LNCS 14703, Social Computing and Social Media: Part I, edited by Adela Coman and Simona Vasilache
21. LNCS 14704, Social Computing and Social Media: Part II, edited by Adela Coman and Simona Vasilache
22. LNCS 14705, Social Computing and Social Media: Part III, edited by Adela Coman and Simona Vasilache

47. LNCS 14730, HCI in Games: Part I, edited by Xiaowen Fang
48. LNCS 14731, HCI in Games: Part II, edited by Xiaowen Fang
49. LNCS 14732, HCI in Mobility, Transport and Automotive Systems: Part I, edited by Heidi Krömker
50. LNCS 14733, HCI in Mobility, Transport and Automotive Systems: Part II, edited by Heidi Krömker
51. LNAI 14734, Artificial Intelligence in HCI: Part I, edited by Helmut Degen and Stavroula Ntoa
52. LNAI 14735, Artificial Intelligence in HCI: Part II, edited by Helmut Degen and Stavroula Ntoa
53. LNAI 14736, Artificial Intelligence in HCI: Part III, edited by Helmut Degen and Stavroula Ntoa
54. LNCS 14737, Design, Operation and Evaluation of Mobile Communications: Part I, edited by June Wei and George Margetis
55. LNCS 14738, Design, Operation and Evaluation of Mobile Communications: Part II, edited by June Wei and George Margetis
56. CCIS 2114, HCI International 2024 Posters - Part I, edited by Constantine Stephanidis, Margherita Antona, Stavroula Ntoa and Gavriel Salvendy
57. CCIS 2115, HCI International 2024 Posters - Part II, edited by Constantine Stephanidis, Margherita Antona, Stavroula Ntoa and Gavriel Salvendy
58. CCIS 2116, HCI International 2024 Posters - Part III, edited by Constantine Stephanidis, Margherita Antona, Stavroula Ntoa and Gavriel Salvendy
59. CCIS 2117, HCI International 2024 Posters - Part IV, edited by Constantine Stephanidis, Margherita Antona, Stavroula Ntoa and Gavriel Salvendy
60. CCIS 2118, HCI International 2024 Posters - Part V, edited by Constantine Stephanidis, Margherita Antona, Stavroula Ntoa and Gavriel Salvendy
61. CCIS 2119, HCI International 2024 Posters - Part VI, edited by Constantine Stephanidis, Margherita Antona, Stavroula Ntoa and Gavriel Salvendy
62. CCIS 2120, HCI International 2024 Posters - Part VII, edited by Constantine Stephanidis, Margherita Antona, Stavroula Ntoa and Gavriel Salvendy

https://2024.hci.international/proceedings

Preface

Software representations of humans, including aspects of anthropometry, biometrics, motion capture and prediction, as well as cognition modeling, are known as Digital Human Models (DHM), and are widely used in a variety of complex application domains where it is important to foresee and simulate human behavior, performance, safety, health and comfort. Automation depicting human emotion, social interaction and functional capabilities can also be modeled to support and assist in predicting human response in real-world settings. Such domains include medical and nursing applications, work, education and learning, ergonomics and design, as well as safety and risk management.

The 16th Digital Human Modeling and Applications in Health, Safety, Ergonomics and Risk Management (DHM) Conference, an affiliated conference of the HCI International Conference 2024, encouraged papers from academics, researchers, industry and professionals, on a broad range of theoretical and applied issues related to Digital Human Modeling and its applications.

The research papers contributed to this year's volumes span across different fields that fall within the scope of the DHM Conference. The role of DHM in the design and evaluation of various technologies has been explored, emphasizing the importance of the field for personalized and useful systems and applications, that advance user experience and foster communication, collaboration and learning. A significant number of submissions addressed DHM in assistive technologies for older adults, individuals with impairments and persons suffering from injuries. Furthermore, contributions have brought to the foreground the significance of DHM in healthcare interventions, and in technologies to support mental health and well-being, bridging the gap between human physiology and technological innovation. Finally, ergonomics constituted a topic that received focus this year, elaborating on the impact of DHM on ergonomic solutions for safety in work environments and the design of smart technologies.

Three volumes of the HCII 2024 proceedings are dedicated to this year's edition of the DHM conference. The first focuses on topics related to Digital Human Modeling for Design and Evaluation; User Experience and Assistive Technologies; and User Experience, Communication, and Collaboration. The second focuses on topics related to Healthcare Design and Support; Technology in Mental Health and Wellbeing; and Artificial Intelligence and Health Applications. The third focuses on topics related to Work, Safety, and Ergonomics; Ergonomics, Artificial Intelligence and Smart Technologies; and Advanced Technologies for Training and Learning.

The papers of these volumes were accepted for publication after a minimum of two single-blind reviews from the members of the DHM Program Board or, in some cases, from members of the Program Boards of other affiliated conferences. I would like to thank all of them for their invaluable contribution, support and efforts.

July 2024   Vincent G. Duffy

15th International Conference on Digital Human Modeling and Applications in Health, Safety, Ergonomics and Risk Management (DHM 2024)

Program Board Chair: **Vincent G. Duffy,** *Purdue University, USA*

- Karthik Adapa, *UNC Chapel Hill, USA*
- Giuseppe Andreoni, *Politecnico di Milano, Italy*
- Pedro Arezes, *University of Minho, Portugal*
- Hasan Ayaz, *Drexel University, USA*
- Aydin Azizi, *Oxford Brookes University, UK*
- Angelos Barmpoutis, *University of Florida, USA*
- Simone Borsci, *University of Twente, Netherlands*
- Andre Calero Valdez, *University of Lübeck, Germany*
- Yaqin Cao, *Anhui Polytechnic University, P.R. China*
- Ignacio Castellucci, *Universidad de Valparaíso, Chile*
- Damien Chablat, *CNRS/LS2N, France*
- Karen Chen, *North Carolina State University, USA*
- Bong Jun Choi, *Soongsil University, Korea*
- Denis Coelho, *Jönköping University, Sweden*
- Clive D'Souza, *University of Pittsburgh, USA*
- H. Onan Demirel, *Oregon State University, USA*
- Yi Ding, *Anhui Polytechnic University, P.R. China*
- Manish Kumar Dixit, *Texas A&M University, USA*
- Ehsan Esfahani, *University at Buffalo, USA*
- Martin Fleischer, *Technical University of Munich, Germany*
- Martin Fränzle, *Oldenburg University, Germany*
- Afzal Godil, *National Institute of Standards and Technology, USA*
- Wenbin Guo, *University of Florida, USA*
- Sogand Hasanzadeh, *Purdue University, USA*
- Bochen Jia, *University of Michigan, USA*
- Genett Isabel Jimenez Delgado, *Institucion Universitaria de Barranquilla IUB, Colombia*
- Jari Kaivo-oja, *Turku School of Economics, University of Turku, Finland*
- Taina Kalliokoski, *University of Helsinki, Finland*
- Jeong Ho Kim, *Oregon State University, USA*
- Woojoo Kim, *Kangwon National University, Korea*
- Steffi Kohl, *Zuyd University of Applied Sciences, Netherlands*
- Richard Lamb, *East Carolina University, USA*
- Nicola Francesco Lopomo, *Università degli Studi di Brescia, Italy*
- Siu Shing Man, *South China University of Technology, P.R. China*
- Alexander Mehler, *Goethe University Frankfurt, Germany*

- Jörg Miehling, *Friedrich-Alexander-Universität Erlangen-Nürnberg (FAU), Germany*
- Salman Nazir, *University of Southeastern Norway, Norway*
- Peter Nickel, *Institute for Occupational Safety and Health of the German Social Accident Insurance (IFA), Germany*
- Ashish Nimbarte, *West Virginia University, USA*
- Joseph Nuamah, *Oklahoma State University, USA*
- Miguel Ortiz-Barrios, *Universitat Politecnica de Valencia, Spain and Universidad de la Costa (CUC), Colombia*
- Nicola Paltrinieri, *NTNU, Norway*
- Thaneswer Patel, *North Eastern Regional Institute of Science and Technology, India*
- Xingda Qu, *Shenzhen University, P.R. China*
- Qing-Xing Qu, *Northeastern University, P.R. China*
- Erwin Rauch, *Free University of Bolzano, Spain*
- Arto Reiman, *University of Oulu, Finland*
- Deep Seth, *Mahindra University, India*
- Fabio Sgarbossa, *NTNU, Norway*
- Jieun Shin, *University of Florida, USA*
- Thitirat Siriborvornratanakul, *National Institute of Development Administration, Thailand*
- Beatriz Sousa Santos, *University of Aveiro, Portugal*
- Hendrik Stern, *Universität Bremen, Germany*
- Lesley Strawderman, *Mississippi State University, USA*
- Youchao Sun, *Nanjing University of Aeronautics and Astronautics, P.R. China*
- Zhengtang Tan, *Hunan Normal University, P.R. China*
- Leonor Teixeira, *University of Aveiro, Portugal*
- Renran Tian, *IUPUI, USA*
- Joseph Timoney, *Maynooth University, Ireland*
- Vinay V. Panicker, *National Institute of Technology Calicut, India*
- Dustin Van der Haar, *University of Johannesburg, South Africa*
- Kuan Yew Wong, *Universiti Teknologi Malaysia (UTM), Malaysia*
- Shuping Xiong, *Korea Advanced Institute of Science and Technology, Korea*
- James Yang, *Texas Tech University, USA*

The full list with the Program Board Chairs and the members of the Program Boards of all thematic areas and affiliated conferences of HCII 2024 is available online at:

http://www.hci.international/board-members-2024.php

HCI International 2025 Conference

The 27th International Conference on Human-Computer Interaction, HCI International 2025, will be held jointly with the affiliated conferences at the Swedish Exhibition & Congress Centre and Gothia Towers Hotel, Gothenburg, Sweden, June 22–27, 2025. It will cover a broad spectrum of themes related to Human-Computer Interaction, including theoretical issues, methods, tools, processes, and case studies in HCI design, as well as novel interaction techniques, interfaces, and applications. The proceedings will be published by Springer. More information will become available on the conference website: https://2025.hci.international/.

General Chair
Prof. Constantine Stephanidis
University of Crete and ICS-FORTH
Heraklion, Crete, Greece
Email: general_chair@2025.hci.international

https://2025.hci.international/

Contents – Part II

Technology in Mental Health and Wellbeing

Artificial Intelligence and Health Applications

Healthcare Design and Support

Comparison of the Accuracy of Markerless Motion Analysis and Optoelectronic System for Measuring Lower Limb Gait Kinematics

Giuseppe Andreoni[1,2(✉)] 🆔 and Luca E. Molteni[2] 🆔

[1] Department of Design, Politecnico di Milano, Milano, Italy
giuseppe.andreoni@polimi.it
[2] Scientific Institute IRCCS "E.Medea", Bosisio Parini, Lecco, Italy

Abstract. Background: Marker-based Optical motion tracking is the gold standard in gait analysis, for their detailed biomechanical modelling and accuracy. Today, in light of developing remote telemonitoring applications, markerless solutions are growing rapidly. Algorithms like Openpose can track human movement from a video. However, only few papers assess the validity of gait analysis using Openpose.

Objective: The purpose of this study was to assess the Openpose reliability to measure kinematics and spatiotemporal gait parameters and to evaluate the minimum technical requirements.

Methods: This analysis used video and optoelectronic motion capture simultaneously recorded. We assessed 4 healthy adults. To compare the accuracy of Openpose respect to optoelectronic system we computed the following indexes: the absolute error (AE) for spatiotemporal parameters and lower limbs kin, the lower limbs Range (ROM) of Motion's intraclass correlation coefficients (ICC), the cross-correlation coefficients (CCC) of normalized gait cycle joint angles computed with two systems.

Results: The spatiotemporal parameter showed an ICC between good to excellent and the absolute error was very small: cadence AE < 0.56 step/min, Mean Velocity AE < 0.11 m/s, Stride length AE < 0.14 cm. The ROM of the lower limbs during gait showed a good to excellent agreement in the sagittal plane.

Also the normalized gait cycle CCC value shown a strong coupling in the sagittal plane.

Conclusion: We found Openpose to be accurate and reliably for sagittal plane gait kinematics and for spatiotemporal gait parameters in healthy adults.

Keywords: Kinematic · Markerless · OpenPose

1 Introduction

Today marker-based Optical motion tracking solutions provides the best metrological performances, in terms of accuracy in the markers' localization (usually in the order of 10ths of millimeters), repeatability and frequency of measurements [1]. In these systems

© The Author(s), under exclusive license to Springer Nature Switzerland AG 2024
V. G. Duffy (Ed.): HCII 2024, LNCS 14710, pp. 3–15, 2024.
https://doi.org/10.1007/978-3-031-61063-9_1

the positions of joints and the orientations body segments are obtained through the three dimensional localization of passive (or sometimes active) markers, fixed on subjects' body and captured by a calibrated multi-camera stereophotogrammetric video system [2].

However, measuring human movement represents an even more open challenge that is constantly evolving. Measuring and analyzing movement is important for many fields, including medicine, sport, entertainments and games, it is fundamental in physical rehabilitation, where more than 1 billion people approximately 15% of the global population suffers from some sort of disability [3]. Treatment of physical impairments could improve if performed in concordance with motion capture. Reliable motion capture would make treatment quantitatively driven and remove the need for qualitative visual assessment, which is prone to evaluator bias and lacks inter-rater reliability [4, 5].

Conventional motion analysis is very useful but shows some disadvantages. Indeed, these technologies are expensive; moreover, time and technical skills are needed to properly attach makers [6]. Therefore, they are used in limited special environments such as laboratories. In most clinical fields, it is difficult to establish an environment where motion evaluations could be performed using conventional motion analysis systems [2, 7, 8].

In light of developing remote telemonitoring applications and with the aim to reduce the cost and to simplify the process, in the last decades the interest into markerless solution has grown rapidly, [9–11]. Markerless systems are based on four main components, namely a camera system, a body model, the image features used and the algorithms that determine shape, pose and location of the model itself [9]. In these approaches two families of camera systems can be used. The first family is camera that produce a so-called "depth map," i.e., an image where each pixel describes the distance of a point in the scene from the camera.

For example, in this family we can find Microsoft Kinect (Microsoft Corporation, Redmond, WA), comprises RGB cameras equipped with an infrared-based depth sensor and can observe motion without requiring the attachment of reflective markers and the use controllers, making it possible to recognize the position and orientation of a part of the human body. The Kinect motion analysis system is easier to operate, more portable, and more economical than conventional motion analysis systems. However, previous studies reported significant differences between Kinect and conventional motion analysis [12–14].

The second family is the traditional camera, and the elaboration of images with novel artificial intelligence (AI) algorithm based on automatic landmarks identification on video images (computer vision). The method opened to a new approach for marker less motion capture, potentially feasible with low-cost hardware [9, 11, 15]. In that, machine learning techniques were exploited to identify the nodes of a skeletal structure describing the posture of a human subject within a given image frame.

Today different processing frameworks are available: OpenPose [15] takes as input color images from simple web-cameras and using a two-branch convolutional neural network (CNN) produces as output confidence maps of keypoints, and affinity for each keypoint pair (that is, belonging to the same skeleton). Although promising results were obtained, the design of markerless systems able to reliably reconstruct human motion in a timely and unobtrusive valid manner is still an open challenge [9]. Among the fast-growing studies on the application to various case studies, only a few focused on the accuracy and reliability of subjects' three-dimensional reconstruction. In particular, only few studies asses the performance of OpenPose in the computation of the lower limbs angles and of the spatiotemporal parameters during movements like walking, compared to a multi-camera marker based system. [16–21]. This is particularly important considering that abnormal gait kinematics and spatiotemporal parameters can occur after injuries and often coincide with disability [22, 23].

The purpose of this study was to compare this pre-trained algorithm, by their reliability to track gait kinematics and spatiotemporal gait parameters and to evaluate the minimum technical requirements.

2 Methods

2.1 Subjects

To conduct this experiment, we used an existing dataset that simultaneously recorded video and motion capture data. From the database, we random extract four gait trials of four different subjects (2 males/2 females; mean age: 28.42 – SD 3.67; age range: 24.9–33.10). All the subject assesses are healthy adult without history of motor impairments. The baseline features of the sample are showed in Table 1.

Table 1. Mean, Standard Deviation (SD) and range for baseline features of sample

Baseline Features (mean –SD; range)	
Numbers of subjects	4
Age [y]	28.42 – SD 3.67; 24.9–33.10
Weight [Kg]	60.50 – SD 6.86; 51.0–66.0
Height [cm]	170.00- SD 9.63; 160.0–183.0
BMI	17.92- SD 3.63; 17.92–25.39

The study was carried out in accordance with the 1964 Helsinki declaration and its later amendments.

2.2 Data Collection

The video data were simultaneously recorded with the optoelectronic system, and with 2 cameras (VIXTA frequency: 25 fps; resolution: 640×480) The two cameras were mounted on a tripod with a height of approximately 90 cm and located respectively, about 3 m from the center of the walkway perpendicular to the sagittal plane of the subject, and at 1,5 m from the start/end of walk perpendicular to the frontal plane of the subject. During the trial the subject walk indifferently from the right to the left of the room or vice versa, (see Fig. 1).

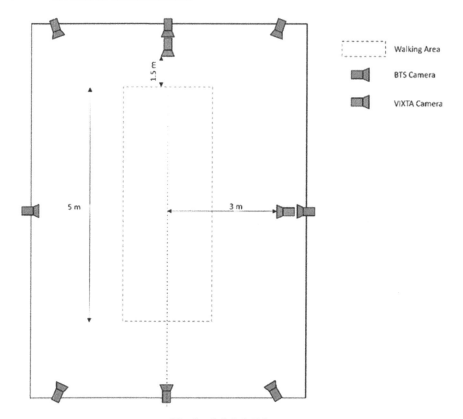

Fig. 1. Gait Lab Scheme

All gold standard measurements were obtained using an optoelectronic multicamera system for human motion analysis (SMART DX, BTS SpA, Milan, Italy) with eight high-resolution cameras with infrared light and a sampling frequency of 100 Hz which recorded the position of passive retroreflective markers directly onto the skin. The experimental protocol required the positioning of 22 markers (plastic spheres covered by reflecting film, 10 mm in diameter), in according to the Davis Protocol [24]. Markers were placed by a physiotherapist with specific training in optoelectronic system for human motion analysis. During the data acquisition protocol, the subject was asked to walking barefoot on a 6 m distance at a self-selected normal-pace speed.

2.3 Data Processing

The raw data acquired from motion capture system were processed with Smart Analyzer software (BTS Bioengineering, Milano, Italy). First, the 3D data were filtered and interpolated in case of missing data for short time. Then spatial–temporal parameters (cycle duration, cadence, gait speed, stance phase, swing phase, double-support phase, stride length and step width) and conventional kinematic parameters of traditional Davis marker-set protocols [24] were computed.

The two video were elaborated using OpenPose that return a set of 25 2D keypoints coordinates for body pose estimation (in pixels) for every videos. Keypoints are located in relevant body landmarks (such as left hand, right hand, face, etc.) and were used to determine the 2D Cartesian coordinates on the sagittal plane and on the frontal plane (see Fig. 2).

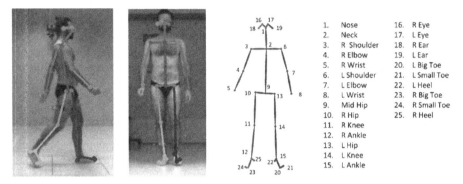

1.	Nose	16.	R Eye
2.	Neck	17.	L Eye
3.	R Shoulder	18.	R Ear
4.	R Elbow	19.	L Ear
5.	R Wrist	20.	L Big Toe
6.	L Shoulder	21.	L Small Toe
7.	L Elbow	22.	L Heel
8.	L Wrist	23.	R Big Toe
9.	Mid Hip	24.	R Small Toe
10.	R Hip	25.	R Heel
11.	R Knee		
12.	R Ankle		
13.	L Hip		
14.	L Knee		
15.	L Ankle		

Fig. 2. Image on sagittal plane, frontal plane respectively and schematic of the anatomical landmark that were extracted from OpenPose.

The data calculated with routines were filtered and interpolated in case of missing data for short time using Matlab. With respect to kinematic parameters from OpenPose data, the segment and joint angles were measured from the estimated feature points of each joint. In particular the segment and joint angles between each feature point were measured from the obtained marker coordinates as shown in Table 2 [20].

Table 2. Definitions of segments and joints based on OpenPose. Abbreviations: Neck: border between cervical and thoracic vertebrae; RHip: right hip joint, LHip: left hip joint, MidHip: center of RHip and LHip, RKnee: right knee joint, Rankle: right ankle joint, RHeel: right heel, RSmallToe: right 5th metatarsophalangeal joint.

Segments and joints Angles	
Hip Flexion/Extension	The angle of a straight line connecting "RHip" and "RKnee" relative to a straight line connecting "Neck" and "MidHip"
Hip Abduction/Adduction	The angle of the straight line connecting "RHip" and "RKnee" relative to the perpendicular line connecting "RHip" and "LHip"
Knee Flexion/Extension	The angle of "RHip", "RKnee" and "RAnkle"
Ankle Dorsiflexion/Plantar flexion	The angle of a straight line connecting "RHeel" and "RSmallToe" relative to a straight line connecting "RKnee" and "RAnkle"

Moreover to identify the gait cycles we detected the heel strike and toe-off events [18, [25]. Thus, spatiotemporal gait parameters were calculated using successive heel strike and toe-off events. For both legs, we calculated the number of frames between successive left and right heel strikes (step time), between heel strike and toe-off of the same leg (stance time), between toe off and heel strike of the same leg (swing time), between heel strike and toe-off of the left and right legs (double support time). The number of frames was then multiplied by the sampling rate to get the time in seconds. Similarly, we measured the number of pixels between the left and right ankle keypoints at successive left and right heel strikes, then multiplied this value by a scaling factor to estimate step length. The scaling factor was estimated by calculating the number of pixels between the tape marks located on the walkway in the video and dividing by the known distance.

2.4 Statistical Analysis

For the accuracy analysis, Absolute errors were calculated for the kinematics parameters and for each spatiotemporal variable by taking the absolute value after subtracting the values obtained using pose estimation methods from the value measured using marker-based motion capture:

$$\text{Absolute Error} = \text{abs}(\text{Motion Capture} - \text{Pose Estimation}) \tag{1}$$

Next, to confirm if the data obtained by OpenPose agreed with the data obtained by optoelectronic system, the ICCs (two-way mixed effects model, absolute agreement, average measurements) between the spatiotemporal and kinematics data obtained by OpenPose and Optoelectronics system. The ICC values were interpreted as poor agreement for ICC < 0.5, as moderate agreement for the values between 0.5 and 0.75 a good agreement for values between 0.75 and 0.9, and as excellent agreement for value greater than 0.90 [26].

Finally, the cross-correlation coefficients r (CCC) between both systems were used to evaluate the similarity of angles during gait cycle. The CCC values were interpreted as weak or no coupling for values $-0.3 < \text{CCC} < 0.3$, moderate coupling for values $0.3 < \text{CCC} < 0.70$ or $-0.7 < \text{CCC} < -0.3$, and strong coupling for values $\text{CCC} > 0.7$ or $\text{CCC} < -0.7$ [27]. The statistical significance was set at $p < 0.05$.

SPSS software (IBM, USA) was used to perform the statistical analysis.

3 Results

3.1 Spatiotemporal Parameters

The mean, standard deviation (SD), mean absolute error (MAE), and the interclass correlation coefficient (ICC) (two-way mixed effects model, absolute agreement), of the spatiotemporal parameters are listed in Table 3.

The ICC values of spatiotemporal parameters were good to excellent, except for only two cases: the double support phase both for right and the left step showed ICC values lesser with a moderate reliability (ICC = 0,553) and a poor reliability (ICC = 0.387) respectively.

Table 3. Mean, SD, MAE, ICC and accuracy levels of spatiotemporal gait parameters (OP: Open-Pose; OS: Optoelectronic System, MAE: Mean Absolute Error, +++= excellent, ++= good, += moderate) [26]

| | OP | OS | MAE | ICC | ICC level |
	mean ± SD	mean ± SD	mean ± SD		
cadence [stepmin]	50.96 ± 6.29	51.23 ± 5.64	0.56 ± 0.36	0.997	+++
Gait Speed [m/s]	1.00 ± 0.21	1.09 ± 0.14	0.11 ± 0.05	0.885	++
Right Stride Lenght [m]	1.17 ± 0.19	1.28 ± 0.12	0.12 ± 0.07	0.841	++
Left Stride Lenght [m]	1.13 ± 0.17	1.27 ± 0.09	0.14 ± 0.09	0.704	++
Step Width [m]	0.11 ± 0.03	0.11 ± 0.05	0.02 ± 0.01	0.896	++
Right Stride time [s]	1.18 ± 0.13	1.17 ± 0.11	0.02 ± 0.02	0.990	+++
Left Stride time [s]	1.21 ± 0.14	1.19 ± 0.13	0.02 ± 0.01	0.994	+++
Right Stance time [s]	0.75 ± 0.08	0.70 ± 0.07	0.05 ± 0.02	0.889	++
Left Stance time [s]	0.79 ± 0.10	0.73 ± 0.10	0.06 ± 0.01	0.913	+++
Right Swing time [s]	0.43 ± 0.05	0.49 ± 0.05	0.06 ± 0.02	0.711	++
Left Swing time [s]	0.42 ± 0.04	0.47 ± 0.05	0.06 ± 0.02	0.788	++
Right-Left Double Support time [s]	0.18 ± 0.02	0.13 ± 0.05	0.05 ± 0.03	0.554	+
Left- Right Double Support time [s]	0.16 ± 0.03	0.11 ± 0.02	0.04 ± 0.01	0.387	–

3.2 Kinematic Parameters

For the kinematic parameters the Table 4 shows mean, SD, MAE and ICC (two-way mixed effects model, absolute agreement) for the Range of Motion (ROM) values of the different considered joint.

Table 4. Mean, SD, MAE, ICC and accuracy levels for articular ROM (OP: OpenPose; OS: optoelectronic System, MAE: Mean Absolute Error (+++= excellent, ++= good, += moderate) [26]

| | OP | OS | MAE | ICC | ICC Level |
	mean ± SD	mean ± SD	mean ± SD		
ROM right hip AA [°]	14.62 ± 26.02	2.30 ± 0.81	14.07 ± 25.07	0.108	–

(continued)

Table 4. (*continued*)

	OP	OS	MAE	ICC	ICC Level
	mean ± SD	mean ± SD	mean ± SD		
ROM left hip AA [°]	3.97 ± 2.76	8.68 ± 0.97	4.70 ± 2.61	0.293	–
ROM right hip FE [°]	5.42 ± 4.05	12.40 ± 0.78	6.98 ± 3.67	0.850	++
ROM left hip FE [°]	7.91 ± 1.89	12.63 ± 2.56	4.71 ± 2.19	0.863	++
ROM right knee FE [°]	41.75 ± 6.77	44.48 ± 4.77	3.98 ± 1.98	0.815	++
ROM left knee FE [°]	39.73 ± 7.16	43.48 ± 4.64	3.75 ± 2.92	0.935	+++
ROM right ankle FE [°]	59.23 ± 3.53	59.00 ± 1.79	1.92 ± 1.00	0.820	++
ROM left ankle FE [°]	58.92 ± 3.81	58.95 ± 5.81	2.15 ± 1.17	0.802	++

The ICC of ROM parameters resulted good to excellent for the angles on the sagittal plane (ICC > 0.802). Instead for the angle on the frontal plane, like hip abduction-adduction, we can found a poor reliability both for the right and for the left hip. The angles normalized on the gait cycle on the frontal plane and in the sagittal plane, for hip, knee and ankle are shown in Fig. 3 and in Fig. 4 respectively.

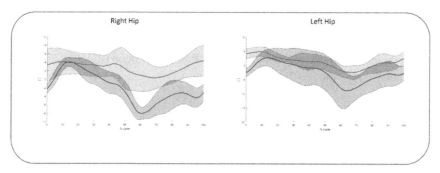

Fig. 3. Hip angles during the gait cycle on the frontal plane (red line: Openpose; blue line: optoelectronic system) (Color figure online)

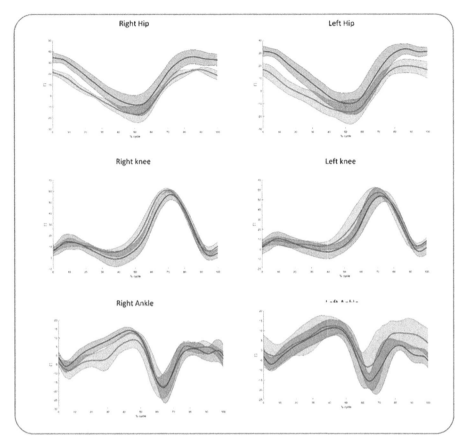

Fig. 4. Hip, knee, ankle angles during the gait cycle on the sagittal plane (*red line: Openpose; blue line: optoelectronic system*) (Color figure online)

To summarize the results, the CCC for each joint are showed in Table 5.

Table 5. CCC values joint angles in every group and their levels (+++= strong, ++= moderate, += weak) [27]

	CCC	CCC level
Right hip AA [°]	0.769	++
Left hip AA [°]	0.901	+++
Right hip FE [°]	0.994	+++
Left hip FE [°]	0.982	+++

(continued)

Table 5. (*continued*)

	CCC	CCC level
Right knee FE [°]	0.970	+++
Left knee FE [°]	0.966	+++
Right ankle FE [°]	0.881	++
Left ankle FE [°]	0.891	++

The CCC of the joint angles in the sagittal plane was strong for the hip, the knee and the ankle joint (CCC > 0.881). For the angles on the frontal plane, the CCC values were moderate (CCC > 0.769).

4 Discussion

This pilot study aimed to investigate the accuracy and of reliability of Openpose method to measure kinematics and spatiotemporal gait parameters in a small sample of four adult healthy subjects. In particular, we studied whether this system could measure parameters like spatiotemporal parameters of gait and kinematics angles, compared to the optoelectronic system.

About the analysis of spatiotemporal gait parameters open pose estimated the parameters with good agreement and consistency. Indeed, the analysis show an overall ICC value between good and excellent reliability, in all different gait patterns, except for the double stance support where the ICC value was from poor to moderate. The best performance to estimate the gait parameters was in the cadence and in the step length both for the right and for the left step, where the reliability was excellent (ICC > 0.994). This results was in concordance with previous studies conducted using a markerless pose estimation systems, where evidence that this system could measure the spatiotemporal parameters almost with good reliability [12, 17, 28]. For the gait speed the ICC value have a good reliability, moreover, the MAE between the OP and OS systems was 1.1 m/s; this error was less than minimum difference with clinical relevance. This result was in concordance with previous studies conducted using a Openpose in the gait speed estimation [29].

About the kinematic parameters the ROM analysis on the sagittal plane the ICC were good to excellent (ICC > 0.802). Instead, the analysis of the ROMs on the frontal plane is less reliable than ROMs in the sagittal plane where the ICC values were poor to moderate. This result was in concordance with previous studies conducted using a Openpose on adult subjects [20].

Also the CCC values for the hip, knee and ankle angles computed are similar to the results found from other studies conduct with OpenPose on adult subjects [17]. In particular, the CCC values show a better performance in the sagittal plane, where the values show a strong coherency. Instead in the frontal plane, the CCC values show only a moderate correspondence.

Thus, considering both the ICC value of the ROM and the CCC value of angles gait cycle seem that for the kinematic parameters in the sagittal plane OP estimated the with high agreement and consistency. Instead, the system estimated the kinematic parameters on the frontal plane with less performance; in particular, for the ROMs it showed some inconsistency and low accuracy. Probably the performance was worse on the frontal plane because of the rotation angles of the hip joints, so the biases between the data obtained by two systems were more influenced from the motions in the transverse plane, as also as assumed in previous studies [20]. Moreover, during the acquisition the subject approaches the camera, changing the distance from the video recording point, and this could affect the measurement.

5   Conclusion

This study introduces a possible setup and validate the use of OpenPose for the markerless assessment of kinematic gait cycle in a population of healthy adults. Our results confirm the reliability found in other previous studies about OpenPose. In particular, this study shows that using a single low-resolution camera positioned parallel to the direction of gait, we can compute ROM and joint angles normalized on the gait cycle of hip, knee and ankle on sagittal plane with more than good accuracy. Not only, with this setting, we can also compute the spatiotemporal gait parameters like cadence, gait speed, stride length, to characterize the walk of the subject. Even if the accuracy and reliability of the optoelectronic system are certainly better than the markerless system, the study shows that OpenPose can be a valid low-cost alternative in some cases.

5.1   Limitations

There are some limitations associated with the present study, such as the relatively small sample size. Moreover, an another limitation can be the resolution of the used camera, precedent studies have demonstrated like a better resolution of the cameras can lead to better results [30]. An interesting development could be to adopt high-resolution cameras to improve the accuracy and the reliability of the system. Another important limitation is that in this experiment we used two cameras, but each video was elaborated individually to estimate the parameters for the anatomical relative plane. This simplification allows simply and fast clinical application, without request of calibration. A future development could be to use two or more cameras and triangulated the data collected to recreate the 3D coordinates of the body points. Future studies on larger population and pathological gait patterns would be needed in order to verify the reliability and the accuracy of the system.

Acknowledgments. This study was supported by "5 per mille" funds for biomedical research, in particular for the project "5x1000/2023 - Sviluppo di nuovi protocolli di valutazione funzionale multifattoriale e relativi indici per l'età pediatrica" awarded to Prof. Giuseppe Andreoni, and by the Italian Ministry of Health (Ricerca Corrente 2024 to Dr. Eng. E. Biffi).

Disclosure of Interests. No conflict of interest exists. The authors wish to confirm that there are no known conflicts of interest associated with this publication and there has been no financial support for this work that could have influenced its outcome.

References

1. Ma'touq, J. , Hu, T., Haddadin, S.: Sub-millimetre accurate human hand kinematics: from surface to skeleton. Comput. Methods Biomech. Biomed. Eng. **21**(2), 113–128 (2018). https://doi.org/10.1080/10255842.2018.1425996
2. Cappozzo, A., Della Croce, U., Leardini, A., Chiari, L.: Human movement analysis using stereophotogrammetry. Part 1: theoretical background. Gait Posture **21**(2), 186–196 (2005). https://doi.org/10.1016/j.gaitpost.2004.01.010
3. Washabaugh, E.P., Shanmugam, T.A., Ranganathan, R., Krishnan, C.: Comparing the accuracy of open-source pose estimation methods for measuring gait kinematics. Gait Posture **97**, 188–195 (2022). https://doi.org/10.1016/j.gaitpost.2022.08.008
4. Viehweger, E., et al.: Influence of clinical and gait analysis experience on reliability of observational gait analysis (Edinburgh Gait Score Reliability). Ann. Phys. Rehabil. Med. **53**(9), 535–546 (2010). https://doi.org/10.1016/j.rehab.2010.09.002
5. Brunnekreef, J.J., Van Uden, C.J.T., Van Moorsel, S., Kooloos, J.G.M.: Reliability of videotaped observational gait analysis in patients with orthopedic impairments. BMC Musculoskelet. Disord. **6**, 1–9 (2005). https://doi.org/10.1186/1471-2474-6-17
6. Baker, R.: Gait analysis methods in rehabilitation. J. Neuroeng. Rehabil. **3**, 1 (2006). https://doi.org/10.1186/1743-0003-3-4
7. Winter, D.A.: Biomechanics and Motor Control of Human Movement, 4th edn. (2009). https://doi.org/10.1002/9780470549148
8. N.P. Access, A. M. J. B. A. manuscript; available in P. 2016 F. 05. P. in final edited form as: J. B. 2015 F. 5; 48(3), 544–548. https://doi.org/10.1016/j.jbiomech.2014.11.048. Krishnan, C., Washabaugh, E.P., Seetharaman, Y: A low cost real-time motion tracking approach using webcam technology. J. Biomech. **48**(3), 544–548 (2015). https://doi.org/10.1016/j.jbiomech.2014.11.048.A
9. Colyer, S.L., Evans, M., Cosker, D.P., Salo, A.I.T.: A review of the evolution of vision-based motion analysis and the integration of advanced computer vision methods towards developing a markerless system. Sport. Med. Open **4**(1), 24 (2018)
10. Tanaka, R., Takimoto, H., Yamasaki, T., Higashi, A.: Validity of time series kinematical data as measured by a markerless motion capture system on a flatland for gait assessment. J. Biomech. **71**, 281–285 (2018). https://doi.org/10.1016/j.jbiomech.2018.01.035
11. Clark, R.A., Mentiplay, B.F., Hough, E., Pua, Y.H.: Three-dimensional cameras and skeleton pose tracking for physical function assessment: a review of uses, validity, current developments and Kinect alternatives. Gait Posture **68**, 193–200 (2019). https://doi.org/10.1016/j.gaitpost.2018.11.029
12. Mentiplay, B.F., et al.: Gait assessment using the Microsoft Xbox One Kinect: concurrent validity and inter-day reliability of spatiotemporal and kinematic variables. J. Biomech. **48**(10), 2166–2170 (2015). https://doi.org/10.1016/j.jbiomech.2015.05.021
13. Pfister, A., West, A.M., Bronner, S., Noah, J.A.: Comparative abilities of Microsoft Kinect and Vicon 3D motion capture for gait analysis. J. Med. Eng. Technol. **38**(5), 274–280 (2014). https://doi.org/10.3109/03091902.2014.909540
14. Springer, S., Seligmann, G.Y.: Validity of the kinect for gait assessment: a focused review. Sensors **16**(2), 1–13 (2016). https://doi.org/10.3390/s16020194
15. Cao, Z., Simon, T., Wei, S.E., Sheikh, Y.: Realtime multi-person 2D pose estimation using part affinity fields. In: Proceedings of the - 30th IEEE Conference on Computer Vision and Pattern Recognition, CVPR 2017, January 2017, pp. 1302–1310, (2017). https://doi.org/10.1109/CVPR.2017.143

16. Gu, X., Deligianni, F., Lo, B., Chen, W., Yang, G.Z.: Markerless gait analysis based on a single RGB camera. In: 2018 IEEE 15th International Conference on Wearable and Implantable Body Sensor Networks, BSN 2018, March 2018, pp. 42–45 (2018). https://doi.org/10.1109/BSN.2018.8329654

17. Yamamoto, M., Shimatani, K., Hasegawa, M., Kurita, Y., Ishige, Y., Takemura, H.: Accuracy of temporo-spatial and lower limb joint kinematics parameters using openpose for various gait patterns with orthosis. IEEE Trans. Neural Syst. Rehabil. Eng. **29**, 2666–2675 (2021). https://doi.org/10.1109/TNSRE.2021.3135879

18. Stenum, J., Rossi, C., Roemmich, R.T.: Two-dimensional video-based analysis of human gait using pose estimation. PLoS Comput. Biol. **17**(4) (2021). https://doi.org/10.1371/journal.pcbi.1008935

19. Mehdizadeh, S., Nabavi, H., Sabo, A., Arora, T., Iaboni, A., Taati, B.: Concurrent validity of human pose tracking in video for measuring gait parameters in older adults: a preliminary analysis with multiple trackers, viewing angles, and walking directions. J. Neuroeng. Rehabil. **18**(1), 1–16 (2021). https://doi.org/10.1186/s12984-021-00933-0

20. Ota, M., Tateuchi, H., Hashiguchi, T., Ichihashi, N.: Verification of validity of gait analysis systems during treadmill walking and running using human pose tracking algorithm. Gait Posture **85**, 290–297 (2021). https://doi.org/10.1016/j.gaitpost.2021.02.006

21. Guo, R., Shao, X., Zhang, C., Qian, X.: Sparse adaptive graph convolutional network for leg agility assessment in Parkinson's disease. IEEE Trans. Neural Syst. Rehabil. Eng. **28**(12), 2837–2848 (2020). https://doi.org/10.1109/TNSRE.2020.3039297

22. Chen, G., Patten, C., Kothari, D.H., Zajac, F.E.: Gait differences between individuals with post-stroke hemiparesis and non-disabled controls at matched speeds. Gait Posture **22**(1), 51–56 (2005). https://doi.org/10.1016/j.gaitpost.2004.06.009

23. Duffell, L.D., Jordan, S.J., Cobb, J.P., McGregor, A.H.: Gait adaptations with aging in healthy participants and people with knee-joint osteoarthritis. Gait Posture **57**, 246–251 (2017). https://doi.org/10.1016/j.gaitpost.2017.06.015

24. Gage, J.R., Davis III, R.B., Õunpuu, S., Tyburski, D.: A gait analysis data collection and reduction technique (i), 1–23 (2016)

25. Zeni, J.A., Richards, J.G., Higginson, J.S.: Two simple methods for determining gait events during treadmill and overground walking using kinematic data. Gait Posture **27**(4), 710–714 (2008). https://doi.org/10.1016/j.gaitpost.2007.07.007

26. Koo, T.K., Li, M.Y.: A guideline of selecting and reporting intraclass correlation coefficients for reliability research. J. Chiropr. Med. **15**(2), 155–163 (2016). https://doi.org/10.1016/j.jcm.2016.02.012

27. Pohl, M.B., Messenger, N., Buckley, J.G.: Forefoot, rearfoot and shank coupling: effect of variations in speed and mode of gait. Gait Posture **25**(2), 295–302 (2007). https://doi.org/10.1016/j.gaitpost.2006.04.012

28. Dolatabadi, E., Taati, B., Mihailidis, A.: Concurrent validity of the microsoft kinect for windows v2 for measuring spatiotemporal gait parameters. Med. Eng. Phys. **38**(9), 952–958 (2016). https://doi.org/10.1016/j.medengphy.2016.06.015

29. Barthuly, A.M., Bohannon, R.W., Gorack, W.: Gait speed is a responsive measure of physical performance for patients undergoing short-term rehabilitation. Gait Posture **36**(1), 61–64 (2012). https://doi.org/10.1016/j.gaitpost.2012.01.002

30. Zago, M., Luzzago, M., Marangoni, T., De Cecco, M., Tarabini, M., Galli, M.: 3D Tracking of human motion using visual skeletonization and stereoscopic vision. Front. Bioeng. Biotechnol. **8**, 1–11 (2020). https://doi.org/10.3389/fbioe.2020.00181

Literature Review on Human-Automation Interaction: Relationship Between Healthcare Automation and Human Error at Work

Min Ho Cho, Yejin Seo(✉), and Vincent G. Duffy

Purdue University, West Lafayette, IN 47906, USA
{cho486,seo104,duffy}@purdue.edu

Abstract. With the development of technology to reduce human errors in medical settings, healthcare has adopted various automation in its systems. This automation system aims to enhance efficiency, accuracy, and patient outcomes. However, the introduction of new systems can change the work environment and lead to undesired outcomes. To examine this relationship, a systematic literature review was conducted using the two keywords 'healthcare automation' and 'human error at work'. The analysis begins by obtaining metadata from different sources, including Google Scholar, Scopus, Web of Science, and Dimension. Various bibliometric tools such as VOSViewer, BibExcel, MaxQDA, CiteSpace, and Google Ngram were utilized to gather insights and relationships between the two topics. These approaches help understand the general trends and climate of the two topics and fields. This comprehensive analysis not only expands our understanding of each topic individually but also highlights the link between the two topics, showcasing the complex relationship of technology, healthcare, and work settings.

Keywords: Healthcare · Automation · Human Error · Dispensing Robot · Medication Error · Reliability

1 Introduction and Background

Due to the shortage of healthcare workers and the intention of reducing human error under various circumstances, healthcare automation using various technologies, dispensing robots, automated patient care, and automated diagnostic, and therapeutic tools, are augmented to exceed human capabilities. Despite various advantages such as improved accuracy in diagnosis, efficiency, patient safety, and communication, there are still numerous medical workers, especially in hospitals where they cannot afford automated systems that could cause human error. Due to communication problems, inadequate information flow, fatigue, and stress, different medical errors can occur such as misdiagnosis, delayed diagnosis, and infection. Medical errors may be reduced by using health information technology, an automated system, which promises to modernize the healthcare system and improve efficiency. Even if health information technology, like electronic health records or personal health records, is correctly built and tested, they may unwittingly add new sorts of mistakes known as technology-induced errors. An error of this kind

© The Author(s), under exclusive license to Springer Nature Switzerland AG 2024
V. G. Duffy (Ed.): HCII 2024, LNCS 14710, pp. 16–34, 2024.
https://doi.org/10.1007/978-3-031-61063-9_2

may occur due to the complicated interaction between healthcare providers, patients, and the health information technology now in use, and they may not be readily apparent until they are put in place. (Khan, B. 2023) Therefore it is crucial to understand various causes of human error in healthcare industries and how to reduce those errors by utilizing automated systems and technologies. Furthermore, understanding potential errors caused by technology-induced errors between medical workers and automated healthcare systems, can minimize negative outcomes and improve significantly in healthcare industries. In this literature review, different relationships between two topics, "Healthcare Automation" and "Human Error at Work" to understand how these topics are related and improved in the future for safer outcomes in healthcare industries. The balance between automation and human expertise is crucial in healthcare delivery, and the deployment of cognitive technology, such as IBM's Watson, exemplifies this need. (Gaynor. M. 2014) (Figs. 1 and 2).

- **Human error at work** can be defined as the inadvertent actions or decisions made by individuals in the workplace, leading to undesired outcomes. This phenomenon is not limited to a specific field but is pervasive across various domains, including medicine, maintenance, construction, and other industries. (Ganiat, T. 1995)
- **Healthcare automation** involves the use of technology, such as artificial intelligence, robotics, and digital systems, to streamline and enhance various processes within the healthcare industry. While the Potential for AI in healthcare is substantial, the large-scale automation of healthcare professional jobs may be hindered by implementation factors. (Davenport. T. 2019)
- **Medication errors** are a significant concern in healthcare, with the potential to cause harm to patients. These errors can occur at various stages of the medication process and are often preventable. A medication error is defined as any preventable event that may cause or lead to inappropriate medication use or patient harm. (Rehan. H. 2015)

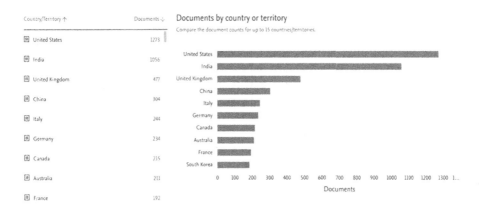

Fig. 1. Publication by Country for the Topic "Healthcare Automation"

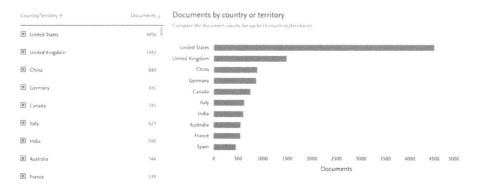

Fig. 2. Publication by Country for the Topic "Human Error at Work"

The two figures above represent the number of publications in different countries on two topics, "Healthcare Automation" and "Human Error at Work". The data on the number of publications was generated by utilizing one of the data sources, Scopus. For the topic "Healthcare Automation", the top five countries with the greatest number of publications are the United States, India, the United Kingdom, China, and Italy. For the topic "Human error at work", the top five countries with the greatest number of publications are the United States, the United Kingdom, China, Germany, and Canada. By analyzing this data of two topics, countries like the United States, the United Kingdom, China, India, and Italy are in common and continuously doing various research.

2   Purpose of Study

The increasing use of healthcare automation systems in the workplace has led to the need to understand the relationship between automation and human error. This study aims to conduct a bibliometric analysis to explore the existing literature on healthcare automation and human error at work, focusing on the relationships among articles, databases, and keywords. This study includes literature from databases such as Web of Science, Scopus, Google Scholar, SpringerLink, and ResearchGate. Several qualitative analysis tools, including BibExcel, CiteSpace, NVIVO, and VOSviewer, were used to visualize key trends. Various analyses were conducted to show the connections and patterns within the literature. The study provides a comprehensive overview of the existing knowledge by comparing findings across databases. While the use of automation in healthcare can improve efficiency, usability challenges must be addressed. Understanding the relationship between healthcare automation and human error is crucial for developing strategies to optimize system performance, enhance user experience, and ultimately improve patient outcomes.

3 Procedure

The figure below represents the step-by-step procedure for the bibliographic review of two topics, "Healthcare Automation" and "Human Error at Work". The main purpose of this bibliographic review is to analyze the relationship between two topics by utilizing different databases, analysis tools, and metadata. The metadata of two topics was gathered from different databases, Scopus, Google Scholar, Dimensions, and Scite.ai. For the comparison of the timeline of the gathered data, one metadata was gathered for the entire year, and other metadata was gathered for recent years. Firstly, by utilizing the Scopus analysis tool, the number of articles per country was generated for the comparison. Secondly, Google Ngram was utilized to perform trend analysis to find the relationship between two topics by analyzing the number of articles per year. Thirdly, Scite.ai was used to see general summaries of different articles within these two topics. Fourthly, VOSviewer was used to perform content and co-citation analysis to analyze the connectivity of two topics. Content analysis uses different keywords in articles on two topics and the map of connectivity was generated. During this process, various conjunctions, numbers, and prepositions were unselected for more accurate results. Co-citation analysis uses different citations in articles of two topics and the map of connectivity was generated. Fifthly, citespace and MAXQDA were utilized to generate Wordcloud and perform cluster analysis to see the various relationships and patterns of keywords between articles within two topics. After gathering all the metadata and performing different bibliographic analyses, the relationship between the two topics was proven. However, these topics are still being researched. By providing potential future work, the significance of these topics and potential problems were discussed (Table 1).

3.1 Relationship to Human Factors and Ergonomics

This topic is closely related to two chapters in the Handbook of Human Factors and Ergonomics: Chapter 20, 'Human Errors and Human Reliability,' and Chapter 53, 'Human Factors and Ergonomics in Health Care'. (Salvendy 2012) As the title suggests, this chapter is closely related to understanding human error and strategies to control it. Additionally, it examines human error in the context of human-automation interaction as part of the emerging field. On the other hand, Chapter 53 provides a more in-depth exploration of the complexity within healthcare industries, where individuals interact with multiple system elements. These two chapters enable us to gain a deeper understanding of the intricacies of the healthcare system and human errors related to automation systems".

Table 1. Sequential Step-by-Step Procedure

Steps	Activities
1	Topic Selection
1.1	Partner Selection
1.2	Analysis Tools Review
1.3	Usage of Databases Review
1.4	Analysis Tools/Databases Selection
2	Data Collection
2.1	Utilize Databases
2.2	Google Ngram for Trend Analysis
2.3	Wordcloud
2.4	Scite.ai
3	Introduction/Abstract
4	Analyze results from 2. ~ 2.4
5	Utilize VOSviewer
5.1	Co-citation Analysis
5.2	Content Analysis
6	Utilize Citespace/MAXQDA
6.1	Create Wordcloud
6.2	Cluster Analysis
7	Discussion/Conclusion
8	Future Work
9	Reference/In Text Citation
10	Final Review
10.1	Final version submission

4   Research Methodology

4.1   Data Collection with Harzing

Two topics "Healthcare Automation" and "Human Error at Work" were searched using Harzing Publish or Perish (through Google Scholar) metadata. The search was limited to 500 articles, with no other restrictions applied. A total of 500 articles using the search terms Healthcare Automation and Human Error at Work were extracted. Both sets of results were saved for further analyses using BibExcel.

4.2   Data Collection

The data of two topics, The data on two topics, "Healthcare Automation" and "Human Error at Work" was collected between three different databases, Google Scholar, Scopus, and Dimensions, the" and "Human Error at Work" was collected between three different databases, Google Scholar, Scopus, and Dimensions, between the entire year and the recent year. From this data collection, the information content of each database was analyzed not only for recent years and entire years but also between different topics (Table 2).

Table 2. "Healthcare Automation" Data Collection from Different Databases for Entire Year vs Recent Year

Database	Keyword	Number of Articles
Google Scholar (Entire Year)	Healthcare Automation	1100000
Google Scholar (After 2018)	Healthcare Automation	21400
Scopus (Entire Year)	Healthcare Automation	5425
Scopus (After 2018)	Healthcare Automation	3237
Dimensions (Entire Year)	Healthcare Automation	280643
Dimensions (After 2018)	Healthcare Automation	178518

The figure above represents the number of articles on the topic "Healthcare Automation" between three databases, Google Scholar, Scopus, and Dimensions, for the entire year and the recent year. From the result, Google Scholar had the greatest number of articles at 1100000 articles. However, Dimension had more recent articles in 178518. Scopus had the least number of articles, but it provides various analysis tools within the results. Despite the result of the number of articles, the articles on the topic "Healthcare Automation" had a high number of articles for the recent year which represents the topic is still being researched (Table 3).

Table 3. "Human Error at Work" Data Collection from Different Databases for Entire Year vs Recent Year

Database	Keyword	Number of Articles
Google Scholar (Entire Year)	Human Error at Work	7720000
Google Scholar (After 2018)	Human Error at Work	135000
Scopus (Entire Year)	Human Error at Work	13506
Scopus (After 2018)	Human Error at Work	5954
Dimensions (Entire Year)	Human Error at Work	8704350
Dimensions (After 2018)	Human Error at Work	3517551

The figure above represents the number of articles on one topic "Human Error at Work" between three databases, Google Scholar, Scopus, and Dimensions, for the entire year and the recent year. From the result, Dimensions had the greatest number of articles at 8704350 and the most recent articles at 3517551. Like the previous result, Scopus had the least number of overall results. Despite the result of the number of articles, the articles on the topic "Human Error at Work" had a high number of articles for the recent year which topic is still being researched (Fig. 3).

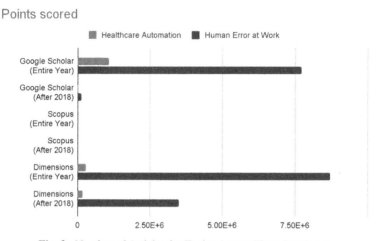

Fig. 3. Number of Articles for Topics Across Three Databases

The figure above represents the overall summary of the total number of articles on two topics, "Healthcare Automation" and "Human Error at Work" within three different databases, Google Scholar, Scopus, and Dimensions. From the result, Scopus contained the least number of articles. However, Scopus provides various analysis tools that can create the results of documents by country, documents by author, document documentation, and documents by subject area. Dimensions had the greatest number of articles for the recent and entire year. Google Scholar and Dimensions could be utilized to gather different metadata of the topics, and Scopus could be utilized to create different analyses to see the insight of the results.

4.3 Trend Analysis

Google Ngram is a groundbreaking analysis tool that allows the user to create trend diagrams that show the number of articles of different keywords of interest. It allows you to choose the options of year, language, and case sensitivity while searching the keyword. For the trend analysis, the keywords, "Healthcare", "Automation", and "Dispensing Robot", were used for the topic, "Healthcare Automation". Also, the keywords, "Human Error", "Medication Error", and "Reliability", were searched for the topic, "Human Error at Work" (Fig. 4).

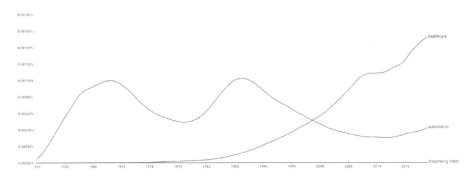

Fig. 4. Google Ngram Visual of "Healthcare Automation"

The figure above represents the trend diagram of the topic, "Healthcare Automation", with three keywords, "Healthcare", "Automation", and "Dispensing Robot". The keyword "Automation" started to increase after the 1950speakedpeaks around the 1960s and the 1990s. The result slightly decreased after the 1990s and increased after the 2010s. The keyword "Healthcare" started to increase around the 1970s and shows constant increment which represents that these two topics are still being researched in many institutes. Unlike the other two keywords, the keyword "Dispensing Robot" has a small number of articles and it starts to increase after 2015 (Fig. 5).

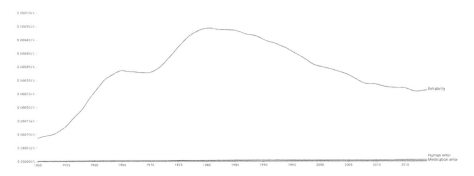

Fig. 5. Google Ngram Visual of "Human Error at Work"

The figure above represents the trend diagram of the topic, "Human Error at Work", with three keywords, "Reliability", "Human Error", and "Medication Error". The keyword "Reliability" started to increase after the 1950s which is like the previous keyword, "Automation". It peaks around the 1980s and slightly decreases until the 2010s and increases again in recent years. However, the keywords, "Human Error" and "Medication Error", have a minor number of results which started to increase after 2010 which represents that these topics are new and starting to be researched.

The keywords, "Automation" and "Reliability", from two different topics show similar trends after the 1980s. Also, the keywords, "Medication Error", "Human Error" and "Dispensing Robot", show similar trends after the 2010s when they just started to get researched by different institutes. By looking at the results of the trend analysis, we can assume that the keywords of the two topics are related, and the relationships are going to be analyzed in the result section.

5   Result

5.1   Co-citation Analysis

VOSviewer is a critical tool that can create various analyses based on metadata of the topics from different databases. A co-citation map consists of nodes representing distinct articles and edges indicating the co-occurrence of these articles. (Leydesdorff, L. 2015) For the topics, "Healthcare Automation" and "Human Error at Work", the metadata was generated in a CSV file format to utilize the VOSviewer from Dimensions and Scopus. For the co-citation analysis, the CSV file from Dimension was used to generate co-citation analysis to see the relationships of different authors of articles in the same topic area which would help the reader to visualize the relationship of the citations in different articles (Fig. 6).

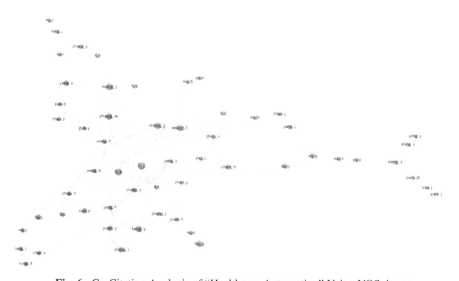

Fig. 6. Co-Citation Analysis of "Healthcare Automation" Using VOSviewer

The figure above represents the co-citation analysis generated with VOSviewer about the topic "Healthcare Automation". A total number of 564 articles were extracted from Dimensions. Since there was a low number of results the parameter of occurrence was reduced to 3 citations which allowed the diagram to be generated with maximized connectivity where the clusters are differentiated by different lines and colors. Despite weak connections due to the lower number of articles, related studies showed some connections based on the co-citation analysis. (Fruehwirt, W. 2021; Singh, N. 2024; Williams, D. 2006) (Fig. 7).

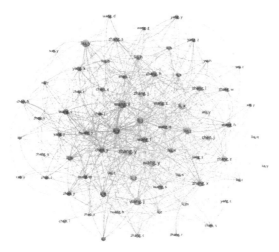

Fig. 7. Co-Citation Analysis of "Human Error at Work" Using VOSviewer

The figure above represents the co-citation analysis generated with VOSviewer about the topic "Human Error at Work". A total number of 6353 articles were extracted from Dimensions. Compared to the last results of "Healthcare Automation", the results of "Human Error at Work" were significantly higher. Due to the high number of results, the parameter of occurrence was increased to 10. Even though the parameter of occurrence was a lot higher than in the last analysis, there was a lot more connectivity between citations and stronger clusters which were differentiated by different lines and colors.

5.2 Content Analysis (Vosviewer)

VOSviewer not only allows the user to perform co-citation analysis but also the content analysis of gathered metadata of different topics. The bibliographic data, network data, and text data of two topics, "Healthcare Automation" and "Human Error at Work" was generated in CSV file form from the database, Scopus. By utilizing VOSviewer, the user is allowed to perform the content analysis which generates the connectivity of keywords from various articles which share different keywords (Fig. 8).

The figures above represent various keywords that were commonly used in the two topics, "Healthcare Automation" and "Human Error at Work". Before creating the diagrams for the content analysis, the user is allowed to see various shared terms, occurrences of the keywords, and the relevance between the keywords on the same topic. However, this map was generated based on the occurrences of the keywords in the article on the same topic. There were a lot of unrelated keywords such as prepositions and conjunctions. Therefore, most conjunctions and prepositions were deselected to generate a more accurate analysis (Fig. 9).

The figure above represents the content analysis of "Healthcare Automation" which was generated by VOSviewer. The user is allowed to change the size of the node, the size of the fonts, and the size of the connectivity depending on the occurrence of the various keywords. The bigger cluster and the bigger node represent that the keywords are

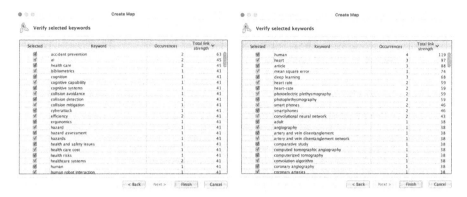

Fig. 8. VOSviewer Keyword Search

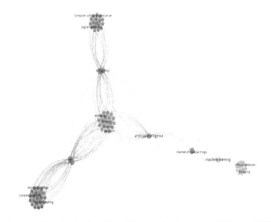

Fig. 9. Content Analysis for "Healthcare Automation" Using VOSviewer

occurring more often. Also, the color of the lines represents the relationships between those keywords between shared articles. The topic "Healthcare Automation", "Accident Prevention", "AI", "Healthcare", and "Bibliometrics" were some of the keywords which were shared among the articles on this topic (Fig. 10).

The figure above represents the content analysis of the topic "Human Error at Work" which was generated by VOSviewer. "Mean square error", "Deep learning". "Heart rate", "Convolutional neural network" and "Angiography" were some of the keywords which were shared in the articles on this topic. By looking at the size of the nodes, the color of the lines, and the clusters, the user can easily define different connectivity and relationships between the topics which allows them to analyze the articles more efficiently.

5.3 Industry Identification with Dimensions

Dimensions.ai was utilized to identify the categories of research publications for our two keywords. Information and computing science were the most dominating fields in

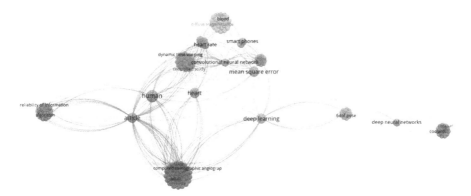

Fig. 10. Content Analysis for "Human Error at Work" Using VOSviewer

healthcare automation. This encompasses fields such as artificial intelligence, machine learning, and data science, playing a significant role in advancing healthcare automation. These technologies offer various opportunities to improve outcomes in the healthcare sector. The Health Science field ranked fifth on the list, but the number was significantly lower compared to information and computing science. The most cited relevant article published by Schmidhuber, J (2015) also came from the information and computer science field (Fig. 11).

Fig. 11. Number of Publications in Category of Industries for "Healthcare Automation"

For the 'Human Error at Work' keyword search, Biomedical and Clinical Science had the most publications, followed by Information and Computing Science. Despite the difference in order, four out of the five research categories were the same: Information and Computing Science, Engineering, Biomedical and Clinical Science, and Health Science (Fig. 12).

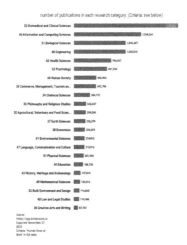

Fig. 12. Number of Publications in Category of Industries for "Human Error at Work"

5.4 Leading Authors and Sources

BibExcel is a tool designed to help analyzation of bibliographic data. We utilized this tool to analyze the articles collected from Harzing Publish or Perish (through Google Scholar) metadata. It is noteworthy that the results of BibExcel's source analysis were found to be incomplete. The program grouped literature sharing identical words within the source, leading to some limitations. Despite this, it became evident that the source "Human factors" predominated among the articles in this domain. Additionally, Carayon, the leading author of our analysis, is also the author of Ch. 53 Human Factors and Ergonomics in Healthcare. In addition, she is one of the authors who created SEIPS 3.0 model which is a fundamental framework utilized widely in healthcare and patient safety fields. (Carayon, P. 2020) (Table 4).

Table 4. Leading authors and sources of "Healthcare automation" and "Human Error at work"

Number	Author	Number	Sources
16	Carayon P	84	Human factors
11	Wickens CD	21	Human â€¦
10	Holden RJ	11	â€¦ on human factors in â€¦
9	Parasuraman R	10	Ergonomics
8	Woods DD	9	Applied Ergonomics
7	Lee JD	6	BMJ quality & safety
6	Cook RI	5	Journal of Biomedical Informatics
6	Hancock PA	5	Proceedings of the Human Factors and â€¦
6	Coiera E	5	Journal of Biomedical â€¦

5.5   Cluster Analysis Word Cloud

Citespace is an analysis tool that enables users to reveal patterns within the literature by generating clusters and citation bursts. This facilitates researchers in gaining insights and understanding relationships. Before conducting the analysis, literature related to the topics "Healthcare Automation" and "Human Errors at Work" was extracted from Web of Science in text format. The articles were organized by the "citation: highest first" option. Due to the limitations of the demo version, the first 150 articles from the "Healthcare Automation" search and the first 40 articles from the "Human Errors at Work" search were included in this study. For "Healthcare Automation," three clusters were generated, and no bursts were found. Keywords identified included lung cancer, early detection, and fluorescence bronchoscopy. The results of the second cluster analysis showed 7 clusters, with no bursts identified. Two articles were identified to have overlap and studied to utilize health technologies to reduce human error. (Ahsen, M. 2019 and Burton, J. 2020) (Figs. 13 and 14).

Fig. 13. Cluster Analysis for "Healthcare Automation" Using Citespace

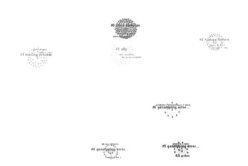

Fig. 14. Cluster Analysis for "Human Error at Work" Using Citespace

5.6   Content Analysis

MAXQDA is an analysis tool that helps the user to utilize different analysis tools such as "Word Explorer", "Text Search", "Profile Comparison Chart", and "Word Cloud". By utilizing these tools, the user can easily understand the text of the articles without reading the entire article. This can help the users to understand the concepts and insights of the topic in a timely and efficient manner. Two topics, "Healthcare Automation" and "Human Error at Work" were searched in ScienceDirect and 10 articles per topic that were highly related and interesting were downloaded in PDF format (Fig. 15).

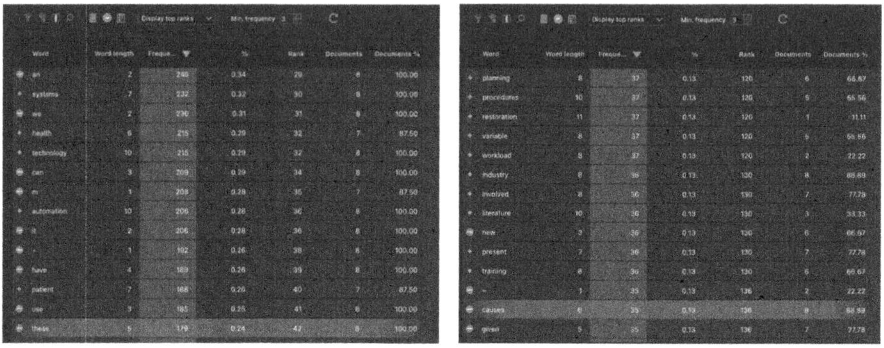

Fig. 15. Lists of Frequently Occurring Words

The figures above represent the lists of words that were frequently used in the articles per topic. For the accuracy of the analysis, the minimum number of occurrences was increased to 10 and a total of 150 words were used to create the "Word Cloud". However, there were a lot of unrelated words such as prepositions, conjunctions, and numbers, which were deselected and moved to the stop list. This process eliminated the unrelated words and increased the visuality and accuracy of the results (Fig. 16).

Fig. 16. Word Clouds of "Healthcare Automation" (Left) and "Human Error at Work" (Right)

The figure on the top and the left side represents the "Word Cloud" of the topic, "Healthcare Automation". For this topic, some of the keywords were healthcare, system, AI, Automation, and Pharmacy. The figure on the top and right side represents the "Word Cloud" of the topic, "Human Error at Work". For this topic, some of the keywords were work, error, performance, tasks, and procedure. Analyzing these figures of "Word Cloud", allows the user to understand the basic concept and insight of the articles which can encourage the user to choose the related topics and articles before reading the entire article.

6   Discussion

There has been a lot of research conducted concerning "Healthcare Automation" and "Human Error at Work" globally. However, the United States stands out as one of the leading countries in terms of research publication. Google Scholar has the highest total number of articles for "Healthcare Automation," while Dimensions yields the higher number of results for articles on "Human Errors at Work". For both topics, approximately 60% and 40% of articles were published after 2018 in Scopus and Dimensions, respectively. The consistent publication of recent articles signifies ongoing exploration and implies that the research areas are constantly changing or evolving. Our search revealed that Dimensions has a robust repository, hosting the most articles, while Google Scholar excels in overall volume. Researchers can utilize the strengths of each database to gather comprehensive metadata and generate diverse analyses, showcasing the multifaceted nature of these critical topics.

The trend analysis provided valuable insights into the evolution of the topic. In the exploration of "Healthcare Automation" "the graph showed that the use of the term "Automation" significantly increased post-1950s, peaking in the 1960s and 1990s. Meanwhile, "Healthcare" demonstrated a consistent upward trajectory since the 1970s, indicating sustained research interest Similarly, for the topic of "Human Error at Work," the trend diagram showed that "Reliability" was a more commonly used term than "Human Error" and "Medication Error". However, when comparing "Human Error" and "Medication Error," a significant difference was identified, with "Human Error" being used more frequently and showing upward trends since the 1920s. This provides a historical view of the evolution of interest in healthcare automation and human error at work, offering valuable insights for researchers.

Co-citation analysis revealed that "Healthcare Automation" has weaker connectivity compared to Human Error at Work. However, this is attributed to the lower number of articles utilized for the analysis of Human Automation. Content analysis was also conducted using VOSviewer. For Healthcare Automation, the following terms are most frequently used: "Accident Prevention," "AI," "Healthcare," and "Bibliometrics." Similarly, "Mean Square Error," "Deep Learning," "Heart Rate," "Convolutional Neural Network," and "Angiography" showed high occurrence in "Human Error at Work." This concludes that "Healthcare Automation" emphasizes terms related to accident prevention and AI, while "Human Error at Work" focuses on concepts like mean square error and deep learning.

Industry identification indicated that despite the variation in order, four out of the top five research categories remained consistent between the two keywords. This suggests a certain degree of overlap in the research landscape, emphasizing the interdisciplinary nature of topics related to human error at work. An analysis of leading authors revealed Pascale Carayon as the top contributor in this field. As an industrial engineering professor and researcher, she specializes in human factors and systems engineering, particularly in healthcare and patient safety research. This highlights the close connection between healthcare automation and human error at work, underscoring the significance of human factors in the context of healthcare.

Cluster analysis was completed using the demo version of CiteSpace and led to a major limitation—reducing the number of articles in this analysis. Only 40 articles from the first topic and 150 articles from the second topic were included. Thus, it is hard to conclude the relationship between the two topics. Lastly, content analysis using MaxQDA emphasizes the efficiency and improved patient care in healthcare automation. The analysis of human error at work expresses the importance of recognizing and reducing errors in different work-related situations. This shows the potential influences of human errors and highlights the complex relationship between technology and healthcare in work settings.

7 Conclusion

Human error in work is closely related to ergonomics due to the impact of human factors and ergonomics on the occurrence of errors which highlights that errors often occur due to the mismatch between the system, technique, and characteristics of the human body. (Mao. X. 2015) Furthermore, the field of human factors and ergonomics has a strong potential in system analysis, design, and improvement, indicating its relevance in addressing human errors. (Karltun. A. 2017) The COVID–19 pandemic has significantly impacted the healthcare industry it generated unique challenges such as elevated levels of stress, burnout, and anxiety toward numerous healthcare professionals which are the main cause of human error in this industry. Automation technologies can contribute to the resilience and sustainability of healthcare systems during and future pandemics. The introduction of automation in healthcare systems can significantly contribute to overcoming reduced human resources and reducing challenges that were caused by various ergonomic reasons. (Dordevic. M. 2021) The bibliographic analysis of two topics, "Healthcare Automation" and "Human Error at Work", utilized various databases, analysis tools, and metadata regarding these topics. The relationship between these two topics was validated through the results of conducting co-citation analysis, content analysis, industry identification, cluster analysis, and content analysis utilizing keywords, citations, articles, and authors. The introduction of automation in various industries, including healthcare, has been aimed at reducing human error and improving overall system performance. However, the relationship between automation and human error is complex and multifaceted. While automation is designed to minimize human error, it can also introduce new types of errors and challenges. Several studies have highlighted the potential for automation to create opportunities for a different class of errors of commission and omission human error. (Iversen. F. 2013) After validating the relationships between the two topics, it is crucial to understand various ergonomics factors that can cause new types of errors and challenges utilizing automation. Developing and training the newly adapted and appropriate automation system will significantly contribute to mitigating the impact of COVID-19 and future crises with minimal consequences.

8 Future Work

The COVID-19 pandemic has stressed the healthcare system to the breaking point and has transformed healthcare delivery, forcing a strong shift to telemedicine. This reduction in in-person healthcare visits is a key strategy for healthcare surge control now and in the future. However, current tele-systems provide mostly communication support, while the physical interactions required for diagnostic procedures, interventional procedures, and bedside care still largely rely on in-person care. (Krieger, A. 2022) Understanding various factors of human errors in Ergonomics would allow healthcare workers to adopt new automated systems using robotics, automated healthcare systems, and dispensing robots with minor human errors where they have a direct impact on the health of the patients. It would be sufficient to understand various factors of causations and correlation in human errors while interacting with the newly adopted system to maximize the result in patient care with minimized errors. Innovative approaches in automation and robotics have the potential to assist and protect healthcare workers in many areas of patient care. The current work develops novel compliant actuators to enable safe physical interactions with patients, thus minimizing the need for physical contact with healthcare providers. The investigators will design robotic systems with varying degrees of autonomy, using a vascular access delivery system as a testbed. The technology developed in this project can be used to mitigate the impact of the next pandemic and spearhead change in healthcare of the future. (Krieger, A. 2022).

References

Ahsen, M.E., Ayvaci, M.U.S., Raghunathan, S.: When algorithmic predictions use human-generated data: a bias-aware classification algorithm for breast cancer diagnosis. Inf. Syst. Res. **30**(1), 97–116 (2019)

Burton, J.W., Stein, M.K., Jensen, T.B.: A systematic review of algorithm aversion in augmented decision making. J. Behav. Decis. Mak. **33**(2), 220–239 (2020)

Carayon, P., Wooldridge, A., Hoonakker, P., Hundt, A.S., Kelly, M.M.: SEIPS 3.0: human-centered design of the patient journey for patient safety. Appl. Ergon. **84**, 103033 (2020). https://doi.org/10.1016/j.apergo.2019.103033

Davenport, T., Kalakota, R.: The potential for artificial intelligence in healthcare. Future Healthc. J. **6**(2), 94–98 (2019). https://doi.org/10.7861/futurehosp.6-2-94

Đorđević, M., et al.: Effects of automation on sustainability of Immunohistochemistry laboratory. Healthcare **9**(7), 866 (2021). https://doi.org/10.3390/healthcare9070866

Fruehwirt, W., Duckworth, P.: Towards better healthcare: What could and should be automated? Technol. Forecast. Soc. Change **172**, 120967 (2021)

Ganiats, T.: Human error in medicine. JAMA J. Am. Med. Assoc. **273**(14), 1156 (1995). https://doi.org/10.1001/jama.1995.03520380092046

Gaynor, M., Wyner, G., & Gupta, A.: Dr. Watson? Balancing automation and human expertise in healthcare delivery. Leveraging applications of formal methods, verification and validation. Spec. Tech. Appl., 561–569 (2014). https://doi.org/10.1007/978-3-662-45231-8_46

Iversen, F., Gressgård, L.J., Thorogood, J.L., Balov, M.K., Hepsø, V.: Drilling automation: Potential for human error. OnePetro (2013). https://onepetro.org/DC/article/28/01/45/204773/Drilling-Automation-Potential-for-Human-Error

Karltun, A., Karltun, J., Berglund, M., Eklund, J.: HTO – a complementary ergonomics approach. Appl. Ergon. **59**, 182–190 (2017). https://doi.org/10.1016/j.apergo.2016.08.024

Khan, B., et al.: Drawbacks of artificial intelligence and their potential solutions in the healthcare sector. Biomed. Mater. Devices (2023). https://doi.org/10.1007/s44174-023-00063-2

Krieger, A.: Safeguarding the health of healthcare workers during future pandemics, using robotics and automation. Principal Investigator (2022). https://www.nsf.gov/awardsearch/showAward?AWD_ID=2222716&HistoricalAwards=false

Leydesdorff, L.: Bibliometrics/citation networks. arXiv preprint arXiv:1502.06378 (2015)

Mao, X.: An evaluation of the effects of human factors and ergonomics on health care and patient safety practices: a systematic review. PLoS ONE (2015). https://journals.plos.org/plosone/article?id=10.1371/journal.pone.0129948

Salvendy, G. (ed.): Handbook of Human Factors and Ergonomics. Wiley, Hoboken (2012)

Schmidhuber, J.: Deep learning in neural networks: an overview. Neural Netw. **61**, 85–117 (2015)

Singh, N., Jain, M., Kamal, M.M., Bodhi, R., Gupta, B.: Technological paradoxes and artificial intelligence implementation in healthcare. An application of paradox theory. Technol. Forecast. Soc. Change **198**, 122967 (2024)

Singh Rehan, H.: Medication errors are preventable. J. Pharmacovigil. **s2** (2015). https://doi.org/10.4172/2329-6887.s2-005

Williams, D.J., Ratchev, S., Chandra, A., Hirani, H.: The application of assembly and automation technologies to healthcare products. CIRP Ann. **55**(2), 617–642 (2006)

NurseAid Monitor: An Ergonomics Dashboard to Help Change Position of Bedridden Patients

Rafael de Pinho André[(⊠)], Almir Fonseca, Lucas Westfal, and Almir Mirabeau

Fundação Getúlio Vargas, Rio de Janeiro, Brazil
rafael.pinho@fgv.br
https://emap.fgv.br/en

Abstract. Wheelchair users and patients who remain bedridden for extended periods are at risk of developing pressure ulcers or bedsores, painful and dangerous wounds that can lead to serious infections if not treated properly. Moreover, prolonged immobility also contributes to muscle atrophy, respiratory and circulatory complications, decreased bone density, and metabolic changes - reducing the patient's autonomy and quality of life after hospital discharge, and hindering the recovery process. We propose an IoT monitoring platform that supports wheelchair users and bedridden patients by assisting nurses and caregivers in an essential routine activity: the changing of positions or turning of patients. An extended experiment was conducted with a diverse base of volunteers and the help of certified health professionals. The collected data is used by a Machine Learning model to power an Ergonomics Dashboard that helps (i) understanding of the right moment to reposition the patient, (ii) deciding on the position for the next change, (iii) inspecting if position changes are occurring according to the medical planning and (iv) probing the patient's position between changes.

Keywords: Health and Ergonomics · IoT Computing and Sensing · Postural Data Visualization

1 Introduction

Wheelchair users and individuals confined to bed for prolonged periods confront significant health challenges that extend far beyond the limitations imposed by their primary conditions. Among the most severe of these secondary complications are pressure ulcers, or bedsores, which develop due to sustained pressure on the skin, cutting off blood supply and leading to tissue necrosis. These lesions are not only painful but can also serve as entry points for infections, posing a serious risk to the patient's health. The development of pressure ulcers is a clear indicator of the need for meticulous care and monitoring, emphasizing the critical nature of regular repositioning and skin assessment [5,6,9]. Furthermore, prolonged immobility contributes to a cascade of physiological deterioration including muscle atrophy, which results in strength loss and reduced mobility, complicating the path to recovery and independence [11].

© The Author(s), under exclusive license to Springer Nature Switzerland AG 2024
V. G. Duffy (Ed.): HCII 2024, LNCS 14710, pp. 35–46, 2024.
https://doi.org/10.1007/978-3-031-61063-9_3

Beyond the physical impairments, the experience of being bedridden or confined to a wheelchair can significantly impact the patient's mental health and overall quality of life. The lack of autonomy and the dependency on caregivers for basic needs can lead to feelings of helplessness and depression, further exacerbating the patient's condition. Additionally, the social isolation experienced by many of these patients can accelerate cognitive decline and diminish their motivation for participation in rehabilitation efforts, making it a pivotal area for intervention. These psychological and social challenges highlight the need for a holistic approach to care that includes not only medical and physical support, but also psychological and social rehabilitation.

In response to these multifaceted challenges, the emergence of Mobile Health technologies offers a promising avenue for enhancing the care and monitoring of bedridden patients and wheelchair users. Mobile Health applications can facilitate more frequent assessments of risk factors for pressure ulcers, enable remote monitoring of patient well-being, and support adherence to repositioning protocols. Moreover, these technologies have the potential to bridge the gap between patients and their care teams, fostering a sense of connection and support that can mitigate feelings of isolation. With the capability to personalize interventions and monitor progress in real time, Mobile Health solutions are poised to transform the management of bedridden and wheelchair-bound patients, ensuring that their care is continuous, comprehensive, and centered on their needs and experiences [8].

Within this context, usage of RPM (Remote Patient Monitoring) to track a patient's clinical status increased significantly in the last ten years, driving investments in the Health Tech sector and commanding increased attention from research institutions [1,15,16,18,19]. Usually, RPM systems are based on two main concepts: medical information collection and medical information display.

As to medical information collection, in addition to the clinical status traditionally collected from bedridden patients, the continuous and automatic collection of posture information in intensive care settings is equally crucial, where subtle changes in a patient's condition can have significant implications and timely decision-making is key to a successful treatment. From garments and bed sheets [17] to smartwatch platforms [10], diverse approaches to posture information collection have been researched. A large number of studies show that maintaining adequate patient posture correlates positively with the outcome of medical interventions, such as, reduced risk of invasive mechanical ventilation in respiratory syndrome or faster recovery in musculoskeletal traumas.

Regarding medical information display, appropriate visual management is indispensable for nurses and caregivers in a medical environment, allowing for a clear and immediate overview of patient statuses, workflows, and potential issues, allowing for more efficient and quicker decision-making. By using visual indicators, such as electronic dashboards, nurses can easily identify priorities, monitor patient progress, and detect abnormalities in real-time. Medical literature, such as [4,7,12], emphasizes that this not only optimizes their workflow, but also enhances patient recovery and reduces the chances of oversight or errors.

In high-pressure medical settings, visual management serves as a cornerstone for maintaining organization, promoting patient safety, and ensuring consistent, high-quality care.

We propose an IoT monitoring platform that employs low-resolution thermal imaging to collect postural data, aiming to protect the patients' privacy and autonomy. It can be deployed on infirmaries, intensive care units (ICU) and home care - due to the non-invasive nature of the sensor - to collect real-time information on the patient's position and ergonomic status, streaming the data into a database server specifically designed to store medical information for future analysis.

Our results show that the platform is accurate to provide reliable long-term postural information and the Ergonomics Dashboard can improve the activities related to the turning of the patients. We are now preparing to deploy the platform on a medical beds at Pedro Ernesto College Hospital and Gaffrée e Guinle College Hospital, both located at Rio de Janeiro, Brazil, to refine the prototype, the Machine Learning Model and the Bed Position Dashboard.

Section 2 presents related work and a brief literature review of pressure ulcer prevention studies. The design of the IoT platform, sensors deployment, replication information and data collection are shown on Sect. 3. Section 4 shows the machine learning model and the medical data dashboard developed from the acquired data. Conclusion and future work are discussed on Sect. 5.

2   Related Work

This section presents an analysis of research projects that collect postural data to support pressure ulcer prevention. We conducted a review of the related works on relevant databases such as, although not limited to, ACM Digital Library, IEEE Xplore, NIH, PubMed and Springer Link.

In [14] the Simultaneously-Collected Multimodal Lying Pose (SLP) dataset is presented, which has been since utilized in numerous other researches for validation or training purposes. This database comprises various types of coverings and images from both RGB cameras and Long Wavelength Infrared (LWIR) cameras, which are vertically aligned with the bed. It primarily categorizes poses into supine, lateral left, and lateral right. For each category, 15 poses are collected. For training, a stacked hourglass (HG) network was used, which, according to the research, is A strong model for pose analysis. The model performed well in dark conditions and with blankets, achieving 96% accuracy with data collected in a hospital setting.

The study presented in [3] aims to analyze obstructive sleep apnea. To this end, the position of the head and the upper body poses is examined during sleep using an infrared camera and Convolutional Neural Networks (CNNs). In the experiment, conducted to differentiate between lateral and supine positions, data from 50 participants was collected. The devised model achieved 87% accuracy and an 87% F1-Score for body position detection, although challenged when the participant's body is heavily covered.

The research in [13] addresses the automatic detection of head and torso positions during sleep, aiming to analyze sleep quality and sleep patterns. It focuses more on the machine learning architecture for that task, proposing a framework that combines motion detection with a convolutional neural network to classify body posture. The architecture comprises two stages: the first detects movement in the video and the second classifies the posture. The results indicate an accuracy of 91.7%, challenged by the patient's cover as the other reviewed studies.

The study presented in [2] investigates automatic body position detection during sleep using RGB and Long-Wave Infrared (LWIR) imagery. To address the challenge of annotating images obtained with LWIR, researchers utilized data from participants laying in bed without blankets and then trained Unsupervised learning models to transform the images to simulate various types of coverage, such as thin, thick, and extreme. Using both real and simulated images, Convolutional Neural Network (CNN) models, including Stacked Hourglass and Simple Baseline, were employed for body position detection. The Simultaneously-Collected Multimodal Lying Pose (SLP) dataset was used to train and test the models. No original data were collected in this study; it primarily focused on testing the simulation of coverage in images and how it affects the outcome.

3   Building the IoT Platform and Data Collection

On this Section, we describe the stages followed to develop the IoT Platform: prototyping the IoT device and implementing the IoT infrastructure for data collection.

In this study, we employed the MLX90640 infrared thermal array sensor from Melexis, notable for its compact form factor and cost-effectiveness, featuring a 32×24 pixel resolution. This sensor is distinguished by its ease of integration, facilitated by an I2C-compatible digital interface, and its capacity for high-precision, non-contact temperature measurements. The MLX90640 offers a broad field of view (FoV) of $110° \times 75°$ and a programmable refresh rate ranging from 0.5 Hz to 64 Hz, ensuring versatility in various applications. Given the focus on continuous monitoring over extended durations (hours or days), we selected a refresh rate of 1 Hz for this project, balancing data resolution with the need for long-term stability.

The MLX90640, encapsulated within the M5 Thermal Unit by M5 Stack, was interfaced with the M5 Stick C Plus - an ESP32-based microcontroller from the same manufacturer. This controller is equipped with a 2.4 GHz 802.11b/g/n WiFi transceiver and dual-mode Bluetooth® (classic and low-energy), enabling efficient data acquisition and transmission. Data, timestamped using Network Time Protocol (NTP) servers, was relayed to a remote real-time database. Communication between these components was achieved using the I^2C protocol via the Groove cables, connecting essential pins (VCC, GND, SDA, SCL) provided by M5 Stack.

To ensure optimal positioning of the thermal sensor and microcontroller above the bedridden patient, we designed a 3D printed folding arm that can be easily mounted and removed from the bed's headboard, shown in Fig. 1. This design emphasizes not only convenience but also the bedridden patient safety, avoiding the risks associated with ceiling-mounted systems or excessively long, unstable arms. This mobile setup allows for quick retraction to not obstruct emergency medical procedures or routine care. The system enters standby mode when the arm is folded and resumes data collection upon returning to its operational position.

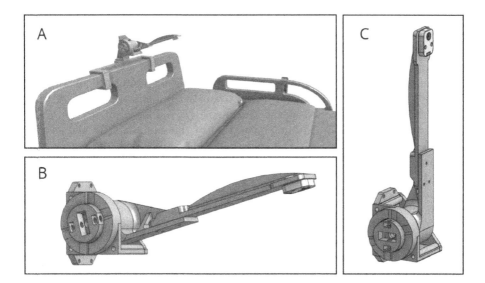

Fig. 1. A: Fastening of the device in an hospital bed - clamping the headboard. B: Extended position configuration. C: Retracted position configuration.

The standard dimensions for the bed mattresses available for the research are 190 cm × 90 cm. We evaluated different sensor positioning schemes aiming to maximize image bed coverage. Table 1 summarizes these sensor positioning schemes. 'Height' refers to the vertical distance measured from the top of the mattress to the sensor. 'Distance' denotes the horizontal length from the sensor to the head of the bed. 'Angle' corresponds to the tilt of the sensor's central infrared beam within the Field of View (FoV) relative to the bed. Figure 1 bellow illustrates the sensor's Field of View (FoV) for each assessed position.

In the process of optimizing bed coverage, four distinct sensor placements were evaluated. The initial strategy involved perpendicular coverage of the bed from a top-view perspective, utilizing the thermal sensor in both landscape (P_1) and portrait (P_2) orientations. Despite the achievement of comprehensive bed coverage, the suboptimal utilization of the Field of View's (FoV) usable area

Table 1. Sensor Placement Specifications.

Position	Height	Distance	Angle	Orientation
P1	124 cm	95 cm	90°	Landscape
P2	66 cm	95 cm	90°	Portrait
P3	56 cm	0 cm	35°	Portrait
P4	60 cm	30 cm	75°	Landscape

and the consequent inclusion of extraneous bed areas led to the rejection of these positionings. Furthermore, the requirement for either ceiling installation or positioning directly above the patient posed significant logistical challenges, ranging from the complexities of installation and maintenance to the practicalities of equipment operation.

To address the challenges associated with overhead mounting, an alternative approach involving an oblique angle towards the bed was explored, with the thermal sensor positioned at the headboard (P_3). This configuration facilitated a more straightforward implementation of the equipment at the cost of producing distorted imagery in the lower extremities and indiscriminately capturing the area in front of the bed, introducing irrelevant noise into the data collected.

In pursuit of an optimal compromise between comprehensive coverage and minimal distortion, further experimentation led to the placement of the sensor directly above the patient's head (P_4), leveraging a slight tilt to enhance FoV coverage. This adjustment yielded images of exceptional clarity, particularly of critical anatomical structures including the head, shoulders, arms, chest, and abdomen. Given these structures' pronounced thermal signatures, this positioning proved superior in facilitating accurate patient position detection. Therefore, this sensor alignment was chosen as the preferred method for data collection, aligning with the objective to enhance the quality and reliability of the postural data acquired.

Figure 3 summarizes the characteristics (age, height, weight, and gender) of the volunteers for the data collection. Non-uniform distributions do not compromise the integrity or reliability of the results obtained by the machine learning model, as this data is not taken into account by the model. However, considerable ranges indicate a diverse set, beneficial for the generalization of this work's findings.

4   Development of the AI Model and the Dashboard

On this Section, we describe the machine learning model and the medical data dashboard developed from the acquired data (Fig. 2).

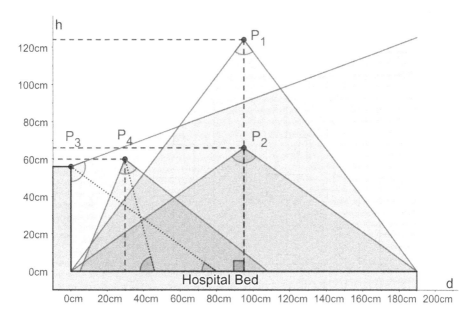

Fig. 2. Assessment of Sensor Coverage Projection from Lateral Perspective of a Hospital Bed.

4.1 Machine Learning Model

To prevent the model from overfitting and achieve greater accuracy, we employed Data Augmentation to increase the training set. We used the Translation technique, shifting the image into various areas along the x-axis or y-axis to increase the participant's body occupancy area in the image, thus addressing the issue of limited data collection and inherent training bias. The empty space created by the translation was filled with the lowest temperature feature and standard noise. Translation was limited to a maximum of 7 pixels, and samples where the body exceeds the bed's boundaries were removed. Figure 4 illustrates the difference between original and augmented images.

The selected model was the Light Gradient Boosting Machine (LGBM). It achieved a base accuracy of 87% boosted to 94% with Data Augmentation. Figure 5 illustrates the frequency with which each pixel in the image was used in the model. The higher the value, the more relevant the pixel is to the model.

4.2 Medical Data Dashboard

The aim of the dashboard is to present a dynamic object, that considers and highlights the delays and inaccuracies of its actual operation. Regarding information design, our objectives were to:

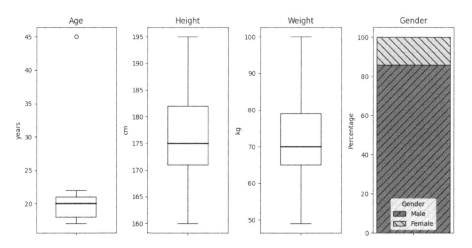

Fig. 3. Anthropometric characteristics and gender distribution over the training dataset.

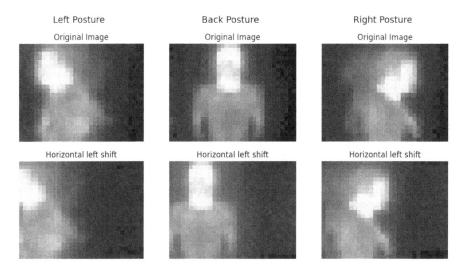

Fig. 4. Original images at the top and augmented images at the bottom.

- Reinforce its resemblance to a clock, including the addition of ticks for better orientation in the hour space and a hand to highlight the current period in the cycle;
- Use of colors instead of text to simplify visualization and interpretation;
- Prioritize the display of actual intervals in each posture. If the time in a given posture exceeds the recommended limit, these intervals are highlighted with red markers;

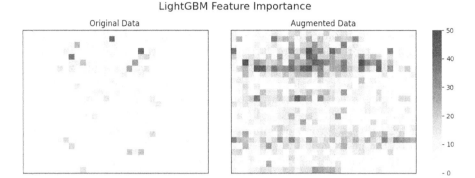

Fig. 5. LightGBM feature importance.

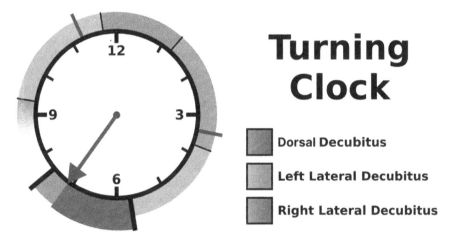

Fig. 6. A decubitus turning clock, representing the current and previous position change periods.

– Visually inform the elapsed time and remaining time of a position; and,
– Avoid overlap of information or the need for the user to reset the clock.

Concerning the represented data, the devised visualization displays the current period in the decubitus change cycle, with emphasis on:

– The beginning of the cycle (last change);
– The anticipated end of the cycle (according to the recommended limit);
– The elapsed time after the recommended limit, if it is exceeded; and,
– The positioning within the current period.

And the previous periods, with emphasis on (i) the actual elapsed time (with start and end marked) and (ii) the recommended limit, if it has been exceeded. Figure 6 illustrates a snapshot of the dashboard.

5   Conclusion and Future Work

This ongoing study introduced an innovative Internet of Things (IoT) monitoring platform aimed at preventing pressure ulcers on wheelchair users and patients confined to prolonged bed rest. Through the integration of a Machine Learning model and an Ergonomics Dashboard, our system assists healthcare professionals in making informed decisions about patient positioning, thereby mitigating the risks of pressure ulcers and associated complications. The extended experiment, supported by a diverse group of volunteers and certified health professionals, demonstrated the platform's potential and represents a significant step forward in utilizing non-invasive privacy-protecting technology to enhance patient autonomy, quality of life, and recovery outcomes post-hospital discharge.

Looking ahead, our focus will extend to refining the Machine Learning model to incorporate real-time feedback mechanisms that allow for the dynamic adjustment of patient care plans. An area of particular interest is the development of predictive analytics capabilities to estimate the Braden Scale for Predicting Pressure Ulcer Risk. Additionally, we plan to explore the integration of wearable sensors to provide a more comprehensive overview of the patient's health status, further enriching the data available for care optimization. A broader deployment of the platform, encompassing a wider range of healthcare settings and patient demographics, will also be pursued to validate its effectiveness and scalability.

To bridge the gap between technological potential and clinical adoption, future work will also emphasize user-centered information design principles, ensuring that the platform remains intuitive and accessible for all healthcare professionals. Engaging directly with end users, including nurses, caregivers, and patients themselves, will be crucial in iterating the design to better meet their needs. Furthermore, the establishment of partnerships with Pedro Ernesto and Gaffrée e Guinle College Hospitals for pilot studies will facilitate real-world insights into the system's impact, allowing for continuous improvement.

References

1. Abranches, D., O'Sullivan, D., Bird, J.: Nurse-led design and development of an expert system for pressure ulcer management. In: Extended Abstracts of the 2019 CHI Conference on Human Factors in Computing Systems, CHI EA 2019, pp. 1–6. Association for Computing Machinery, New York (2019). https://doi.org/10.1145/3290607.3312958
2. Afham, M., Haputhanthri, U., Pradeepkumar, J., Anandakumar, M., Silva, A.D., Edussooriya, C.U.S.: Towards accurate cross-domain in-bed human pose estimation. CoRR **abs/2110.03578** (2021). https://arxiv.org/abs/2110.03578
3. Akbarian, S., Delfi, G., Zhu, K., Yadollahi, A., Taati, B.: Automated non-contact detection of head and body positions during sleep. IEEE Access **7**, 72826–72834 (2019). https://doi.org/10.1109/ACCESS.2019.2920025
4. Arora, T., Balasubramanian, V., Mai, S.: Prioritization of clinical alarms using semantic features of vital signs in remote patient monitoring. In: Proceedings of the 2022 Australasian Computer Science Week, ACSW 2022, pp. 242–245. Association for Computing Machinery (2022). https://doi.org/10.1145/3511616.3513124

5. Bergstrom, N., Braden, B.J., Laguzza, A., Holman, V.: The braden scale for predicting pressure sore risk. Nurs. Res. **36**, 205–210 (1987)
6. Bergstrom, N., Braden, B., Kemp, M., Champagne, M., Ruby, E.: Predicting pressure ulcer risk. A multisite study of the predictive validy of the Braden scale. Nurs. Res. **47**(5) (1998). https://doi.org/10.1097/00006199-199809000-00005
7. Enshaeifar, S., Barnaghi, P., Skillman, S., Sharp, D., Nilforooshan, R., Rostill, H.: A digital platform for remote healthcare monitoring. In: Companion Proceedings of the Web Conference 2020, WWW 2020, pp. 203–206. Association for Computing Machinery, New York (2020). https://doi.org/10.1145/3366424.3383541
8. Free C., Phillips G., W.L., et al.: The effectiveness of mobile-health technologies to improve health care service delivery processes: a systematic review and meta-analysis. PLoS Med. **10**(1), e1001363 (2013). https://doi.org/10.1371/journal.pmed.1001363
9. Huang, C., et al.: Predictive validity of the Braden scale for pressure injury risk assessment in adults: a systematic review and meta-analysis. Nurs. Open **8**(5), 2194–2207 (2021). https://doi.org/10.1002/nop2.792
10. Karnati, Y., et al.: ROAMM: a customizable and interactive smartwatch platform for patient-generated health data. In: Proceedings of the 2021 Thirteenth International Conference on Contemporary Computing, IC3 2021, pp. 150–158. Association for Computing Machinery, New York (2021). https://doi.org/10.1145/3474124.3474144
11. Kortebein, P.: Rehabilitation for hospital-associated deconditioning. Am. J. Phys. Med. Rehabil. **88**(1), 66–77 (2009)
12. Kuge, J., Grundgeiger, T., Schlosser, P., Sanderson, P., Happel, O.: Design and evaluation of a head-worn display application for multi-patient monitoring. In: Proceedings of the 2021 ACM Designing Interactive Systems Conference, DIS 2021, pp. 879–890. Association for Computing Machinery, New York (2021). https://doi.org/10.1145/3461778.3462011
13. Li, Y.Y., Wang, S.J., Hung, Y.P.: A vision-based system for in-sleep upper-body and head pose classification. Sensors **22**(5) (2022). https://doi.org/10.3390/s22052014
14. Liu, S., Ostadabbas, S.: Seeing under the cover: a physics guided learning approach for in-bed pose estimation. CoRR **abs/1907.02161** (2019). http://arxiv.org/abs/1907.02161
15. Liu, W.M., Chen, C.L., Chang, L.Y., Pong, S.C., Chen, H.M.: Multimodal and multispectral imaging for chronic pressure ulcer assessment. In: Proceedings of the 2nd International Conference on Biomedical Signal and Image Processing, ICBIP 2017, pp. 47–52. Association for Computing Machinery, New York (2017). https://doi.org/10.1145/3133793.3133802
16. Matthies, D.J., Haescher, M., Chodan, W., Bieber, G.: DIY-PressMat: a smart sensor mat for posture detection applicable for bed-exit intention detection, pressure ulcer prevention, and sleep apnea mitigation. In: Proceedings of the 14th PErvasive Technologies Related to Assistive Environments Conference, PETRA 2021, pp. 76–80. Association for Computing Machinery (2021). https://doi.org/10.1145/3453892.3454001
17. Onose, R., Enokibori, Y., Mase, K.: Garment vs. bed-sheet sensors: to deal with pressure dispersion cushion use in pressure ulcer prevention. In: Proceedings of the 2017 ACM International Joint Conference on Pervasive and Ubiquitous Computing and Proceedings of the 2017 ACM International Symposium on Wearable Computers, UbiComp 2017, pp. 169–172. Association for Computing Machinery, New York (2017). https://doi.org/10.1145/3123024.3123143

18. Onose, R., Harasawa, Y., Enokibori, Y., Mase, K.: Textile sensor-based visualization to enhance skills to understand the body-pressure distribution for pressure ulcer prevention. In: Proceedings of the 2018 ACM International Joint Conference and 2018 International Symposium on Pervasive and Ubiquitous Computing and Wearable Computers, UbiComp 2018, pp. 194–197. Association for Computing Machinery, New York (2018). https://doi.org/10.1145/3267305.3267644
19. Sung, C.S., Park, J.Y.: A monitoring sensor-based ehealth image system for pressure ulcer prevention. Multimedia Tools Appl. **78**(5), 5255–5267 (2019). https://doi.org/10.1007/s11042-017-4992-3

Enhancing User Experience: Innovations in Blood Glucose Meter Design for Improved Efficiency and Convenience

Jennifer Gohumpu[1,2]([✉]) [iD], Win Kee Lim[1,2], Yujie Peng[1,2][iD], Mengru Xue[1,2], and Yichuan Hu[1,2][iD]

[1] Ningbo Innovation Center, Zhejiang University, Ningbo, China
jennifergohumpu@163.com
[2] Zhejiang University, Hangzhou, China

Abstract. The surging prevalence of diabetes, attributed to sedentary lifestyles and poor dietary choices, has precipitated a global health crisis marked by a substantial increase in overweight individuals. The incorporation of blood glucose meters for diabetes management is impeded by multifaceted challenges, including complexities in usage procedures, concerns regarding the hygiene of test strip retrieval, and storage issues. In this study, the primary emphasis is placed on the development of a finger-prick blood glucose meter featuring an embedded test strip vial that aims to improve user convenience and ensure the sanitary retrieval of test strips. A user study was conducted, engaging 30 participants, with a balanced distribution across genders and a lack of prior experience in using blood glucose meters. The study aimed to assess the efficiency and user experience of the designated product in comparison to two commercially available alternatives. The results show the superiority of the proposed blood glucose meter, with shorter task times, a reduced number of procedural steps, and a flawless error record. These findings support the improved efficiency and reliability of the designated product, fundamentally elevating the user experience and setting the stage for future advancements in medical device design.

Keywords: Blood Glucose Meter · Diabetes · Medical Devices · Product Design · User Experience

1 Introduction

Diabetes mellitus (DM), a multifaceted and widespread metabolic disorder, poses a substantial global public health challenge. Marked by elevated blood glucose levels, this condition is intricately connected to lifestyle factors, particularly physical inactivity and dietary choices, contributing to its relentless rise. The escalating prevalence of diabetes has transformed into an urgent global health crisis, necessitating diverse strategies for its effective management and care. Beyond its numerical implications, diabetes emerges as a profound global health challenge, exerting far-reaching consequences on mortality and overall quality of life.

V. G. Duffy (Ed.): HCII 2024, LNCS 14710, pp. 47–69, 2024.
https://doi.org/10.1007/978-3-031-61063-9_4

In 2021, the grim toll of diabetes manifested in approximately 6.7 million lives lost, signifying a devastating occurrence every second. These meticulously compiled statistics from the International Diabetes Federation (IDF) underscore a significant surge in diabetes prevalence. From 2011 to 2021, the global diabetic population soared from 366 million to 537 million, with over 70% of cases concentrated in rural, low- to middle-income regions [1]. Authoritative projections from organizations like the World Health Organization (WHO) anticipate a continual increase to 643 million affected individuals by 2030, and a forecasted 784 million by 2045 [2,3].

Examining the intricacies of this surge reveals impediments in the integration of blood glucose meters for diabetes management, significantly contributing to the escalating prevalence. Our prior investigation, conducted through interviews and questionnaires within diabetes communities, unveiled multifaceted challenges. Following an analysis of feedback and suggestions from previous research, which encompass complexities in usage procedures, concerns about the hygiene of test strip retrieval, and storage issues, these challenges hinder the seamless assimilation of these essential devices into daily life. The intricate nature of usage procedures poses barriers to regular monitoring, compromising effective management. Apprehensions related to hygiene during test strip retrieval raise questions about safety, while storage challenges impact device accessibility and reliability over time.

Addressing these challenges is crucial for effective diabetes management and the mitigation of rising cases. A purpose-designed product that streamlines the usage of blood glucose meters, ensures hygienic practices and resolves storage concerns is pivotal in promoting the widespread and sustained adoption of these vital devices. This scientific approach underscores the necessity for innovative solutions to enhance the usability and integration of blood glucose meters, fundamentally elevating the user experience and laying the foundation for future advancements in medical device design.

The two main contributions of this research are:

1. This study introduces an innovative blood glucose meter design featuring integrated test strips, representing a pioneering advancement in blood glucose monitoring technology. This design offers users a more efficient and convenient approach to the application procedure of the blood glucose meter. The integration of test strips enhances overall usability, addressing challenges associated with conventional meters.
2. Anticipated improvements in ease of use, reduced operating steps, and innovative features, highlighted through comprehensive user feedback, promise an enhanced user experience in blood glucose monitoring. The study focuses on optimizing the device's efficiency and user-friendliness, essential for advancing blood glucose monitoring technology. These improvements offer not only enhanced reliability but also a seamless and user-friendly experience for individuals managing diabetes.

The study aimed to integrate design research and technology to develop a product focused on enhancing the user experience in blood glucose meters. Conducting a thorough user needs analysis, literature review, and user test, the product was tailored to provide a more efficient and convenient approach to the application procedure of the blood glucose meter. Furthermore, the study anticipated contributing to the advancement of the field by substantiating the enhanced efficiency and reliability of the designated product, fundamentally elevating the user experience, and laying the foundation for future innovations in medical device design.

2   Related Work

2.1   Importance of Blood Glucose Meter in Diabetes Management

Diabetes management strategies exhibit global variation and are tailored to meet regional and population-specific needs. These strategies encompass education, community care, self-management, technology integration, glucose level monitoring, and dietary guidance [4]. Guided by a global guideline, Diabetes Self-Management (DSM) interventions aim to regulate glycosylated hemoglobin (HbA1c) levels [5]. Aligned with the American Association of Diabetes Educators' "AADE 7," these interventions cover various aspects, including adopting healthier eating habits, engaging in more physical activity, occasional blood glucose monitoring, proper medication management, and risk reduction [6].

This comprehensive approach seeks to improve diabetes management globally. The pivotal role of blood glucose meters in diabetes management is paramount. The introduction of home blood glucose monitoring four decades ago marked a revolutionary leap in diabetes self-management, providing invaluable glucose data that have significantly benefited many people with diabetes in optimizing their glycemic control [7]. These devices are indispensable tools for individuals with diabetes, offering effective means to monitor and regulate their blood glucose levels. Additionally, monitoring conducted outside clinical facilities, such as at home, provides enhanced convenience [8].

Furthermore, blood glucose meters play a crucial role in facilitating personalized diabetes management plans. This capability allows healthcare professionals to tailor interventions based on individualized data, promoting a personalized approach that enhances the overall efficacy of diabetes care [9,10]. This personalized strategy contributes to better health outcomes for those living with the condition.

2.2   Comparison of Different Blood Glucose Monitoring Technologies

Biochemical Laboratory Testing. Biochemical laboratory testing, characterized by automation, enhances convenience and safety, offering improved efficiency in blood glucose testing. This method, known for its sensitivity, accuracy, and standardization [11], primarily employs spectrophotometry in clinical biochemical testing. Hospitals predominantly use fully automated biochemical testing for blood glucose assessments to ensure precision and convenience.

While biochemical laboratory testing plays a crucial role in medical diagnostics, it has drawbacks. Notably, the associated costs can be a significant financial burden for patients, potentially limiting access to necessary healthcare services [12]. Extended turnaround times [13] may lead to delayed diagnoses, particularly problematic in cases requiring swift action. Precise sample collection requirements, such as fasting or specific preparation, can be inconvenient and time-consuming. Additionally, certain tests, like blood draws [14], can be invasive and discomforting, potentially discouraging individuals from undergoing necessary testing. Limited accessibility is another concern, especially in underserved or rural regions [15], where access to biochemical laboratory testing may be restricted, requiring significant travel for patients.

Point-of-Care Testing. Point-of-care testing (POCT) presents numerous advantages, transforming medical diagnostics by delivering rapid results. This accessibility allows a broader range of healthcare professionals to perform diagnostic tests confidently, reducing reliance on specialized laboratory technicians. POCT simplifies the diagnostic process with user-friendly devices, eliminating complex laboratory techniques and sample preparation [16]. This expedites results, ensures accuracy and reliability by minimizing human errors, and has a decentralized nature with lower turnaround times and a lower risk of sample degradation.

However, challenges hinder the widespread adoption of currently available POCT systems, including issues related to costs, complexity, and strict usage conditions, such as heat or humidity [17]. Discrepancies in accuracy, especially in glucose dehydrogenase (GDH) methodology, and potential interference from other sugars pose risks of clinical treatment errors [18–20]. Inaccuracies in intensive care units (ICUs) due to various factors further complicate the adoption of POCT.

Self-monitoring of Blood Glucose. Self-monitoring of blood glucose (SMBG) is a crucial tool for people with diabetes, particularly those on insulin, helping maintain near-normal blood glucose levels. While type 1 diabetes mellitus (T1DM) often performs SMBG at least three times per day, the optimal frequency for type 2 diabetes mellitus (T2DM) is not clearly defined, requiring adjustment based on personalized glucose goals [20]. SMBG provides personalized blood glucose profiles to guide individualized treatment plans, aiding in informed daily decisions about diet, exercise, and medication choices. As an educational tool, it enhances patient understanding of how lifestyle and medication affect glycemic control, although its full potential in glycemic control enhancement warrants further investigation.

However, the SMBG method has limitations, causing physical and psychological distress, limiting continuous monitoring of blood glucose fluctuations, and impacting the prevention of complications, especially related to hypoglycemia [14]. Result reliability is influenced by environmental factors, operator actions, patient conditions, medications, and metabolic variables, requiring consideration for accurate interpretation of blood glucose results [21].

Continuous Glucose Monitoring. Continuous glucose monitoring (CGM) offers numerous advantages, particularly during nighttime and busy hours. It effectively addresses concerns related to nighttime hypoglycemia, improves the quality of sleep, and empowers users by enhancing daily life and ensuring more peaceful nights. CGM provides real-time glucose data, enables early detection of glycemic imbalances, offers comprehensive trend analysis, facilitates precise insulin adjustments, minimizes the need for invasive fingerstick testing, and enhances patient empowerment.

The primary barrier hindering the adoption of CGM technology is its cost, as health plans, insurance companies, and governments typically do not offer coverage globally. Additional factors impacting CGM adoption include wear discomfort and social considerations, influencing clinicians' willingness to prescribe CGM devices. Addressing these challenges requires providing sufficient time and clinic resources to support ongoing CGM device use and imposing specific criteria on individuals before prescribing a CGM system. The longevity of the CGM sensor, adhesive durability, and calibration introduces additional considerations related to cost, convenience, and user acceptance. Improvements in these aspects are expected to enhance user acceptance and adoption of CGM technology [22].

2.3   Importance of Self-Monitoring Blood Glucose Meter

The 21st century grapples with the pervasive global health challenge of diabetes, impacting millions worldwide with significant health, economic, and societal implications [1]. Amidst the technological advancements integrating insulin pumps and continuous glucose monitoring (CGM), Self-Monitoring of Blood Glucose (SMBG) tools, such as meters and test strips, retain a pivotal role, especially in resource-constrained settings [14,23].

SMBG through glucose meters proves cost-effective, clinically validated, and conducive to multiple daily measurements, fostering overall well-being [24,25]. These portable devices empower individuals to regularly monitor their blood glucose levels, providing insights into the effects of dietary choices, physical activity, and medication management [19,26,27]. This valuable data facilitates informed decisions about diabetes care, promoting a deeper understanding of how lifestyle choices influence blood sugar levels.

Regular SMBG not only assists in promptly adjusting glucose levels but also contributes to the long-term management of diabetes. It allows healthcare providers to customize treatment plans according to individual needs, empowering individuals to actively engage in their healthcare journey [28–30]. By monitoring changes in blood glucose levels, patients and their healthcare teams can make real-time adjustments, striving for optimal glycemic control.

SMBG is particularly crucial for individuals with diabetes on insulin therapy, helping them determine the correct insulin dosage based on current blood

sugar levels, activity, and food intake. This proactive approach prevents hypo-
or hyperglycemia, minimizing complications.

In conclusion, SMBG tools, including glucose meters, play an indispensable
role in the global landscape of diabetes care. They assist individuals in making informed decisions and provide trackable data for healthcare professionals
to guide or revise treatment plans. Integrating SMBG into daily routines can
enhance glycemic control, ultimately improving the quality of life for those managing diabetes. The enduring significance of SMBG is emphasized by its market
valuation of approximately US$6.4 billion across 71 countries, highlighting its
enduring importance in diabetes management [23,31].

3   Methodology

3.1   Design Research Plan

Design Thinking, a dynamic human-centered problem-solving framework
employed across diverse industries, unfolds through five stages, nurturing collaboration and an experimental mindset [32,33]. The involvement of cross-
functional teams is pivotal, introducing diverse perspectives for a comprehensive
and innovative approach. Recognized as a cornerstone for business innovation,
design thinking, with its roots in design, seamlessly permeates various sectors.
It strategically incorporates fundamental design principles, heightening its effectiveness in crafting solutions attuned to human experiences. This study specifically applied the model to design and develop human-centered innovations in
blood glucose meter design. In essence, design thinking serves as a powerful cata-
lyst for innovation, harmonizing collaboration and design principles in problem-
solving across a spectrum of business landscapes. The five phases of the design
process are illustrated in Fig. 1.

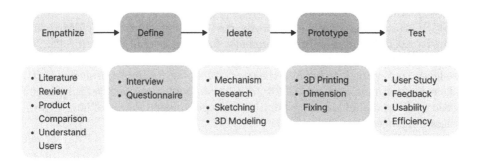

Fig. 1. Design Thinking Model (Design Process of This Study)

3.2   Design Research

3.2.1   Empathize Phase During this phase, an extensive review and analysis of related works and past studies on blood glucose meters were undertaken. Different blood glucose meter technologies were compared, and a comprehensive assessment of their advantages and disadvantages was conducted.

3.2.2   Define Phase To comprehend the requirements and obstacles faced by individuals managing diabetes while monitoring their blood glucose levels with blood glucose meters and test strips, a detailed research initiative was undertaken. The methodology encompassed two distinct phases, each dedicated to gathering, analyzing, and prioritizing user feedback.

Phase 1: Individual Interviews. The initial phase involved a focused survey with 15 diabetes patients regularly using blood glucose meters and test strips for monitoring. The objective was to explore challenges encountered during daily SMBG. Insights gained from this phase provided real-world experiences and information about challenges during SMBG application. Identified issues included accidental strip contact, complex operational procedures, system fragmentation, cost-effectiveness concerns, storage inconveniences, blood collection challenges, and accuracy apprehensions (Table 1).

Table 1. Phase 1 User Needs and Frequency Distribution

Description	Number
Accidental contact with adjacent test strips occurred during test strip retrieval from the vial	3
The operational procedure was complex and lengthy.	5
The system had many components, making it fragmented	2
It had a low cost-effectiveness	1
Its efficiency was sub-optimal	1
Required larger storage, causing inconvenience.	4
Blood collection was inconvenience.	2
Finger lacerations resulted from contact with test strip edges during test strip retrieval from the vial	1
Accidental spillage of multiple test strips occurred during closing the test strip vial	1
It was challenging to close the test strip vial with single-handed	1
Issues arose from test strip misalignment with the blood glucose meter interface	2
Test strips were often inserted incorrectly	1
Inadvertent contact with the test strip's blood inlet during handling was problematic	1
The blood glucose meter had a limited lifespan	1
Accuracy was a significant concern.	1

Phase 2: Community Questionnaire. Building on Phase 1 findings, a community questionnaire that are multiple choices was distributed to local diabetes communities. The aim was to obtain a broader perspective on challenges during daily blood glucose monitoring. Participants identified and ranked challenges based on their experiences. Quantitative analysis of questionnaire responses revealed the most prevalent issues: complex operational procedures (90.24%), accidental strip contact (82.93%), system fragmentation (73.17%), storage inconveniences (63.41%), and accidental strip spillage (41.46%).

The study emphasizes the need for streamlined operational procedures, addressing test strip retrieval and storage issues, and enhancing overall user experience in blood glucose meter applications. The research approach, combining individual interviews and community questionnaires, provided valuable user feedback. These findings lay the groundwork for designing blood glucose meter devices and test strips tailored to the specific needs of diabetes patients. Prioritizing these challenges offers insights for refining blood glucose meter devices to better serve the diabetes patient community at large (Table 2).

Table 2. Phase 2 User Needs and Frequency Distribution

Description	Number	Percentage
The operational procedure was complex and lengthy	333	90.24
Accidental contact with adjacent test strips occurred during test strip retrieval from the vial	306	82.93
The system had many components, making it fragmented.	270	73.17
Required larger storage, causing inconvenience	234	63.41
Accidental spillage of multiple test strips occurred during closing the test strip vial	153	41.46
It was challenging to close the test strip vial with single-handed	126	34.15
Test strips were often inserted incorrectly.	90	24.39
Its efficiency was sub-optimal	81	21.95
Inadvertent contact with the test strip's blood inlet during handling was problematic.	81	21.95
Issues arose from test strip misalignment with the blood glucose meter interface	72	19.51
Blood collection was inconvenience.	63	17.07
It had a low cost-effectiveness	45	12.20
Accuracy was a significant concern	45	12.20
Finger lacerations resulted from contact with test strip edges during test strip retrieval from the vial	36	9.76
The blood glucose meter had a limited lifespan	36	9.76

3.2.3   Ideate Phase Based on the survey, identified needs for Simplified Operational Procedures, Test Strip Retrieval and Storage, and Efficient Space Utilization will be integrated into the product design.

1. Simplified Operational Procedures: The device will feature intuitive and user-friendly procedures, streamlining the testing process for enhanced usability.
2. Test Strip Retrieval and Storage: Addressing issues like accidental contact and improving storage will ensure easy, safe test strip retrieval, minimizing contamination risks.
3. Efficient Use of Space: Designing for optimal space utilization is crucial for portability. The device will maintain functionality while minimizing its footprint for user convenience.

This focused approach aims to develop a self-monitoring blood glucose meter that prioritizes simplicity, effective storage, and space efficiency, ultimately improving the user experience for diabetes management.

Mechanism Research Stage. During the mechanism research stage, an investigation into the motion and push-out mechanism of the test strip from the blood glucose meter's body was conducted.

The inspiration for the push mechanism, employing a retractable spring method, draws from the efficient and secure mechanisms utilized in retractable utility knives. This method offers controlled and precise ejection of the test strip, aligning seamlessly with the design objectives of the blood glucose meter.

The research indicates that the push with retractable spring method is well-suited for our design requirements, especially in terms of product size. It promises to provide a reliable, user-friendly mechanism, contributing to an enhanced user experience (Fig. 2).

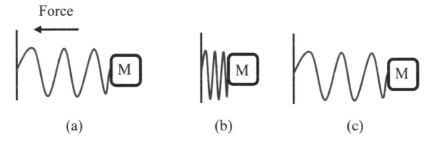

Fig. 2. The Push and Retractable Spring Method. (a) When a Force is Applied (b) The Spring is Compressed (c) When it is Released the Spring Return

Sketching and 3D Modeling. In the sketching and 3D modeling phase, the design team translated identified requirements and specifications into tangible visual representations. This crucial stage aimed to conceptualize the final product while refining intricate details. Key considerations included form factor, ergonomic design, operational simplicity, test strip retrieval and storage mechanisms, space optimization, integration of researched mechanisms, and the overall enhancement of the user experience.

The 3D modeling phase stands as a pivotal step in the research flow, dedicated to transitioning the initial sketches from the conceptual design phase into a comprehensive and precise 3D model. This transformation was facilitated using Autodesk Fusion 360, a sophisticated Computer-Aided Design (CAD) software recognized for its capability to generate highly accurate digital representations of the product. The utilization of such advanced tools ensures the precision and reliability of the developed model, laying the groundwork for subsequent prototyping and testing stages. This iterative process allows for continuous refinement based on feedback, ultimately contributing to the creation of an optimized and well-designed final product (Fig. 3).

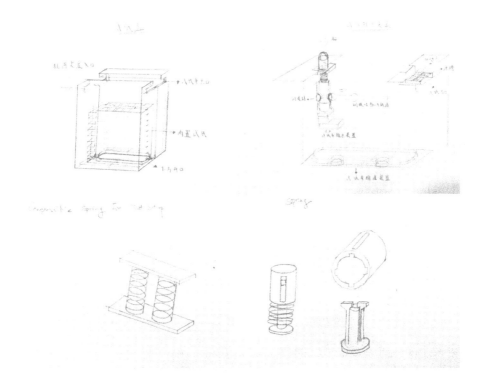

Fig. 3. The Draft Sketches

3.2.4 Prototype Phase The rapid prototyping stage is critical, seamlessly transforming the digital blueprint into a tangible prototype using our advanced Fused Deposition Modeling (FDM) and Stereolithography (SLA) 3D printers.

This process ensures precision and intricate detailing, enabling a comprehensive evaluation of both structural integrity and functional attributes.

Subsequent to the printing phase, a meticulous manual sanding procedure is judiciously applied to refine and polish the prototype's surface. This precision-driven surface treatment guarantees a flawless and visually appealing finish, essential for a detailed assessment of the product's aesthetic and ergonomic attributes (Figs. 4, 5, 6, 7, 8).

Fig. 4. Prototyping with different Materials and Materials Waste from Faulty

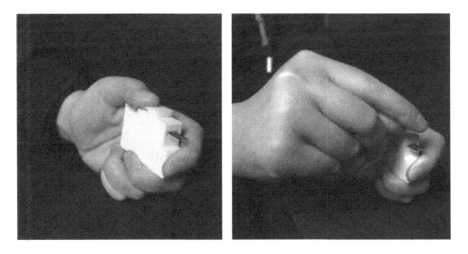

Fig. 5. The Application Views for the Final Product

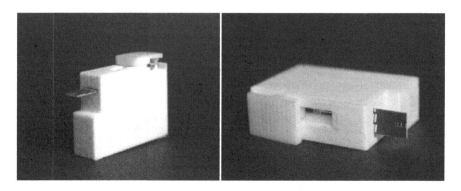

Fig. 6. The Different Views for the Final Product

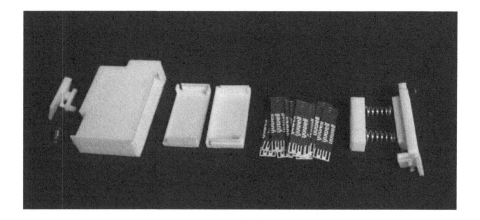

Fig. 7. The Exploded View for the Final Product

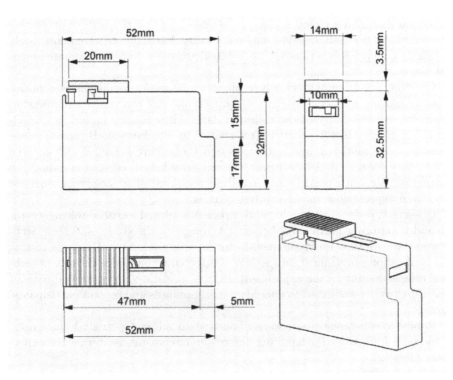

Fig. 8. The Multiple Views with Dimensions for the Final Product

4   Test Phase and Evaluation Methods

4.1   Participant

A total of 30 participants were selected to actively engage in a comparative experiment study on blood glucose meters. To ensure an impartial evaluation, individuals with no prior experience in using blood glucose meters were deliberately included. The participant group was carefully balanced in terms of gender, with an equal representation of male and female participants. Furthermore, the group comprised 15 individuals of Chinese nationality and 15 individuals of non-Chinese nationality. The mean age of the study group was 24.9 years, with a standard deviation of 4.68, encompassing a diverse yet representative age range from 19 to 45 years. The experiment solely simulates the scenario of applying a blood glucose meter. There are no wounds, and no real blood is taken from the participants.

4.2   Setting up

Preparations for the experiment were meticulously undertaken to ensure its smooth execution and the reliability of obtained results. Key components of the preparation phase included the careful selection of participants, representing a balanced distribution of gender and nationality. Participants were deliberately chosen with no prior experience in using blood glucose meters to eliminate potential biases.

Creating a setting that closely replicates real-world conditions was prioritized to provide participants with a comfortable and controlled environment, enhancing the reliability of the collected data. All necessary materials, including blood glucose meter products (referred to as Products A, B, and C), user manuals, questionnaires, and data collection tools, were arranged and ensured to be ready for use. A detailed protocol was established, offering standardized instructions for both participants and observers, outlining specific procedures, tasks, and expectations for all involved parties.

Observers, possessing training and experience, played a crucial role in recording and monitoring participant behavior throughout the study, and their accuracy in data capture was fundamental to the study's success. Rigorous testing and verification of technical setups were conducted to minimize the risk of technical difficulties during the experiment. Ethical guidelines and informed consent procedures were established to uphold ethical standards and protect participants' rights.

Robust contingency plans were developed to address potential challenges, providing a framework for handling unforeseen circumstances during the experiment (Figs. 9).

Fig. 9. Product A -Sinocare Dnurse Smart Glucometer, Product B - Yuwell Conventional Home Use Blood Glucose Meter, and Product C - Designated Product

4.3   Procedure

Before commencing the experiment, participants are provided with a comprehensive briefing on the experiment's objectives and procedural steps. This introductory session aims to create a comfortable environment, and participants are encouraged to ask questions or seek clarification to ensure their full understanding. Warm and informal communication is employed, and consent forms are thoughtfully provided to secure participants' approval for participation.

The experiment procedure is outlined as follows:

1. The experimenter engages in open and relaxed communication with participants, presenting the experiment's objectives and procedures in simple and understandable language. Participants are encouraged to ask questions, and small tokens of appreciation are offered to alleviate any nervousness.
2. Detailed explanations of the experiment's objectives and essential procedures are provided, with a strong emphasis on safety. Consent forms are distributed, and participant details are recorded. The experiment solely simulates the scenario of applying a blood glucose meter, and it is important to note that there are no wounds, and no real blood is extracted from the participants.
3. In the Learning Phase, participants are given product-specific user manuals, allowing them to familiarize themselves with the blood glucose meter within 1 min, ensuring a fundamental understanding of its operation.
4. In the Task Phase, participants perform a test strip replacement procedure, repeating the task three times in each trial to eliminate time bias.
5. An experienced observer meticulously documents participant behavior and key variables during the Learning and Task Phases, recording task completion time, the number of steps taken, errors encountered, and descriptions of significant events.
6. During the Evaluation Phase, participants provide feedback and evaluate their experiences with the three products using Standard Usability Scale (SUS) and System Usability Scale (SEQ) questionnaires, along with qualitative questions in the questionnaire.
7. Each participant undergoes three rounds of the experiment, evaluating Product A, Product B, and Product C.
8. The entire experiment is video-recorded for comprehensive data collection and subsequent analysis (Figs. 10, 11, 12).
9. After completing the experimental phases, participants engage in interviews to share their satisfaction perspectives with the three products. Insights into potential modifications for better usability and functionality of Product C are recorded, allowing for a well-rounded assessment and the incorporation of user feedback into product development.

Fig. 10. The Experiment Procedure

Fig. 11. At the Beginning, Participants are Reading and Signing Consent Letter

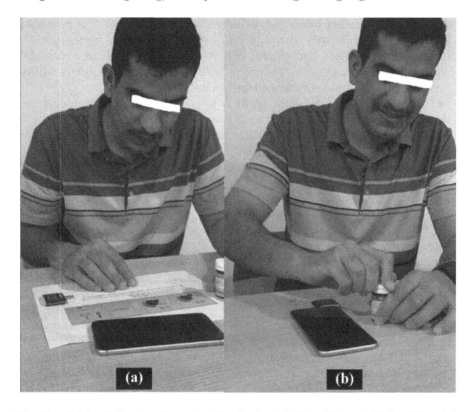

Fig. 12. (a) Participant is Learning the Product A User Manual (b) Participant is Completing the Task

4.4   Measurements

In the conducted research, a total of 30 participants were involved, and the data documented includes various aspects. Firstly, participant profiles were compiled, encompassing demographic details such as age, nationality, and gender. Behavioral data, which includes participants' responses, actions, and reactions throughout the experiment, was meticulously recorded. Attitudinal data was collected to understand participants' opinions, attitudes, and perspectives. Observational data played a significant role, capturing participant behavior and non-verbal cues during their interactions with the products, thus providing a comprehensive insight into user behavior.

Quantitative data, including metrics like task completion times, the number of steps taken to complete tasks, and errors, were measured and quantitatively compared to evaluate the performance of the products. It's noteworthy that the number of steps taken to complete tasks was detailed in the user manual distributed to the candidates during the learning phase. Any deviation from these steps during the task phase contributed to the recorded error count.

5   Result and Discussion

5.1   Quantitative Analysis

The hypothesis that need to be study, Hypothesis 1: It is postulated that Product C will manifest superior performance metrics, reflected in reduced task completion time, minimized task steps, and a diminished error rate. 2. Hypothesis 2: Product C is hypothesized to yield the utmost System Usability Scale (SUS) score among the evaluated products.

The outcomes on the three products, including Mean Task Time, Steps Taken, and Errors are detailed in Table 3, Table 4 and Table 5. The calculated metrics encompass the mean. 95% confidence interval (CI), median, standard deviation, minimum and maximum for each product. These results suggest that Product C, features by a shorter task time, fewer steps, and a flawless error record, exhibits enhanced efficiency and reliability in comparison to Products A and B. The narrow CI associated with Product C underscore the statistical significance of these distinctions.

Table 3. The standard analysis for mean task time

Product Type	Mean	95% Confidence Level		Median	SD	Min	Max
		Lower	Upper				
A	28.17	25.91	30.43	27.98	6.06	19.09	40.10
B	17.14	15.58	18.71	16.34	4.19	9.71	25.90
C	7.13	6.34	7.92	7.39	2.11	3.15	11.50

Table 4. The standard analysis for steps taken

Product Type	Mean	95% Confidence Level		Median	SD	Min	Max
		Lower	Upper				
A	22.77	22.06	23.48	24.00	1.91	19.00	26.00
B	17.10	16.51	17.69	18.00	1.58	13.00	18.00
C	9.00	9.00	9.00	9.00	9.00	9.00	9.00

Table 5. The standard analysis for errors

Product Type	Mean	95% Confidence Level		Median	SD	Min	Max
		Lower	Upper				
A	2.27	1.53	3.00	2.00	1.96	0.00	6.00
B	1.63	0.99	2.27	1.00	1.71	0.00	6.00
C	0.00	0.00	0.00	0.00	0.00	0.00	0.00

For the System Usability Scale (SUS) scores for Products A, B and C, in Table 6 provides a nuanced understanding of user perceptions and experiences in the experimental context. Product C emerges with the highest mean score at 72.2, boasting a 95 between 67.8 and 76.6, signifying superior perceived usability in contrast to Products A and B. This is reinforced by the narrower CI, underscoring the robustness of this assessment. The SUS scores for Product A were significantly lower than those for Product. However, no significant difference emerged between Product B and C. In essence, this analysis suggests that Product C exhibits superior usability compared to the other blood glucose meter options.

Table 6. The standard analysis for SUS scores

Product Type	Mean	95% Confidence Level		Median	SD	Min	Max
		Lower	Upper				
A	63.87	58.05	69.70	64.90	15.60	26.40	85.80
B	68.79	64.78	72.79	68.20	10.73	46.20	88.00
C	72.16	67.77	76.55	70.40	11.76	33.0	88.00

Besides standard analysis, repeated measures ANOVA was conducted to study the effect of different products on Mean Task Time, Steps Taken and Errors. These findings highlight that Product C exhibited significantly different Mean Task Times compared to both Product A and Product B. This result also aligns with the proposed hypotheses, as the p-values are < 0.001, indicating a statistically significant relationship.

5.2   Qualitative Analysis

User Feedback on Usability and Innovative Design. Participant feedback overwhelmingly emphasizes the user-friendly aspects of Product C, particularly its ease of use and streamlined operational steps. Among the 30 participants, 25 specifically lauded the product's user-friendly design, with 10 highlighting its reduced operational steps (Tables 7, 8, 9, 10, 11, 12).

Table 7. Repeated measures ANOVA for mean task time

Sphericity Correction	Sum of Square	df	Mean square	F	p	n^2
Huynh-Feldt	6646	1.71	3889.00	250	<.001	0.796

Table 8. Post hoc tests - Tukey for mean task time

Product Type 1	Product Type 2	Mean Differenc	SE	df	t	Ptukey
A	C	21.00	1.091	29.00	19.30	<.001
B	C	10.00	0.691	29.00	14.50	<.001

Table 9. Friedman's test for steps taken

X^2	df	P
54.20	2	<.001

Table 10. Pairwise comparison (Durbin-Conover) for steps taken

Product Type	Product Type 2	Statistic	P
A	C	23.30	<.001
B	C	12.20	<.001

Table 11. Friedman's test for errors

X^2	df	P
30.70	2	<.001

Table 12. Pairwise comparison (Durbin-Conover) for errors

Product Type 1	Product Type 2	Statistic	P
A	C	7.33	<.001
B	C	5.93	<.001

For example, participant P4 mentioned, "Product C is user-friendly, requiring fewer steps as there's no need to insert the test strip into the meter." Similarly, participant P18 commended the simplicity of changing the test strip, praising Product C for integrating the test strip vial with the meter, minimizing space requirements, and enhancing overall user-friendliness.

Moreover, four participants appreciated the innovative design of embedding the test strip vial into the body, eliminating direct finger contact with the test strip and promoting hygiene. Participant P9 remarked, "Product C's design is innovative and ensures hygiene during the test strip retrieval process," while P29 highlighted pollution prevention and hygiene benefits by avoiding direct contact with the test strip during retrieval. Additionally, three participants specifically mentioned the compact size of Product C, making it easy to carry around. Participant P21, for example, stated, "Product C is user-friendly and portable."

In summary, participant feedback underscores the positive reception of Product C's design, acknowledging its ease of use, reduced operational steps, innovative features, hygienic benefits, and compact size, contributing to an overall positive user experience.

Identified Challenges and Drawbacks. Among the 30 participants, 11 reported no limitations with Product C. Most of these participants focused on ergonomic aspects, with P2 suggesting, "Needs refinement in the ergonomic aspects," and P3 mentioning the need for customization with better materials.

Participants also brought attention to the push button on Product C. P13 noted, "The push button is a bit rough, maybe there is friction," and P16 shared a similar view, stating, "Push button is a bit rough, maybe there is friction."

Another highlighted issue was the motion of the test strip during the push-out process. P6 mentioned, "There was a slight lag when the test strip was pushed out," while P29 stated, "There is a bit of lag during the test strip being pushed out."

Additional concerns included P16 noting that "the test strip push-out length is not uniform," and P18 expressing that "the remaining quantity of test strips inside the product is not visually intuitive."

6 Future Work and Conclusion

In conclusion, this study aimed to design an innovative blood glucose meter, addressing user challenges and feedback through A/B Testing, experiment observations, questionnaires, and interviews for Products A, B, and C. The emphasized aspects were Simplified Operational Procedures, Test Strip Retrieval and Storage, and Efficient Use of Space.

Product C was designed to have fewer operational procedures, eliminate the test strip retrieval step to prevent contamination, and reduce components. Thirty participants underwent validation experiments, evaluating task time, steps, and errors for Products A, B, and C. The results indicated that Product C improved overall efficiency and required less effort during the blood glucose monitoring process.

The main innovations and outcomes include:

1. Identification of user needs through interviews and questionnaires, highlighting priorities such as reducing operational procedures, preventing contamination during test strip retrieval, and minimizing components. 2. Exploration of an innovative blood glucose meter featuring an embedded test strip and a novel test strip ejection method inspired by the structure of a gun. 3. Meticulous design and construction of a prototype that proficiently addressed all user requirements, undergoing systematic usability testing. Experimental results confirmed the efficiency and convenience of Product C through quantitative and qualitative analyses.

While providing valuable insights into the design and evaluation of an innovative blood glucose meter, this study is subject to certain limitations. Temporal constraints on experimentation, predominantly centered on laboratory investigations, highlight the need for extended evaluations in domiciliary settings to address the real-time dynamics of blood glucose fluctuations integral to diabetes management. The constraining focus on university students as the experimental cohort and the absence of a diverse age spectrum underscore limitations in comprehending age-dependent variations. Moreover, technological constraints, restricting the glucose meter's current design to the simulation of strip ejection without actual glucose concentration quantification, emphasize the necessity for iterative advancements and refined technological integration.

Future works in this study aim to overcome these limitations and drive innovation in blood glucose monitoring devices. The integration of electronic components with the physical structure of the blood glucose meter holds promise for a holistic, efficient, and compact monitoring device. Smartphone connectivity, utilizing Bluetooth functionality, can provide seamless data transmission for personalized insights, optimizing health monitoring practices. Adhering to ergonomic design principles ensures a safer and more user-friendly experience, addressing concerns raised during the evaluation.

Implementation of feedback mechanisms and continuous iteration based on user input are vital for refining the blood glucose meter. These enhancements contribute to improved usability, functionality, and overall user satisfaction. Despite the current limitations, the study sets the stage for future research endeavors, encouraging comprehensive investigations across diverse demographic spectra and refining technological facets to elevate the overall experiential paradigm of blood glucose monitoring devices.

References

1. IDF Diabetes Atlas. https://diabetesatlas.org/. Accessed 25 Jan 2024
2. Kahkoska, A., Dabelea, D.: Diabetes in youth: a global perspective. Endocrinol. Metabol. Clin. North America. **50**, 491–512 (2021). https://www.sciencedirect.com/science/article/pii/S0889852921000414, Pandemic of Diabetes and Prediabetes: Prevention and Control

3. Diabetes. https://www.who.int/news-room/fact-sheets/detail/diabetes. Accessed 25 Nov 2023
4. Glasgow, R., Davis, C., Funnell, M., Beck, A.: Implementing practical interventions to support chronic illness self-management. Joint Comm. J. Qual. Safety. **29**, 563–574 (2003)
5. Organization, W.: Glycated haemoglobin (HbA1c) for the diagnosis of diabetes. (2011). https://www.ncbi.nlm.nih.gov/books/NBK304271/
6. Sherifali, D., Jones, H., Mullan, Y.: Diabetes self-management: what are we really talking about? Can. J. Diabetes **37**, 2–3 (2013)
7. Weinstock, R., et al.: The role of blood glucose monitoring in diabetes management. Compendia. **2020** (Oct 2020). https://doi.org/10.2337/db2020-31
8. Mathew, T.: Blood glucose monitoring. (2023). https://www.ncbi.nlm.nih.gov/books/NBK555976/
9. Heisler, M., Bouknight, R., Hayward, R., Smith, D., Kerr, E.: The relative importance of physician communication, participatory decision making, and patient understanding in diabetes self-management. J. Gen. Intern. Med. **17**, 243–252 (2002)
10. Shillington, A., Col, N., Bailey, R., Jewell, M.: Development of a patient decision aid for type 2 diabetes mellitus for patients not achieving glycemic control on metformin alone. Patient Preference and Adherence, pp. 609–617 (2015)
11. Krha, M., Lovrenić, M.: Update on biomarkers of glycemic control. World J. Diab.**10**, 1–15 (2019). https://api.semanticscholar.org/CorpusID:59337865
12. Sherwani, S., Khan, H., Ekhzaimy, A., Masood, A., Sakharkar, M. Significance of HbA1c test in diagnosis and prognosis of diabetic patients. Biomarker Insights. **11**, 95–104 (2016). https://api.semanticscholar.org/CorpusID:15571196
13. Shen, Y., et al.: Association between 1,5-Anhydroglucitol and acute C peptide response to arginine among patients with type 2 diabetes. J. Diab. Res. **2020** (2020). https://api.semanticscholar.org/CorpusID:221008085
14. Jing, Y., Chang, S., Chen, C., Liu, J.: Review-glucose monitoring sensors: history, principle, and challenges. J. Electrochem. Society (2022). https://api.semanticscholar.org/CorpusID:248359808
15. Kehlenbrink, S., Ansbro, Besançon, S., Hassan, S., Roberts, B., Jobanputra, K.: Strengthening diabetes care in humanitarian crises in low- and middle-income settings. J. Clin. Endocrinol. Metabol. (2022). https://api.semanticscholar.org/CorpusID:249234875
16. Matteucci, E., Giampietro, O.: The point-of-care testing in diabetology. Clin. Manage. Issues. **5**, 107–112 (2011). https://api.semanticscholar.org/CorpusID:70851278
17. Ortiz, D., Loeffelholz, M.: Practical challenges of point-of-care testing. Clin. Lab. Med. **43 2**, 155–165 (2023). https://api.semanticscholar.org/CorpusID:257710727
18. ElSayed, N., et al.: R. 7. Diabetes technology: standards of care in diabetes-2024. Diabetes Care. **47 Suppl 1**, S126–S144 (2023). https://api.semanticscholar.org/CorpusID:266227263
19. Zhou, Y., Liao, L., Sun, M., He, G.: Self-care practices of Chinese individuals with diabetes. Exper. Therap. Med. **5**, 1137–1142 (2013). https://api.semanticscholar.org/CorpusID:1922138
20. Pleus, S., et al.: Self-monitoring of blood glucose as an integral part in the management of people with type 2 diabetes mellitus. Diabetes Therapy. **13**, 829–846 (2022). https://api.semanticscholar.org/CorpusID:248120816

21. Smigoc Schweiger, D., Battelino, T.: Chapter 1 - Introduction to SMBG. Glucose Monitoring Devices, pp. 3–31 (2020). https://www.sciencedirect.com/science/article/pii/B9780128167144000016

22. Miller, E.: Using continuous glucose monitoring in clinical practice. Clin. Diabetes : Public. American Diabetes Assoc. **38**, 429– 438 (2020). https://api.semanticscholar.org/CorpusID:229162361

23. Klatman, E., Jenkins, A., Ahmedani, M., Ogle, G.: Blood glucose meters and test strips: global market and challenges to access in low-resource settings. Lancet. Diabetes Endocrinol. **7 2**, 150–160 (2019). https://api.semanticscholar.org/CorpusID:51907630

24. Baird, H., Webb, T., Martin, J., Sirois, F.: The relationship between a balanced time perspective and self-monitoring of blood glucose among people with type 1 diabetes. Ann. Behav. Med.: A Public. Society Behav. Med. **53 2**, 196–209 (2019). https://api.semanticscholar.org/CorpusID:13710458

25. Wang, X., Luo, J., Qi, L., Long, Q., Guo, J.: Hong-Wang Adherence to self-monitoring of blood glucose in Chinese patients with type 2 diabetes: current status and influential factors based on electronic questionnaires. Patient Preference Adherence. **13**, 1269–1282 (2019). https://api.semanticscholar.org/CorpusID:199571699

26. Zhong, X., Li, S., Luo, M., Ma, X., Fisher, E.: Peer support self-management intervention for individuals with type 2 diabetes in rural primary care settings: protocol for a mixed methods study. JMIR Res. Protocols. **12** (2023). https://api.semanticscholar.org/CorpusID:260235584

27. Liang, D., Fan, G.: Social support and user characteristics in online diabetes communities: an in-depth survey of a large-scale Chinese population. Int. J. Environ. Res. Public Health. **17** (2020). https://api.semanticscholar.org/CorpusID:216108532

28. Bao, Y., Zhu, D.: Clinical application guidelines for blood glucose monitoring in China (2022 edition). Diabetes/Metabol. Res. Rev. **38** (2022). https://api.semanticscholar.org/CorpusID:252916005

29. Jankowska, A., Golicki, D.: Self-reported diabetes and quality of life: findings from a general population survey with the short form-12 (sf-12) health survey. Arch. Med. Sci.: AMS. **18**, 1157–1168 (2021). https://api.semanticscholar.org/CorpusID:234871535

30. Gisinger, T., et al.: Sex and gender aspects in diabetes mellitus: focus on access to health care and cardiovascular outcomes. Front. Public Health. **11** (2023). https://api.semanticscholar.org/CorpusID:256462142

31. Continuous glucose monitoring. https://www.iqvia.com/library/infographics/continuous-glucose-monitoring. Accessed 25 Jan 2024

32. Kwon, M., Remøy, H.: User-centred design thinking. A Handbook Of Management Theories and Models for Office Environments and Services. (2021). https://api.semanticscholar.org/CorpusID:237703642

33. Mueller-Roterberg, C.: Handbook of Design Thinking: Tips and Tools for How to Design Thinking. (Independently Published,2018). https://books.google.com.my/books?id=qUQjvwEACAAJ

Review of Research Status and Development Expectation of Health Smart Clothing

Ruoyin Huang[✉] and Yurong Yan

South China University of Technology, Guangzhou, China
2661728380@qq.com

Abstract. With the intensification of the global ageing population, the consumption needs of the elderly are gradually being taken seriously. Against the backdrop of strengthening health awareness, Chinese residents' per capita healthcare consumption expenditure continues to increase. It is urgent to develop smart clothing that meets the consumption needs of the elderly.

Smart clothing, as a new trend in the electronics and computer industries, has emerged - designing high-tech products that can be integrated with clothing. Among them, medical smart clothing is a vital application direction, gradually developing into an emerging health monitoring technology. For example, physiological monitoring smart clothing can monitor physiological indicators of the human body, such as heart rate, electrocardiogram, blood pressure, body temperature, pulse, pressure, and electromyographic signals.

This study analyzed the current application status of smart clothing in health monitoring, focusing on market size, technological innovation, application areas, brand competition, and development trends. Meanwhile, this study explored the promotion and application prospects of smart clothing in an ageing society, summarized the problems faced by smart clothing for the elderly, and looked forward to the future development trends of smart clothing for the elderly. In addition, to understand Chinese consumers' expectations for healthy smart clothing, a questionnaire survey was conducted. The collected data were analyzed to determine the demand and expectations of the Chinese elderly for health smart clothing.

In summary, the development of health smart clothing requires attention to technological innovation, intelligent design, customized services, brand building, cross-border cooperation, and compliance with regulations and standards.

Keywords: health smart clothing · Health Monitoring · Development Trend

1 Introduction

In recent years, with the development of science and technology, smart clothing has gradually entered the public view. At present, the smart clothing market is rapidly developing. According to market research company data, the size of the smart clothing market has reached $3.5 billion in 2022 and is expected to grow to $10 billion by 2026. In the same time, the number and proportion of elderly population are increasing; The growth rate of the population over 65 years old exceeds that of the population under 65 years

V. G. Duffy (Ed.): HCII 2024, LNCS 14710, pp. 70–86, 2024.
https://doi.org/10.1007/978-3-031-61063-9_5

old; The proportion of the global population aged 65 and above is expected to increase from 10% in 2022 to 16% by 2050 [1]. The large number of elderly people and the huge demand for elderly products present infinite potential for the consumer market. Against the backdrop of increasing health awareness, the per capita medical and health care consumption expenditure of Chinese residents continues to increase, and the proportion of it in per capita consumption expenditure continues to rise. In the future, per capita medical and health care consumption expenditure is expected to continue to grow. Consumers pay more attention to consumption in areas such as medical care and health to improve their quality of life, thereby promoting the continuous growth of the wearable device market. The development of functional clothing that meets the consumption needs of the elderly is imminent.

People's attention to health issues has led to the emergence of intelligent clothing for real-time monitoring of physical health, providing a more convenient and comfortable experience for exercise health, disease prevention, and post disease recovery.

Improving human health and living standards is one of the important aspects of current research in the field of biomedical engineering on a global scale. In this case, one of the main issues is focused on the development of wearable electronic devices, including smartwatches, bracelets, or clothing, for real-time monitoring of biological activity [2–6].

Therefore, this article starts with the basic concept of healthy smart clothing, summarizes the development history of health monitoring smart clothing at home and abroad, analyzes the basic principles, core components, specific applications and development status of healthy smart clothing for different uses, elaborates on the design points of health monitoring smart clothing, and summarizes its shortcomings and looks forward to its development direction. Finally, based on the existing technology and development trend, suggestions and trends for the future development of healthy smart clothing are proposed. This study has certain reference value for the further research and development and market promotion of healthy smart clothing.

2   Definition and Classification of Healthy Smart Clothing

Intelligent clothing combines clothing with information technology, implanting miniaturized and flexible electronic components into advanced textile materials and technology, enabling them to have functions such as information perception, computational analysis, and communication [7].

Among them, intelligent health clothing can be summarized into the following categories (Fig. 1).

1. Sports monitoring: This type of intelligent health clothing is mainly used in the fields of sports and fitness, and can monitor exercise related data such as heart rate, step count, exercise distance, calorie consumption, etc. They are typically equipped with sensors and algorithms to provide real-time motion feedback and data analysis.
2. Health monitoring: This type of intelligent health clothing focuses on monitoring and tracking physiological parameters of the human body, such as heart rate, blood pressure, body temperature, respiration, etc. They can help users understand their health status in real-time and provide health warnings and advice.

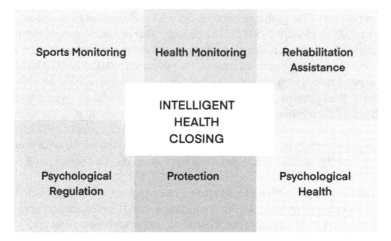

Fig. 1. Classification of intelligent health clothing

3. Rehabilitation assistance: This type of intelligent health clothing is designed to assist rehabilitation patients in rehabilitation training and physical therapy. They can monitor the execution of rehabilitation exercises, provide posture correction feedback, record rehabilitation progress, and assist patients in better completing rehabilitation training.

4. Physiological regulation: This type of intelligent health clothing has the function of regulating human physiological functions, such as intelligent heating, cooling, or massage. They can provide comfortable temperature and stimulation according to user needs and environmental conditions, promote blood circulation, alleviate fatigue, etc.

5. Protection: This type of intelligent health clothing is mainly used to provide protective functions, such as anti-fall, collision, bulletproof, etc. They typically use special materials and designs to provide users with additional safety measures in specific environments or activities.

6. Psychological health category: A small number of intelligent health clothing focuses on the psychological health of users, monitors indicators such as stress and emotions through sensors and analysis technology, and provides corresponding relaxation and psychological support [8].

3 The Application of Smart Clothing

Different from the traditional smart clothing, the smart clothing used for medical and health functions pays more attention to its environmental protection and health needs. Initially, in this industry, textiles are more like a carrier, a carrier of electronic products that can monitor human vital signs and collect data [11]. With the development of science and technology, people begin to explore the greater possibility of this kind of intelligent clothing, that is, on the basis of the data obtained by intelligent monitoring, with the support of big data and the algorithm, the huge monitoring data will be converted into easy-to-understand analysis results, so that doctors can grasp the patient's physical condition at any time and adjust the treatment plan in time.

3.1 Healthy Smart Clothing for Infants and Young Children

Breathing is an important parameter to judge the health status of infants. Once apnea or instantaneous breath holding occurs, it may cause unusually serious consequences. At present, most of the baby monitoring products on the market are placed at the bedside or under the mattress, the effect of respiratory monitoring for infants is not ideal. JAKUBAS Adam etc. [9] the Textronic system developed for the above phenomenon can detect the change of electrical resistance of conductive rib fabric through respiratory rhythm sensor, so as to monitor the respiratory status of infants [10]. The abdomen of the baby fluctuates most when breathing, and the sensor is installed on the belt of the rib material, which helps to obtain reliable respiratory data, and the knitted material is soft and has good elasticity and recovery. Will not bind the baby. With the ups and downs of the abdomen when the baby is breathing, the length of the rib fabric changes accordingly, the resistance also changes, and then passes through the transmission output of the sensor, and finally achieves the purpose of detecting the baby's breath condition. It reduces the pressure of the caregiver and improves the safety of the baby during sleep.

3.2 Healthy Smart Clothing for Elderly

Research shows that the elderly population is a high-risk population of diabetes, hypertension, coronary heart disease and other diseases. Some elderly guardians cannot accompany them for a long time, and cannot timely find and treat the physical problems of the elderly [12]. Psychologically, most of the elderly are reluctant to go to the hospital for physical examination frequently, and are more reluctant to inform their guardians of their personal physiological parameters, which leads to the occurrence of abnormal physical conditions but missed the best period of treatment without timely detection. Physiologically speaking, the physiological functions of the elderly gradually weaken, making it more difficult for them to resist external harm. It is said that elderly people are more prone to falls due to their physical decline, ranging from sprains and strains to fractures and even life-threatening injuries [13]. Most elderly people suffer from osteoporosis, lower back pain, fear of cold and heat, which are common and common problems. In addition, the timely detection of physical abnormalities through various physiological parameters plays an important role in emergency treatment before hospitalization, which helps to reduce the incidence rate of patients and the probability of other emergencies, thus reducing medical costs [14].

Therefore, in order to meet the above needs, the main functions of health smart clothing include real-time monitoring of heart rate, blood sugar, and blood pressure.

4 The Application of Healthy Smart Clothing in the Context of Aging Population

1. Health monitoring: Old people are easy to fall, and it will be very dangerous for old people living alone to have a child. E-Vone anti-fall smart shoes mainly rely on sensors hidden in the sole interlayer, including GPS, accelerometer, pressure system and gyroscope. When a human body falls, the shoe will send the wearer fall information to family, friends and nearby medical sites to ensure timely rescue [15]. Zhang Haijun [16] developed an ECG monitoring clothing for the elderly, which formed an ecological and healthy monitoring system with portable ECG monitors, positive and negative electrodes, flexible lead wires and other devices, which were fixed by Velcro and vest to facilitate disassembly and washing. Zheng Zejian etc. [17]. Combined the Bluetooth communication module with the mobile phone control module to design an intelligent control software that integrates the functions of collecting and controlling temperature, which makes the intelligent heating clothing easier to monitor and control.

2. Rehabilitation therapy: The LEGSTM posture (Motion Evaluation and Gait system) developed by Biosensics is a portable gait evaluation system based on wearable motion sensors. It supports multiple high-precision inertial sensors, captures many leg motion details in real time, and transmits the data to APP via Bluetooth for easy viewing and evaluation [18]. The biggest advantage of the system is that it is not limited to the laboratory, and users can use it for a long time on different floors and wearing different shoes. This kind of gait analysis plays an important role in the rehabilitation of nervous system, and sometimes it can even be used to change hands. The smart kit for stroke patients includes blouse, trousers, shoes and gloves, equipped with EMG textile electrodes, kpf goniometer, Force Sensitive Resistor (FSR) in different parts, monitoring the daily activities of stroke patients and training the motor ability of upper and lower limbs [19].

3. Security protection: Old people are easy to fall, and it will be very dangerous for old people living alone to have a child. E-Vone anti-fall smart shoes mainly rely on sensors hidden in the sole interlayer, including GPS, accelerometer, pressure system and gyroscope. When a human body falls, the shoe will send the wearer fall information to family, friends and nearby medical sites to ensure timely rescue.

4. Social interaction (Mental Health): With the aging becoming more and more serious, the number of the elderly in the society has risen sharply. The elderly's social interaction ability will be greatly reduced due to the growth of their age and physical deterioration, resulting in anxiety, loneliness and other negative emotions, which may have serious consequences for human health and mental health. This situation is a negative trend, which will bring many problems to the elderly: reduce their cognitive ability, exacerbate the deterioration of their physiological conditions, and cause diseases of the elderly. Therefore, the most important thing for the elderly is to learn to adjust their emotions to avoid the impact of negative emotions, so the monitoring of the elderly's emotions is very critical [20]. Through the use of wearable devices, provide scientific methods to improve users' mental health. As in jebelli Houtan's 《wearable biosensors to understand construction workers' mental and physical stress 》, through wearable EEG headphones and wrist band biosensors, can find and relieve

the pressure of construction workers, help researchers better understand the stressors in the workplace, ensure the physical and mental health of workers, and improve productivity [21]. In 《Eazytrack: exploring next gen technology and user experience design to help relieve stress》, kaiy proposed to use data visualization and user interface design to help people determine their stress level and provide customized scientific methods to relieve stress. Help them understand their stress and manage it in a more relaxed, intuitive and accessible way [22].

5 Application Technology of Health Intelligent Clothing

The key technologies of intelligent clothing applications can be divided into three categories: sensing technology; data transmission, processing and storage technology; smart fiber and textiles.

5.1 Sensing Technology

Sensing technology is the key to intelligent clothing, which acts as a bridge between human and machine. The flexibility and miniaturization of electronic components are the basis for the combination of electronic components and clothing to form intelligent clothing. There are many electronic components for smart clothing, including flexible electrodes, sensors, conduction circuits and so on. These electronic components need to cooperate with each other to complete data monitoring, but at present, most of the integration technologies of these electronic modules are in the laboratory stage and have not yet reached standardized production.

As a part of smart clothing, electronic components must also meet the wearing performance of clothing [23]. For example, long-term voyage, washable, etc.; minimize wiring, improve clothing comfort; reasonably optimize the layout and enhance aesthetics. In addition, the sensors such as ECG monitoring, respiratory rate and temperature should be accurately placed in the corresponding position of the human body according to the monitoring principle of human physiological signals. At the same time, the information processing module should take into account the wearable area of the human body in the design and placement, avoid dislocation due to differences in consumer size, and select areas with relatively fixed and large load-bearing surface area during exercise, so as to reduce the clothing burden of consumers [24].

Photo plethysmography (PPG) sensor [25] tests heart rate by converting pulsating signal changes of blood transmittance into electrical signals, which is cheap and easy to operate, so it is widely used in wearable devices. Electrocardiography (ECG) sensor [26] through the electrode changes collected from the body surface, the ECG is obtained by algorithm processing, which can be used for a single accurate test to measure heart rate variability.

5.2 Data Transmission

With the development of computer technology, the data transmission of the monitoring system will be wireless and integrated gradually. All kinds of sensors and electrodes integrated on clothing will greatly reduce the use of leads if wireless signal transmission is used. Through the centralized integration of the signal port, the test is more convenient and flexible, and the port can be expanded, which makes it possible to add function in the future. Therefore, the wireless and integration of signal processing and communication technology is also one of the difficulties that the intelligent clothing industry needs to break through.

Embedded single chip microcomputer is a special computer system which is embedded into the object system with the controller as the core control unit. The electronic platforms used in wearable devices are Arduino, STM32 and so on, which play an important role in the human-computer interaction of wearable technology [27]. Wireless communication technology realizes the short-distance data transmission between intelligent clothing and terminal, which makes intelligent clothing more efficient and convenient. Wireless communication technology mainly includes Bluetooth, Near Field Communication (near field communication, NFC), Radio Frequency Identification (radio frequency identification, RFID), ZigBee and so on.

5.3 Processing and Storage Technology

Cloud storage of human body-related physical parameters enriches the sample size for future health monitoring data analysis [28]. The establishment of cloud storage platform can not only let people know their own physical conditions, but also be of great significance to the research in the field of health through the analysis of a large number of human body data in the future.

5.4 Smart Fiber and Textiles

Electronic textiles are usually formed by knitting, knitting or embroidering functional fibers in a coaxial or twisted layout into the fabric or directly embedding functional nanoparticles into the fabric [29–31]. Different types of methods have their own advantages and disadvantages [32]. The weaving of textiles can promote the manufacture of multiple layers, which can hide conductive yarns in braided textiles to prevent short circuit, but the resulting braided structure requires a predetermined position of weft or warp, which limits the degree of freedom of manufacturing. Knitted textiles are relatively stretchable, but the conductivity of the transmission line is significantly higher than that of the yarn in the sensing area to adapt to the deformation of the yarn ring. Textile embroidery has a high degree of freedom in the placement of wires, but it causes a high level of stress on the yarn during the embroidery process, thus limiting the choice of yarn.

6 Market Prospects and Challenges of Health Smart Clothing

At present, most of the smart clothing stay in the laboratory products, have not really entered the market. The reason is that the production cost of this kind of intelligent products is too high and has not yet been industrialized, which leads to its high price. Therefore, it is very necessary to establish an intelligent clothing factory based on automation system to improve productivity, reduce production costs and carry out responsive production in the market. Only by walking down the altar and entering the factory can smart clothing make people enjoy the convenience it brings. Only in this way can smart clothing be constantly updated and improved in practice and coruscate a long-term vitality.

Therefore, this report conducted a sampling questionnaire survey on the potential users of smart clothing in China, in order to get a more realistic future development trend and market demand of healthy smart clothing.

Summary of Smart Clothing Market Questionnaire. A total of 385 questionnaires were collected and 383 were valid. In this survey, 43.6% were male and 56.4% were female. The sex ratio in the survey is relatively balanced, with women in the majority. Among the surveyed population, 3.38% were under 18 years old, 50.31% were between 18 and 25 years old, 21.15% were between 25 and 30 years old, 21.15% were between 30 and 50 years old, and only 4.18% were over 50 years old. The survey population is of all ages. Generally speaking, the survey population is mainly 18 to 25 years old.

Basic Information of Respondents

1. The vast majority of respondents are students, blue collar and white-collar workers, with the largest proportion of students.
2. Conclusion: the vast majority of respondents' monthly income is between 2000 and 8000 yuan, and there are many people without income in the middle. The vast majority of respondents' monthly income is between 2000 and 8000 yuan, and there are also many people without income in the middle.
3. Most of the cities surveyed are new frontlines, but a large number of people have only heard of smart clothing, and 20% have not even heard of smart clothing at all.
4. Most of the respondents obtained smart clothing information through fashion magazines and periodicals, as well as through school courses or short video platforms.

Respondents' Expectations for Smart Clothing

1. The vast majority of respondents hope that smart clothing has a life span of more than five years.
2. For smart clothing, most respondents are more concerned about its safety, but people are also concerned about environmental protection, beauty, entertainment, health and other issues:
   1. On the issue of environmental protection, people pay more attention to the problem of degradable recycling of materials, and people also pay attention to anti-pollution and non-cleaning.
   2. As for aesthetics, people pay more attention to changes in color appearance and style, and size adjustment is also more important for people.
   3. As for entertainment, people pay more attention to whether there are mobile Hotspots or not, and game functions are less valued by people.
   4. As for health, people pay more attention to whether smart clothing has intelligent monitoring, and hope that smart clothing can provide some sports guidance.
   5. With regard to safety, respondents paid more attention to the protective performance of smart clothing to protect human body. Secondly, they hoped that smart clothing would have some positioning functions.

a. If there are smart clothes on the market, the vast majority of respondents hope that smart clothes have the functions of body monitoring and clothing status monitoring. Respondents hoped that smart clothing in health care would have the functions of life and rest tips and disease monitoring, and real-time synchronization with the hospital
b. Other unilateral specific expectations:
   a. Smart clothing that can protect the body has the function of decompression and sterilization
   b. It has the function of monitoring blood pressure, blood oxygen, heart rate, respiration
   c. Smart clothing with environmental monitoring function has the function of monitoring temperature and humidity
   d. Smart clothes that can monitor the state of clothes can display the cleanliness of clothes
   e. It is hoped that smart clothing with leisure entertainment function can change colors and show mood.

Respondents' Purchase Intention and Expectation for Smart Clothing Market

1. the most acceptable price for smart clothing is 1000–3000 yuan. They are more willing to buy smart clothing from Taobao or personalized customization channels, because they love technology, bring convenience to life, like novelty, and catch up with the trend of the times. Three quarters of respondents are willing to buy smart clothing just launched in the market
2. respondents are reluctant to buy smart clothing because they are worried about the security of new things, worry about the high price, lack of practicability and complex operation. The main factors influencing respondents' purchase of smart clothing are: fabric, technical function, durability and safety (Fig. 2).

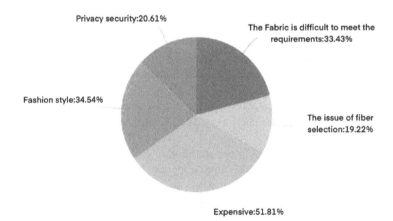

Fig. 2. Why the respondents are reluctant to buy smart clothing.

3. respondents most expect smart clothing that can detect their own health. People think that the popularity of smart clothing is mainly reflected in its functionality. Respondents felt that the portability of smart clothing was the most important, followed by accuracy, and finally popularity. In the survey, most respondents were willing to wear smart clothing to go out.

To sum up, it is not difficult to draw a conclusion that the future development trend of health smart clothing will be more intelligent, personalized, multifunctional and fashionable, providing people with more comprehensive, convenient and efficient health management and life support. The technical difficulties in the development of intelligent clothing lie in the monitoring technology of human physiological signals, the integration of sensing elements and clothing platform, the technology of signal processing and system communication, and the research on the dynamic interaction between clothing and skin. At the same time, smart clothing is currently facing some problems, such as product safety, high cost, limitation of use, application of big data and so on. In addition to the key technologies at the scientific research level need to be further studied, in terms of industry standards, it is necessary to uniformly formulate intelligent clothing safety norms in order to guide and restrict the development of this intelligent clothing. At the same time, it is necessary to integrate the textile industry, because only comprehensive industry integration can form a complete industrial chain, and further promote smart clothing to reduce costs and move towards the public.

Appendix Survey Questionnaire

Smart clothing market questionnaire survey

Dear interviewee: Hello! We are fashion design students from South China University of Technology. In order to better understand people's views and use of smart clothing, we have specially made a smart clothing questionnaire. We hope you can spare a few minutes to fill it out and submit it. Your comments and suggestions will be very helpful to our research. We promise that the information you provide will only be used for research analysis and will not be disclosed to any third party institutions or individuals. Please click on the following link to enter the questionnaire: (Link) Thankyou for your patience! If you have any questions, please feel free to contact us. Have a nice life!

Students from School of Design, South China University of Technology
Contact number:
Person in charge:
Year month

Guidance:
We have set multiple-choice and sorting questions, please pay attention to the question type
Please answer according to your real situation

Welcome to this quiz

1. Your gender
male
Female

2 Your age
Under 18 years of age
18 -25 years old
25-30 years old
30-50 years old
50 +

3 Your occupational status
Students
White collar, blue collar
Businessman
Freelancers
(elderly) retirees
Others (please specify)

4 Your current monthly income

No income yet
Less than 2,000 yuan
2,000-8,000 yuan
8000- 15000 yuan
15,000-40,000 yuan
Over 40,000

5. What do you know about smart clothing

I've never heard of it
Only heard of
Vaguely aware but feeling distant

Interested, usually pay more attention to this information

Very understand, think it will soon be marketable

6. How do you get the information about smart clothing? (multiple choice)
At a physical Store
Fashion magazines
Social platforms
Introductions from friends
TV commercials
Email
Other (please specify)

9 How long do you want smart clothing to last

0- 1 years

1-3 years

3-5 years

5 + years

10. For smart clothing, which of the following points do you pay more attention to (please select the corresponding question according to the answer) (multiple choice)
Environmental Protection
Aesthetic
Entertainment
Health
Secure

11.Which of the following do you value most about environmental protection (multiple choices),

Materials that are degradable and recyclable

Energy can be stored through motion

Stain resistant and clean free
12. Which of the following do you value most in terms of aesthetics

Size adjustment

Style changes

Anti-pressure and anti-wrinkle

Color appearance change

13. Which of the following do you value most about entertainment

Games

WIFI hotspot

Multimedia library

AR Entertainment

Dazzle Vision

14. Which of the following do you value most about health
Sports coaching

Smart temperature regulation

Healthcare

Smart monitoring

15. Which of the following do you value most about safety

The protection of the human body

Pocket with anti-theft function

Location function

16. If there are smart clothes on the market at present, what functions do you want smart clothes to have?
Health care
Body protection
Body monitoring
Environmental monitoring
Clothing condition monitoring
Laid-back entertainment (comes with cameras, screens, etc.)
Communication positioning
Automatically fit body shape
Automatic cleaning
Temperature regulation
Other, please specify:

17. What aspects of health care function do you want smart clothing to have?
Massage
Acupuncture

Disease surveillance synced with hospitals in realtime

Lifestyle tips

Other, please specify:

18. What aspects of body protection functions do you want smart clothing to include [multiple choices]

Germicidal

Enhanced sense of balance

Shock absorption

Decompression

Others, please specify:

19. What aspects of body monitoring function do you want smart clothing to have?

Weight, body fat ratio

Blood pressure, blood oxygen, heart rate, breathing

Body temperature, heat expenditure

Muscle fatigue, body dehydration tips

Mental stress, psychological condition

Athletic posture

20. What environmental monitoring functions do you want smart clothing to include?

Temperature, humidity

Air quality

Noise, electromagnetic radiation

Radioactive contamination

Light, heat, ultraviolet rays

Other, please specify:

21. What aspects of clothing condition monitoring do you want smart clothing to include [check]

Degree of cleanliness

Degree of wear and tear

Level of flatness

Color retention

Others, please specify:

22. What leisure and entertainment functions do you want smart clothing to include?

【Multiple choices 】

Multimedia

Mood display

Changing colors

Other, please specify:

23. What kind of smart clothing are you willing to buy for your pet

GPS location function

Health check

Tear-resistant

Assisted movement to increase weight bearing

Pet profile Contact owner

Unwilling to buy

No pets

23. What is the highest price you can accept if smart clothing enters everyday life

200 to 1000 yuan

1000-3000 yuan

3000-5000 yuan

5000- 10000 yuan

10,000 to 30,000 yuan

More than 30,000 yuan

24. Which channel do you prefer to buy smart clothing from

Taobao (online shopping)

Official website

Specialty Stores

Personalization

Through-shop

Others (please specify)

25. If smart clothing has just been launched in the market, would you like to buy it and try it? (Please select the corresponding question according to the answer.)

Yes.

Disinclination

26. Why are you willing to buy smart clothing (in order of preference)
4. You like novelty
A love of technology
Bringing convenience to life
Catchup with The Times

27. The reasons you don't want to buy smart clothing (in order of preference)
Fear of high prices
Safety concerns about new things
No practicality
Complex operation

28. What is your attitude towards the prospect of smart clothing

Expectations: Believe that technology changes lives

Optimism: Maybe there is a real possibility that it will become popular and mainstream in the future

Neutral: The future is unpredictable

Skeptical: Because it feels like smart clothing is far away from people's lives, there are too many problems to solve

Pessimism: smart clothing has never replaced traditional clothing, it is only a demonstration of science and technology,
cannot be market, people are difficult to accept

29. Do you want smart clothing to be different from ordinary clothing in appearance? [Single choice]

Very hopeful
Hope
Doesn't matter

Not wished

Very much not
30. If () smart clothing is introduced, to what extent will you buy it? 【Single choice】

Definitely going to buy

May buy
Not sure
May not buy
Definitely not buying

31. What are the factors that influence whether you buy smart clothing? 【Check the check box, select a maximum of 3 】
brand
Exterior styles
Fabric
Workmanship
Comfort
Safety
Durability
Technical features
Price
Ease of operation
Practicality
Other, please specify:

32. What kind of smart clothing are you looking forward to

Smart clothing that can check your own health

changeable
Emotion-regulating

Energy saving reusable type
34. Why do you think the development of smart clothing is limited

The fabric is difficult to meet the requirements

The choice of fiber is a problem

Expensive
Style restrictions
Privacy concerns

35. What do you think the popularity of smart clothing reflects

Features
Style

36. Which advantages of smart clothing do you like better

More portable
More accurate
More mass

37. Do you think smart clothing should focus more on function or style?

Function
pattern

38. Would you like to go out in smart clothes

Yes.

Disinclination
39. In your opinion, does smart clothing open a new century for the garment industry and textile industry

YES
No

40. If you were building smart clothing, what other features would you give it?

References

1. World Population Prospects 2022: Summary of Results July 2022. https://www.un.org/dev elopment/desa/pd/
2. Gentile, F., et al.: A mathematical model of OECTs with variable internal geometry. Sens. Actuators Phys. **304**, 111894 (2020)
3. Zhou, Z., et al.: All-carbon positive electrodes for stable aluminium batteries. J. Energy Chem. **42**, 17–26 (2020)
4. Bhagwat, S., Mukherji, P.: Electromyogram (EMG) based fingers movement recognition using sparse filtering of wavelet packet coefficients. Sādhanā **45**(1), 3 (2020)
5. Yu, T., et al.: Recursive decomposition of electromyographic signals with a varying number of active sources: bayesian modeling and filtering. IEEE Trans. Biomed. Eng. **67**(2), 428–440 (2020)
6. Li, M., Xiong, W., Li, Y.: Wearable measurement of ECG signals based on smart clothing. Int. J. Telemed. Appl. (2020)
7. Li, S., Zhang, H., Teng, W.: Application status and development prospect of smart clothing. Prog. Text. Sci. Technol. (4), 4Mel 7 (2019). (Chinese)
8. Hao, J., Li, Y.: Development status and trend of intelligent clothing. Text. Guide (4), 4 (2020). https://doi.org/10.16481/j.cnki.ctl.2020.04.015. (Chinese)
9. Jakubas, A., Łada-Tondyra, E.: A study on application of the ribbing stitch as sensor of respiratory rhythm in smart clothing designed for infants. J. Text. Inst. **109**(9), 1208–1216 (2018)
10. Lada-Tondyra, E., Jakubas, A.: The concept of a textronic system limiting bacterial growth. In: 2018 Progress in Applied Electrical Engineering (PAEE), pp. 1–4 (2018)
11. Long, R: Health care industry has become the biggest potential market of smart clothing industry. China Fiber Insp. (Z1), 174175 (2020). (Chinese)
12. Lindeman, R.D., et al.: Prevalences of type 2 diabetes, the insulin resistance syndrome, and coronary heart disease in an elderly, biethnic population. Diabetes Care **21**, 959–966 (1998)
13. Tanwar, R., et al.: Pathway of trends and technologies in fall detection: a systematic review. Healthcare **10** (2022)
14. Liu, S.: The importance of regular physical examination for early prevention and treatment of diseases in the middle-aged and elderly. Chin. Conval. Med. **18**(5), 2 (2009). (Chinese)
15. Blain, H., et al.: Anti-fall plan for the elderly in France 2022–2024: objectives and methodology. Geriatrie et psychologie neuropsychiatrie du vieillissement **21**(3), 286–294 (2023)
16. Zhang, H., Chen, Y.: Design and development of ECG monitoring clothing for the elderly. Shanghai Text. Sci. Technol. (6), 18Mel 21 (2018). (Chinese)
17. Zheng, Z., Liu, H.: Design of intelligent heating clothing control software based on Android and Bluetooth communication. Tianjin Text. Sci. Technol. (2), 26Mui 28 (2015). (Chinese)
18. Chen, B.R.: LEGSys: wireless gait evaluation system using wearable sensors. In: Proceedings of Wireless Health (2011)
19. Tognetti, A., Lorussi, F., Car-Bonaro, N., et al.: Daily–life monitoring of stroke survivors motor performance: the interaction sensing system. In: Conference Proceedings of Annual International Conference of the IEEE Engineering in Medicine and Biology Society, Chicago. Annual International Conference of the IEEE Engineering in Medicine and Biology Society, pp 4099–4102 (2014)
20. Ren, X., Shen, L., Xue, Z.B., Tang, Y.: The construction of intelligent wearable clothing collaborative design system for the elderly. Decoration (4), 4 (2020). (Chinese)
21. Jebelli, H.: Wearable biosensors to understand construction workers' mental and physical stress (2019)

22. Dong, K.: EazyTrack: Exploring Next-Gen Technology and User Experience Design to Help Relieve Stress. Rochester Institute of Technology (2018)
23. Liang, S., Xu, P.: Intelligent underwear design based on physiological signal monitoring. J. Wuhan Text. Univ. **31**(6), 38 (2018). (Chinese)
24. Feng, J.M., Liu, Y.: Application analysis of new flexible energy storage components in clothing. Int. Text. Guide **44**(2), 60, 65 (2016). (Chinese)
25. Jong, G.J., Aripriharta, Horng, G.J.: The PPG physiological signal for heart rate variability analysis. Wirel. Pers. Commun. **97**(4), 5229–5276 (2017)
26. Kida, N., Tsubakihara, Y., Kida, H., et al.: Usefulness of measurement of heart rate variability by holter ECG in hemodialysis patients. BMC Nephrol. **18**(1), 8 (2017)
27. Liu, Y., Cong, S.: Progress in the application of wearable technology in human health monitoring. Acta Text. Sinica **39**(10), 180Mel 184 (2018). (Chinese)
28. Pei, L.: Research and Development of Intelligent clothing for exercise and body temperature Monitoring. Suzhou University, Suzhou (2017). (Chinese)
29. Wang, L., et al.: Application challenges in fiber and textile electronics. Adv. Mater. **32**, 1901971 (2019)
30. Ismar, E., Tao, X., Rault, F., Dassonville, F., Cochrane, C.: Towards embroidered circuit board from conductive yarns for e-textiles. IEEE Access **8**, 155329–155336 (2020)
31. Lund, A., et al.: Roll-to-roll dyed conducting silk yarns: a versatile material for e-textile devices. Adv. Mater. Technol. **3**, 1800251 (2018)
32. Atalay, O., Kalaoglu, F., Bahadir, S.K.: Development of textile-based transmission lines using conductive yarns and ultrasonic welding technology for e-textile applications. J. Eng. Fibers Fabr. **14**, 1558925019856603 (2019)

Inclusive Medicine Packaging for the Geriatric Population: Bridging Accessibility Gaps

Mrishika Kannan Nair$^{(\boxtimes)}$ and Richa Gupta

Accessible and Inclusive Design Lab, Indraprastha Institute of Information Technology, Delhi, New Delhi, India
mrishnair@gmail.com

Abstract. The geriatric population is the largest and most consistent consumer of medications [6]. Age-related changes impacting visual and tactile acuity pose barriers to effective medication management. The primary reason for this, is the neglect of inclusive and accessible design practices in medicine strips. This research uncovers the exclusionary design of medication packaging and emphasises the imperative shift towards a more inclusive design. A mixed-method study was employed to understand the major physical and cognitive challenges faced by the elderly in medication management. Amongst the different design interventions explored, augmented reality QR tags emerged as a versatile solution, offering easy, magnified, text-to-speech content on mobile devices. To validate the proposed prototype and approach, an experiment was conducted. Our design reduced task completion time, minimised the chances of medication errors and reduced the reliance on assistance. The qualitative interview post-experiment revealed enhanced user satisfaction and ease of use. This research has illuminated the possibilities for enhancing healthcare accessibility and medication management through the thoughtful integration of technology into medicine strip design. By offering a more inclusive and user-friendly approach, the study bridges the accessibility gap, empowering individuals of all ages and abilities to manage their medications safely and effectively.

Keywords: Assistive Technology · Geriatric · QR tags · Inclusion · Polymedication

1 Introduction

The design of medicine strips, an indispensable medium in healthcare, has long overlooked the critical element of inclusion. These slender, foil-wrapped carriers of vital medications are integral to saving countless lives. Despite their ubiquity, their design has often been exclusionary, inadvertently sidelining a significant portion of the population and erecting barriers to healthcare accessibility. This oversight is particularly detrimental to vulnerable demographics, including the

V. G. Duffy (Ed.): HCII 2024, LNCS 14710, pp. 87–102, 2024.
https://doi.org/10.1007/978-3-031-61063-9_6

elderly, visually impaired individuals, and those with diminished tactile sensitivities. Our research is a comprehensive exploration of the challenges faced by these diverse demographic groups [19], with a specific focus on the geriatric population, to unravel the intricacies of exclusionary design practices within the context of Human-Computer Interaction (HCI) for medication management.

As physiological transformations accompany the ageing process, there is a notable decline in visual acuity [18] and diminishing tactile sensitivities [12], which present formidable impediments to proficient medicine handling, comprehension, and adherence. These challenges underscore the pressing need for a paradigm shift toward inclusion in medicine strip design, emphasising equitable accessibility as a paramount goal.

The impact of age-related conditions collectively precipitates a reduction in visual sharpness, hindering the deciphering of minuscule fonts, intricate instructions, and compact dosage information typical of prevailing medication packaging [1]. As individuals age, their ability to perceive and comprehend these critical details on medicine strips diminishes significantly. Concurrently, ageing brings about the erosion of tactile sensitivities, presenting yet another multifaceted challenge within HCI. The repercussions of this decline are manifold as geriatric individuals struggle with grasping minuscule pills, navigating intricate packaging mechanisms, and avoiding accidental medication mishaps [6]. These impediments compromise medication adherence and elicit safety concerns, underscoring the necessity for innovation and transformation in medication packaging.

Throughout this research, a wide range of challenges faced by the target population was observed. By analysing their current methods of interacting with and accommodating the contemporary design of medications, valuable insights emerged, guiding toward innovative design solutions. Among a spectrum of potential options, augmented reality QR tags emerged as a versatile solution with the potential to address a wide range of needs. They enable users to access magnified content on their mobile devices, effectively prioritising essential information while minimising the visual clutter often found on traditional medicine strips. Furthermore, this technology is highly adaptable, as family members can easily apply QR stickers that can be annotated with audio messages using a simple app. This user-friendly approach ensures that the technology can be personalised and accessible to individuals according to their unique requirements. To test the premise, an experiment with pretest and posttest phases was designed, where participants were initially asked to perform a set of tasks with the traditional medicine strip design. Subsequently, during the posttest phase, participants were asked to repeat the same tasks with the proposed prototype. The evaluation of their performance was done on the basis of key parameters, including accuracy, the time taken to complete each task, user satisfaction and ease of use through qualitative comments. The later sections will present a comprehensive data analysis of these results.

This paper is structured as follows: Sect. 2 has a detailed literature review; in Sect. 3 reviews the design of the existing medicine strip; Sect. 4 has the detailed research methodology followed; Sect. 5 and 6 dives into the results and observations obtained from the research; Sect. 7 highlights future research possibilities.

2   Literature Review

2.1   Geriatric and Medicines

The geriatric population is often susceptible to multiple health and chronic conditions, leading to polymedication - the concurrent usage of multiple medications due to multimorbidity [6,13]. This increases the complexity of their medication regimens, demanding careful management and coordination [5]. Ageing poses challenges on multiple fronts. Physical challenges like weak hands and vision problems make medication handling difficult. With age, there is a significant cognitive decline and forgetfulness to take medicines on time according to the dosage schedule [2]. Language barriers and lack of information about the medication add another layer of complexity. These factors collectively impact an individual's ability to administer, manage and keep track of the medication schedule. The combination of physical, cognitive and sensory decline complicates the daily routines of the geriatric population and also poses significant barriers to achieving optimal medication adherence. Despite these challenges self-medication is still a prevalent choice in this age group [9]. Major reasons for this include repetitive, common or already experienced symptoms, and factors such as time constraints, misinformation and lack of accessible healthcare.

2.2   Age-Related Challenges

Ageing causes a lot of physiological changes, majorly related to sensory perception. Generally after the age of 50, individuals traverse various stages of their lives marked by a substantial decline in vision and tactile sensations.

Vision Challenges: According to World Health Organisation data, the prevalence of blindness varies across different age groups. It ranges from 0.1% in people ages 55 to 64 to 3.9% in people aged 85 or older. The presence of any sort of visual impairment in this age group ranged from 0.1% to 11.8% [10]. The reason for visual impairment in people under the age of 75 is mainly myopic degeneration and for those aged older, macular degeneration becomes the leading cause of blindness. The onset of presbyopia within this age group stands as a significant factor [17]. Presbyopia is characterised by the loss of flexibility in the eye lens, which reduces the ability to focus on nearby objects. Individuals with this condition face difficulties in reading small fonts, discerning intricate details, and, particularly relevant to the study, comprehending important information presented on medicine strips like the name, expiry date and dosage. This would hinder their ability to comprehend the key details presented on the medicine strips like the name, expiry date and dosage. These details , if misinterpreted, can lead to catastrophic consequences.

Tactile Sensation Challenges: Ageing induces transformation of skin characteristics, including a reduction in skin elasticity and changes in the morphology of tactile receptors. In individuals aged 50 and above, there is a gradual decline in the density and functionality of skin tactile receptors, leading to decreased tactile acuity [12]. Additionally, ageing contributes to demyelination in the central and peripheral nervous system, intensifying the impact on tactile function [12]. The reduction in tactile sensitivity can impede the ability to handle small objects, such as pills from medicine strips, making it difficult to navigate complex packaging structures effectively. This decline in tactile capabilities hinders the ability to manage medications with precision.

2.3   Medication Errors

Among elderly, polymedicated people, the probability of medication errors at home is high. Around the world, the rates of non-adherence of medication dosage range from 7.1% to 66.2% and exceed 50% among the polymedicated elderly [15]. Through a study done in the USA and European countries, polymedicated elderly reported the reasons for their medication errors. Skipping a dose or not taking it regularly or at the prescribed frequency (reported by 50% of respondents), not remembering doctor's instructions (42.9%), and getting confused with different medications and not taking the right one (24.9%) were the major reasons [15]. The conclusion of the study was that when the number of prescriptions rises, it is more common to confuse medications since their understanding and memory of the correct dosage for each decreases. This is a significant consideration as the prevalence of polymedication in patients aged 65 or above is 50%. In another study, there was a survey conducted of 100 people impaired with colour vision, 2% reported that they had confused their medication because they had mistaken the colour of tablets [7], this shows how people sometimes just rely on the external characteristics of the medicine like the colour and shape, and don't always pay attention to the details on the medicine blister foil information. So medication errors among the polymedicated elderly are often attributed to factors such as forgetting dosage instructions, reliance on external characteristics like medicine colour or shape, and confusion with different medications.

2.4   Intervention of Technology in Medication Management

There have been a lot of technological interventions to ease medication management. Some solutions catering to the needs of the geriatric population encompass Android phone applications for medicine reminders, smart dispensers, audio-prescription readers, touch-to-speech devices, continuous glucose monitoring systems, etc. [8]. Smart packaging has revolutionised medication management, prioritising user convenience and safety [11]. These packaging have features such as temperature monitoring, tamper-evident seals, RFID tracking systems, offering real-time insights into the condition and location of medicines, ensuring medication efficacy [4,16]. Despite these advancements in medication handling, there is a pressing need to improve and reduce the difficulty of identifying crucial information, such as expiration dates and dosage details on the medicines. A gap remains in ensuring easy and comprehensive accessibility to vital medication-related information. Ongoing developments and innovations are essential to create holistic solutions that not only streamline the medication process but also prioritise accessibility to important information for individuals, particularly the elderly, ensuring their well-being and adherence to prescribed regimens.

2.5   Technology Usage Amongst Elderly

The older population faces difficulty in using smartphones due to a lack of knowledge in using technological devices and their advanced functionalities. In a study that focused on understanding barriers to smartphone usage among the elderly, the findings indicated that ease of use and actual need of the services are an important criteria for them, and they tend to avoid more complex functions [14]. Their opinion was that making a call is the easiest functionality of a smartphone, and they prefer tactile buttons over touch screen features. In recent years, senior citizens have become increasingly reliant on smartphones compared to the younger generation. According to a report, a substantial 67% of India's urban online population, with the largest majority falling between the ages of 60 and 65, couldn't imagine life without their smartphones [3]. This underscores the significant role smartphones play in the daily lives of senior citizens, they use it to perform daily tasks like shopping, booking appointments, etc. highlighting the growing smartphone adoption within this demographic.

3   Studying the Existing Medicine Strip Design

Medicine strips are ubiquitous due to their integral role in healthcare. But a closer examination revealed that these slender blister foils fall short in addressing critical elements of inclusion. There are several inherent problems in their design which impact different user groups.

Small Font Size: The text on medicine strips is often very small, making it non-legible and difficult for individuals with visual impairments or those experiencing age-related decline in vision. Reading important information like the medication name, expiration date and dosage becomes a daunting task. This leads to misinterpretation and errors in medication management. So this induces a tendency in the older population to identify medicines on the basis of their external characteristics like shape and colour.

Low Colour Contrast: Solely relying on external characteristics is also dangerous because medicine strips have low colour contrast and the colours used in general are mostly not distinguishable by various colour blindness types-

- Yellow-blue colour blindness (tritanopia)
- Red-green colour blindness (protanopia and deuteranopia)
- Total colour blindness (Fig. 1)

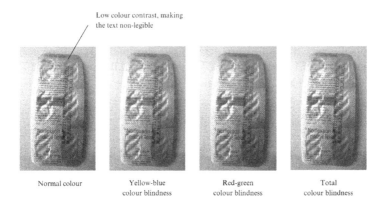

Low colour contrast, making the text non-legible

| Normal colour | Yellow-blue colour blindness | Red-green colour blindness | Total colour blindness |

Fig. 1. The low colour contrast of medicine strips, non-legible for different color blindness types

Placement and Layout: Different medicines have different layouts of textual information. There is no universal placement or hierarchy in key information like the expiration date and dosage details. Mostly the expiry date is engraved on the places that get peeled off while taking a medicine, and ultimately, the user is left with no other option but to throw the medicine. Cluttered information makes navigation tedious, and an oversight can lead to potentially jeopardising the effectiveness and safety of the medication.

Too Much Information: Medicine strips have a lot of information, not all of which are essential to the user. The information overload can be overwhelming for older adults because they already face challenges in cognitive progression. The confusion may result in difficulty in understanding essential information, leading to poor adherence and medical errors. Simplifying and just including the required information can enhance user comprehension.

Dexterity and Safety Concerns: Blister packaging, commonly used for medicine strips, often incorporates a level of resistance to make it childproof and secure. This introduces challenges for individuals experiencing limitations in dexterity, a prevalent issue associated with ageing. The need to peel back or push through blister foils to access each dose makes it challenging and time-consuming for the elderly due to their diminished tactile grasp and manual coordination. The struggle to extract individual doses sometimes results in accidental double dosing or missed doses. Thus handling blister packaging impedes efficient medicine administration. Another problem with these blister foils is that their edges are very sharp; they pose a risk of cuts when handling the packaging, a concern that becomes particularly significant for the older population, given their susceptibility to multimorbidity. For individuals with diabetes, in particular, the consequences of these cuts can be perilous. The compromised healing ability associated with diabetes makes such cuts more than just a minor inconvenience; they can escalate into severe complications.

4   Methodology

The research methodology consists of three key stages. Initially, a need validation survey was conducted among the target audience to ascertain whether the identified problems resonated with users and if they encountered similar challenges with the current design of medicine strips. Following this, the current adaptation techniques employed by users were explored; using this information, accommodations to the existing design were devised. A radically disruptive redesign of the product was proposed towards the end of this phase. In the final stage an experimental study was conducted to validate the viability and efficacy of the proposed new design.

4.1   Need Validation Survey

To verify the problems identified, a need validation study was done through surveys, targeting the geriatric demographic - aged 50 and above. The questions covered three broad categories - their demographic, problems they face with the current design and whether they wish to have a new and accessible design.

An expansive number of 273 participants participated in the survey study.

Result Analysis

Demographic
Majority of the participants were in the age range 50–70. 29 participants were in the age group 70–100, the reduced participation was because engaging participants proved challenging due to the online survey format. To address this limitation, outreach was extended to several retirement homes with continuous medical support. This facilitated direct collaboration with the medical teams overseeing the well-being of elderly residents. During these interactions, they highlighted the prevalence of medication errors, particularly regarding incorrect administration and dosage among this age group. This firsthand information emphasised the substantial reliance of this age group on external assistance for the effective management of their medication routines. Out of the participants almost 25% were polymedicated, 66% had some sort of visual impairment and 69% had reduced tactile grasp.

Problems Faced
Many participants wished to manage their medications independently, suggesting a preference for self-sufficiency in this age group. However, more than half of the study population mentioned their struggles with the current design of medicine strips. The problems they faced were either administering the wrong dosage (41%), difficulty in reading the medication instructions due to small fonts (73.4%), struggles with finding the expiration date (58.5%) or accidentally peeled out the expiration date while administering the medicine (75.6%). This highlighted a crucial gap in the accessibility of information, signalling a pressing need

for intervention in medication packaging design. Most of the participants(88%) were also in support of an accessible intervention in medicine packaging design.

To understand the viewpoint of the pharmacists a semi-structured interview across 16 pharmaceuticals was conducted, the professional were asked questions that mainly targeted the use of the intricate textual info on the hind side of the medicine strip, and whether they have got complaints from the geriatric age group related to medicine management difficulties. Understanding their perspective not only validates practicality but also explores collaborative opportunities for effective medication management solutions. The feedback revealed a significant finding: a considerable number of patients struggle to interpret information on the back of the strip, often requiring constant assistance from pharmacists over calls. Interestingly, when questioned about the necessity of detailed textual information, pharmacists emphasised its importance for accurate medication comprehension. This key insight led us to recognize the need for distinct designs tailored to different user groups - patients and pharmacists. When asked about the concept of inclusive medicine strips featuring QR codes, a noteworthy 17 out of 20 pharmacists expressed their support. These discussions emphasised the potential value of incorporating innovative solutions that prioritise accessibility and streamline information retrieval (Fig. 2).

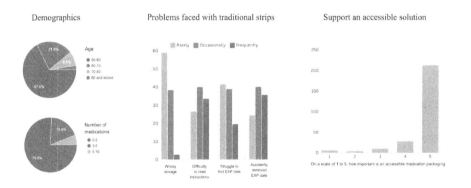

Fig. 2. Data gathered through surveys and interviews

4.2 User Adaptation Techniques

After gaining a comprehensive understanding of the user's needs, their current adaptation techniques to temporarily solve the problems they face was explored. For medicine identification, one prevalent approach involves relying on physical characteristics, such as the shape and size of the medicine. They also use tactile markers such as rubber bands, adhesive labels, and stickers. For remembering the dosage details, they majorly use pill organisers; some have pictograms on them that cater to individuals facing language barriers or literacy challenges. Another segment of the population also uses smartphone apps to set reminders for their medication schedule. To address the challenge of opening blister packaging, individuals with limited hand mobility and strength tend to use safety pins or knives to peel off these foils. However, recognising the inherent limitations of all these methods, most elderly still rely on assistance from others, such as family members or caretakers, to presort or organise their pills to ensure accurate dosage and administration.

4.3   Proposed Design Solutions

Accomodations to Existing Design

Analysing the accessibility challenges and problems posed by conventional medicine strip designs, during the research possible accommodations were devised to the existing design, and the merits and drawbacks of each were discussed. Some of the explored additions were:

Tactile Markers
Pros: Tactile markers, such as rubber bands, offer a solution that can benefit a wide demographic. Shapes, colours and numbers are easier to organise in your head than complex textual information. This method can prove helpful for individuals who have visual impairments (permanent, temporary, or situational). It is also a low cost solution and users can customise the markers based on personal preferences.
Cons: This solution may not be ideal for polymedicated individuals, as it requires remembering which marker corresponds to each medication, which can be a cognitive challenge. These markers provide minimal information about the medication apart from identification cues. Continuous use of tactile markers contribute to more environmental waste, because they need to be frequently replaced as they can wear out. Additionally, the process of creating and attaching these tactile markers for each medicine can be time consuming.

NFC Audio Token
Pros: NFC (Near Field Communication) audio tokens assist individuals with visual impairments, particularly those with permanent visual impairments. These tokens enable users to access medication information audibly, eliminating the need for text-based information. It also lowers the amount of cognitive load in medication management.
Cons: The adoption of audio tokens presents certain limitations. It necessitates the availability of audio card scanning machines, which can be a costly investment. This technology may not be suitable for emergencies, as individuals may not have immediate access to the required equipment or there could be technical issues such as device malfunctions or low battery. NFC tokens are small and portable, making it susceptible to easy damage. Moreover, these tokens provide one-way audio information and there is a limitation to interactive features, which demands a level of sustained focus while listening to the audio.

QR Codes
Pros: QR codes represent a versatile solution with potential benefits for diverse populations. They prove helpful for older individuals and the visually impaired (permanent, temporary, or situational). QR codes can be easily updated, scanned and interpreted using mobile devices with screen readers, providing immediate and accurate medication information. QR codes seamlessly integrate with technology, making it a compatible, convenient and accessible option for a larger population. These codes can also overcome language barriers as the information can be presented in multiple languages. They can also contribute to minimising the cluttered information on the medicine strips, thereby limiting the cognitive load.
Cons: Nevertheless, challenges remain in ensuring that blind individuals can independently locate and scan QR codes. This also has a huge reliance on smartphones, and the accessibility of this solution may be compromised in emergency situations where individuals may not have immediate access to their devices.

In conclusion, while various accommodations have been considered to enhance the accessibility of medicine strips, QR codes, strategically placed at tactile corners for easy location, emerged as a promising solution. Their versatility, coupled with the potential for zoomed content and decluttering, positions QR codes as a robust option to promote inclusion in medication management, catering to a wide range of needs and enhancing the autonomy of users.

Redesigning - Radically Disruptive Design

Based on the findings, the radically disruptive design introduces a more accessible and user-friendly medicine packaging. It is a flip-top packaging inspired from the lids of a tissue paper box, and it comprises two different sides:

Top Side: This side gives a prominent display of essential information such as the medicine's name, expiry date, and QR codes placed near the tactile opening area, which makes it easy for a visually impaired person to navigate to the code. This QR code serves as a multifunctional tool, enhancing accessibility for various user groups.
Bottom Side: The opposite side features the front area of the medicine strip, where the pills are visible through individual compartments.

Upon opening the flip-top lid, users encounter a designed interior:
Inner Lid: It houses reusable dosage instructions, which can be tailored to different medications. This ensures consistency and possible digital customisation in dosage management.
Blister Side: The adjacent inner lid section accommodates the blister side of the medicine strip. The clever design minimises the force required to open the packaging since users can press against a rigid surface, making it user-friendly (Fig. 3).

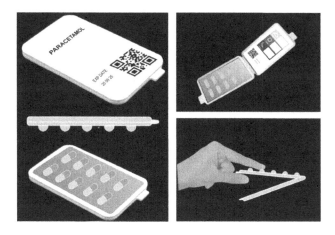

Fig. 3. Sketches of proposed design of medicine packaging

Benefits of the Redesigned Solution

Improved Accessibility and Inclusion: The placement of the QR codes near the tactile lid projection makes it easy to locate for a person with limited vision. This also benefits colour-blind individuals and those experiencing situational blindness (such as not having access to their eyeglasses).

Reduced Cognitive Load: The minimalist approach to presenting only the important information ensures that individuals find it easier to read and understand the information rather than being overwhelmed with cluttered text.

Efficient Dosage Management: The inclusion of reusable dosage details with a possibility of digital intervention for respective medicines on the inner side improves medication management and reduces the chances of errors.

Improved Pill Retrieval: Users can effortlessly pop a pill with minimal force since they press against a rigid case. The popped pill conveniently lands on the side where dosage instructions are mentioned, minimising the risk of spillage.

User-Friendly Design: The flip-top lid and sleek packaging make it easy to handle and stack. Moreover, this packaging method provides more pill security, since it reduces the chances of errors like spillage or accidental dosage.

Prototype Design

To conduct a field study and assess the effectiveness of our proposed solution, a mid-fidelity prototype was designed. A medicine strip was inserted into the flip-top lid of wet wipes. QR codes were printed specific to the medication on the outer side, accompanied by clear labelling. An app was developed to make the procedure of QR scanning easier. The app has minimal components, just a scan button that gives you important medication information like the medicine name, expiry date and dosage details. Then there is an audio button to read out the information if required. This feature allows users to access important medication information through audio narration, making it effortless for people with visual impairments (Fig. 4).

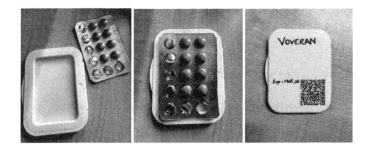

Fig. 4. Mid-fidelity prototype of the redesigned medicine packaging

4.4   Experiment Design - Prototype Validation

To test the effectiveness of QR codes over traditional medicine strips an experiment was devised. It had two parts a pretest and a posttest, where participants have to perform a set of tasks with 5 different medicine strips:

Task 1: Participants are prompted to identify the name, expiration date and dosage details of each medicine. This task assesses their ability to recognize and locate medications efficiently.

Task 2: Participants were asked to sort each medicine in the increasing order of their expiration date. This was done to understand the learnability of the participant.

Task 3: Participants are required to extract a pill from each medication strip. This task assesses their proficiency in pill removal, a fundamental aspect of medication management.

In the **Pretest**, the participants performed the tasks with traditional medicine strips.

In the **Posttest**, the participants performed the tasks while using the app and prototype.

During both the stages participants were provided with clear instructions regarding the tasks before starting and upon completing each task.

The following data was recorded while the users performed the three tasks:

- Time taken to do the three tasks (The mean and standard deviation was calculated)
- Accuracy of completing the tasks (The number mistakes committed in reporting medicine information was recorded)
- Assistance requested (Binary scale evaluation on whether the participants requested for assistance)
- Ease of doing the tasks (Users were given a few design parameters to rate their preference using a 5-point Likert scale)

Hypothesis

Out of the two designs (traditional packaging and proposed prototype) participants would find one design better over the other in terms of usability and accessibility.

5   Results

The experiment was conducted with 10 participants whose age ranged from 51 to 84 (mean age = 65.5 years, SD = 8.11). The proposed prototype reduced the time taken to interpret the medicine information by 80%. The task accuracy increased from 70% to 96%. In the pretest 6 out of 10 participants requested assistance to perform the task; however, with the proposed prototype in the posttest, this number reduced to 2 participants requesting assistance.

For detailed statistics, please refer to Table 1 (Fig. 5).

Table 1. Results of the experiment

	Traditional medicine packaging	Redesigned prototype
Time taken to complete the tasks	Mean = 396.8 sec (6 min 37 sec) SD = 26.38	Mean = 82.5 sec (1min 22sec) SD = 21.28
Assistance requested	6 out of 10 participants	2 out of 10 participants
Accuracy	70% (3 wrong in every 10 medication)	96%

Fig. 5. Participants performing the experiment

After the prototype evaluation experiment, a comparative qualitative study was conducted with the same group of participants. Participants were instructed to rate their preferences using a 5-point Likert scale, where a rating of 1 indicated a strong preference for the traditional packaging, and a rating of 5 indicated a strong preference for the proposed prototype. The mean of the ratings provided by the participants were calculated and is given in detail in Table 2.

Table 2. Comparison between the user ratings of traditional and redesigned packaging

Design Parameters	Participant rating (1 = prefers traditional design, 5 = prefers proposed prototype)	Overall Preference
Finding the important information	Mean = 5, SD = 0	Proposed prototype
Easy to use	Mean = 4.5, SD = 0.67	Proposed prototype
Safety - blister foil cuts	Mean = 4.5, SD = 0.5	Proposed prototype
Easier to hold and remove the pill	Mean = 3.3, SD = 0.64	Comparable
Size and storage	Mean = 3.8, SD = 0.6	Proposed prototype
Would you use it?	Mean = 4.6, SD = 0.66	Proposed prototype

6   Observation and Discussion

In the prototype evaluation experiment, the results indicated that the time taken to interpret and report the important medicine information(name, expiration date and dosage) was reduced considerably when participants used the redesigned prototype. The error rate was considerably low, thereby the participants task accuracy increased in the posttest. More participants requested for assistance while performing the tasks with the traditional medicine strips in comparison to when they used the proposed design prototype. This shows that the proposed design has increased the ease of use, and provides information in a more accessible manner. This would enhance participants self-reliance in managing their medication schedule.

The results of the comparative study clearly indicate a strong preference among participants for the proposed prototype over traditional medicine packaging. This preference was in terms of usability, safety and easily finding the medication information. However, some participants expressed concerns regarding the perceived difficulty in removing pills from the packaging and the potential increase in storage space required. These feedback points will be carefully considered in the future iterations of the design.

7   Conclusion and Future Work

Through this research, substantial gaps in medication packaging were identified and opportunities to make medication packaging more accessible and inclusive were discovered. The need for this change has been convincingly demonstrated through user studies, and the geriatric population is highly supportive of it. They expressed a desire for self-reliance in managing medications easily and efficiently. The incorporation of an intuitive QR code scanning feature into medicine packaging reduced both the time and errors associated with medication management. Our study participants' positive and suggestive comments helped us lay the foundation for future improvements. Moving forward, the focus would be on refining the design in terms of size and customisation to cater to various medicines to ensure that the end product is effective and user-friendly.

The overarching goal is to revolutionise this segment of the healthcare industry and make it a holistic, easy-to-manage ecosystem. We aim to do this through the digital dosage intervention in the package. This intervention would go beyond reminders; incorporate natural language processing to remove language barriers in understanding medication instructions, facilitate medication orders, and aid in scheduling timely appointments with healthcare professionals. This system would reduce the burden on both patients and doctors by ensuring everyone is up-to-date with the medication regimen. The research propels towards a future where medication management is seamless, inclusive, and empowering for users across diverse demographics.

Acknowledgment. This work was done under the affiliation of the Accessible and Inclusive Design Lab, Indraprastha Institute of Information Technology Delhi. I would like to thank my family and professors for their constant support and assistance throughout this research endeavor.

References

1. Common Age-Related Eye Problems
2. Medication errors in the older people population. ISSN 1751-2433
3. Senior citizens rely more on smartphone than youth in India - Tech Observer, March 2018. Section: Gadgets
4. Auctores: New Methods and Technology of Pharmaceutical Packaging in the Future
5. Barry, H.E., Hughes, C.M.: An update on medication use in older adults: a narrative review. Curr. Epidemiol. Rep. **8**(3), 108–115 (2021)
6. Christopher, C.M., et al.: Medication use problems and factors affecting older adults in primary healthcare. Res. Social Adm. Pharm. **19**(12), 1520–1530 (2023)
7. Cole, B.L., Harris, R.W.: Caution: coloured medication and the colour blind. Lancet **374**(9691), 720 (2009)
8. Cooper, L., et al.: Assistive technologies and strategies to support the medication management of individuals with hearing and/or visual impairment: a scoping review. Disabil. Health J. **16**(4), 101500 (2023)
9. Ghodkhande, K.P., Choudhari, S.G., Gaidhane, A.: Self-medication practices among the geriatric population: a systematic literature review. Cureus **15**(7), e42282 (2023)
10. Klaver, C.C.W., Wolfs, R.C.W., Vingerling, J.R., Hofman, A., de Jong, P.T.V.M.: Age-specific prevalence and causes of blindness and visual impairment in an older population: the Rotterdam study. Arch. Ophthalmol. **116**(5), 653–658 (1998)
11. Li, Y.Y., Zhang, D.: Application of augmented reality in the medicine packaging box. In: 2021 4th International Conference on Information Systems and Computer Aided Education, Dalian China, September 2021, pp. 2923–2927. ACM (2021)
12. McIntyre, S., Nagi, S.S., McGlone, F., Olausson, H.: The effects of ageing on tactile function in humans. Neuroscience **464**, 53–58 (2021)
13. Meredith, S., Feldman, P.H., Frey, D., Hall, K., Arnold, K., Brown, N.J., Ray, W.A.: Possible medication errors in home healthcare patients. J. Am. Geriatr. Soc. **49**(6), 719–724 (2001). _eprint. https://onlinelibrary.wiley.com/doi/pdf/10.1046/j.1532-5415.2001.49147.x
14. Mitzner, T.L., et al.: Older adults' training preferences for learning to use technology. In: Proceedings of the Human Factors and Ergonomics Society ... Annual Meeting. Human Factors and Ergonomics Society. Annual Meeting, vol. 52, no. 26, pp. 2047–2051, September 2008
15. Pérez-Jover, V., et al.: Inappropriate use of medication by elderly, polymedicated, or multipathological patients with chronic diseases. Int. J. Environ. Res. Public Health **15**(2), 310 (2018)
16. Rydzkowski, T., Wróblewska-Krepsztul, J., Thakur, V.K., Królikowski, T.: Current trends of intelligent, smart packagings in new medical applications. Procedia Comput. Sci. **207**, 1271–1282 (2022)
17. Singh, P., Tripathy, K.: Presbyopia. In: StatPearls. StatPearls Publishing, Treasure Island (FL) (2023)
18. Sjöstrand, J., Laatikainen, L., Hirvelä, H., Popovic, Z., Jonsson, R.: The decline in visual acuity in elderly people with healthy eyes or eyes with early age-related maculopathy in two Scandinavian population samples. Acta Ophthalmol. **89**(2), 116–123 (2011). _eprint. https://onlinelibrary.wiley.com/doi/pdf/10.1111/j.1755-3768.2009.01653.x
19. Weeraratne, C.L., Opatha, S.T., Rosa, C.T.: Challenges faced by visually disabled people in use of medicines, self-adopted coping strategies and medicine-related mishaps. WHO South-East Asia J. Publ. Health **1**(3), 256 (2012)

Experience Design Assisted in Improving the Efficiency of Adolescent Invisible Orthodontic Treatment

Silin Lei, Zijia Xu, Ziyi Ma, Yunchang Jiang, and Siu Shing Man[⊠]

School of Design, South China University of Technology, Guangzhou 510006, China
ssman6@scut.edu.cn

Abstract. Malocclusion is a prevalent oral condition that typically necessitates orthodontic treatment to adjust the arrangement of teeth. Among orthodontic patients, the majority are adolescents, and nowadays, adolescents increasingly prefer opting for invisible orthodontics. During invisible orthodontic treatment, the patient's user experience often influences the treatment outcomes. However, current research on the design of user experiences for invisible orthodontics in non-clinical settings remains relatively scarce. Therefore, this study aims to apply the Double Diamond Model to propose an experience design solution that effectively enhances orthodontic outcomes. In the Discover and Define stage of the Double Diamond model, this research delved into the challenges and obstacles adolescents face in invisible orthodontic treatment, explicitly defining the core issue: adolescents struggle with self-discipline in wearing orthodontic braces during treatment. Subsequently, in the Develop and Deliver phases, this study explored design solutions to address the core problem, ultimately devising a digital orthodontic treatment system and an old orthodontic brace recycling system. This study provides a novel approach to user experience design for adolescents undergoing invisible orthodontic treatment in non-clinical environments.

Keywords: Invisible orthodontics · Experience design · User experience · Double Diamond Design Model · Adolescent

1 Introduction

1.1 Background

Oral diseases affect nearly 3.5 billion people worldwide [1], with malocclusion always being a common condition [2, 3]. Adolescents frequently have crowded teeth due to insufficient space in the dental arch [4, 5]. In today's society, a person's dentition is an essential component of facial attractiveness, which can affect their self-esteem and self-image [6]. Misalignment of teeth affects physical health and impairs quality of life by affecting function, appearance, relationships, socialization, self-esteem, and mental health [7]. Orthodontic treatment can effectively improve oral function and facial aesthetics [8, 9]. The demand for orthodontic treatment for aesthetic reasons is common

© The Author(s), under exclusive license to Springer Nature Switzerland AG 2024
V. G. Duffy (Ed.): HCII 2024, LNCS 14710, pp. 103–120, 2024.
https://doi.org/10.1007/978-3-031-61063-9_7

in young and adult patients, and more and more people are undergoing orthodontic treatment [10]. The orthodontic market has also witnessed rapid growth in the development of orthodontic appliances to attract patients for consumption. The paradigm shift toward dental aesthetics, the increased demand for orthodontic treatment, and the highly competitive orthodontic industry have contributed to the development and production of orthodontic appliances, which have primarily reduced the visibility of the appliances [11–14].

1.2 Invisalign

In 1999, Align Technology pioneered the invisible orthodontics market by introducing the Invisalign System. The Invisalign System is used for straightening teeth with a series of custom-made aligners for each patient. It combines proprietary virtual modelling software, rapid manufacturing processes, mass customization, and custom-made aligners with patented material. Over time, several generations of Invisalign have been released, involving changes in appliance materials, tooth attachment design, and software simulation. Although initially confined to the treatment of adults, an aligner approach aimed at teenage patients was introduced in 2008 (Invisalign Teen System). It has reached more than 4.7 million adolescent patients in the last decade [15–17].

Invisalign is aesthetically pleasing, comfortable to use, easy to wear, and easy to manage for oral health [18, 19]. It is more efficient in treatment than fixed appliance treatment [20]. Therefore, Invisalign has been extensively used to replace conventional ligating brackets [21]. Teenage patients are a large user group of Invisalign [16, 22].

1.3 User Experience

User Experience (UX) covers various concepts, from traditional usability to emotional, experiential, hedonic, and aesthetic variables.

Hassenzahl and Tractinsky define UX as the "consequence of a user's internal state (predispositions, expectations, needs, motivation, mood, etc.), the characteristics of the designed system (e.g., complexity, purpose, usability, functionality, etc.) and the context (or the environment) within which the interaction occurs (e.g., organizational/social setting, the meaningfulness of the activity, voluntariness of use, etc.)" [23].

UX design also plays an essential role in the field of orthodontics. It can help designers and engineers develop innovative orthodontic devices, build human-computer interfaces, and explore artificial intelligence-assisted remote orthodontic care [24–26].

1.4 Research Status and Aim of the Study

Poor compliance is a prevalent problem during invisible orthodontic treatment [27]. Factors such as pain, discomfort, and forgetfulness can reduce patient compliance [28, 29]. How to improve the compliance of adolescent patients during invisible orthodontic treatment has not been well investigated?

Current research on the orthodontic experience focuses on public settings such as clinics and hospitals, and there is a lack of research on the orthodontic experience in home treatment settings [30–32].

In conclusion, this study aims to explore the problems and needs faced by adolescent patients during invisible orthodontic sessions. Moreover, this study proposes a set of experiential protocols applicable to non-clinic scenarios to enhance adolescents' orthodontic experience and compliance for better treatment outcomes.

2 Methods

The design process of the Double Diamond Model [33, 34] was applied as the logical framework in this paper to describe a detailed account of the research process for the efficient experiential design of invisible orthodontic treatment tailored to adolescents.

The Double Diamond Model, initially introduced by the British Design Council in 2004, stands as a design thinking model widely utilized in user experience design [35]. Its core objective is to unearth genuine problems and identify corresponding solutions. The design model is divided into two main stages: Research and Design, each consisting of two steps. The Double Diamond Model encompasses four steps: Discover, Define, Develop, and Deliver [36].

In the Discover stage, information regarding potential issues users face is extensively gathered. This research employed desktop research, expert interviews, and competitive analysis to collect information on the current problems adolescents encounter in invisible orthodontic treatment. Moving to the Define stage involves refining the identified problem and establishing a framework for its solution. This study utilized user interviews, log analysis, user personas, and user journey maps to define the core issues addressed by this design in adolescent invisible orthodontics. Proceeding to the Develop stage, solutions are created and explored. This paper presents conceptual design solutions and outlines improvements based on user testing during this stage. Finally, in the Deliver stage, the ultimate design solutions are presented. This paper will elaborate on the final experiential design solution and introduce the tangible product outcomes in this stage.

2.1 Discover

Desktop Research. Firstly, this study conducted extensive desk research. The data from the 4th National Oral Health Survey indicates that in 2017, the prevalence of malocclusion in China was as high as 74%, with nearly 70% of the affected individuals being adolescents. Consequently, focusing on orthodontic treatment for adolescents is highly meaningful in this research.

However, for adolescents, numerous factors impede the smooth progress of the therapeutic process, ultimately resulting in suboptimal orthodontic outcomes.

Thus, more extensive literature research is needed to gain a comprehensive understanding of the factors influencing the outcomes of orthodontic treatment in adolescents. During dental correction, careful attention to the daily diet is necessary; however, some adolescents face challenges in adhering to dietary recommendations during orthodontic procedures [37]. Due to the discomfort caused by orthodontic appliances, adolescents may exhibit poor compliance during the treatment, potentially leading to premature termination [38]. Furthermore, adolescents, influenced by factors such as busy academic schedules, are more prone to irregular follow-up visits to dental clinics. This can result in doctors being unable to promptly assess the current status of the orthodontic treatment, thereby affecting the efficiency of orthodontic procedures. Following the completion of orthodontic treatment, patients are often required to wear retainers for a specified period to solidify the achieved orthodontic outcomes. However, adolescents are inclined to non-compliance with retainer-wearing instructions, adversely impacting the effectiveness of orthodontic therapy and potentially necessitating a repeat of orthodontic treatment [39].

Field Research. Field research in dental clinics is necessary to gain a more in-depth understanding of the current invisible orthodontic processes and the actual orthodontic situations among adolescents.

A dental clinic in the Huangpu District of Guangzhou City was selected for field research. The invisible orthodontic treatment process at the clinic involves the following steps: utilizing an intraoral scanner to scan the patient's oral cavity, simultaneously automatically constructing a three-dimensional model in the computer; the computer generating several treatment options; the doctor examining the intraoral model on the computer and devising the orthodontic plan; production of braces; providing the patient with 4–5 sets of aligners at one time; instructing the patient to change their worn aligner every two weeks; and scheduling regular follow-up visits to the clinic for the patient.

After gaining an understanding of the fundamental processes of invisible orthodontics, expert interviews are advantageous for further in-depth research. The purpose of the interview was to gain insights into the real situations of adolescent orthodontics and the user experience of adolescents during the orthodontic process through face-to-face communication with a senior orthodontist in the clinic. The interview, conducted with an experienced doctor, lasted for 30 min and primarily revolved around three main themes:

- What types of orthodontic treatments do adolescents tend to prefer?
- What challenges are encountered when providing orthodontic treatment to teenagers?
- What kind of assistance is currently needed by the clinic?
- The interview results can be summarized as follows:
- Adolescent patients, driven by considerations related to external appearance and other factors, are more inclined to choose invisible orthodontics for teeth correction.
- Adolescents tend to exhibit poor self-discipline in wearing orthodontic appliances during invisible orthodontic treatment, making it challenging to wear the aligners for a minimum of 22 h per day.
- A complete course of invisible orthodontic treatment typically spans 2–3 years, requiring patients to wear approximately 50 sets of braces. Following the conclusion of orthodontic treatment, these discarded old braces are ultimately disposed of.
- Managing a substantial quantity of orthodontic braces and ensuring the correct pair of braces are worn poses a challenge for adolescents.

After field research and expert interviews, the research focus has been determined to center around the field of invisible orthodontics for adolescents primarily. The clinic's equipment related to invisible orthodontic treatment is relatively advanced and comprehensive. However, insights from the orthodontist reveal that adolescents often struggle to consistently wear orthodontic appliances for 22 h a day outside the clinic setting. Additionally, the lack of a proper mechanism for recycling old appliances is also a noteworthy concern.

Therefore, the following central area of research in this study was to optimize the experience of adolescents in wearing braces during invisible orthodontic treatment and to improve the recycling process of old discarded braces.

Competitor Analysis. Having determined the overarching direction of the research, it is imperative to analyze relevant competitors currently available in the market. The competitive analysis is bifurcated into two major dimensions: auxiliary products for invisible orthodontics and recycling old orthodontic braces. Initially, this study undertakes a competitive analysis of the top three orthodontic auxiliary physical products on Amazon [40] and the top three downloaded applications [41] on AppStore from 2020 to 2023. This analysis aims to comprehend the existing shortcomings and functional requirements of auxiliary orthodontic products in the current market landscape.

"Tray Minder", "Orbits", and "JIYA" were chosen to analyze and compare (see Fig. 1).

"Tray Minder" primarily assists users in documenting their usage of the invisible orthodontic system. Its core functionalities include reminding users to wear the orthodontic braces, recording the duration of daily braces wearing hours each day, and documenting changes in tooth alignment.

"Orbits" is primarily designed for tracking the progress of braces wear, timely notifying users to replace their current braces and daily reminders for on-time orthodontic braces usage.

"JIYA" is primarily aimed at helping users record the number of days during orthodontic treatment, reminding them of follow-up appointments, and providing features for comparing orthodontic outcomes and measuring the degree of maxillary protrusion, among other functionalities.

These apps serve as tools for users to record and monitor their orthodontic progress. Users can also perceive the orthodontic effects by comparing changes in their teeth. However, these apps still have the following shortcomings:

- Lack of incentive: Current competing apps lack reward systems and incentive policies, making it challenging for users to consistently wear orthodontic braces and maintain regular uploads of orthodontic progress records.
- Absence of orthodontic appliance recycling functionality: A module for orthodontic appliance recycling is absent, leaving this aspect virtually unaddressed.
- Weak visualization feedback of orthodontic effects: Given the prolonged orthodontic treatment cycles and subtle changes in the short term, these apps fail to provide effective visual feedback on orthodontic effects within a short period.
- Inadequate resource integration: The target users of competing apps are patients, but the information on patients' orthodontic conditions is challenging to integrate and share with clinics, indicating a lack of adequate resource integration.

For evaluating the orthodontic auxiliary physical products, the "Yile", "Y-kelin", and "Vinlley" were chosen to analyze and compare (see Fig. 2).

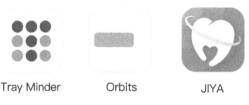

Tray Minder   Orbits   JIYA

Fig. 1. Logo of the apps

Yile   Y–kelin   Vinlley

Fig. 2. Product picture

"Yile" is an invisible orthodontic appliance storage and soaking box. It can be used for storing and soaking orthodontic appliances in cleaning solutions. It features a drainage layer for easy drying.

"Y-kelin" is a portable invisible orthodontic braces storage box with a mirror. It can accommodate orthodontic appliances and oral care accessories. Its compact size allows for easy portability, and the mirror assists in placing orthodontic appliances.

"Vinlley" is a cleaning box for orthodontic appliances that utilizes ultrasonic technology for deep cleaning. It includes a drainage tray to maintain the cleanliness and dryness of the orthodontic braces.

These physical products for auxiliary orthodontics generally have the function of orthodontic braces storage, with some also offering orthodontic appliance cleaning capabilities. Through the analysis of the aforementioned competing products, the following shortcomings in auxiliary orthodontic products are identified:

- The dual attainment of cleaning functionality and portability is unattainable: Products with soaking or cleaning functions for braces are excessively bulky, making them inconvenient for portable use. However, smaller products with limited size cannot clean and dry braces effectively.
- Reminders lack functionality: Inability to remind users to wear braces on time.

Through the aforementioned competitive analysis of current auxiliary products for invisible orthodontics, it can be summarized that such products need to possess the following functional characteristics:

1. The product should be capable of motivating orthodontic patients to consistently wear invisible braces.
2. Possess the capability to assist in documenting changes in patients' teeth during the orthodontic process.

3. Provision of convenience to patients, alleviating the treatment burden through features such as appointment reminders and synchronization of treatment data with the hospital.
4. Physical products should be as compact and portable as possible, offering a function for storing braces and the ability to clean them. Ideally, they should include a mirror to assist patients in removing and wearing braces.

In the context of recycling old orthodontic braces, there are currently no search results for products and apps related to recycling old discarded braces. Further research and data retrieval are still necessary in this regard.

Case Study. In order to gain a deeper understanding of information related to recycling old orthodontic braces, this study conducted a case study.

China currently lacks a comprehensive system for the recycling of old braces. Conversely, there are relevant cases of old orthodontic braces recycling abroad [42]. In one such case, patients concluding orthodontic treatment need only to place their old orthodontic braces into the recycling bin at Impress Clinic. Subsequently, these discarded old braces can be utilized for power generation or in producing materials for various industries, as well as in manufacturing fertilizers or soil amendments.

From this case, it can be observed that the materials used in the production of invisible braces are recyclable, and they have inherent value for recycling and reuse.

2.2 Define

User Interviews. After gaining a preliminary understanding of the issues encountered by adolescents during invisible orthodontic treatment, it is essential to further focus on the core problems. Consequently, interviews were conducted with five patients aged between 16–20 years old to comprehend their habits of wearing invisible braces and their experiences with orthodontic treatment. Two of these patients had previously worn invisible braces, while the remaining three were wearing them. The interviews primarily revolved around three aspects:

- Fundamental treatment conditions.
- Daily wearing of braces (adherence to prescribed wearing duration, challenges encountered during the wearing period).
- How to dispose of discarding old orthodontic braces and perspectives on braces recycling?

Through user interviews, it was observed that adolescent orthodontic patients commonly face the issue of insufficient duration of wearing invisible braces. The reasons behind this include discomfort during brace wear, reluctance to wear them for extended periods, and forgetting to put them back on promptly after removal. During the therapeutic process, the changes in tooth alignment were minimal, and nearly all interviewees were instructed by their parents to wear orthodontic braces, potentially contributing to their lack of initiative and motivation. Additionally, all participants expressed willingness to participate in the recycling of old braces; however, they hoped that the recycling process would not be overly cumbersome and could be conveniently accomplished during follow-up appointments.

Web Research. Web research becomes essential to validate further the universality of the challenges raised by adolescent interviewees in the interviews regarding difficulties in self-discipline and the reluctance to recycle old braces.

By examining a substantial amount of content on social platforms, it was observed that adolescents undergoing invisible orthodontic treatment often struggle with self-discipline in wearing braces, leading to suboptimal treatment outcomes. Furthermore, they tend to hoard used braces due to a desire to preserve memories of their orthodontic journey. However, limited storage space eventually results in the disposal of old braces. This hoarding behavior stems from individuals wishing to retain the corrective memories associated with the braces, hoping that old braces can regain physical value. Additionally, there is a perception that directly discarding braces is deemed regrettable by users.

User Persona. Based on preliminary research and the results of user interviews, user profiles were constructed, incorporating information such as user motivations, experiential objectives, and pain points (see Fig. 3).

Fig. 3. User persona

User Journey Map. Based on the analysis of user behavior, a user journey map was created.

Patients typically only remove their braces during meals throughout the day, which is the most likely period for instances of lack of discipline, so the mealtime segment was chosen for mapping the user journey. In addition to this, the journey map also encompasses the process of discarding old braces (see Fig. 4).

User Requirements Sorting. After the aforementioned research, the needs of adolescents undergoing invisible orthodontic treatment were identified. Subsequently, these needs were categorized and can be summarized into the following classifications:

- Optimization of removal process: users could be reminded when they forget to put on their braces after eating.
- Getting motivated to wear: users could view the changes in their teeth and get inspired to wear braces in a more entertaining form.

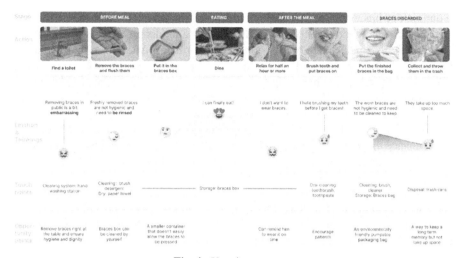

Fig. 4. User journey map

- Disposal of old braces: users could dispose of discarded braces better and more meaningfully.

Elevator Manifesto. In accordance with user needs, the design directions for proposed solutions were initially formulated. Subsequently, an elevator manifesto for the product is presented: To address the issues of adolescents' lack of discipline and low enthusiasm for wearing braces, our system is designed to optimize the self-wearing process. It achieves this by simplifying the carrying and removal procedures, motivating proactive wearing, and creating a ceremonial experience for discarding. This system aims to assist users in wearing braces with a more enjoyable mindset and a more convenient approach.

2.3 Develop and Deliver

Concept Statement. The conceptual design closely aligns with the core issues identified during the preliminary research phase and, based on the product definition, presents an innovative experiential solution tailored for the adolescent orthodontic patient demographic. The objective is to enhance the user experience of adolescents in non-clinical settings, thereby improving the efficiency of invisible orthodontics. The design comprises a digital orthodontic treatment system and an old orthodontic brace recycling system.

The digital orthodontic treatment system comprises an intelligent hardware product, the smart orthodontic case, and an associated mobile application (APP) connected to the orthodontic case for data transmission.

The design of the hardware product focuses on addressing issues faced by adolescents, such as the need to remove and clean orthodontic braces during meals and the tendency to forget to reapply them after meals. A sketch of the product is shown in Fig. 5. Its core functionalities include storage and cleaning of braces, automatic detection of the duration of braces placement, and reminders for the patient to wear them. To min-imize the burden on adolescents, the product adopts a modular design. The upper part of the product is a detachable braces storage compartment. After cleaning the braces, adolescents can remove and carry the upper part of the product. Additionally, placing the braces into the product automatically starts recording the duration of braces placement. If the user exceeds a specific duration without wearing the braces, the LED strip at the bottom of the product will flash to remind them to wear it.

The APP is primarily designed for data transmission with the orthodontic brace box and to enhance the motivation for patients to wear their braces. To achieve this purpose, an information architecture diagram was first established (see Fig. 6). The app com-prises five functional sections: "Homepage", "Statistics", "Growth", "Recycling", and "Me". The "Homepage" and "Statistics" sections primarily record and visualize patients' orthodontic information. The "Growth" section features a placement-type game where patients can receive rewards for wearing disciplined orthodontic braces to decorate the teeth character in the game. The "Recycling" section primarily showcases the recycling status of patients' old orthodontic braces. The "Me" section includes basic settings and synchronized data with the clinic, such as follow-up appointment times and visit details.

The recycling system proposes a recycling service process, offering a viable solution to effectively conserve material resources for invisible orthodontic braces and achieve the recycling and reuse of resources circularly. Simultaneously, it enhances the sense of accomplishment for orthodontic patients without increasing their treatment burden.

Fig. 5. Design sketch of the orthodontic case.

User Testing. To enhance usability and user-friendliness, three adolescents (two high school students wearing braces for three months and a college student who used to wear braces) were invited to participate in user testing. Due to the relatively straightforward interaction process between the recycling system and users, user testing was conducted solely on the output of the digital orthodontic treatment system. The testing consisted of two parts.

Fig. 6. App Information Architecture Diagram

The first part focused on evaluating the usability of the intelligent orthodontic case, which was a rough prototype made of stiff cardboard. Participants were instructed to imagine themselves in a classroom scenario where they needed to eat and remove their braces, utilizing the orthodontic case. After the test, researchers conducted inquiries with the participants from the perspectives of ergonomics, functionality, and aesthetics. Two adjustments were identified for the product based on the feedback:

1. Reducing the size of the product. Participants perceived the orthodontic case as too large, making it inconvenient to carry.
2. Modifying the flashing mode of the bottom LED strip. Participants expressed confusion about the meaning of the LED strip lighting up as a reminder to wear braces.

The second part involved testing the app's interface. Participants were instructed to perform the following tasks on a paper prototype:

• Utilize the "Daily Wear" page.
• Browse the statistical records page, view a facial shape record, observe tooth changes, and add a record.
• Change the number of braces currently being worn.

Following the test, participants were instructed to complete a System Usability Scale (SUS) questionnaire designed to measure the usability of a system [43, 44]. The scores on the scale serve as indicators of their satisfaction with the product, with higher scores suggesting more excellent usability [45]. The average score across all participants was 3.66 out of 5. Additionally, researchers conducted inquiries with participants from the perspectives of functional settings, interface layout, and motivational effects. Combining observations during the testing process, two adjustments were identified for the APP:

1. Simplify the presentation of orthodontic-related information. Participants expressed confusion about whether the pie charts on the "Statistics" interface represented self-discipline achievements or time.

2. Optimize the main interface's tooth images. Participants were unaware of the functionality allowing them to view data on the corrective movement of a tooth by clicking on an illuminated tooth icon on the main page.

3   Results

This study ultimately designed a system to enhance the experience of invisible orthodontic treatment for adolescents in non-clinical settings. The system consists of a digital orthodontic treatment system and an old orthodontic brace recycling system. The final output was a smart braces box, an app, and a recycling service process.

3.1   Digital Orthodontic Treatment System

The system includes an intelligent orthodontic brace box and a mobile application (see Fig. 7).

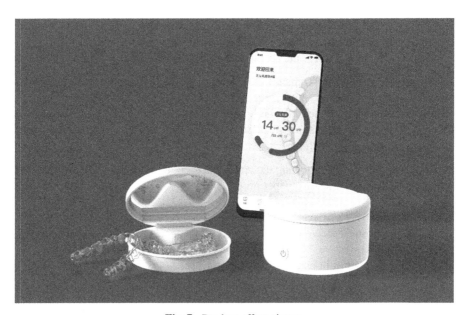

Fig. 7. Product effect picture

Smart Orthodontic Brace Box. The smart orthodontic appliance box utilizes ultrasonic cleaning technology to achieve quiet and efficient orthodontic brace cleaning. Due to the size increase resulting from the ultrasonic cleaning functionality, the product adopts a modular design to meet users' portability requirements. The orthodontic brace box employs infrared detection technology to monitor the duration of orthodontic brace placement. Simultaneously, the bottom LED light strip's illumination range is proportional to the time, reminding the patient if the orthodontic brace has been removed for a duration beyond the set range. The orthodontic appliance box also integrates Bluetooth transmission technology, enabling it to connect with the mobile app. It transfers daily data on orthodontic appliance placement duration to the phone and receives data from the mobile app. Users can customize the duration for which the orthodontic brace box emits light reminders through the APP.

APP. The core functions of the APP include recording and visually displaying orthodontic information and providing motivational games. The APP employs data analysis and processing techniques to visualize patients' orthodontic information precisely. It can connect to the intelligent orthodontic brace box, retrieve data on orthodontic brace wear time, perform data statistics, and display user wear duration on the APP. Additionally, users can adjust reminder duration and form through the APP. The APP also incorporates image comparison technology, comparing facial photos taken by patients during the orthodontic process, allowing patients to assess their orthodontic progress visually. To enhance the sense of companionship during treatment without overly captivating the attention of adolescents, the motivational game in the APP is a placement-type game. Adolescents can earn coins by wearing braces diligently to decorate the teeth character in the game. After completing a treatment cycle, the APP generates a new teeth model based on the patient's digital oral model. Additionally, the APP shares data with the clinic, facilitating timely reminders for follow-up visits and enabling efficient online supervision, reducing the utilization of offline medical resources. High-fidelity prototypes and primary interactive processes of the APP are shown in Fig. 8.

3.2 Old Orthodontic Brace Recycling System

The old orthodontic brace recycling system proposes a service process for patients to handle their old orthodontic braces conveniently (see Fig. 9). Patients only need to perform a simple action during follow-up visits—disposing of their old braces into a designated recycling bin to complete the recycling of the old braces. Subsequently, the recycling company will regularly collect discarded braces from the clinic and transport them to the corresponding factory, producing new materials that other industries can utilize. Additionally, patients can view the recycling process and destination of discarded braces in the app, further incentivizing adolescents to efficiently complete orthodontic treatment while contributing to the resource reuse of discarded braces.

The aforementioned research can assist in streamlining the orthodontic brace wear and removal process, visualizing and digitizing wear data, and dental changes. This approach aims to enhance user motivation, leading to improved treatment outcomes. Additionally, it facilitates more efficient hospital management and holds the potential for remote follow-ups and supervision. Furthermore, the design proposed in this study is conducive to promoting the recycling of old orthodontic braces, increasing resource utilization efficiency, and aiding hospitals in generating additional revenue.

The research ultimately resulted in the physical production of the intelligent orthodontic case, a hardware product.

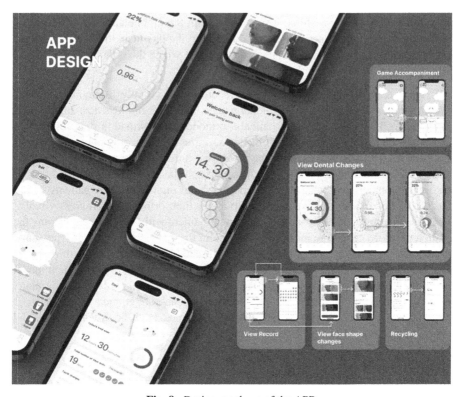

Fig. 8. Design mockups of the APP

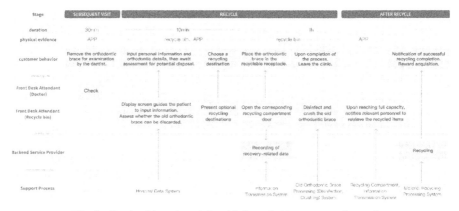

Fig. 9. Service blueprint of the old discarded braces recycle service

Initially, modifications were made to the model created using computer modelling software. The model reserved areas for placing circuit components to achieve the desired functionality. After the modifications, the model was 3D printed to produce a physical prototype. Simultaneously, circuit design was conducted. Finally, the circuit components were soldered together, and the circuit was assembled with the physical prototype, resulting in the tangible output of the intelligent orthodontic case (see Fig. 10).

Fig. 10. The final assembled orthodontic brace box

After the product assembly was completed, the intelligent orthodontic case underwent further testing. The following is the validated usage process based on the test results:

- Injection of cleaning fluid.
- Take off the braces.
- Press the power button on the orthodontic case to initiate the brace-cleaning process.
- Start eating.
- The bottom LED progress bar is about to end, prompting the patient to put on the braces.

4 Conclusion

This paper focuses on exploring the challenges and issues faced by adolescents during orthodontic treatment, proposing a design solution for invisible orthodontic experiences applicable in non-clinical settings.

The derived experiential design solution includes a digital orthodontic treatment system and a recycling system, resulting in an intelligent orthodontic case and APP design. The two systems are interrelated, aiming to enhance the user experience of adolescents in non-clinical settings, thereby improving the efficiency of orthodontic treatment. Additionally, it increases the recycling rate of orthodontic materials, achieving the circular utilization of resources.

This user experience project focuses on everyday life scenarios, providing new perspectives to enhance the compliance and effectiveness of invisible orthodontics for adolescents, making contributions to the global invisible orthodontic experience design field. Simultaneously, this research is dedicated to filling the gap in domestic abandoned braces recycling, contributing to the circular utilization of orthodontic materials, and aligning with the current trend of sustainable development in society.

5 Limitation

This study has limitations due to a relatively small sample size. The interviews and research samples in the study are limited, which may impact the accuracy of the research results, particularly in expert interviews where access to orthodontists from different cities was constrained.

In the future, it is envisioned to develop the APP as a mini-program, concurrently initiating mass production of the intelligent orthodontic case product. Subsequently, recruiting additional adolescent orthodontic patients for testing is intended to facilitate further optimization of this experiential solution.

References

1. Global oral health status report: towards universal health coverage for oral health by 2030. https://www.who.int/publications-detail-redirect/9789240061484
2. Arabiun, H., Mirzaye, M., Dehghani-Nazhvani, A., Ajami, S., Faridi, S., Bahrpeima, F.: The prevalence of malocclusion among 14–18 years old students in Shiraz. J. Oral Health Oral Epidemiol. **3**, 8–11 (2014)
3. Shrestha, B.K., Yadav, R., Basel, P.: Prevalence of malocclusion among high school students in Kathmandu valley. Orthod. J. Nep. **2**, 1–5 (2012)
4. Bourzgui, F., Sebbar, M., Hamza, M., Lazrak, L., Abidine, Z., El Quars, F.: Prevalence of malocclusions and orthodontic treatment need in 8- to 12-year-old schoolchildren in Casablanca, Morocco. Prog. Orthod. **13**, 164–172 (2012). https://doi.org/10.1016/j.pio.2011.09.005
5. Šidlauskas, A., Lopatienė, K.: The prevalence of malocclusion among 7–15-year-old Lithuanian schoolchildren. Medicina **45**, 147 (2009). https://doi.org/10.3390/medicina45020019
6. Buttke, T.M., Proffit, W.R.: Referring adult patients for orthodontic treatment. J. Am. Dent. Assoc. **130**, 73–79 (1999). https://doi.org/10.14219/jada.archive.1999.0031
7. Need of minimal important difference for oral health-related quality of life measures - Masood - 2014 - Journal of Public Health Dentistry - Wiley Online Library. https://onlinelibrary.wiley.com/doi/abs/10.1111/j.1752-7325.2012.00374.x
8. Chang, C.C., Lin, J.S., Yeh, H.Y.: Extra-alveolar bone screws for conservative correction of severe malocclusion without extractions or orthognathic surgery. Curr. Osteoporos. Rep. **16**, 387–394 (2018). https://link.springer.com/article/10.1007/s11914-018-0465-5
9. Comparative Assessment of Facial Asymmetry in Malocclusion using Posteroanterior View. - Abstract - Europe PMC. https://europepmc.org/article/med/29959301

10. Nanda, R.S., Kierl, M.J.: Prediction of cooperation in orthodontic treatment. Am. J. Orthod. Dentofac. Orthop. **102**, 15–21 (1992). https://doi.org/10.1016/0889-5406(92)70010-8
11. Sarvera, D.M., Ackermanb, J.L.: Orthodontics about face: the re-emergence of the esthetic paradigm. Am. J. Orthod. Dentofac. Orthop. **117**, 575–576 (2000). https://doi.org/10.1016/S0889-5406(00)70204-6
12. Keim, R.G., Gottlieb, E.L., Nelson, A.H., Vogels, D.S.: 2007 JCO orthodontic practice study. Part 1: trends. J. Clin. Orthod. **41**, 617–626 (2007)
13. Willems, G., Carels, C.E.: Developments in fixed orthodontic appliances. Ned. Tijdschr. Tandheelkd. **107**, 155–159 (2000)
14. Current Products and Practice: Aesthetic Orthodontic Brackets - J. S. Russell (2005). https://journals.sagepub.com/doi/abs/10.1179/146531205225021024
15. Investors | Align Technology. https://investor.aligntech.com/
16. Align Technology. https://www.aligntech.com/solutions
17. Braces recommended | Patent-approved braces | Invisalign Braces - Invisalign Hong Kong. https://www.invisalign.com.hk/
18. Are clear aligners as effective as conventional fixed appliances? | Evidence-Based Dentistry. https://www.nature.com/articles/s41432-020-0079-5
19. Invisalign®: Early Experiences - L. Joffe (2003). https://journals.sagepub.com/doi/abs/10.1093/ortho.30.4.348
20. Outcome assessment of orthodontic clear aligner vs fixed appliance treatment in a teenage population with mild malocclusions | The Angle Orthodontist. https://meridian.allenpress.com/angle-orthodontist/article/90/4/485/431828/Outcome-assessment-of-orthodontic-clear-aligner-vs
21. Yang, L., Yin, G., Liao, X., Yin, X., Ye, N.: A novel customized ceramic bracket for esthetic orthodontics: in vitro study. Prog. Orthod. **20**, 1–10 (2019) https://link.springer.com/article/10.1186/s40510-019-0292-y
22. Seeling, S., Prütz, F.: Inanspruchnahme kieferorthopädischer Behandlung durch Kinder und Jugendliche in Deutschland – Querschnittergebnisse aus KiGGS Welle 2 und Trends. (2018). https://doi.org/10.17886/RKI-GBE-2018-094
23. User experience - a research agenda. Behav. Inf. Technol. **25**(2). https://www.tandfonline.com/doi/abs/10.1080/01449290500330331
24. Filippi, S., Grigolato, L., Savio, G.: UX concerns in developing functional orthodontic appliances. In: Marcus, A., Rosenzweig, E. (eds.) HCII 2020. LNCS, vol. 12202, pp. 229–241. Springer, Cham (2020). https://doi.org/10.1007/978-3-030-49757-6_16
25. Aurelie, M., Jérôme, D.: Recommendations for an innovative distance continuing education device intended for orthodontic practitioners. In: Salopek Čubrić, I., Čubrić, G., Jambrošić, K., Jurčević Lulić, T., Sumpor, D. (eds.) ERGONOMICS 2022. LNNS, vol. 701, pp. 181–190. Springer, Cham (2023). https://doi.org/10.1007/978-3-031-33986-8_20
26. A Co-Design Methodology: Design Guidelines for Tele-Orthodontics Tool to Reduce Adult Patients' Anxiety: Understanding Concerns and Expectations of AI-Assisted Remote Orthodontic Care – ProQuest. https://www.proquest.com/openview/bbf481dd1f15f8d1443eba3d455b5cb0/1?pq-origsite=gscholar&cbl=18750&diss=y
27. Applied Sciences | Free Full-Text | Factors Influencing Appliance Wearing Time during Orthodontic Treatments: A Literature Review. https://www.mdpi.com/2076-3417/12/15/7807
28. Functional and social discomfort during orthodontic treatment - effects on compliance and prediction of patients' adaptation by personality variables | European Journal of Orthodontics | Oxford Academic. https://academic.oup.com/ejo/article/22/3/307/470345
29. Patients' attitudes towards compliance with retainer wear | Australian Orthodontic Journal. https://search.informit.org/doi/abs/10.3316/INFORMIT.963161047257686
30. Ellis, P.E., Silverton, S.: Using the experience-based design approach to improve orthodontic care. J. Orthod. **41**, 337–344 (2014). https://doi.org/10.1179/1465313314Y.0000000105

31. Factors influencing satisfaction with the process of orthodontic treatment in adult patients. https://www.sciencedirect.com/science/article/abs/pii/S0889540617308934

32. Extent and provision of orthodontic services for children and adolescents in Finland - Pietilä - 1997 - Community Dentistry and Oral Epidemiology - Wiley Online Library. https://online library.wiley.com/doi/abs/10.1111/j.1600-0528.1997.tb00913.xx

33. Bischof, A.C., et al.: Diamond Model user guide (2022)

34. Kochanowska, M., Gagliardi, W.R.: The double diamond model: in pursuit of simplicity and flexibility. In: Raposo, D., Neves, J., Silva, J. (eds.) Perspectives on Design II. Springer Series in Design and Innovation, vol. 16, pp. 19–32. Springer, Cham (2022). https://doi.org/10.1007/978-3-030-79879-6_2. with reference to Jonathan Ball

35. Velloso, L.M.R., Barros, G.: Recurrent techniques used in UX design: a report from user survey and interviews with professional designers. J. Des. Res. **21**, 47–61 (2023). https://doi.org/10.1504/JDR.2023.133264

36. Gustafsson, D.: Analysing the double diamond design process through research & implementation (2019)

37. Bukhari, O.M., Sohrabi, K., Tavares, M.: Factors affecting patients' adherence to orthodontic appointments. Am. J. Orthod. Dentofac. Orthop. **149**, 319–324 (2016). https://doi.org/10.1016/j.ajodo.2015.07.040

38. Albino, J.E.N.: Factors influencing adolescent cooperation inorthodontic treatment. Semin. Orthod. **6**, 214–223 (2000). https://doi.org/10.1053/sodo.2000.19007

39. Liu, D.: Analysis of factors affecting orthodontic efficacy in adolescent orthodontic patients

40. iSellerPal. https://www.isellerpal.com/

41. https://app.diandian.com/

42. https://smile2impress.com/

43. Lewis, J.R.: The system usability scale: past, present, and future. Int. J. Hum. Comput. Interact. **34**(7). https://www.tandfonline.com/doi/abs/10.1080/10447318.2018.1455307

44. Wang, Y.: System Usability Scale: A Quick and Efficient User Study Methodology – IXD@Pratt. https://ixd.prattsi.org/2018/04/system-usability-scale-a-quick-and-efficient-user-study-methodology/

45. SUS: A Retrospective – JUXJUX. https://uxpajournal.org/sus-a-retrospective/

Incorporating Regional Brain Connectivity Profiles into the Inference of Exposure-Related Neurobehavioral Burden in Explosive Ordnance Disposal Veterans

Jeffrey Page[1], Hyuk Oh[2], Thomas Chacko[1,4], Immanuel B. H. Samuel[3,4], Calvin Lu[3,4], Robert D. Forsten[3,4,5], Matthew J. Reinhard[3,4], Michelle E. Costanzo[3,4,5], and Gordon Broderick[1,4(✉)]

[1] Center for Clinical Systems Biology, Rochester General Hospital, Rochester, NY, USA
gordonbroderick55@gmail.com
[2] Department of Kinesiology, University of Maryland, College Park, MD, USA
[3] Department of Veterans Affairs, War Related Illness and Injury Study Center, Washington, DC, USA
[4] Department of Veterans Affairs, Complex Exposures Threats Center, Washington, DC, USA
[5] Uniformed Services University, Washington, DC, USA

Abstract. Conventional data-driven investigation into novel and complex health outcomes is often impeded by sparse and incomplete data fragmented across platforms and studies. To address this, we propose a knowledge-driven framework for assembling mechanistically informed regulatory networks and simulating their dynamic behavior. We apply the Natural Language Processing (NLP) engine MedScan to the Elsevier ontology and full text corpus (>7.2 million journal articles) to extract documented relationships linking 40 bilateral Brodmann Area (BA) regions, to 9 self-reported neurobehavioral measures of mood, quality of life, resilience and symptom burden. A Constraint Programming problem was defined to determine the direction and mode of action for each network interaction as well as logic parameters describing signal transmission thresholds and decisional weights dictating each node's state transition. Parameter values were identified such that the predicted behavior of this integrated neurobehavioral regulatory network would jointly explain 1) two distinct neurobehavioral profiles associated with subjective military exposure histories in a pilot cohort ($n = 13$) of deployed Explosive Ordnance Disposal (EOD) veterans, and 2) EEG regional source activation patterns (theta/alpha spectral power ratio) previously reported during acute mild Traumatic Brain Injury (acute mTBI), chronic mild-moderate Traumatic Brain Injury (chronic mmTBI), as well as control subjects from a publicly available database. Outcomes from the resulting family of competing models unanimously predicted distinct shifts in neural activity in the dorsolateral prefrontal cortex (Brodmann Areas 9 and 46) presenting primarily in the right hemisphere for self-reported exposure to ionizing radiation sources and in the left hemisphere in the case of non-ionizing radiation.

Keywords: Natural Language Processing · Constraint Programming · Electroencephalogram

© The Author(s), under exclusive license to Springer Nature Switzerland AG 2024
V. G. Duffy (Ed.): HCII 2024, LNCS 14710, pp. 121–139, 2024.
https://doi.org/10.1007/978-3-031-61063-9_8

1   Introduction

Explosive Ordnance Disposal (EOD) specialists regularly engage in high-stress, life-threatening situations, and are frequently exposed to repetitive sub-concussive blasts and other environmental conditions such as heat, dust, toxic fumes, electronic counter measures and heavy metals both during training and deployment with unknown health repercussions. EOD can be assigned to conventional forces as well as embedded with Special Operation Forces thus presenting with complex exposure histories and injuries. The co-occurrence of post-traumatic stress disorder (PTSD) and mild traumatic brain injury (mTBI) along with the allostatic effects, recently characterized as Operator Syndrome (OS), may be one of many potential health consequences in such elite groups [1, 2]. Because research into health outcomes in EOD veterans is still limited, conventional data-driven analyses are impeded by the small size, fragmented, and incomplete nature of available study data. Data integration methods aimed at interpreting different data sources to address specific research questions will be a key contributor to knowledge development in these specialized populations.

A number of data augmentation strategies exist for dealing with data sparsity and typically involve adding noise, duplicating, reweighting or dropping data records, or perturbing numerical features. Unfortunately, data augmentation is generally applied within the feature space of a specific data set and the success of a given method in one instance, does not extend easily to other datasets and applications (e.g. classification) [3]. While a number of methods have been proposed for the fusion of data sets based on the numerical reconciliation of the different feature spaces [4, 5], these typically require at least some degree of overlap in data elements or a common outcome class describing the same or very similar study participants. Moreover, these strategies generally focus specifically on experimental data, in particular structured numerical data, with little or no integration of prior factual domain knowledge or more general conceptual first-principles knowledge. A possible exception to this is the inference of regulatory networks from the predicted physical interactions between macromolecules by leveraging fundamental molecular properties such as binding affinities and basic thermodynamic laws [6]. In order to work beyond the molecular scale and seamlessly integrate clinical measures for example, more generic knowledge-driven methods have been proposed that leverage context-dependency [7]. These derive and use central ontologies in the reconciliation of disjoint structured and unstructured data sets [8]. Though powerful in their own right, these data fusion techniques remain relatively static and do not directly enforce the cohesiveness of diverse data sources in jointly describing the dynamic behavior of a system. In this study, we propose a hypothesis-development approach that builds on knowledge-driven data fusion techniques inclusive of published findings to reconcile disjoint data sets from structured and unstructured sources with the additional requirement that specific dynamic response properties of the system must be captured. Specifically, we leverage automated text-mining to extract a prior knowledge network scaffold which is further augmented with empirically derived interactions. Sparse and incomplete data are then used to validate or invalidate competing variants of this aggregate network and corresponding sets if decisional logic rules instead of supporting the de novo identification of these. As a representative case study, we apply this approach to the reverse engineering of a regulatory network describing the dynamic response behavior in EOD veterans based on prior knowledge extracted from the literature and separate empirical analyses of publicly available neuroimaging TBI data set and limited neurobehavioral profiling in a small study cohort these veterans. The resulting predictions about regional brain activity point to potential underlying mechanisms linking heterogenous military occupational exposure, neurobehavioral symptoms as well as acute and chronic TBI injury types.

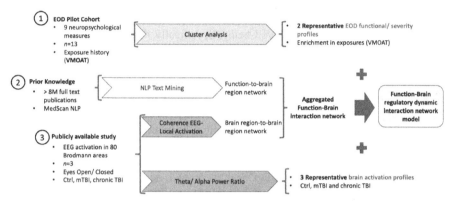

Fig. 1. A data flow diagram describing the reconciliation of 3 disparate sources of data in constructing a dynamic regulatory model describing brain region interactivity and its relationships with function and mood. VMOAT: Veterans - Military and Occupational Environmental Assessment Tool.

2   Methods

The principal challenges of data sparsity, partial observability and fragmentation across multiple disjoint and disparate data sources is addressed by 1) broadening the definition of data to include text and prior knowledge elements, 2) combining all forms of data in a qualitative-descriptive representation, and 3) enforcing consistency between these partial descriptions by leveraging known and posited interdependencies in the assembly of a logical decision network that is expected to explain real-world observations. These concepts are applied to the analytical steps outlined in Fig. 1 and described in the following sections. We apply a cluster analysis to neurobehavioral profiles observed in a small cohort of EOD veterans (1) to define characteristic exposure-relevant symptom burden profiles. Similarly, we conduct a separate empirical analysis of publicly available EEG data (3) to generate brain activation profiles. Relationships linking brain regions and neurobehavioral are extracted from peer-reviewed literature using text mining (2) with additional brain region connectivity being inferred from an empirical coherence analysis of said EEG data. These three elements in Fig. 1 are combined by requiring that any plausible model must explain all observed neurobehavioral and brain activation profiles as stable resting states using the proposed network of regulatory interactions extracted from text and available data.

2.1 Characteristic Symptom Profiles in a Small Cohort

We utilized data from a cohort of n = 12 male and n = 1 female EOD veterans enrolled in a pilot study of TBI (severe TBI was excluded) conducted at the Washington D.C. War Related Illness and Injury Study Center (DC WRIISC). On average, male participants were Caucasian, 50.6 years of age (std dev. 9.2), with a body mass index (BMI) of 31.6 (std dev 6.6), and with 14.4 years of military service (std dev. 8.9). The female subject was African American, 57 years of age, with a BMI of 28.8 and 24 years of military service. Subjects were assessed using 9 standardized self-report questionnaires for resilience, behavioral traits and psychological well-being. Specifically, data was collected using the Holmes-Rahe [9], a history of exposure to 43 stressful common life events; the Connor-Davidson Resilience Scale (CD-RISC) [10], a measure that assesses one's perception of their ability to "thrive in the face of adversity; the Social Connectedness Scale (SCS) [11], a measure of one's feelings of belongingness and relations with others; Five Facet Mindfulness Questionnaire (FFMQ) [12], a widely used 39-item measure of mindfulness in 5 basic domains; the Neurobehavioral Symptom Inventory (NSI) [13], a measure of physical, cognitive and emotional symptoms that occur after a mild traumatic brain injury; the Neuro-Quality of Life (NQOL) [14], an inventory of symptoms related to general cognitive concern; the PTSD Checklist 5 (PCL-5) [15], a screening measure used to assess the 20 DSM-5 symptoms of PTSD; the Pittsburg Sleep Quality Index (PSQI) [16], a measure that assesses sleep quality over a 1-month time interval; and the Patient Health Questionnaire (PHQ-9) [17], a screening measure that assessed the presence and severity of cognitive and somatic symptoms of depression.

Data from each of these behavioral and functional scales were individually range-adjusted and translated onto an ordinal discrete qualitative scale whereby values considered below average were assigned to bin 0, values comparable to average were assigned to bin 1 and those considered above average to bin 2. The boundaries separating these bins and the assignment of values were computed using a simple k-means clustering, reseeded 10 times for k = 3 clusters, based on Lloyd's algorithm [18] available under the *sklearn.cluster.KMeans* function in the Python package *scikit-learn*, version 1.3.2. Representative subgroups were then identified in the cohort of *n = 13* EOD veterans based on characteristic patterns of co-expression in these 9 neurobehavioral measures using the spectral co-clustering algorithm proposed by Dhillon [19]. Given the small group size, only 2 clusters were prescribed. And analysis was performed using the *sklearn.cluster.SpectralCoclustering* function also available under the Python package *scikit-learn*, version 1.3.2. Representative neurobehavioral profiles were selected in each group as the *actual* profile observed in the veteran found closest based on Manhattan distance to the centroid of his or her assigned cluster. The relevance of service-related environmental exposure to the subgrouping of the veterans in this neurobehavioral space was assessed by a simple group-wise univariate chi-squared test of the frequency of self-reported exposure in each group to each of 65 individual sources listed in the Veterans - Military and Occupational Assessment Tool (V-MOAT) [20]. The latter assesses subjective military occupational exposures across well-defined occupational and environmental medicine domains of chemical, physical, biological, ergonomic/injury, and psychosocial hazards.

2.2   Extracting a Prior Knowledge Scaffold

Neuroanatomy was first coarse-grained and described in terms of 52 Brodmann brain areas (BA) either by region number (e.g. Brodmann 40) or by the corresponding term assigned under the Yale ontology (e.g. Supramarginal gyrus) (https://brain-language.yale.edu/brodmann-areas). Similarly, the neurobehavioral measures described in Sect. 2.1 were assigned manually curated proxy terms when necessary. Using original or proxy labels, the Elsevier Biology Knowledge Graph database (Elsevier, Amsterdam) [21] was queried using the Pathway Studio and EmBiology graphical interface [22] for documented relationships linking Brodmann brain areas (BA) and the above-mentioned neuropsychological measures of mood, quality of life, resilience and symptom burden. The Elsevier Biology Knowledge Graph database includes entries from the Elsevier ResNet Mammal database [23], ChemEffect, DiseaseFX, and Reaxys databases as well as the DrugBank and BioGRID databases. This overarching database is updated weekly and recognizes in excess of 1.4M (million) biological entities (molecules, cell types, diseases, clinical measures, etc....) connected through over 15.7M relationships (co-expression, regulatory, binding interactions, etc.). These relationships were extracted by deploying the MedScan natural language processing (NLP) engine [24, 25] and the Elsevier ontology to over 7.2M full-text peer-reviewed publications. In addition, over 34M PubMed abstracts were text-mined describing in vitro as well as in vivo animal and human studies (including results from over 430,000 clinical trials). MedScan is a rule-based NLP engine that applies known grammatical rules to infer specific source-target direction and effect (target activation or inactivation) as well as the type of relationship linking any two entities. These range in nature from undirected associative relationships like simple co-expression, to more functional causative directed relationships like molecular synthesis or molecular transport. Of particular value in this work are relationships where the stated evidence is strong enough to infer the regulation or direct regulation of a target by an upstream mediator. Whether associative or causative, only relationships supported by at least 3 citations were retained in this analysis. Brodmann areas reported in the literature as one region were aggregated and represented as a single node in the network model. Lastly, nodes that were orphaned from the greater network by enforcing this level of literature support were removed from further analysis.

2.3   Network Reverse Engineering from Open Neuro-Imaging Databases

To better inform the network in brain region interactivity, we also leveraged the publicly accessible OpenNeuro database version 4.21.1 [26] which holds 977 public data sets describing over 39,000 participants. We used a subset of OpenNeuro Accession Number ds003522 contributed by Cavanagh and Quinn [27] consisting of a 64-channel resting-state electroencephalography (EEG) montage collected during two eyes open (EO) and two eyes closed (EC) conditions for 61 s in representative male subjects from the control (CTRL) (subject 002, age 30), acute mild traumatic brain injury (mTBI) (subject 046, age 30) and chronic mild-moderate traumatic brain injury (TBI) (subject 078, age 29) groups. EEG recorded at the sampling rate of 500 Hz in the 10–10 system with the ground at AFz and the reference at CPz using the actiCHamp (Brain Products GmbH) [28]. These EEG recordings were analyzed within the Brodmann Area source space to produce empirical estimates of regional resting-state brain activity as well as neural electrical interactivity under eyes open and eyes closed conditions. All signal processing analyses were conducted using the MATLAB R2023a (The MathWorks, Inc.), EEGLAB v2023.0 [29], and Brainstorm 21-Jun-2023 [30] software libraries.

Specifically, EEG signals were processed in the forward and backward directions using a Kaiser window-based finite impulse response (FIR) bandpass filter at the passband edges of 1 and 30 Hz with the maximum passband deviations of 0.01 dB, and the stopband edges of 0.1 and 31 Hz with the maximum stopband attenuation of 60 dB, respectively. Next, an automated EEG quality assessment algorithm [31] was employed to identify EEG channels with significant task-irrelevant activities. Any irremediable EEG channels were removed and restored with a spherical interpolation algorithm. EEG signals were then re-referenced with the common average reference, which allowed for examining hemisphere unbiased cortical activities. Furthermore, after reducing dimensionality of rank-deficient EEG by principal component analysis, an extended infomax algorithm [32] was employed to obtain the independent components (ICs) of EEG. Then, Multiple Artifact Rejection Algorithm (MARA) [33] was used to retain the task-related neural components in reconstructing task-relevant clean EEG signals. Next, the registration between EEG sensors and the ICBM152 anatomy template distributed with Brainstorm was executed, and a realistic head model was created using symmetric boundary element method so that the cortical space is represented with 15002 vertices that correspond to 45006 dipoles. The cortical distribution of current density was estimated using the standardized Low Resolution Electromagnetic Tomography (sLORETA) [34] along with the noise covariance over the first 1 s time window and the data covariance over the last 60 s time window. The regional source activation was estimated by averaging the sLORETA dipoles mapped on the 79 regions of interest (ROIs) represented by the PALS-B12 Brodmann atlas [35]. Lastly, the magnitude-squared coherence of the average spectral power was computed using Welch's method to examine the spectral associations of the default mode network in the theta (4–8 Hz) and the alpha (8–13 Hz) frequency bands with a Hamming window of 4 s and the hop size of 1 s. Estimates of regional resting-state brain activity were based on the ratio of power in the theta frequency band to power in the alpha frequency band, or the theta-alpha ratio (TAR), shown to be a relevant correlate of cognitive impairment with higher metrics associated with cognitive deficits [36]. As with the neurobehavioral measures described previously, all TAR values were normalized and translated onto the discrete ordinal scale range [0, 1, 2]. Specifically, TAR values were range adjusted within each EEG recording separately and each value assigned to a Low, Nominal or High bin using thresholds computed with a K-means clustering using Lloyd's algorithm as described above. This normalization and discrete scale transformation was conducted within each time series separately to correct for recording-to-recording variability and to preserve time series integrity based on the assumption that all regions have same effective range available [37, 38].

The resulting default mode matrices were then filtered using Otsu's method [39] for threshold detection. Foreground coherence values exceeding a threshold value that minimized the weighted sum of within set variances were considered significant. Background coherence values below this threshold were remove the latter from further analysis. In this work background and foreground variances were assigned equal weights in determining the optimal threshold coherence value (Fig. 2). The initial empirical region-to-region coherence map was created using the union of significant interactions from all 6 matrices (EO, EC x CTR, acute mTBI, chronic mmTBI). Finally, this empirical brain region connectome was overlaid and reconciled with the literature-informed neurobehavioral network to define architecture of the initial putative network model. In the latter all undirected associations (connectome) were translated into pairs of opposite directed interactions (interactome).

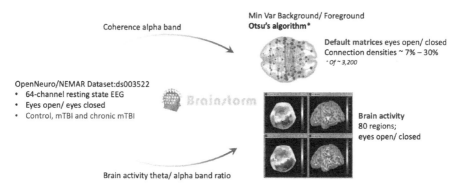

Fig. 2. Augmenting a literature-informed neurobehavioral network with detailed map of brain region connectivity reverse engineered from publicly available eyes-closed and eyes-open resting-state electroencephalography (EEG) profiling of control, acute mTBI, and chronic mmTBI subjects.

2.4 Enforcing Consistent Overarching Dynamic Behavior Across Data Sources

The flow of information through this directed network is modeled by applying to each node a simple discrete decisional logic originally proposed by proposed by Thomas [40] and further developed by Mendoza and Xenarios [41]. Each network regulatory interaction is defined by a direction (i.e., a source and a target), and a mode of action (i.e., inactivating or activating its downstream target). The activation level of each neurologic or behavioral node is described as one of three discrete qualitative states, namely Low (0), Nominal (1), or High (2). An increase or decrease in the activation level of any given node is determined by the states and actions of its upstream neighbors. The competing actions of upstream neighbors activated to levels above their respective perception thresholds were then aggregated using a simple piece-wise linear function where the actions of weak inactivators were weighed against those of strong activators, and vice versa. Based on this combinatorial context-specific process, an increase or decrease the activation of the node in question is proposed for update in the next iteration [42]. Therefore, in this parameter space, each network node carries a baseline activation term and every regulatory interaction is characterized by a perception threshold and a strength of action weight.

A Constraint Satisfaction (SAT) problem [43] was defined to determine the direction and mode of action for each network interaction where unspecified as well as logic parameters describing signal transmission thresholds and decisional weights dictating each node's state transition [44, 45]. Additional free variables consisted of unmeasured states, namely brain region activation values corresponding to 2 characteristic exposure-driven behavioral profiles extracted from the pilot cohort of veterans, as well as values for the behavioral measures corresponding to each of the 6 EEG active connectivity maps (Fig. 3). In addition to requiring the exact recovery of observed values in both the neurologic and behavioral domains as hard constraints, additional constraints were imposed by describing these 8 observed states as dynamically stable resting states. In other words, not only must the current partially observed state be recovered exactly, but the next predicted state must also be identical to the current state (i.e., it must be explained as a steady state). Therefore, any allowable solution set must consist of free variable values whereby the predicted behavior of this integrated neurobehavioral regulatory network jointly explains 1) two distinct symptom profiles enriched in subjective military exposure histories in deployed veterans, and 2) EEG regional source activation patterns (theta/alpha spectral power ratio) in chronic mmTBI, acute mTBI and control subjects, all as stable resting states. This parameter search problem was encoded using the open-source Constraint Programming and Modeling in Python (CPMpy) library [46]. Solutions were generated by invoking the CP-SAT solver [47] within the Google OR-Tools optimization toolbox [48]. CP-SAT applies lazy clause generation, a hybrid approach which combines the strengths of finite domain propagation in Constraint Programming (CP) with the efficiency of Boolean Satisfiability (SAT) solvers. In the current example, we allow for the possibility that the constraints imposed under steady state assumptions may make the problem unsolvable. To identify individual constraints that if relaxed might allow for the identification of solution sets, we conducted an analysis of minimal unsatisfiable sets (MUS) of constraints [49–51].

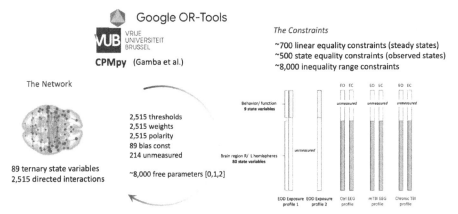

Fig. 3. Applying constraint satisfaction to reconcile and integrate a literature-informed neurobehavioral network with a detailed empirical map of brain region connectivity such that regulatory logic programs exist whereby the predicted network dynamic behaviors explain the 9 partially observed neurobehavioral and EEG brain activation profiles.

3 Results

3.1 Meaningful Exposure-Related Symptom Profiles

We applied spectral co-clustering to profiles in 9 neurobehavioral and psychosocial constructs (i.e., neurobehavioral symptoms, depression, PTSD, sleep disorders, stress, social support, resilience, quality of life, mindfulness) describing n = 13 EOD veterans, encoded into low (0), nominal (1), and high (2) levels of expression. A simple Principal Component Analysis (PCA) was used to reduce dimensionality, demonstrating separability of subjects into distinct symptom profile groups (Fig. 4). An enrichment analysis was applied to determine overrepresentation in any of 64 distinct exposures sources recorded using the Veterans - Military and Occupational Assessment Tool (V-MOAT). This analysis pointed to 2 distinct symptom profile clusters that also aligned with statistically distinct exposure profiles. In each cluster, the individual with the neurobehavioral profile closest in terms of Manhattan distance to that cluster's centroid profile was selected as representative of that group. Encoded neurobehavioral profiles for subject EOD_TBI_002 in cluster 0 and EOD_TBI_005 in cluster 1 are shown in Table 1. Cluster 0 (n = 8) captured individuals presenting increasing neurobehavioral symptom burden, PTSD severity, reduced quality of life and lower protective factors coincided with increased exposures to non-ionizing radiation (4 of 8), inhaled contaminants such as paint and dust (7 of 8) as well as fog oils (5 of 8). Confounding factors

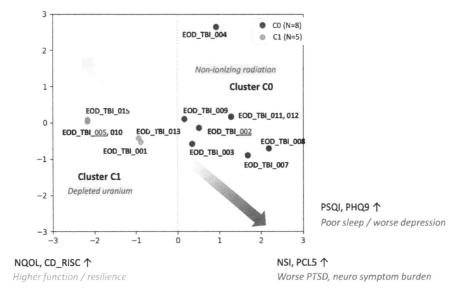

Fig. 4. A principal component analysis (PCA) linear projection of *n = 13* subjects described by 9 neurobehavioral measures of cognition and mood. Agglomerative clustering identified 2 groups each with a characteristic symptom-performance and exposure history (VMOAT: Veterans - Military and Occupational Environmental Assessment Tool) documenting >60 exposure sources. Two subjects each closest to their respective cluster centroids were identified as especially representative of each group (EOD TBI subject 002 and 005).

notwithstanding, comparatively higher resilience, neurological function and quality of life were reported in Cluster 1 (n = 5) despite higher exposure to depleted uranium (4 of 5), diesel fuels (5 of 5), and more frequent musculoskeletal injuries (4 of 5) (Fig. 5).

Table 1. Characteristic neurobehavioral profiles (0 = Low, 1 = Nominal and 2 = High expression).

Profile	Holmes	CD_RISC	SCS	FFMQ	NSI	NQOL	PCL5	PSQI	PHQ9
Centroid C0	1.4	0.8	1.5	1.0	1.5	0.5	1.8	1.8	1.8
EOD_TBI_002	1.0	1.0	2.0	1.0	1.0	1.0	2.0	2.0	2.0
Centroid C1	0.8	2.0	1.4	1.8	0.4	1.6	0.2	2.0	2.0
EOD_TBI_005	1.0	2.0	2.0	2.0	0.0	2.0	0.0	2.0	2.0

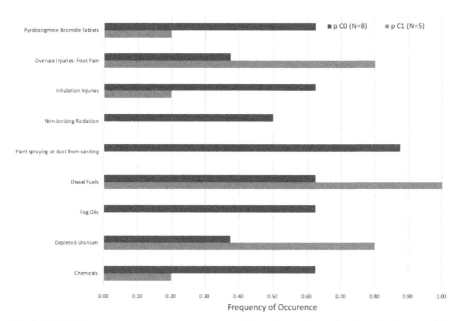

Fig. 5. V-MOAT exposure sources overrepresented in each neurobehavioral profile cluster with a frequency difference to noise ratio $Z > Z_{crit}$ ($p < 0.15$) and a minimum frequency of occurrence >0.5. Cluster C0 (n = 8) contains all 4 of 8 non-ionizing radiation exposures, all 7 of 8 paint and dust exposures, all 5 of 8 fog oil exposures. Cluster C1 (n = 5) is enriched in depleted uranium exposures (4 of 5), overuse injuries - foot pain (4 of 5), and diesel fuel exposures (5 of 5).

3.2   A Literature-Informed Biobehavioral Scaffold

Reconciliation with the Elsevier ontology and query of the MedScan-informed Elsevier Biology Knowledge Graph resulted in the use of some proxy terms for the 9 neurobehavioral measures as well as the omission of some brain regions that were poorly documented leaving 39 of the initial 52 Brodmann regions. Automated text-mining of the literature recovered 131 documented relationships linking these 48 nodes with most of these consisting of undirected associations. Interestingly, relationships bridging across the brain and behavioral domains were better represented in the literature than relationships between elements within the same domain. Of the 111 undirected relationships linking a behavioral construct and a brain region, only 50 (45%) were supported by at least 3 citations. Relationships between any two brain regions were poorly represented in the literature with only 17 such relationships recovered and only 2 (12%) being supported by at least 3 citations. Likewise of the 19 relationships linking any 2 behavioral constructs, only 9 (47%) were supported by at least 3 citations. Aggregating brain regions to improve membership in the network, removing orphan nodes and duplicating brain regions to represent both left and right hemispheres resulted in an initial literature-informed network consisting of 51 nodes connected by 186 directed interactions supported by at least 3 citations for a total overall support of over 900 citations (Fig. 6).

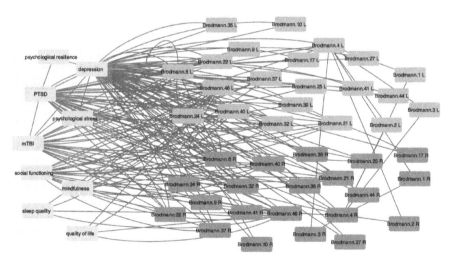

Fig. 6. A literature-informed network consisting of 51 nodes connected by 186 directed interactions supported by at least 3 citations each for a total overall support of over 900 citations. Brain regions were duplicated to represent both hemispheres. Undirected associations were translated into pairs of opposite direction relationships. Literature supported a connection density of on 7% with brain-region connectivity being especially sparse in documented support.

3.3 An Empirical Brain Region- Neurobehavioral Interactome

To improve representation of brain region connectivity in the network model, we conducted an empirical analysis of publicly available 64-channel EEG recordings at rest with eyes open and eyes closed in a representative control subject as well as in a representative subject with acute mTBI and one with chronic mmTBI. Coherence arrays were computed for each of these 6 matrices as an estimate of brain region connectivity. Non-zero coherence values were recovered for 79 Brodmann brain regions across both hemispheres. A threshold coherence value separating significant foreground coherence values from background values by applying Otus's methods to the unique values of squared coherence in the upper triangular matrix from each array as this is an undirected measure of association. The number of brain region interactions varied from roughly 14% in the control subject eyes open survey to almost 60% in the chronic mTBI subject eyes open survey (Table 2). An interaction between brain regions found significant in any of the surveys in Table 2 were retained and used to construct the final aggregate empirical brain connectivity network. Once again, these undirected interactions were translated into pairs of oppositely directed interactions. These were then combined with the precursor literature-informed network (Fig. 6) as the union of all candidate interactions to create the overall aggregate biobehavioral network. The latter now counts 89 nodes connected by a total of 2,515 directed interactions or a connection density of roughly 30% (Fig. 7).

Table 2. Foreground threshold coherence values and number of unique values.

Survey	Threshold Coherence^2	Associations Retained (of 3081)
Control eyes closed (subject 002)	0.24	479
Control eyes open (subject 002)	0.23	440
Acute mTBI eyes closed (subject 46)	0.41	997
Acute mTBI eyes open (subject 46)	0.36	1640
Chronic mTBI eyes closed (subject 78)	0.43	900
Chronic mTBI eyes open (subject 78)	0.33	1838

3.4 Plausible Regulatory Logic Programs Explaining Observations

A discrete decisional logic was applied to the above-mentioned aggregate network whereby the actions of each network edge are described in terms of a perception threshold, a mode of action or polarity (i.e. regional brain activity), and an effectiveness weight (i.e., strong activation vs weak deactivation and vice versa). Likewise, each node is assigned a bias term dictating its baseline activation level in the absence of input from neighboring nodes. This translates into a free variable parameter space consisting of 3

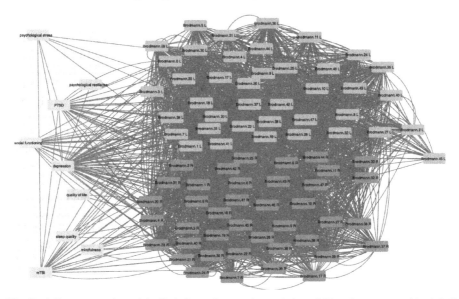

Fig. 7. A literature and empirically informed network consisting of 89 nodes connected by 2,515 directed interactions supported by at least 3 citations each or exceeding the coherence threshold determined by Otsu's method. This represents a connection density in excess of 30%. Brain regions were duplicated as required to represent both hemispheres. Undirected associations were translated into pairs of oppositely directed regulatory relationships.

parameters for each of the 2,515 edges and an additional 89 baseline activation terms for a total of 7,634 decisional logic parameters. Unmeasured state variables at each partially observed steady state are also free variables to which values must be assigned. Specifically, values must be inferred for the 40 brain region activation levels in each of the 2 veteran behavioral profiles as well as for 9 behavioral measures corresponding to each of the 6 EEG-inferred brain region profiles, adding another 214 free variables to the optimization problem for an overall solution space of close to 8,000 free variables. Allowable estimates for these integer free variables were first required to lie within the set [0, 1, 2] in the case of a state variable, an edge effectiveness weight and a node baseline activation, with mode of action polarity estimates constrained to [−1, 0, 1]. For each of the 8 partially observed states, we require that observed values be recovered exactly, adding over 500 equality constraints. For these partially observed profiles we also require that the next predicted state be the same as the current state i.e. a steady state. This is formulated as a set of linear equality constraints based on each node's state transition function output in each of the 8 postulated steady states. Altogether this resulted in over 1,200 linear equality constraints and close to 8,000 inequality range constraints (Fig. 3).

Applying the CP-SAT solver under Google OR-Tools to this problem as initially stated resulted in no valid solution sets. However, a minimal unsatisfiable set (MUS) analysis revealed that as few as 7 state variable constraints corresponding to values assigned to activation of Brodmann region 3 in the right hemisphere in all 6 EEG-inferred profiles as well as the level of PTSD severity specified in the behavioral profile for veteran cluster C1 were especially difficult to satisfy. Re-assigning these state variable values to unspecified and removing the corresponding 7 of over 9,000 constraints resulted in a family of over 10,000 feasible competing regulatory network models. Despite this large number, analysis of these parameter sets indicated that these solutions were overwhelmingly similar to one another with 86% of all network edges being conserved unanimously (2,169/2,515) across all solutions. Moreover, only roughly 2% (53) of the edges in this core conserved sub-network were regulated differently (variance ratio >0). Most importantly perhaps, despite these differences, these network models unanimously predicted that veteran subjects who reported exposure to non-ionizing radiation could possibly be characterized by decreased activation of right BA 5, and left BA 32, with concurrent increases in left BA 3 and BA 9 compared to controls. In contrast, EOD subjects reporting exposure to depleted uranium are predicted to show increased activation of right BA 4, 40 and 46 with decreased activation of left BA 6 and right BA 9 and 44 (Fig. 8).

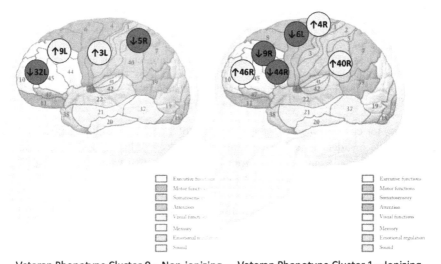

Veteran Phenotype Cluster 0 – Non-ionizing   Veteran Phenotype Cluster 1 – Ionizing

Fig. 8. Brain regions predicted to show increased (green) or decreased (red) resting state activation on EEG-inferred mappings when subjects present with characteristic neurobehavioral profiles in 2 exposure-relevant clusters in a cohort of n = 13 veterans. (Color figure online)

4   Discussion

This study demonstrates a formal analytical framework that leverages prior knowledge to infer cortical regions of interest that may be characteristic of exposure-related health outcomes in EOD veterans. This approach uses experimental and clinical observations to constrain and validate a regulatory network model rather than to the latter model de novo. It is important to emphasize that the objective of this framework is not to produce a definitive prediction. Rather, the objective is to generate a reasonable family of hypotheses to inform the early phase design for a formal study when there are few or no preliminary data available. In doing so, we attempt to bring together and reconcile as much prior knowledge and observation as possible from whatever source and in whatever form accessible. Nonetheless, these different sources each have their share of uncertainty and error. For example, we have found that reverse engineering of networks from experimental data alone may produce accuracies in the order of 50–60% to recover 40–60% of the true network (recall) [52] (depending on the type more than the abundance of data). Likewise, although the accuracy of predicting causal relationships from text continues to evolve [53], basic challenges regarding the assembly and use of valid benchmark data sets remain [54]. Our own group's domain expert performed a manual curation of close to 700 relationships describing female endocrine-immune signaling extracted from the Elsevier corpus using the MedScan NLP engine text and found 80–90% agreement (unpublished data). However, broader more formal studies describing the recovery of expert stated cause-and-effect statements with more generic language models report accuracies as low as 60% and recall levels of roughly 70% [55]. Rather than work with a single method, we attempt to boost overall performance by combining the strength of both data-driven and text-driven recovery methods. Specifically, we propose a hybrid framework to cross-validate imperfect and incomplete knowledge elements, extracted from various sources, and recovered by various method. This is accomplished by forcing agreement where these knowledge elements overlap, and where they do not, by forcing consistency with other interconnected knowledge elements extracted from other sources as well as those recovered from the same source.

The consistency we expect is not just a static recovery of observations. More importantly, we also apply our hypotheses regarding the system's dynamic behavior. To be more specific, we assign the observed conditions that we expect to be stable resting states or persistent illness states (i.e., dynamically stable), and separate them from those that we might consider transient responses. When using the simple logic applied here to manage network dynamics, the resulting discrete combinatorial optimization problems grow very quickly. Moreover, to allow for the discovery of multiple competing explanations, we apply a constraint satisfaction approach which despite recent advances in SAT divide and conquer strategies [56] remains very challenging to scaleup. Our group continues to work on implementing these strategies and is also looking at opportunities to leverage the power of emerging quantum computing systems by redefining this parameter search as a quantum annealing problem [57]. Finally, despite the important advantages of this data fusion, gaps in our current knowledge and observation will inevitably emerge. These gaps typically lead to the generation of many potentially competing explanations. Interestingly, more often than not, these share a significant degree of agreement. It is this commonly agreed-upon insight that we believe can be instrumental in helping focus a study design, point to specific knowledge gaps, and improve the efficiency of future experimentation [58]. We also propose that use of multiple competing hypotheses is of special value when, as with the example presented here, we are searching for relevant features in neuroimaging. As is generally the case with most medical imaging, the latter typically performs better clinically when used in a confirmatory rather than discovery role and in that respect benefits greatly from *a priori* defined regions of interest (ROI). For example, in this case, the rather large family of models unanimously agree on brain ROI in the dorsolateral prefrontal cortex (BA 9 & 46) as being of special interest in this group of veterans. These same regions have been associated in several studies with changes in brain signaling incurred in post-traumatic stress disorder (PTSD) as well acute and chronic brain dynamics following TBI [59, 60].

Acknowledgments. This work was supported by Rochester Regional Health in conjunction with Elsevier BV (Amsterdam) under a collaborative research sponsorship (Broderick, PI) and the US Department of Veterans Affairs through an Interagency Personnel Agreement (IPA) (Broderick, Chacko, Page) award. Pathway Studio (© 2020), Elsevier Text Mining and Elsevier Knowledge Graph are trademarks of Elsevier Limited. Copyright Elsevier Limited except certain content provided by third parties.

Mandatory Disclosure. The opinions and assertions contained herein are the private views of the authors and are not to be construed as official or as reflecting the views of the US Department of Veterans Affairs, the US Department of Defense, Rochester Regional Health, or Elsevier BV.

Disclosure of Interests. The authors have no competing interests to declare that are relevant to the content of this article.

References

1. Frueh, B.C., et al.: "Operator syndrome": a unique constellation of medical and behavioral health-care needs of military special operation forces. Int. J. Psychiatry Med. **55**(4), 281–295 (2020)
2. Stewart, W., Trujillo, K.: Modern Warfare Destroys Brains. Paper, Belfer Center for Science and International Affairs, Harvard Kennedy School. https://www.belfercenter.org/sites/def ault/files/2020-07/ModernWarfareDestroysBrains.pdf. Accessed 20 Dec 2023
3. Khan, A.A., Chaudhari, O., Chandra, R.: A review of ensemble learning and data augmentation models for class imbalanced problems: combination, implementation and evaluation. Expert Syst. Appl. **244**(15), 122778 (2024)
4. Bengio, Y., Courville, A., Vincent, P.: Representation learning: a review and new perspectives. IEEE Trans. Pattern Anal. Mach. Intell. **35**(8), 1798–1828 (2013)
5. Lahat, D., Adali, T., Jutten, C.: Multimodal data fusion: an overview of methods, challenges, and prospects. Proc. IEEE **103**(9), 1449–1477 (2015)
6. Kortemme, T., Baker, D.: Computational design of protein-protein interactions. Curr. Opin. Chem. Biol. **8**(1), 91–97 (2004)
7. Gangemi, A., Mika, P.: Understanding the semantic web through descriptions and situations. In: Meersman, R., Tari, Z., Schmidt, D.C. (eds.) OTM 2003. LNCS, vol. 2888, pp. 689–706. Springer, Heidelberg (2003). https://doi.org/10.1007/978-3-540-39964-3_44
8. Ali, I.M.: Ontology-driven semantic data integration in open environment. Electronic Thesis and dissertation repository, 7230 (2020). https://ir.lib.uwo.ca/etd/7230. https://www.scienc edirect.com/science/article/pii/S0957417423032803. Accessed 12 Dec 2023
9. Holmes, T.H., Rahe, R.H.: The social readjustment rating scale. J. Psychosom. Res. **11**(2), 213–218 (1967)
10. Connor, K.M., Davidson, J.R.T.: Development of a new resilience scale: the connor-davidson resilience scale(CD-RISC). Depress. Anxiety **18**(2), 76–82 (2003)

11. Lee, R.M., Draper, M., Lee, S.: Social connectedness, dysfunctional interpersonal behaviors, and psychological distress: testing a mediator model. J. Couns. Psychol. **48**(3), 310–318 (2001)
12. Baer, R.A., et al.: Construct validity of the five facet mindfulness questionnaire in meditating and nonmeditating samples. Assessment **15**(3), 329–342 (2008)
13. Cicerone, K.D., Kalmar, K.: Persistent postconcussion syndrome: the structure of subjective complaints after mild traumatic brain injury. J. Head Trauma Rehabil. **10**(3), 1–17 (1995)
14. Cella, D., et al.: Neuro-QOL: brief measures of health-related quality of life for clinical research in neurology. Neurology **78**(23), 1860–1867 (2012)
15. Blevins, C.A., Weathers, F.W., Davis, M.T., Witte, T.K., Domino, J.L.: The posttraumatic stress disorder checklist for DSM-5 (PCL-5): development and initial psychometric evaluation. J. Trauma Stress **28**(6), 489–498 (2015)
16. Buysse, D.J., Reynolds, C.F., Monk, T.H., Berman, S.R., Kupfer, D.J.: The Pittsburgh sleep quality index: a new instrument for psychiatric practice and research. Psychiatry Res. **28**(2), 193–213 (1989)
17. Kroenke, K., Spitzer, R.L.: The phq-9: A new depression diagnostic and severity measure. Psychiatr. Ann. **32**(9), 509–515 (2002)
18. Hamerly, G., Drake, J.: Accelerating Lloyd's algorithm for k-means clustering. In: Celebi, M. (ed.) Partitional Clustering Algorithms, pp. 41–78. Springer, Cham (2015). https://doi.org/10.1007/978-3-319-09259-1_2
19. Dhillon, I.S.: Co-clustering documents and words using bipartite spectral graph partitioning. In: Proceedings of the Seventh ACM SIGKDD International Conference on Knowledge Discovery and Data Mining, Charlottesville, August 2001, pp. 269–274. Association for Computing Machinery (ACM) (2001)
20. Samuel, I. et al.: Effects of military occupational exposures on home-based assessment of veterans' self-reported health, sleep and cognitive performance measures. In: Schmorrow, D.D., Fidopiastis, C.M. (eds.) HCII 2022. LNCS, vol. 13310, pp. 91–102. Springer, Cham (2022). https://doi.org/10.1007/978-3-031-05457-0_8
21. Kamdar, M.R., et al.: Text snippets to corroborate medical relations: an unsupervised approach using a knowledge graph and embeddings. In: AMIA Joint Summits on Translational Science proceedings. AMIA Joint Summits on Translational Science, pp. 288–297 (2020)
22. Nikitin, A., Egorov, S., Daraselia, N., Mazo, I.: Pathway studio—the analysis and navigation of molecular networks. Bioinformatics **19**(16), 2155–2157 (2003)
23. Yuryev, A.: Targeting transcription factors in cell regulation. Expert Opin. Ther. Targets **10**(3), 345–349 (2006)
24. Novichkova, S., Egorov, S., Daraselia, N.: MedScan, a natural language processing engine for MEDLINE abstracts. Bioinformatics **19**(13), 1699–1706 (2003)
25. Daraselia, N., Yuryev, A., Egorov, S., Novichkova, S., Nikitin, A., Mazo, I.: Extracting human protein interactions from MEDLINE using a full-sentence parser. Bioinformatics **20**(5), 604–611 (2004)
26. Markiewicz, C.J., et al.: The OpenNeuro resource for sharing of neuroscience data. Elife **10**, e71774 (2021)
27. Cavanagh, J.F., Quinn, D.: EEG: three-stim auditory oddball and rest in acute and chronic TBI. OpenNeuro. Dataset (2021). https://doi.org/10.18112/openneuro.ds003522.v1.1.0. Accessed 12 Dec 2023
28. Delorme, A., et al.: NEMAR: an open access data, tools and compute resource operating on neuroelectromagnetic data. Database **2022**, baac096 (2022)
29. Delorme, A., Makeig, S.: EEGLAB: an open source toolbox for analysis of single-trial EEG dynamics including independent component analysis. J. Neurosci. Methods **134**(1), 9–21 (2004)

30. Tadel, F., Baillet, S., Mosher, J.C., Pantazis, D., Leahy, R.M.: Brainstorm: a user-friendly application for MEG/EEG analysis. Comput. Intell. Neurosci. **2011**, 879716 (2011)
31. Kothe, C.A., Makeig, S.: BCILAB: a platform for brain-computer interface development. J. Neural Eng. **10**(5), 056014 (2013)
32. Lee, T.W., Girolami, M., Sejnowski, T.J.: Independent component analysis using an extended infomax algorithm for mixed subgaussian and supergaussian sources. Neural Comput. **11**(2), 417–441 (1999)
33. Winkler, I., Haufe, S., Tangermann, M.: Automatic classification of artifactual ICA-components for artifact removal in EEG signals. Behav. Brain Funct. **7**, 1–15 (2011)
34. Pascual-Marqui, R.D.: Standardized low-resolution brain electromagnetic tomography (sLORETA): technical details. Methods Find. Exp. Clin. Pharmacol. **24**(Suppl. D), 5–12 (2002)
35. Van Essen, D.C.: A population-average, landmark-and surface-based (PALS) atlas of human cerebral cortex. Neuroimage **28**(3), 635–662 (2005)
36. Trammell, J.P., MacRae, P.G., Davis, G., Bergstedt, D., Anderson, A.E.: The relationship of cognitive performance and the theta-alpha power ratio is age-dependent: an EEG study of short term memory and reasoning during task and resting-state in healthy young and old adults. Front. Aging Neurosci. **9**, 364 (2017)
37. Zhao, Y., Wong, L., Goh, W.W.B.: How to do quantile normalization correctly for gene expression data analyses. Sci. Rep. **10**(1), 15534 (2020)
38. Amjad, A.M., Halliday, D.M., Rosenberg, J.R., Conway, B.A.: An extended difference of coherence test for comparing and combining several independent coherence estimates: theory and application to the study of motor units and physiological tremor. J. Neurosci. Methods **73**(1), 69–79 (1997)
39. Otsu, N.: A threshold selection method from gray-level histograms. IEEE Trans. Syst. Man Cybern. **9**(1), 62–66 (1979)
40. Thomas, R.: Regulatory networks seen as asynchronous automata: a logical description. J. Theor. Biol. **153**, 1–23 (1991)
41. Mendoza, L., Xenarios, I.: A method for the generation of standardized qualitative dynamical systems of regulatory networks. Theor. Biol. Med. Model. **3**, 13 (2006)
42. Sedghamiz, H., Morris, M., Craddock, T.J.A., Whitley, D., Broderick, G.: High-fidelity discrete modeling of the HPA axis: a study of regulatory plasticity in biology. BMC Syst. Biol. **12**(1), 76 (2018)
43. Barták, R.: Constraint programming: in pursuit of the holy grail. Theor. Comput. Sci. **17**(12), 555–564 (1999)
44. Sedghamiz, H., Chen, W., Rice, M., Whitley, D., Broderick, G.: Selecting optimal models based on efficiency and robustness in multi-valued biological networks. In: 2017 IEEE 17th International Conference on Bioinformatics and Bioengineering (BIBE), October 2017, pp. 200–205. IEEE, New York (2017)
45. Sedghamiz, H., Morris, M., Craddock, T.J.A., Whitley, D., Broderick, G.: Bio-ModelChecker: using bounded constraint satisfaction to seamlessly integrate observed behavior with prior knowledge of biological networks. Front. Bioeng. Biotechnol. **7**, 48 (2019)
46. Guns, T.: Increasing modeling language convenience with a universal n-dimensional array, CPpy as python- embedded example. In: The 18th Workshop on Constraint Modelling and Reformulation (ModRef 2019), University of Connecticut, Stanmford (2019)
47. Stuckey, P.J.: Lazy clause generation: combining the power of SAT and CP (and MIP?) solving. In: Lodi, A., Milano, M., Toth, P. (eds.) CPAIOR 2010. LNCS, vol. 6140, pp. 5–9. Springer, Heidelberg (2010). https://doi.org/10.1007/978-3-642-13520-0_3
48. Cuvelier, T., Didier, F., Furnon, V., Gay, S., Mohajeri, S., Perron, L.: OR-tools' vehicle routing solver: a generic constraint-programming solver with heuristic search for routing problems.

In: 24e congrès annuel de la société française de recherche opérationnelle et d'aide à la décision, ROADEF, Rennes, France, ⟨hal-04015496⟩ (2023)

49. Liffiton, M.H., Sakallah, K.A.: Algorithms for computing minimal unsatisfiable subsets of constraints. J. Autom. Reason. **40**(1), 1–33 (2008)

50. Bleukx, I., Devriendt, J., Gamba, E., Bogaerts, B., Guns, T.: Simplifying step-wise explanation sequences. In: 29th International Conference on Principles and Practice of Constraint Programming (CP 2023), vol. 280, no. 11, pp. 11:1–11:20. Schloss Dagstuhl-Leibniz-Zentrum für Informatik (2023)

51. Gamba, E., Bogaerts, B., Guns, T.: Efficiently explaining CSPs with unsatisfiable subset optimization. J. Artif. Intell. Res. **78**, 709–746 (2023)

52. Vashishtha, S., Broderick, G., Craddock, T.J., Fletcher, M.A., Klimas, N.G.: Inferring broad regulatory biology from time course data: have we reached an upper bound under constraints typical of in vivo studies? PLoS ONE **10**(5), e0127364 (2015)

53. Feder, A., et al.: Causal inference in natural language processing: estimation, prediction, interpretation and beyond. Trans. Assoc. Comput. Linguist. **10**, 1138–1158 (2022)

54. Keith, K.A., Jensen, D., O'Connor, B.: Text and causal inference: a review of using text to remove confounding from causal estimates. arXiv preprint arXiv:2005.00649 (2020)

55. Hassanzadeh, O., et al.: Answering binary causal questions through large-scale text mining: an evaluation using cause-effect pairs from human experts. In: 2019 International Joint Conference on Artificial Intelligence (IJCAI 2019), Macao, pp. 5003–5009 (2019)

56. Le Frioux, L., Baarir, S., Sopena, J., Kordon, F.: PaInleSS: a framework for parallel SAT solving. In: Gaspers, S., Walsh, T. (eds.) SAT 2017. LNCS, vol. 10491, pp. 233–250. Springer, Cham (2017). https://doi.org/10.1007/978-3-319-66263-3_15

57. Campbell, E., Khurana, A., Montanaro, A.: Applying quantum algorithms to constraint satisfaction problems. Quantum **3**, 167 (2019)

58. Videla, S., et al.: Designing experiments to discriminate families of logic models. Front. Bioeng. Biotechnol. **3**, 131 (2015)

59. Pang, E.W.: Different neural mechanisms underlie deficits in mental flexibility in post-traumatic stress disorder compared to mild traumatic brain injury. Front. Psych. **6**, 170 (2015)

60. Eierud, C., et al.: Neuroimaging after mild traumatic brain injury: review and meta-analysis. NeuroImage Clin. **4**, 283–294 (2014)

Improving the Accessibility and Legibility of Prescription Medicine Labels for the Elderly in China: A Study on Enhanced Design and Usability Testing

Wei Xiong, Boxian Qiu$^{(\boxtimes)}$, Keyu Li, Jintao Lin, and Zhongbo Liu

South China University of Technology, Guangzhou, China
qiuboxian1101@163.com

Abstract. This study examined the effects of enhanced design of prescription medication labels on label legibility among elderly individuals in China. The layout, structuring, and visual representation of drug labels were enhanced. A group of thirty Chinese elderly participants was recruited to evaluate their comprehension and satisfaction with both the newly designed and conventional labels through a series of comprehension tests and satisfaction assessments. Participants in the experimental group demonstrated superior performance in label reading efficiency and comprehension compared to the control group. The redesigned prescription medication labels improved the elderly's understanding of medication information, enhancing legibility and accessibility. The findings suggested that substantial improvements to the layout and presentation of information on prescription medication labels could enhance satisfaction with the label and improve medication adherence accuracy among the elderly.

Keywords: Chinese typographic cues · Elderly · legibility · Medicine labelling · Medications/prescriptions · Usability test

1 Background

With the increasingly serious aging of Chinese population, the elderly medication group is growing. Patients' correct understanding of the drug is essential to ensure that they take the drug correctly according to the doctor's advice and to ensure the safety of the drug. Understanding the role, indications, usage, dosage, and possible side effects of medications can help patients better manage their health and avoid unnecessary risks [1]. Consequently, promoting accurate medication comprehension among elderly patients will have a positive impact on their treatment outcomes and overall health status. In response to the global challenges posed by population aging, the World Health Organization has proposed the Global Age-friendly Cities Guide [2], which specifically addresses the design of medication labels. The guide emphasizes that information designed for elderly individuals should be clearly legible and easily comprehensible. In China, medication labels are strictly regulated [3], however, these regulations do not specify requirements

© The Author(s), under exclusive license to Springer Nature Switzerland AG 2024
V. G. Duffy (Ed.): HCII 2024, LNCS 14710, pp. 140–150, 2024.
https://doi.org/10.1007/978-3-031-61063-9_9

for font type, size, and color, nor do they address the issue of label readability. Many elderly individuals in China still face challenges in reading these labels. Improper design of prescription drug labels may lead to medication errors, which may result in serious consequences such as gastric bleeding or poisoning. Compared to young individuals, the elderly rely more on drug labels and are also more susceptible to misinterpreting the information presented [4]. Therefore, the legibility of prescription drug labels is particularly crucial for older adults [5]. Accurate comprehension of these labels by older adults is essential to safeguard the therapeutic efficacy of their medications and to mitigate the risks of medication misuse or overuse.

Modifications to the font and format of drug labels can affect their legibility [6]. In order to provide elderly clearer and more understandable prescription information, it is crucial to thoroughly investigate the relationship between the layout of prescription label information, its readability, and its comprehensibility [7]. Simple improvements to medication instructions can cost-effectively enhance patient adherence [8] and accuracy in taking medicines, particularly for elderly patients with limited literacy and more complex medication regimens [9]. In Singapore, enhancing elderly patients' understanding of prescription medication labels may be achieved by incorporating bilingual text and visual aids such as graphics into the label design [10].

In China, it had been identified that prescription instructions often suffer from small font sizes, dense and complex information, highlighting a need for redesigns tailored to the elderly. However, focused research on the design specifics of prescription drug labels remains remarkably limited. As the public becomes more conscious of their rights, there is an escalating demand for more accessible drug label information. Given the difficulties many elderly individuals face in deciphering these labels, the imperative to investigate design improvements aimed at enhancing the clarity and legibility of prescription drug labels for this population is clear [11].

The purpose of this study was to investigate whether prescription drug labels, redesigned to align with the cognitive abilities and usage habits of the elderly in China, can optimize user experience and enhance reading efficiency. To validate the improvements, a group of senior participants were invited to participate in comprehension test and satisfaction evaluation comparing the new and old labels. The findings of this research will offer healthcare professionals targeted strategies to refine the prescription label system for Chinese elders, thus promoting and ensuring the accurate transmission and understanding of medication information.

2 Method

2.1 Preliminary Experiment on the Comprehension of USP Pictograms Among Chinese Elderly

The United States Pharmacopeial (USP) Convention [12] created a collection of 81 pharmaceutical pictograms to serve as "standardized graphic images that help convey medication instructions, precautions and/or warnings to patients and consumers". The use of pictograms to enhance patient comprehension of prescription medication instructions has been widely adopted internationally [13] and its feasibility was empirically validated [14]. Taking into account the linguistic and cognitive disparities between domestic and international contexts, this study embarked on a preliminary experiment to assess the potential of USP pictograms in boosting the readability of Chinese medication labels, starting with evaluating Chinese seniors' understanding of these pictograms. A group of Chinese elderly was tasked with interpreting medical information conveyed through three USP pictograms. These pictograms, representing common medication-related instructions, were displayed to the participants. The experimental protocol unfolded as follows: 1) Three pictograms that signify commonly understood concepts were selected from the USP series (Fig. 1); 2) Participants were shown the pictograms one at a time, informed that they were related to medication instructions, and then asked to explain their understanding of the information each pictogram conveyed; 3) The responses were recorded and subsequently compared with the intended meanings to evaluate the pictograms' readability and the perception and comprehension of the Chinese elderly. The following Table 1 gives a summary of the pre-experimental results.

Pic.1.Take by mouth   Pic.2.Drink additional water   Pic.3.Nasal spray

Fig. 1. Three pictograms for pre-experiment.

Table 1. Results of fifteen participants' comprehension test for USP pictograms.

Pictograms	Number of correct responses	Number of incorrect responses	Accurate rate
Pic.1	6	9	40.00%
Pic.2	3	12	20.00%
Pic.3	5	10	33.33%

The findings indicate that the comprehension of USP pictograms among Chinese elderly individuals was limited. This implied that the older population needed to devote extra time to learning the interpretation of these symbols. Consequently, the incorporation of pictograms into prescription drug labels might not enhance the understanding of medication information for the elderly in China.

2.2   Prescription Drug Label Improvement Design

In the process of user research conducted with elderly participants, it was discovered that current prescription drug labels exhibit shortcomings in terms of comprehensiveness and logical structuring of information hierarchy. Subsequent empirical and desktop research into the prescription drug details that concern older adults revealed that their attention is primarily focused on the following aspects: therapeutic effects, instructions for use and dosage, side effects, expiration date, and applicable symptoms.

In terms of textual elements, correct interpretation of drug labels instructions was crucial for the safe administration and better adherence to prescribed drugs. Textual elements that aid patients in the correct interpretation of drug labels included: employing explicit time periods in dosage instructions, using language that was simple and easy to understand, presenting numbers in a numeric format, and providing medication instructions in the patient's native language [15]. To assist the elderly in accessing and understanding medication information with greater accuracy, this study was dedicated to designing a clear prescription drug label that provided tiered and distinct levels of information. Reflecting the elderly's prioritization of information, the drug information was categorized into three levels of priority: primary information (basic drug facts and dosage instructions), secondary information (the duration of medication use, precautionary advice, and expiration dates) and tertiary information (personal details, hospital information, and the prescription number).

In terms of font design, Heiti was a more suitable typeface for the elderly to read because it possessed a strong visual impact and a sense of weight. Regarding font size, the optimal readability for older adults was achieved with a font size ranging from 14 to 16 points [16]. Using red, boldface, or contrast could help differentiate drug information [17]. Boldface and contrast could be used in prescription drug labels to enhance information discrimination, while red was considered inappropriate due to concerns about the cost of printing.

In the layout design, the following three aspects were considered: (1) The directional orientation of the typesetting was primarily horizontal, as it was observed that the elderly have a better reading habit with horizontal text, which aids in improving visual search efficiency. (2) In the arrangement of text, appropriate font sizes were chosen based on the layout, the information to be conveyed, and the visual characteristics of the elderly. (3) On the page, striking graphics and shapes were employed to enhance the visibility of information, which, through the use of sensible layout designs, aimed to increase the elderly's perception of information and to reduce their reading time and memory difficulties. Finally, the prescription drug label after improved design is shown in Fig. 2 (taking the Third Affiliated Hospital of Sun Yat-Sen University as an example).

Fig. 2. Prescription drug label after improved design.

2.3   Usability Testing of the Improved Labels

A group of Chinese older adults (aged 65 and above) were asked to complete a task assessing their understanding of prescription drug label information. A total of 30 Chinese elderly participants—17 males and 13 females—were involved in the study, with ages ranging from 60 to 85 years. These participants possessed basic literacy skills and were capable of engaging in user testing dialogues without any language barriers. None of the participants were healthcare professionals (HCPs), whether practicing or retired.

Participants in the experimental group (15 subjects) were presented with the redesigned prescription drug labels, while the control group participants (15 subjects) were shown the original labels (Fig. 3). Both groups were provided with a sheet of pills and several small bowls to simulate the medication dispensing process. The specific experimental process was as follows:

a) Simulated Pill Retrieval Task. After reading and comprehending the labels, participants were tasked with a medication retrieval exercise—extracting a day's dosage of medication and distributing the pills into small bowls according to the quantity required for each intake. During this process, the time taken to read the labels was recorded.

Fig. 3. The labels used in control group (left) and the labels used in experimental group (right).

b) Comprehension Test. The comprehension test questionnaire (Table 2) was designed in accordance with the usability guidelines for consumer medical information developed by Sless et al. [18]. The guideline suggests a set of questions that are extensively used to assess the usability of medical information leaflets and to ensure they meet the required performance benchmarks. The questionnaire comprised ten questions aimed at understanding the label design's readability and accessibility from the user's perspective. Participants were required to answer these ten label-related questions, after which their responses were scored for correctness according to a grading scale (1–5 points).

Table 2. Comprehension test questionnaire of drug labels.

Number	Question
Q.1	When was this medicine prescribed?
Q.2	When will the drug expired?
Q.3	How should this medicine be stored
Q.4	Please describe how to take this medicine and how many tablets at a time?
Q.5	When is this medicine taken every day? (Before/after meals/on an empty stomach/before bed)
Q.6	Is it permissible to drink alcohol while taking this medication?
Q.7	Is it permissible to smoke while taking this medication?
Q.8	What are the possible side effects of taking this medicine?
Q.9	Can this medication be taken on an empty stomach?
Q.10	If you experience any discomfort while taking the medication, what should you do?

c) Satisfaction Evaluation. At the conclusion of the experiment, participants in the experimental group were asked to express their overall satisfaction with the performance of the revised labels, which was to be carried out through completing a satisfaction questionnaire (Table 3). This questionnaire was designed based on a Likert five-point scale [19], where responses to each question spanned five levels, specifically: (1) Strongly Disagree (1 point), (2) Disagree (2 points), (3) Neutral (3 points), (4) Agree (4 points), and (5) Strongly Agree (5 points). Subjects were required to evaluate the label across five distinct aspects. This method allowed participants to indicate their satisfaction with the overall performance of the modified drug labels after the experiment (in the form of scoring).

Table 3. Satisfaction evaluation questionnaire.

Number	Question
Q.1	I agree that the font and layout of the new label are very clear and distinct
Q.2	I agree that with the new label, I can immediately obtain the most critical information
Q.3	I agree that reading the new label allows for higher reading efficiency compared to the old label
Q.4	I agree that there is no need for further improvement on this label

3   Results

The label reading time for both the control group (with original prescription drug labels) and the experimental group (with improved prescription drug labels) were presented in Fig. 4. Wilcoxon signed ranks tests [20] were used to examine the reading duration for each drug between control and experimental groups. According to the results of the Wilcoxon signed-rank test, the p-value for the comparison of reading times between the new and old labels is less than 0.05 ($Z = -3.298$, $P = 0.001$), suggesting that the difference in reading times for the labels is statistically significant. The median reading time for the control group was 27 s, which is longer than the median reading time of 16 s for the experimental group.

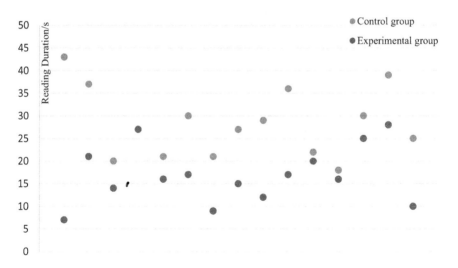

Fig. 4. The label reading duration of participants.

The comprehension test scores for the control group (using the original prescription drug labels) and the experimental group (using the improved prescription drug labels) were depicted in Table 4. After calculating the average score for each question, the data from the two groups were analyzed using the Wilcoxon signed-rank test. The test results revealed a statistically significant difference in label reading times between the two groups, with a p-value less than 0.05 ($Z = -2.803$, $P = 0.001$). The median reading time of the control group (2.667) was observed to be lower than that of the experimental group (3.646).

Table 4. The comprehension test questionnaire scores of participants.

Factor	Average score per question (Total points: 5)										
	Number of participants	Q1	Q2	Q3	Q4	Q5	Q6	Q7	Q8	Q9	Q10
Original label	15	2.933	1.800	3.133	4.533	2.733	2.600	2.375	1.375	2.467	3.125
Improved Label	15	4.133	3.200	3.625	4.875	3.333	3.867	3.667	2.733	3.467	4.133

In evaluating the reliability of the collected data, a Cronbach's alpha analysis was performed on the satisfaction evaluation data [21]. The Cronbach's alpha coefficient, a measure of internal consistency within the questionnaire, ranges from 0 to 1, with higher values indicating better reliability and internal consistency. The satisfaction assessment questionnaire for the experimental group, which considered the revised prescription drug labels, was detailed in the Table 5. The Cronbach's alpha test results displayed $\alpha \geq 0.8$ ($\alpha = 0.818$), signifying very good reliability for the test or scale. With all Corrected Item-Total Correlation (CITC) values exceeding 0.4, there was a strong correlation between the items, which also confirmed a good reliability level. The assessment revealed that participants showed a higher level of satisfaction with the improved labels, particularly in terms of layout, primary information, and reading efficiency.

4   Discussion

The results indicated that the experimental group (with the improved labels) experienced significantly reduced comprehension times compared to the control group (with the original labels), suggesting that design enhancements to prescription drug labels can increase the efficiency with which the elderly read these labels. The redesigned labels were tailored to reflect the reading and cognitive preferences of older adults, establishing a clear and well-prioritized information hierarchy. Furthermore, medication-related information of greatest relevance to the elderly was prominently displayed on the improved labels, as determined by user surveys and interviews. Consequently, the elderly were able to access and analyze medication information more accurately. The experimental findings affirmed that such a design could optimize user experience and thereby improve reading efficiency.

Table 5. The satisfaction evaluation of participants (Experimental group)

Participants	Q1	Q2	Q3	Q4
P1	Neutral	Neutral	Neutral	Agree
P2	Agree	Strongly Agree	Agree	Agree
P3	Strongly Agree	Strongly Agree	Strongly Agree	Strongly Agree
P4	Agree	Strongly Agree	Strongly Agree	Strongly Agree
P5	Strongly Agree	Strongly Agree	Strongly Agree	Strongly Agree
P6	Strongly Agree	Strongly Agree	Strongly Agree	Agree
P7	Agree	Agree	Agree	Strongly Agree
P8	Agree	Neutral	Agree	Agree
P9	Agree	Strongly Agree	Strongly Agree	Strongly Agree
P10	Strongly Agree	Strongly Agree	Strongly Agree	Strongly Agree
P11	Strongly Agree	Agree	Agree	Agree
P12	Neutral	Neutral	Agree	Agree
P13	Agree	Strongly Agree	Strongly Agree	Strongly Agree
P14	Neutral	Agree	Agree	Strongly Agree
P15	Strongly Agree	Agree	Agree	Strongly Agree

The data analysis of the comprehension test questionnaire revealed that the experimental group (with the improved labels) scored significantly higher than the control group (with the original labels). A higher score on the comprehension test questionnaire indicated a better understanding of the medication information by the elderly during reading. This suggested that the improved design has enhanced the readability and accessibility of prescription drug labels. To ensure patients take their medications correctly, the presentation of drug information must be easily understandable. The findings of this study demonstrated that refinements in the layout design and information presentation of prescription drug labels could improve their readability, thereby aiding the elderly in better comprehending medication information.

The satisfaction assessment questionnaire results for the experimental group (with the improved labels) showed that the elderly were generally more satisfied with the new labels. This satisfaction was specifically reflected in the participants' approval of the new label's layout design, the presentation of key information, and the efficiency of reading.

In this study, prescription drug labels were redesigned to enhance readability and comprehension for the elderly in China. The experimental results confirmed that the modified drug labels indeed possess improved readability. This suggested that making improvements in the layout design of prescription medication labels could significantly enhance the understanding and reading efficiency of Chinese seniors when it comes to these labels. Moreover, it was discovered that comprehensive knowledge of medication information through prescription drug labels can increase the elderly's satisfaction with the labels and improve the accuracy of their medication administration. This assisted the elderly in better understanding and adhering to medication usage instructions.

The issue of reading barriers faced by the elderly in relation to prescription drug labels had been extensively studied by scholars. The innovation and focus of this research were on the user characteristics and cognitive habits of the elderly in China. It had been demonstrated that the addition of pictograms to medication information could enhance older adults' understanding, and this improvement had been proven to be related to the number of used pictograms [14]. However, preliminary experiments conducted with Chinese seniors suggest that their understanding of pictograms is very low. The use of pictograms on prescription drug labels did not improve the comprehension of medication information among Chinese seniors. This insight revealed that due to differences in language and cognitive habits, the experimental results could be significantly influenced by users from different countries. This was a factor that would require special attention in future research.

5 Conclusion

This study demonstrated that enhancements in the layout design and information presentation of prescription drug labels could foster a better understanding of medication information among the elderly. Experimental results indicated that, compared to the old labels, the enhanced labels performed better in terms of user comprehension and had better legibility. In the experiments, the elderly participants were more satisfied with aspects of the new labels such as layout design, the presentation of key information, and reading efficiency. As awareness of patient rights continued to increase, design emerged as an increasingly significant and effective approach to dealing with issues of information accessibility and readability on drug labels. The research explored prescription drug label design forms and content suitable for the elderly in China, which could provide assistance in enhancing China's prescription drug labeling system. Encouraging the practical application of improved prescription drug label designs will facilitate elderly individuals' understanding of medication information, decrease the frequency of medication errors, and improve drug compliance.

Disclosure of Interests. The authors have no competing interests to declare that are relevant to the content of this article.

References

1. Brown, M.T., Bussell, J.K.: Medication adherence: WHO cares? Mayo Clin. Proc. (2011)
2. World Health Organization (WHO): Global Age-friendly Cities: A Guide (2007)
3. Drug Administration Law of the People's Republic of China, No. (2019)
4. Hong, S.H., Liu, J., Tak, S., Vaidya, V.: The impact of patient knowledge of patient-centered medication label content on quality of life among older adults. Res. Soc. Adm. Pharm. **9**, 37–48 (2013)
5. Moisan, J., Gaudet, M., Grégoire, J.P., Bouchard, R.: Noncompliance with drug treatment and reading difficulties with regard to prescription labelling among seniors. Gerontology **48**, 44–51 (2002)

6. Kwok, B.S.H.: Accessibility and legibility for the elderly in Hong Kong: an empirical study of Chinese typographic cues on prescribed medicine labelling. Des. J. **21**, 625–645 (2018)
7. Bailey, S.C., Navaratnam, P., Black, H., Russell, A.L., Wolf, M.S.: Advancing best practices for prescription drug labeling. Ann. Pharmacother. **49**, 1222–1236 (2015)
8. Conn, V.S., Hafdahl, A.R., Cooper, P.S., Ruppar, T.M., Mehr, D.R., Russell, C.L.: Interventions to improve medication adherence among older adults: meta-analysis of adherence outcomes among randomized controlled trials. Gerontologist **49**, 447–462 (2009)
9. Wolf, M.S., Davis, T.C., Curtis, L.M., et al.: A patient-centered prescription drug label to promote appropriate medication use and adherence. J. Gener. Intern. Med. **31**, 1482–1489 (2016)
10. Malhotra, R., Bautista, M.A.C., Tan, N.C., et al.: Bilingual text with or without pictograms improves elderly Singaporeans' understanding of prescription medication labels. Gerontologist **59**, 378–390 (2019)
11. Sahm, L., Gallwey, H., Brennan, M., Behan, R., Carthy, S.M.: Enhanced prescription label design to improve patients' understanding of their medication. Int. J. Pharm. Pract. (2011)
12. United States Pharmacopeial Convention. USP Pictograms (2015). http://www.usp.org/usp-healthcare-professionals/relatedtopics-resources/usp-pictograms. Accessed 31 Aug 2015
13. Ferreira-Alfaya, F.J., Zarzuelo-Romero, M.J., Cura, Y.: Pharmaceutical pictograms to improve textual comprehension: a systematic review. Res. Soc. Adm. Pharm. (2024)
14. Ng, A.W.Y., Chan, A.H.S., Ho, V.W.S.: Comprehension by older people of medication information with or without supplementary pharmaceutical pictograms. Appl. Ergon. **58**, 167–175 (2017)
15. Maghroudi, E., van Hooijdonk, C.M.J., van de Bruinhorst, H., van Dijk, L., Rademakers, J., Borgsteede, S.D.: The impact of textual elements on the comprehensibility of drug label instructions (DLIs): a systematic review. PLoS ONE **16**, e0250238 (2021)
16. Kwok, S.H.: Examining the legibility of Chinese typefaces used in medicine label design for the elderly people. Paper presented at: Typography and Education Conference (2016)
17. Wang, H., Tao, D., Yan, M.: Effects of text enhancement on reduction of look-alike drug name confusion: a systematic review and meta-analysis. Qual. Manag. Health Care **30**, 233–243 (2021)
18. Sless, D., Wiseman, R., Hall, R., Wooller, H.: Writing about Medicines for People: Usability Guidelines and Glossary for Consumer Product Information. Department of Human Services and Health, Canberra (1994)
19. Taherdoost, H.: What is the best response scale for survey and questionnaire design; review of different lengths of rating scale/attitude, scale/Likert scale. Int. J. Acad. Res. Manag. **8**, 1–10 (2019)
20. Woolson, R.F.: Wilcoxon signed-rank test. In: D'Agostino, R.B., Sullivan, L., Massaro, J. (eds.) Wiley Encyclopedia of Clinical Trials (2008)
21. Schrepp, M: On the usage of Cronbach's alpha to measure reliability of UX scales. J. User Exp. (2020)

Technology in Mental Health
and Wellbeing

Switching Off to Switch On: An Ontological Inquiry into the Many Facets of Digital Well-Being

Mariangela Nascimento[1]([✉]), Claudia Motta[1,2], António Correia[3],
and Daniel Schneider[1,2]

[1] Postgraduate Program in Informatics, PPGI/UFRJ, Rio de Janeiro, Brazil
marigsn.br@gmail.com
[2] Tércio Pacitti Institute of Computer Applications and Research (NCE), Federal University of
Rio de Janeiro, Rio de Janeiro, Brazil
[3] Faculty of Information Technology, University of Jyväskylä, P.O. Box 35, 40014 Jyväskylä,
Finland

Abstract. In the last couple of years, there has been widespread recognition that digital well-being requires an initial conceptualization and a multidisciplinary approach to characterize the technological and human infrastructures behind the surge of applications intended to trigger behavioral and attitudinal transformations. From self-monitoring functionalities to screen dimming and real-time notifications, digital well-being applications present a distinct set of affordances and design requirements when compared to other media-based solutions. In line with this, the purpose of this research design is to delineate an initial ontology-based scheme for digital well-being taking into consideration the different building blocks, harms, challenges, and players in this transformative ecosystem at both micro and macro levels. By starting from the most basic situational contexts within which digital practices shape and are shaped by technology use, this study employs a domain-specific approach towards an ontological inquiry aimed at providing a description of the concepts and architectural elements underlying persuasive technology applications that promote digital well-being interventions. The goal is to encourage the development of a new route for more holistic and accurate depictions in this emerging phenomenon.

Keywords: Digital health · Digital wellness · Ontology · Persuasive technology Research design · Social media use · Digital well-being

1 Introduction

In an increasingly digitized society, human interactions are shifting from a limited face-to-face setup to a pervasive, uninterrupted format. As the use of mobile devices such as smartphones and other wearables grows and becomes pervasive, digital media becomes available 24 h a day, 7 days a week for users with diverse well-being support needs in their daily leisure and work activities. However, the abuse of what was originally conceived to

© The Author(s), under exclusive license to Springer Nature Switzerland AG 2024
V. G. Duffy (Ed.): HCII 2024, LNCS 14710, pp. 153–162, 2024.
https://doi.org/10.1007/978-3-031-61063-9_10

promote quality of life, enhance productivity, and facilitate communication and access to information has become an issue. Depression, anxiety, fear of missing out (FOMO), and other psychological disorders have grown and are being studied as consequences of uncontrolled digital technology usage. The amount of time spent on digital social interaction appears to be the primary factor triggering other disorders [1, 2]. In this regard, digital or behavioral mechanisms intended to take some time out from digital life have been proposed as digital detox practices. Building on the definition provided in [3], Mirbabaie and colleagues [4] describe digital detox as *"a periodic disconnection from information technology (IT) as well as strategies which help to reduce the engagement with IT."* However, the awareness of the level of personal engagement on social media seems to be more effective in preventing further damage.

Digital well-being is not a simple subject to define as it adds the digital dimension to the multidisciplinary wellness approach. As scholarship evolves, additional complexity shows up in the analysis and conceptualization of digital well-being. If in the beginning most of the responsibility for well-being was attributed to the user and the detractors derived from screen time, other dimensions have been added to the scene on both sides [5, 6]. As a multifaceted phenomenon, digital well-being has largely been observed by scientists from distinct disciplines with a particular focus on the negative effects of excessive usage or connection to technology, no matter if it is a smartphone, a wearable device, or social media. Amidst this fog of heterogeneous practices and media-based technological advances, many scholars have postulated that behavioral, emotional, and even physical diseases are consequences of excessive, uncontrolled, and somewhat chaotic exposure to the nuances of the evolving digital world.

Disease severity varies across a wide range of factors impairing well-being in the current digital sphere. From a digital citizenship viewpoint, the full spectrum of notions encompassing digital skills, identity, and accessibility within the frame of digital inequality [7] profoundly affect the perception of comfort and discomfort that individuals experience when engaging in activities mediated by technological devices. When seen from a design perspective, some mechanisms have also been pointed out as triggers of health disorders: notifications, messages, posts, likes, rewards, and a bunch of other functions that promote an intrinsic psychological desire to "hunt" are directly associated with some level of emotional disorders [8]. At a glance, these aspects are predominantly influenced by the level of awareness users can perceive through their daily interactions within the digital environment.

Primarily research for possible solutions to mitigate major effects has relied on promoting a pause in continuous and ubiquitous connection through digital detox mechanisms. For instance, Radtke and co-authors [9] framed the effectiveness of digital detox into five distinct categories: duration of use, performance (i.e., cognitive, physical), self-control (i.e., self-regulation, procrastination), health and well-being (e.g., sleep, life satisfaction, anxiety, stress, depression, addiction), and social relationships (e.g., FOMO, loneliness, social connectedness). Among the possible scenarios, disorders like depression, anxiety, and addiction seem to be among the most frequently cited in the literature as primary factors or a consequence of a composition of other behavioral or emotional disorders.

Given the emergence of many new persuasive technologies promoting digital well-being in both clinical and non-clinical settings, this conceptual paper challenges dominant discourses and presents a brief introductory description of the major digital well-being detractors. The key goal is to propose an initial ontological representation that can be used by designers and researchers in the field of human-computer interaction (HCI) to self-assess how detracting their applications and research prototypes are to the users' digital well-being. In addition, we also aim to apply an initial ontology-based approach to model and clarify the concept of digital well-being in its many forms and varieties. To this end, we followed the ontology engineering method proposed in [10], as shown in Fig. 1.

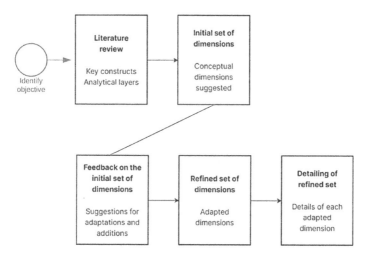

Fig. 1. Overview of the ontology engineering method leading to the initial ontological structure representation of digital well-being (adapted from Eide et al. [10]).

These methodological procedures allowed us to dissect the vast array of conceptual structures underlying the digital well-being phenomenon. The objective is to contribute to digital well-being research by putting together the major dimensions currently under discussion and thus provide an overview of this increasingly complex and transdisciplinary domain. Through a literature review, we have identified the initial set of dimensions and challenges to reach a common understanding of what are the current conceptual and technological problems associated with the digital well-being phenomenon. A series of feedback loops led to a refined set of dimensions which are discussed in the following sections of this paper.

2   Digital Well-Being Concepts

One basic yet fundamental challenge to digital well-being research pertains to the foundational assumption of what digital well-being entails. What are its building blocks? Is it a static concept? How might it evolve as novel technologies emerge? Extant literature exhibits distinct definitions for well-being, depending on the subject area. Despite these conceptual differences, some common factors seem to lean towards a shared conceptual consensus. Mostly mixed with health and happiness definitions and abstract perceptions of feelings, environment, and social relations, well-being comprises physical, psychological, social, and even spiritual dimensions affecting human abilities to deal with ordinary challenges in life [11]. Once human relations are increasingly being mediated by digital technology, the previous state of well-being remains with an additional dimension: the digital world. In any case, this is quite an abstract analysis and requires a deeper understanding.

As a common sense notion, the user's choices and actions are in the central analysis of what factors promote digital well-being. Yea and associates [12] have developed a framework for assessing digital well-being on a citizenship standpoint where each dimension characterizes the ability to think about the data critically. As said before, digital well-being encompasses a myriad of dimensions, making it even more complex to define [13]. At a general level, Yea et al. [12] claim that digital well-being can be defined as the ability to:

- Craft and maintain healthy relationships with technology that can be used in a balanced and civic way.
- Identify and understand the positive and negative impacts of engaging with digital activities.
- Be aware of ways to manage and control factors that contribute to digital well-being.

Note that the user's ability for self-assessment and self-control is crucial to the starting point of the digital well-being discussion. However, as research evolves, other important parameters are added to this context; more than that, complex and dynamic constructs shall be taken into consideration to build what we seek as a definition of digital well-being. Now, not only the time spent on a digital connection (e.g., screen time) matters, but who the individual using the devices is, what kind of device this individual is connected to, and what content and individual cognitive factors are involved.

3 Detractors of Digital Well-Being

Although it is hard to find a single or simple definition for digital well-being, harms as a consequence of the abuse of digital media are recognized and observed in ordinary life. The absence or lack of social relations intensified during COVID-19 pandemic has caused severe psychological disorders in the general population. However, a direct relation between application characteristics and psychological fragility is still not clear. In an experiment focused on teenagerhood, Twenger [14] analyzes possible causes for suicides and self-harm in teenagers, with considerable growth in the last decade. Despite the great number of factors influencing the subtle increase in mental issues, there is a growing consensus that the decline in mental health may be linked to the increasing popularity of smartphones and social media during the same period of time. That is, technology has been in the middle of this problem and some common factors seem to appear more often in the literature. For instance, Radtke and colleagues [9] synthesize empirical evidence and provide further insight on a decline of both smartphone or social media duration and depression symptoms after digital detox interventions. As mentioned before, depression, anxiety, and addiction are among the most addressed factors as reported in the literature as a primary factor or a consequence of other behavioral symptoms.

From a social media research lens, attention and data are considered to be the most valuable goods in the digitized world. Giraldo-Luque and co-authors [8] emphasize attention struggling as part of a strategy to increase consumption, as attention serves to predict the future behavior, while Hanin [15] discusses attention effects on digital relations in distinct levels and with different consequences on cognitive functions. In [16], the author discusses social inequality as a major element to differentiate attention effects due to digital excessive connection. FOMO is largely present in the discussion of social media excessive usage effect. Defined as *"a pervasive apprehension that others might be having a rewarding experience from which one is absent"* [17], FOMO has been studied in the context of social relations established through a digital media. A deeper neurophysiological perspective identifies the sensory mechanisms that trigger the FOMO effect [8]. In fact, social media deals with sophisticated economics, neurophysiology and neuropsychology mechanisms to retain users' attention and lead to one of the most cited well-being detractors: addiction. In any case, not only abuse but also the excessive engagement with digital technology may trigger most of the detractors.

4 On the Intervention of Persuasive Technology in Digital Well-Being

While it is more or less clear that some disorders are derived from excessive use of digital media and that user abuse of the media can trigger some of them, it has been an ongoing investigation to discover which elements of digital products promote or change user behavior, and even whether these are deliberately designed to absorb the user's attention and self-control. Continuous, uninterrupted, and somewhat hazardous social media usage has been attributed to an intentional design of the tools. A cycle of Trigger → Action → Reward → Investment commonly known as "Hook Method" [18] is a digital strategy based on psychological vulnerabilities which is used to attain human interest and attention to keep users consistently connected to social media applications or any other software designed to maintain a continuous and consistent connection. In a similar vein, the customer smartphone distraction (CSD) [19] research approach points to some directions in leveraging a dimension of digital well-being understanding: environmental stimuli, psychological state, social-cultural influences, and individual characteristics as a combination of elements with behavioral and psychological consequences.

4.1 Digital Detox and Screen Limits as a Solution

If ubiquitous contact with digital technologies is a pervasive cause of stress, it would be obvious to figure out that some period of time free from this contact would be a solution to mitigate the problem. This is the simplest conception of digital detox as a *"period of time during which a person refrains from using their electronic devices, such as smartphones, regarded as an opportunity to reduce stress or focus on social interaction in the physical world"* [20]. In a more sophisticated description, digital detox emphasizes an effort to raise awareness of excessive use and boost self-optimization to reduce stress [9]. This approach advocates an individual balance between exposition and pause, as awareness is the main trigger to detox.

Recent studies bring a deeper discussion and detailed approach for deliberate "disconnection", "detoxing", among other terms related to the interruption of connection sequence to promote well-being. Additional factors need to come to the scene when discussing the type of harm and the "prophylaxis" proposed to avoid ill-being, including user's behavioral factors, the type of usage, the device, and content consumed as examples of variables added to the increasingly complex equation of promoting and maintaining digital well-being [6]. Considering the individual drivers, some useful detox practices proposed by Kärki [16] can be expanded to non-organizational environments as they consider behavioral needs.

4.2 Developers, Designers, and Sponsor's Roles in Digital Well-Being Application Development

So far, major responsibility to avoid digital ill-being rests in the user's ability to recognize connection limitations [21], even if supported by a notification mechanism to promote awareness [18]. However, this approach is based on the assumption that the user is under cognitive and emotional control and able to take decisions over an eventual warning to the harms of excessive exposure or connection. Using the research literature as the primary data source, Roffarello and De Russis [22] synthesize a set of practical challenges and ethical concerns in designing for digital self-control.

Once it is known that addiction and cognitive issues have been studied as a consequence of excessive exposure to digital media, not all responsibility shall be assigned to end-users once they may not have full control of their choices. In fact, persuasive and immersive design techniques are used to guide user's behaviors and leverage engagement [23], which lead us to other actors in this process: the designers, developers, and those who request digital products to capture customer's attention and guide decisions to monetize or get more profitability.

As the digital ecosystem may be designed to promote continuous connection and profitability while supporting actions or choices, a long journey to balance distinct responsibilities and involvement in an increasingly complex environment is in place. While scholars, enterprises, technicians, and customers drive the transformation, governmental entities are involved in discussing the limitations, ethics, and rules with the challenge of keeping the freedom of choice of all the parts involved in the pace that the transformation occurs. In such a dynamic environment, open discussions based on promoting well-being are required by involving all parts of society.

5   Challenges in Finding Primary Building Blocks in a Dynamic Digital Environment: An Initial Ontological Exercise

As previously stated in this paper, well-being is a multidisciplinary subject ranging from biological to technological sciences. As the technological era escalates, the word "digital" is also applied to well-being. However, it is also challenging to drive research with such a mixed range of elements, measurements, and concepts. Moreover, the main issue refers not to the well-being but to its components that are jeopardized as a consequence of digital life.

A considerable portion of publications point out that excessive connection is the main cause of harm [24]. More recent studies report on other factors, while a more robust methodology is also required to aggregate findings and propose evidence-based solutions [9]. Therefore, a common understanding of causes, harms, consequences, and relationships between those elements would help to achieve interoperability and consensus between different disciplines involved in digital well-being research.

As a starting point, the studies on the known disorders would be a reference to baseline upcoming actions. As most disorders are known from psychological and sociological dimensions, it is natural to associate their composition with their "digital version". It is also important to highlight that what is called excessive today may not be considered excessive in the future as users get familiar with new technologies and environments. Thus, as we have discussed, putting together the elements and disciplines that need deeper understanding would guide the investigation on what is being designed as a very complex subject area. The diagram shown in Fig. 2 presents the primary building blocks and components of this proposed research design with distinct levels of detail.

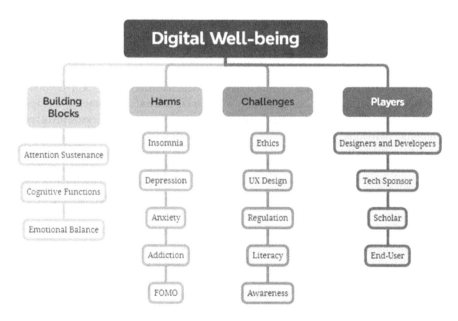

Fig. 2. Proposal of an initial ontology-based representation for digital well-being.

This preliminary ontological exercise represents a call for arms for more reality-oriented scenarios and in-situ interventions where observation practices with different players can play an active role in determining the success of a digital well-being initiative. Further explorations are needed at the conceptual level to mitigate ontology heterogeneity problems and augment their practical usage. The main contribution is an enhanced awareness and understanding around the richness of the interventional value that a persuasive technology can offer in terms of digital well-being, along with the formalization of the challenges that may hinder their successful implementation and adoption. By addressing individual and societal aspects in an integrative manner, this initial ontological inquiry contributes a bottom-up discovery of research gaps and solutions to consolidate the knowledge base in the digital well-being domain from an HCI perspective.

Ranging from philosophy to artificial intelligence (AI) and ethics, human well-being is affected by distinct elements of the hyper-digital lifestyle [25]. Thus, as a starting point for a more robust research, we bring up some important questions towards a common ground in this domain of inquiry:

- What defines digital well-being? What are the main "building blocks"?
- How does research evolve? Keeping previous well-being states when dealing with the digital world? Developing digital products to promote well-being?
- Which are the main digital well-being detractors? Insomnia, anxiety, lack of concentration, depression, FOMO?
- Which elements contribute more and less as digital well-being detractors? User's previous organic issues, user's digital literacy, excessive screen time, attention retention algorithms, inappropriate content consumption, social isolation?

6   Discussion and Future Ontology Mapping Representations

As digital well-being merges human and technological factors, the disciplinary discussion around this emerging phenomenon has become increasingly complex. The volatility of the digital ecosystem reflected in social, commercial, or academic dimensions triggers researchers' attention to deeply understand the components and processes involved in maintaining individual and collective wellness. In the same vein, the multiple disciplines and actors come to the scene to build an instigating and complex framework of behavioral, emotional, political, technological, and commercial elements. Instead of having a single answer to the open questions that have been posed in the literature, this paper proposes an initial discussion on the components and a common understanding of what each component means.

This is not a discussion of what is good or bad, but where and how we are going to establish the baselines of physical, mental, and emotional relations. How free we really are when taking decisions or making choices in a digital environment? How distinct are the effects of digitalization in distinct cultures and what are the actions needed to keep a healthy life in such a complex and fast-changing digital world? These and other questions need to be answered in order to provide future guidance for more effective digital well-being interventions.

References

1. Elhai, J.D., Levine, J.C., Dvorak, R.D., Hall, B.J.: Fear of missing out, need for touch, anxiety and depression are related to problematic smartphone use. Comput. Hum. Behav. **63**, 509–516 (2016)

2. Dhir, A., Yossatorn, Y., Kaur, P., Chen, S.: Online social media fatigue and psychological wellbeing—a study of compulsive use, fear of missing out, fatigue, anxiety and depression. Int. J. Inf. Manag. **40**, 141–152 (2018)
3. Syvertsen, T., Enli, G.: Digital detox: media resistance and the promise of authenticity. Convergence **26**(5–6), 1269–1283 (2020)
4. Mirbabaie, M., Stieglitz, S., Marx, J.: Digital detox. Bus. Inf. Syst. Eng. **64**(2), 239–246 (2022)
5. Büchi, M.: Digital well-being theory and research. New Media Soc. **26**(1), 172–189 (2024)
6. Vanden Abeele, M.M.: Digital wellbeing as a dynamic construct. Commun. Theory **31**(4), 932–955 (2021)
7. Robinson, L., Ragnedda, M., Schulz, J.: Digital inequalities: contextualizing problems and solutions. J. Inf. Commun. Ethics Soc. **18**(3), 323–327 (2020)
8. Giraldo-Luque, S., Afanador, P.N.A., Fernández-Rovira, C.: The struggle for human attention: between the abuse of social media and digital wellbeing. Healthcare **8**(4), 497 (2020)
9. Radtke, T., Apel, T., Schenkel, K., Keller, J., von Lindern, E.: Digital detox: an effective solution in the smartphone era? A systematic literature review. Mob. Media Commun. **10**(2), 190–215 (2022)
10. Eide, A.W., et al.: Human-machine networks: towards a typology and profiling framework. In: Proceedings of the 18th International Conference on Human-Computer Interaction, pp. 11–22 (2016)
11. Johnson, S.S., Tisdale, S., Mechlinski, J., Öste, H.F.: Knowing well, being well: well-being born of understanding. Am. J. Health Promot. **34**(7), 809–820 (2020)
12. Yue, A., Pang, N., Torres, F., Mambra, S.: Developing an indicator framework for digital well-being: perspectives from digital citizenship. NUSCTIC Working Paper Series, no. 1 (2021)
13. Cecchinato, M.E., et al.: Designing for digital wellbeing: a research & practice agenda. In: Extended Abstracts of the 2019 CHI Conference on Human Factors in Computing Systems, pp. 1–8 (2019)
14. Twenge, J.M.: Increases in depression, self-harm, and suicide among U.S. adolescents after 2012 and links to technology use: possible mechanisms. Psychiatric Res. Clin. Pract. **2**(1), 19–25 (2020)
15. Hanin, M.L.: Theorizing digital distraction. Philos. Technol. **34**(2), 395–406 (2021)
16. Kärki, K.: Digital distraction, attention regulation, and inequality. Philos. Technol. **37**(1), 1–21 (2024)
17. Przybylski, A.K., Murayama, K., DeHaan, C.R., Gladwell, V.: Motivational, emotional, and behavioral correlates of fear of missing out. Comput. Hum. Behav. **29**(4), 1841–1848 (2013)
18. Purohit, A.K., Barclay, L., Holzer, A.: Designing for digital detox: making social media less addictive with digital nudges. In: Extended Abstracts of the 2020 CHI Conference on Human Factors in Computing Systems, pp. 1–9 (2020)
19. Taylor, A., Hook, M., Carlson, J., Gudergan, S., Falk, T.: Appetite for distraction? A systematic literature review on customer smartphone distraction. Int. J. Inf. Manag., 102722 (2023)
20. Oxford Dictionaries: Definition of digital detox in English (2019)
21. Docherty, N., Biega, A.J.: (Re)politicizing digital well-being: beyond user engagements. In: Proceedings of the 2022 CHI Conference on Human Factors in Computing Systems, pp. 1–13 (2022)
22. Roffarello, A.M., De Russis, L.: Achieving digital wellbeing through digital self-control tools: a systematic review and meta-analysis. ACM Trans. Comput. Hum. Interact. **30**(4), 1–66 (2023)
23. Al-Mansoori, R.S., Al-Thani, D., Ali, R.: Digital wellbeing: designers' perspectives on where the responsibility lies. In: Proceedings of the 9th International Conference on Behavioural and Social Computing, pp. 1–6 (2022)

24. Baym, N.K., Wagman, K.B., Persaud, C.J.: Mindfully scrolling: rethinking Facebook after time deactivated. Soc. Media Soc. **6**(2), 2056305120919105 (2020)
25. Arora, A., Belk, R.W., Patra, S.K.: Digi & the metaverse. In: Heggde, G.S., Patra, S.K., Panda, R. (eds.) Immersive Technology and Experiences: Implications for Business and Society, Singapore, pp. 45–54. Springer, Singapore (2023). https://doi.org/10.1007/978-981-99-883 4-1_3

Understanding Chinese University Students' Perspectives on and Challenges with the Technology Based on Cognitive Behavioral Therapy for Insomnia: A Qualitative Exploration

Qing Peng$^{(\boxtimes)}$, Siu Shing Man, and Hua Ming Peng

School of Design, South China University of Technology, Guangzhou 510006,
People's Republic of China
pengqing0323@gmail.com

Abstract. While the technology based on Cognitive Behavioral Therapy for insomnia (TCBTI) has been found effective in treating insomnia, its adoption among Chinese university students remains limited. This study explored the perspectives, attitudes, and potential challenges related to TCBTI among Chinese university students. The research involved 30 participants from the South China University of Technology who had experienced or are dealing with insomnia. The majority of participants expressed a willingness to explore therapy-based apps as a means to improve their insomnia condition. However, a notable barrier exists due to a lack of understanding of therapeutic principles, leading to reluctance to execute certain tasks. Therefore, therapy apps must convey relevant principles quickly and straightforwardly, enabling users to comprehend and willingly engage in the therapeutic process. Some participants preferred the app to take effect within the first week, to reduce anxiety and improve sleep efficiency. They emphasized that their motivation to continue using the app might diminish if the effects are not noticeable within a relatively short time. To enhance app adherence, designers should consider addressing potential challenges college students face and aligning app functionalities with user expectations. This involves compiling insights on adherence challenges and incorporating them into the app design to encourage sustained usage among college students.

Keywords: Cognitive Behavioral Therapy · Insomnia · University Students · User Experience

1 Introduction

Insomnia is defined as difficulty falling or staying asleep accompanied by daytime impairments [1]. The prevalence of insomnia disorder in Europe varies, ranging from a minimum of 5.7% in Germany to a maximum of 19% in France [2]. The combined prevalence of insomnia in China was 15.0% [3]. Insomnia prevalence in university students

© The Author(s), under exclusive license to Springer Nature Switzerland AG 2024
V. G. Duffy (Ed.): HCII 2024, LNCS 14710, pp. 163–176, 2024.
https://doi.org/10.1007/978-3-031-61063-9_11

was considerably higher than in the general population, accounting for 18.5% [4]. Insomnia profoundly influences physical and mental health [5]. Individuals with insomnia face an increased risk of developing cardiovascular conditions, including arterial hypertension, myocardial infarction, and chronic heart failure [2]. Moreover, there appears to be a potential connection to the onset of type 2 diabetes [6]. Furthermore, insomnia is intricately linked with mental health disorders, acting as a significant risk factor for the emergence of conditions such as depression, anxiety, and suicidal tendencies [7].

The treatment of insomnia is mainly psychotherapy, medication, and physical therapy. As the most well-known psychotherapy, cognitive behavioral therapy for insomnia (CBT-I) is recommended as the first-line treatment for chronic insomnia in Europe [2], American [8], and China [9]. CBT-I is a structured therapy consisting of several components [10]. The therapy typically includes educational, behavioral, cognitive, and relaxation components [11]. It focuses on adjusting individuals' unhealthy sleep habits and eliminating negative cognitions contributing to insomnia. Treatment progresses using information typically gathered with sleep diaries completed by the patient throughout the course of treatment (typically 4–8 sessions). CBT-I is an effective treatment for insomnia in college students [12]. Figure 1 shows the structure of CBT-I components.

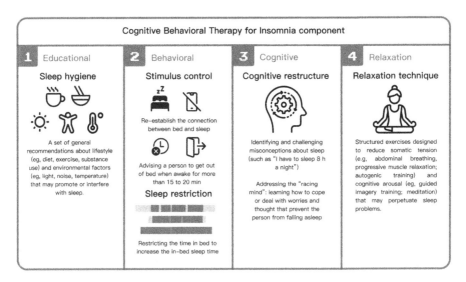

Fig. 1. The structure of CBT-I components

CBT for insomnia is not widely accessible, primarily due to a scarcity of therapists and resources. Over the past fifteen years, technology-based CBT-I (TCBT-I, also called digital CBT-I, dCBT-I) has emerged as a preferred alternative, providing patients with a more flexible and personalized approach to managing insomnia. These technologies, including online platforms and mobile applications, are accessible through rich media interactions and personalized (algorithm-based) information delivery [13]. Different versions of digital CBT-I exist, such as supportive dCBT, therapist-guided dCBT, and fully automated digital CBT-I [14].

Most of the scientific evidence and emphasis is given to clinical effectiveness [15]; however, the problem of adherence continues to exist for the present dCBT-I platforms. Adherence is persistence in the practice and maintenance of desired health behaviors and results from the patient's active participation in an agreement with treatment recommendations [16].

University students' acceptance of these technologies and concerns regarding their adherence to practical usage still pose uncertainties. Qualitative research is deemed necessary to gain a more comprehensive understanding of students' perspectives on these technologies and potential issues related to adherence. By delving into individual experiences, we can better guide the design and implementation of these technologies, enhancing their effectiveness among university students with insomnia and promoting broader adoption.

2 Method

Qualitative methods are valuable for investigating experiences related to insomnia and adherence to CBT-I [17, 18]. Consistent with prior research, this study utilized in-depth semi-structured interviews to acknowledge the unique experiences of individuals with insomnia and their attitudes toward technology.

2.1 Participants

Participants were recruited at the South China University of Technology through a combination of random sampling and snowball sampling. The inclusion criteria required participants to have experienced or been dealing with insomnia. Participants received a small incentive of 5 RMB or an equivalent token of appreciation for participating in the study. Before the interviews, informed consent was obtained from each participant.

2.2 Semi-structured Interviews

The semi-structured interviews were conducted face-to-face by the researcher Qing Peng. Before the interviews, an interview guide was drafted to provide a framework for the discussions. During the interviews, key research topics were explored according to the interview guide, and subtle modifications were made based on new questions raised by participants. The a priori questions addressed in the interview guide are presented in Fig. 2. Each interview was digitally recorded using an Aigo digital voice recorder (model: R3312C) and transcribed verbatim for analysis using the Sonicloud speech-to-text transcription system. Participants were also asked to complete the Insomnia Severity Index (ISI) [19].

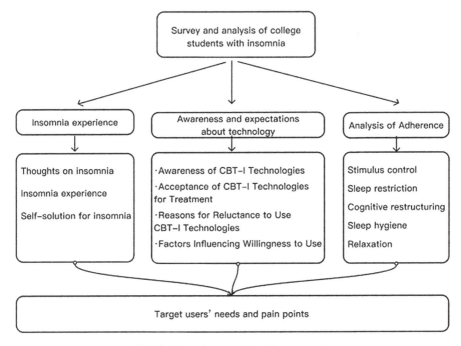

Fig. 2. Interview questions Framenwork

3 Result

Between October 11, 2023, and November 30, 2023, a total of 30 semi-structured interviews were conducted, all of which were face-to-face. The duration of the interviews ranged from 13 to 36 min. Every participant admitted to experiencing insomnia. According to the Insomnia Severity Index (ISI) results, 33.3% of participants reported no current symptoms of insomnia, 53.3% were in a subclinical insomnia state, and 13.3% were classified as having moderate symptoms of clinical insomnia. 27% of the participants were undergraduates, while 73% were master's degree students. A summary of participant characteristics is presented in Table 1.

Table 1. Summary of Participants' Characteristics

Variable	n	%
Gender		
Male	16	53
Female	14	47

(continued)

Table 1. (*continued*)

Variable	n	%
Age (in years)		
Mean	23.5	
SD	2.5	
Range	19–27	
ISI score		
0–7	10	33.3
8–14	16	53.3
15–21	4	13.3
Mean	9.3	
SD	4.3	
Range	2–18	

Note. ISI = Insomnia Severity Index.

3.1 Insomnia Experience

Thoughts on Insomnia. 26% of the participants were deeply concerned about their insomnia and were eager to improve their sleep condition. This could be attributed to an excessive emphasis on sleep, which negatively impacted their sleep quality. The remaining participants maintained a relatively positive attitude toward insomnia. Despite impacting their daily lives and causing some concerns, it is within a tolerable range.

Self-help Solution for Insomnia. Many participants took at least an hour or more to fall asleep, and some experienced insomnia for several years or even close to a decade. Upon entering university, the flexible schedule of college life seems to have alleviated insomnia for some students. Participants typically did not seek hospital assistance for insomnia and instead relied on self-regulation methods. These methods can be categorized as adjusting routines, engaging in physical activities, and using external aids.

3.2 Awareness and Expectations About the Technology

Awareness of the Technology. When presented with the term "Cognitive Behavioral Therapy for Insomnia (CBT-I)," only 13% of participants indicated that they had heard of it, and their understanding of the specifics was limited. Some participants found information about CBT-I while searching for sleep solutions but chose not to explore it further because they thought it was too complex. Some others had some familiarity with cognitive behavioral therapy. None of the participants had used a CBT-I app. This could be attributed to the tendency of college students to rarely seek professional help for sleep issues. Furthermore, even if sleep-related apps drawed inspiration from therapeutic approaches, they may not necessarily include the name of the therapy. Despite having limited awareness of comprehensive CBT-I, many participants unintentionally applied certain aspects of the therapy to alleviate their insomnia. During discussions about their previous efforts to address insomnia, all participants actively sought information related to sleep, which aligns with the goals of sleep hygiene education. A minority of people participated in relaxation therapy, using techniques such as meditation, breathing exercises, and muscle relaxation. Some participants utilized cognitive therapy to identify and correct specific cognitive patterns that were affecting their sleep.

Acceptance of CBT-I Technologies for Treatment. The majority of participants were willing to try therapy-based apps, hoping to improve their insomnia condition. They had a strong desire to use these apps, motivated by a need to alleviate the discomfort of insomnia and a willingness to explore different solutions. However, participants anticipated that the therapy will yield results within a timeframe of one week to one month.

Reasons for Reluctance to use CBT-I Technologies. Only 13% of individuals expressed reluctance to use such technology. The reasons for this reluctance can be categorized into two types. One group was skeptical about the therapy's effectiveness and its ability to cure their insomnia. The opposing group believed that using such technology is unnecessary. They argued that individuals should refrain from using phones during sleep and instead rely on their willpower after understanding the principles of the therapy.

Factors Influencing Willingness. For students entering college, university credits and tangible financial rewards were highly valued. Participants indicated a strong willingness to use such apps if they offer credit or monetary incentives, indicating that the integration of these features may need to be coordinated with the university. Some participants desired a more engaging user experience through design, especially by incorporating motivational mechanisms that encourage persistent app usage. Others hoped for a more engaging user experience and suggested incorporating fun and simple quizzes to convey knowledge about sleep hygiene.

Participants were also looking forward to features such as real-time reminders to reduce the cognitive load on users and personalized reminders based on device motion detection for a more individualized and intelligent approach. Participants expected a user-friendly experience and visually appealing design, believing that simple operation, smoother interaction, and aesthetically pleasing design would increase their willingness to use the app. Indeed, the time it takes for the app to demonstrate effectiveness is a crucial factor that influences user engagement. Some participants preferred the app to take effect within the first week, to reduce anxiety and improve sleep efficiency. They emphasized that their motivation to continue using the app might diminish if the effects are not noticeable within a relatively short time.

On the other hand, some participants were willing to wait up to a month for the app to demonstrate its effectiveness. They recognized the importance of personal dedication and anticipated that the app would help establish consistent sleep patterns, enhance mental well-being, and offer intuitive data to monitor therapeutic progress. Given their prolonged struggle with insomnia, they were willing to be patient if the app proves to be effective. They hoped for genuine assistance in addressing their sleep issues.

3.3 Analysis of Adherence

Stimulus Control. Stimulus Control [8] aims to eliminate the association between the bed/bedroom and wakefulness, promoting the reassociation of the bed/bedroom with sleep. Simultaneously, it involves establishing a consistent wake-up time.The principles of stimulus control are as follows: (a) Only go to bed when feeling sleepy. (b) Get out of bed if unable to fall asleep. (c) Use the bed/bedroom only for sleep and sexual activities, avoiding activities like using the phone or contemplating issues in bed. (d) Wake up at the same time every morning. (e) Avoid daytime napping.

Only Go to Bed When Feeling Sleepy. Some participants expressed dissenting views regarding these principles. Some people believed that inducing a sense of sleepiness in bed is essential, while others advocated that going to bed early is healthier and more appropriate. This study recognized that the belief in favor of an early bedtime is deeply ingrained in the minds of most participants. The strong desire for an early bedtime contributes to the difficulty that some participants experience in accepting insomnia.

Get Out of Bed if Unable to Fall Asleep. Stimulus control therapy suggests that individuals with insomnia should leave the bed and room if they have not fallen asleep within 15–20 min and return only when they feel sleepy again. Some participants found this suggestion difficult to follow. Some participants were not motivated to get out of bed after 20 min because they believed they would fall asleep if given more time or that the 20-min limit was too short. This resulted in a lower motivation to follow this advice. Some participants found it challenging to implement this recommendation, particularly in cold weather or when the bed is exceptionally comfortable in terms of capability. Some participants felt uncertain about what to do after getting out of bed. However, most participants considered this practice to be effective and not too difficult to implement.

Use the Bed/Bedroom Only for Sleep and Sexual Activities, Avoiding Activities Like Using the Phone or Contemplating Issues in Bed. Restricting the bed solely for sleep and avoiding activities such as using phones or contemplating issues is challenging for most individuals. Some people struggle due to a lack of motivation, while others find it difficult due to their capabilities. Some participants were motivated by a desire to use their phones in bed, and they lacked the motivation to break this habit. Regarding capability, some participants had a low motivation to refrain from using their phones in bed but lacked the self-discipline to follow through. Limited space in dormitory environments could be another factor, leaving participants with no alternative furniture for relaxation. Contemplating issues in bed is common because thinking is an effortless activity, making it easy for individuals to engage in such behavior while in bed.

Get Up at the Same Time Every Morning. For half of the participants, getting up simultaneously every morning was challenging, but others felt it was not difficult if necessary. This suggested that these participants had stronger motivation and capability to accomplish this task when it is necessary to address their sleep issues.

Avoid Daytime Napping. Avoiding daytime napping did not pose significant difficulties for most participants. This may be attributed to waking up late, or not having a fixed habit of taking naps during the day. Executing this task for a short duration did not seem challenging for them.

Sleep Restriction Therapy. Sleep Restriction Therapy [20]: This method enhances sleep drive and consolidates sleep by initially restricting time in bed to match the patient's estimated sleep duration (typically based on daily sleep diaries). The time in bed is initially limited to the average sleep duration, and it is subsequently adjusted based on sleep efficiency thresholds until a sufficient sleep duration and overall sleep satisfaction are achieved. Since many patients with insomnia have difficulty falling asleep due to excessive anxiety, implementing sleep restriction therapy may initially worsen insomnia symptoms. During the treatment, patients are continually asked to adjust the length of time spent in bed. By reducing time in bed, milder sleep deprivation is induced, leading to improved sleep efficiency. The advantage of this therapy is its simplicity, but long-term patient compliance can be challenging, potentially impacting the effectiveness of Cognitive Behavioral Therapy for Insomnia (CBT-I) [21].

Key Implementation Points: Firstly, refer to the patient's sleep diary for two weeks or more, calculate the average total sleep time per day, and use it as the adjusted time allowed in bed. Secondly, calculate sleep efficiency, and if sleep efficiency is ≥90%, increase time in bed by 15–20 min. If efficiency is ≤80%, reduce time in bed by 15–20 min. If sleep efficiency falls between these two ranges, no change is needed.

Concerns Were Raised About the Accuracy of Data Collected by Smart Wristbands. In the context of this study, where a CBT-I application utilized smart wristbands to record sleep duration and employs technology to calculate sleep efficiency, some participants expressed skepticism regarding the precision of the wristband measurements and doubted its ability to provide accurate calculations. However, the majority of participants were accustomed to using smart wristbands for tracking, and they expressed confidence in this method, anticipating advancements and improvements in the future.

Coordinating and Negotiating Bedtime and Wake-Up Time with Users. After calculating the user's average sleep duration based on a two-week sleep diary, the user need to reduce time in bed to match this average sleep duration. This setting requires users to choose a suitable bedtime and wake-up time and adhere to these designated times. Achieving this may involve users delaying their current bedtime or waking up earlier.

In the event of delaying bedtime, some participants expressed disagreement. Some believed in cultivating a sense of sleepiness, while others considered going to bed early as a healthier and correct practice. Inspired by these viewpoints, this study suggested that when users use the therapy app, it is important to quickly and simply make users understand and accept the relevant principles to encourage their willingness to execute the therapy.

Some participants expressed difficulty based on their experiences when waking up at the set time. People living with Insomnia may have difficulty waking up promptly due to their low mental alertness at that time. When there are no essential tasks during the day, it became challenging for them to wake up promptly and stay alert.

Other Concerns. Some participants were concerned that implementing sleep restriction may result in a poor mental state the next day, affecting work efficiency, and thus, they were unwilling to try this therapy.

Cognitive Therapy. Cognitive Therapy [22] aims to change erroneous beliefs and attitudes about sleep. For example, individuals with insomnia often exhibit significant concerns about bedtime and performance anxiety when attempting to control the process of falling asleep. Some may even harbor catastrophic thoughts about the potential consequences of insomnia, all of which can exacerbate their emotional reactions to poor sleep. The goal of cognitive therapy is to break the vicious cycle of insomnia, emotional distress, cognitive dysfunction, and further sleep disturbances. Cognitive therapy involves identifying specific dysfunctional sleep cognitions in patients, questioning their effectiveness, and replacing them with more adaptive attitudes using restructuring techniques (such as reattribution training), de-dramatization, hypothesis testing, reevaluation, and attention redirection.

Examples of target beliefs include:

(a) Unrealistic sleep expectations (e.g., "I must sleep 8 h every night");
(b) Misunderstandings about the causes of insomnia (e.g., "My insomnia is entirely due to a chemical imbalance");
(c) Magnifying the consequences (e.g., "After a night of poor sleep, I can't accomplish anything");
(d) Performance anxiety resulting from excessive attempts to control the sleep process.

- **Some cognitions that may impact sleep were collected:**

  1. Feeling lonely and hopeless when it is very late and not asleep yet, makes me feel that there is no hope for tomorrow, and I perceive myself as worthless.
  2. Worrying about not having energy and experiencing poor mood tomorrow, anticipating a decline in physical well-being.
  3. Feeling that time spent awake during the night is wasted.
  4. Despite making efforts to sleep, avoiding phone use, lying with eyes closed, and even attempting meditation, I still cannot fall asleep.
  5. I had a period where I was afraid to sleep every night. As soon as I laid down, I knew I would not fall asleep for one or two hours, and I felt fearful.
  6. I hope I can relax and fall asleep when I should, for example, at 11:00, or at least I must be asleep by 2:00.
  7. Sleeping late affects my state the next day, especially impacting my studies. I have a lot of academic pressure, and only in college did it improve slightly. I greatly value my studies and feel that sleeping late affects my rest.
  8. I feel that sleep should involve falling asleep, such as during a nap. If I do not fall asleep, I feel like I have not restored my energy.
  9. When I am sleeping, I suddenly realize I have not fallen asleep. I check my phone, and it is 3:00. Then I feel very annoyed, thinking I will probably have a headache or something similar tomorrow. Definitely not good for my health.

Participants Found It Challenging to Change Their Thoughts or Attitudes Through Cognitive Therapy. Some participants were pessimistic about changing their thoughts, believing it is impossible. Others perceived difficulty in the event of changing thoughts. They may not be aware of the specific cognitions affecting sleep or struggle to recall their thoughts upon waking. Additionally, they expressed uncertainty about how to reconstruct accurate cognitions.

Participants Had Some Suggestions for This Part of the APP Function

1. Participants suggested having recording and reminder features. When experiencing negative thoughts during sleep, symbols on the smart bracelet or emotional tests could be used to record the thoughts. Upon waking up, looking at the symbols helps recall the emotions, and thoughts can be documented.
2. Participants proposed providing concrete cues during the thought recording process, such as suggesting common anxiety-inducing thoughts related to unhealthy sleep patterns or concerns about the next day's mental and physical state.
3. During sleep, participants recommended using the smart bracelet to detect patient anxiety, allowing subjective and objective measurements. Users could subjectively rate their anxiety levels, helping them record insomnia thoughts the next day. Different anxiety levels may correspond to different thoughts.
4. Participants believed insomnia may not only stem from sleep beliefs but also other anxieties like academic stress. They hoped to personalize the discovery of each person's stressors and receive suggestions, such as planning daily tasks, to alleviate insomnia when anxiety reduces.
5. One participant, unfamiliar with cognitive therapy but inadvertently using it, found it crucial. Emphasizing a user-friendly app experience, he valued aesthetics and accurate content, emphasizing the importance of designing the interface appropriately.
6. Another participant using cognitive therapy highlighted the importance of repeatedly reviewing new viewpoints to replace old ones, suggesting that the app could focus on this aspect in its design.

Relaxation Training. Relaxation Training [22]: Insomniacs typically exhibit high levels of arousal (physiological and cognitive) during both nighttime and daytime. Relaxation methods are employed to deactivate arousal systems to stop physiological or cognitive arousal. Most of these relaxation techniques require regular practice over several weeks, often with professional guidance in the initial stages of training.

- Aimed at reducing physiological arousal (e.g., muscle tension):

  1. Progressive Muscle Relaxation (a method involving the tension and relaxation of different muscle groups throughout the body).
  2. Biofeedback [23] (a self-regulation technique, guided by trained practitioners, that translates physiological signals into meaningful visual and auditory cues through specialized equipment, training individuals to control their physiological functions such as breathing, heart rate, brainwaves, etc.).

Reducing pre-sleep cognitive arousal (e.g., intrusive thoughts, racing thoughts):
Attention-focused programs, such as Imagery Training (visual techniques that concentrate attention on pleasant or neutral images).
Thought Stopping (blocking and replacing distressing thoughts).

Other relaxation training: Additional relaxation therapies, including diaphragmatic breathing, meditation, and hypnosis.

For relaxation training, some participants had previously used related techniques. Some found them highly effective, providing immediate results, while others felt ineffective, causing distraction and making it difficult to complete.

Sleep Hygiene Education. Sleep hygiene education [22]: General education that provides users with knowledge about sleep (e.g., sleep cycles), habits that may be detrimental or beneficial to sleep health (e.g., diet, exercise, substance use), and environmental factors (e.g., light, noise, temperature, and mattress). While these factors are rarely severe enough to be the primary cause of chronic insomnia, they may complicate existing sleep problems and hinder treatment progress [24]. Although individuals with poor sleep quality are often more knowledgeable about sleep hygiene, they also tend to engage in more unhealthy behaviors than those with good sleep quality.

1. Avoid consuming caffeine and nicotine 4–6 h before bedtime.
2. Avoid using alcohol as a sleep aid.
3. Engage in regular physical exercise daily, but avoid vigorous exercise within 3 h of bedtime.
4. Avoid consuming heavy or hard-to-digest foods within 2 h of bedtime.
5. Control water intake after dinner to reduce the frequency of nighttime urination and improve sleep quality.
6. Use earplugs, blackout curtains, or adjust heating/cooling systems to minimize noise, light, and excessive temperature during sleep.
7. Avoid stimulating or overly active environments before bedtime.
8. Other recommendations often overlap with stimulus control and sleep restriction, including minimizing daytime naps, restricting bed activities to sleep only, engaging in activities or resting in a chair rather than bed, and establishing a pre-sleep routine.

Regarding sleep hygiene education, many participants had actively sought information on the topic to varying extents. Some mentioned that the advice provided may not necessarily impact their sleep due to individual differences. Some participants indicated that although they know about sleep hygiene, it didn't always translate into practical actions. Some suggested the introduction of reminder features to avoid the need to memorize the information. However, opinions diverged, with some expressing concerns about the effectiveness of phone reminders and suggesting integration with smart devices for more intelligent and reliable reminders. Additionally, some participants wished for a more engaging and attractive presentation of the information.

4   Discussion

Regarding participants' experiences and thoughts on insomnia, the majority demonstrated a relatively high level of acceptance towards insomnia. Despite the impact insomnia has on their lives, most participants could still accept it, indicating a generally healthy belief system and cognitive understanding of insomnia. Only a small number of participants felt anxious about insomnia and its consequences, and it was possible that their cognitions exacerbated the severity of insomnia.

Almost all participants did not seek help from hospitals for their insomnia but instead engaged in self-regulation, including activities such as exercise, adjusting their daily routines, using melatonin, and practicing relaxation techniques and meditation.

Collecting participants' understanding and expectations of CBT-I showed that few participants were aware of the comprehensive CBT-I therapy, and none had used related apps. The low awareness of CBT-I might be attributed to insomnia participants not seeking hospital help and thus not being informed through official channels. Additionally, limited information about this therapy on the internet and insufficient popularity of related apps could contribute to this lack of awareness. Furthermore, the complex nomenclature of this Western therapy might hinder participants' understanding without a desire for in-depth exploration.

Most participants expressed willingness to try CBT-I apps with the hope of improving their insomnia condition. The motivation to use such apps was strong, driven by a desire to alleviate the suffering caused by insomnia and a willingness to explore solutions. However, they expected the apps to show effectiveness within a relatively short timeframe, ranging from one week to one month.

A small percentage of participants were unwilling to use such technologies either due to skepticism about the efficacy of this therapy or strong confidence in their willpower, leaning towards self-implementation.

Regarding expectations for app design, participants primarily emphasized motivational incentives (monetary rewards, academic credits, app-specific currency), gamified elements for engagement, personalized reminders for important events, visually appealing aesthetics, and comfortable user interaction experience.

Based on the investigation into the challenges of compliance with the five therapies around CBT-I, we have gathered reasons why participants might abandon the use of the app. In the Stimulus Control module, participants found it challenging to adhere to principles such as only going to bed when sleepy, getting out of bed if unable to sleep, refraining from using the phone or contemplating issues in bed, and waking up at the same time every morning. The key insight is that when designing corresponding therapy features, the app should help users understand and acknowledge the related principles so that users can implement them actively. If users have the motivation but cannot accomplish a task, the app can adopt persuasive mechanisms to assist users in reducing the difficulty of completing the task, ensuring user success and long-term implementation of a particular function.

For the Sleep Restriction module, participants, especially college students, found it challenging to maintain compliance with traditional therapy, which requires manually filling out sleep diaries. Therefore, the app should preferably use wearable devices to record relevant behaviors and calculate sleep efficiency.

Regarding the Cognitive Restructuring module, simplicity, ease of operation, minimal thinking, and abundant prompts should be the principles followed when designing this functionality. Users should not be burdened with excessive typing tasks, and a choice of tasks filled with prompts could potentially increase user compliance. It may be beneficial to assess users' sleep beliefs; if there are no detrimental sleep-related cognitions, users can reduce the associated operational content.

Relaxation Training is a feature experienced by many users, and there are some details of differentiation between relaxing the body and mind. Since most users do not have prior experience in this area, the design can offer users a choice between these two classifications.

Sleep Hygiene Education is the most familiar knowledge for most insomnia participants. Many participants actively sought a lot of information and may feel that this module is unnecessary. However, some participants suggested the need for reminders. When designing this module, allowing users to choose events that need reminders could personalize the prompts for users.

In summary, participants may be unwilling to execute certain tasks due to a lack of understanding of the therapeutic intent. Therefore, when users use therapy apps, it is crucial to quickly and simply make them understand and acknowledge the relevant principles to willingly execute the therapy. When designing app features, external factors influencing users should also be considered to provide recommendations. For instance, users were suggested to replace lying on the bed with a comfortable chair if they prefer to relax leisurely. If schools can provide more comfortable accommodation environments, it may be more convenient for some insomnia patients who like to lie on the bed when not sleepy. Additionally, addressing users' potential lack of trust in smart device accuracy requires a reasonable implementation plan and a credible explanation of the functionality.

References

1. Diagnostic and Statistical Manual of Mental Disorders: DSM-5^{TM}, 5th edn., pp. xliv, 947. American Psychiatric Publishing, Inc., Arlington (2013). https://doi.org/10.1176/appi.books.9780890425596
2. Riemann, D., et al.: European guideline for the diagnosis and treatment of insomnia. J. Sleep Res. **26**(6), 675–700 (2017). https://doi.org/10.1111/jsr.12594
3. Cao, X.-L., et al.: The prevalence of insomnia in the general population in China: a meta-analysis. PLoS ONE **12**(2), e0170772 (2017). https://doi.org/10.1371/journal.pone.0170772
4. Jiang, X.-l., et al.: A systematic review of studies on the prevalence of insomnia in university students. Public Health **129**(12), 1579–1584 (2015). https://doi.org/10.1016/j.puhe.2015.07.030
5. Fernandez-Mendoza, J., Vgontzas, A.N.: Insomnia and its impact on physical and mental health. Curr. Psychiatry Rep. **15**(12), 418 (2013). https://doi.org/10.1007/s11920-013-0418-8
6. Anothaisintawee, T., Reutrakul, S., Van Cauter, E., Thakkinstian, A.: Sleep disturbances compared to traditional risk factors for diabetes development: systematic review and meta-analysis. Sleep Med. Rev. **30**, 11–24 (2016). https://doi.org/10.1016/j.smrv.2015.10.002
7. Baglioni, C., et al.: Insomnia as a predictor of depression: a meta-analytic evaluation of longitudinal epidemiological studies. J. Affect. Disord. **135**(1), 10–19 (2011). https://doi.org/10.1016/j.jad.2011.01.011
8. Edinger, J.D., et al.: Behavioral and psychological treatments for chronic insomnia disorder in adults: an American Academy of Sleep Medicine clinical practice guideline. J. Clin. Sleep Med. JCSM Off. Publ. Am. Acad. Sleep Med. **17**(2), 255–262 (2021). https://doi.org/10.5664/jcsm.8986
9. Guidelines for the diagnosis and treatment of insomnia in China. Natl. Med. J. China **97**(24), Article no. 24 (2017). https://doi.org/10.3760/cma.j.issn.0376-2491.2017.24.002

10. Edinger, J.D., Carney, C.E.: Overcoming Insomnia: A Cognitive-Behavioral Therapy Approach, Therapist Guide. Oxford University Press, Oxford (2014) https://doi.org/10.1093/med:psych/9780199339389.001.0001

11. Luik, A.I., Van Der Zweerde, T., Van Straten, A., Lancee, J.: Digital delivery of cognitive behavioral therapy for insomnia. Curr. Psychiatry Rep. **21**(7), 50 (2019). https://doi.org/10.1007/s11920-019-1041-0

12. Taylor, D.J., et al.: A pilot randomized controlled trial of the effects of cognitive-behavioral therapy for insomnia on sleep and daytime functioning in college students. Behav. Ther. **45**(3), 376–389 (2014). https://doi.org/10.1016/j.beth.2013.12.010

13. Espie, C.A., Hames, P., McKinstry, B.: Use of the internet and mobile media for delivery of cognitive behavioral insomnia therapy. Sleep Med. Clin. **8**(3), 407–419 (2013). https://doi.org/10.1016/j.jsmc.2013.06.001

14. Luik, A.I., Kyle, S.D., Espie, C.A.: Digital cognitive behavioral therapy (dCBT) for insomnia: a state-of-the-science review. Curr. Sleep Med. Rep. **3**(2), 48–56 (2017). https://doi.org/10.1007/s40675-017-0065-4

15. Ritterband, L.M., et al.: Efficacy of an internet-based behavioral intervention for adults with insomnia. Arch. Gen. Psychiatry **66**(7), 692 (2009). https://doi.org/10.1001/archgenpsychiatry.2009.66

16. Matthews, E.E., Arnedt, J.T., McCarthy, M.S., Cuddihy, L.J., Aloia, M.S.: Adherence to cognitive behavioral therapy for insomnia: a systematic review. Sleep Med. Rev. **17**(6), 453–464 (2013). https://doi.org/10.1016/j.smrv.2013.01.001

17. Cheung, J.M.Y., Bartlett, D.J., Armour, C.L., Glozier, N., Saini, B.: Insomnia patients' help-seeking experiences. Behav. Sleep Med. **12**(2), 106–122 (2014). https://doi.org/10.1080/15402002.2013.764529

18. Dyrberg, H., Juel, A., Kragh, M.: Experience of treatment and adherence to cognitive behavioral therapy for insomnia for patients with depression: an interview study. Behav. Sleep Med. **19**(4), 481–491 (2021). https://doi.org/10.1080/15402002.2020.1788033

19. Morin, C.M., Belleville, G., Bélanger, L., Ivers, H.: The insomnia severity index: psychometric indicators to detect insomnia cases and evaluate treatment response. Sleep **34**(5), 601–608 (2011). https://doi.org/10.1093/sleep/34.5.601

20. Spielman, A.J., Saskin, P., Thorpy, M.J.: Treatment of chronic insomnia by restriction of time in bed. Sleep **10**(1), 45–56 (1987). https://doi.org/10.1093/sleep/10.1.45

21. Ren, X., Wang, J., Guo, J., Chen, Y.: Factors influencing cognitive behavioral therapy and sleep belief correction. Chin. J. Health Psychol. **30**(4), 491–498 (2022). https://doi.org/10.13342/j.cnki.cjhp.2022.04.003

22. Morin, C.M., Hauri, P.J., Espie, C.A., Spielman, A.J., Buysse, D.J., Bootzin, R.R.: Nonpharmacologic treatment of chronic insomnia. Sleep **22**(8), 1134–1156 (1999). https://doi.org/10.1093/sleep/22.8.1134

23. Frank, D.L., Khorshid, L., Kiffer, J.F., Moravec, C.S., McKee, M.G.: Biofeedback in medicine: who, when, why and how? Ment. Health Fam. Med. **7**(2), 85–91 (2010)

24. Reynolds, C.F., Kupfer, D.J., Buysse, D.J., Coble, P.A., Yeager, A.: Subtyping DSM-III-R primary insomnia: a literature review by the DSM-IV work group on sleep disorders. Am. J. Psychiatry **148**(4), 432–438 (1991). https://doi.org/10.1176/ajp.148.4.432

Chatbot-Based Mood and Activity Journaling for Resource-Oriented CBT Support of Students

Julian Striegl[(✉)], Farah Fekih, Gerhard Weber, and Claudia Loitsch

ScaDS.AI Dresden/Leipzig Center for Scalable Data Analytics
and Artificial Intelligence, Dresden, Germany
{julian.striegl,gerhard.weber,claudia.loitsch}@tu-dresden.de,
farah.fekih@mailbox.tu-dresden.de

Abstract. A high prevalence of mental health disorders among students combined with a lack of sufficient psychological counseling and treatment options makes new approaches to mental health support necessary. One possibility to strengthen the resilience and mental well-being of students in a scalable, low-threshold approach is the use of chatbots. While numerous work exists on chatbot-based cognitive behavioral therapy (CBT), the acceptance and usability of a resource-oriented approach to chatbot-based CBT has thus far not been investigated. Moreover, existing chatbot-based systems use a categorical model for the tracking of emotional states, thereby limiting the complexity of tracked emotions. This paper presents a chatbot-based approach for the tracking of dimensional emotional states and activities in the scope of resource-oriented CBT support for students. The developed concept and system are presented and investigated in a single-arm user study focusing on the usability and acceptance of the system with the primary target group (N=9). Results indicate excellent usability and good acceptance with some room for improvement for future iterations of the system.

Keywords: Conversational Agents · Chatbots · Cognitive Behavioral Therapy · Resource-oriented Psychotherapy · Salutogenesis

1 Introduction

In recent years, students' mental health issues have drawn substantial attention on a global scale as nearly 20% of students are suffering from mental disorders such as anxiety and depression [16,28]. Despite this high prevalence, there is a tendency for the younger generation to exhibit reluctance in seeking mental health support [5]. As one consequence of this predicament, along with the connected treatment gap in the mental health sector [24], research on the use of chatbots in mental health has gained popularity. While first studies yielded promising results in terms of acceptance and efficacy [17], further research in

V. G. Duffy (Ed.): HCII 2024, LNCS 14710, pp. 177–188, 2024.
https://doi.org/10.1007/978-3-031-61063-9_12

the field is needed to draw more concise conclusions [30]. Moreover, so far developed systems focus mostly on providing exercises and content based on classical cognitive behavioral therapy (CBT) [1]. Systems incorporating approaches from resource-oriented psychotherapy (ROT) are still lacking.

ROT follows the salutogenesis approach to healthcare, focusing on a person's resources and capacity to create health rather than taking the pathogenic approach of focusing on health risks and diseases [21]. According to Priebe et al. [31], highlighting positive personal and social experiences of patients may lead to a beneficial advancement in their mental state. Lately, resource-oriented approaches have moreover been incorporated into CBT-based treatments. CBT is based on the idea that thoughts, feelings, and behaviors are interconnected and that altering any of these components can result in a positive impact on the others [6]. There is strong evidence for the effectiveness of CBT for a variety of mental health conditions such as anxiety and affective disorders [14,27]. Furthermore, some studies imply that internet-based CBT in primary care may be more efficacious than face-to-face therapy under certain conditions [18]. To focus more on the patient's mental well-being during treatment, a combination of both ROT and CBT was introduced by Willutzki et al. [35]. They showed that the combination of resource-oriented approaches and CBT can have a beneficial long-term effect on the treatment of social anxiety. Furthermore, they showed that life satisfaction and attachment to therapy increased within patients following resource-oriented CBT programs in comparison to those following only a cognitive therapy (CT) program [34].

A method used in resource-oriented CBT is mood journaling and activity tracking, as keeping up a mood journal, especially in stressful or traumatic situations, can be a beneficial tool for recovery and lead to a better mental health state [31]. As described by Susan Brokin [7], mood journaling can help patients accept, tolerate and manage their unpleasant emotions, and journaling and tracking of activities can be seen as a central component of an overall treatment plan. Furthermore, the identification and appraisal of personal resources by analyzing the effect certain activities have on one's mood is a central part of resource-oriented therapy [34,35].

In the context of chatbot-based therapy, research has shown that journaling through chatbots is effective and can contain more honest self-disclosures compared to human face-to-face interaction [2], probably due to the fear of criticism or rejection when interacting with other humans [2]. Related studies [22] have, moreover, shown that it is possible to extract the emotional and mental health state from one's journaling behavior with a chatbot. However, interpreting, and accurately determining a patient's emotions based on their utterances can be a challenging task for both humans and chatbots, as the expression of emotions can vary from person to person [12]. Hence, existing chatbot-based CBT approaches focus exclusively on the tracking of emotional states using categorical emotional models, thereby limiting the trackable emotional states to predefined emotional categories [15].

To address this gap, this paper presents the concept and implementation of a web application for chatbot-based resource-oriented CBT support through journaling-based tracking of daily activities and connected changes in emotional states with students as the main target group. The recognition of emotional states is done by applying the circumplex model by Russell [33] as a dimensional emotional model. Therefore, emotional states in the valence-arousal spectrum are mapped to the utterances that users disclose to the chatbot while chatting about their current mood and their daily activities. The acceptance and usability of the developed system are investigated in a single-arm pilot study with 9 participants.

In Sect. 2 related work is presented and analyzed. Section 3 introduces the concept of chatbot-based resource-oriented CBT support and briefly displays the implemented system components and user interface. In Sect. 4 the study design and results of a conducted user study are presented and consequently discussed in Sect. 5. Section 6 draws a concise conclusion and proposes future work.

2   Related Work

While research on resource-oriented chatbot-based therapy approaches is still lacking, some promising systems focusing on chatbot-based CBT have been introduced in recent years.

The chatbot system *Woebot*[1] is a digital mental health application that primarily aims to provide content and techniques based on CBT to users with depression and anxiety disorders. Users have the opportunity to track their emotions using the chatbot by selecting predefined emotional states and by categorizing their moods through questions and answers. The tracking of emotional states uses a categorical emotional model without transforming the presented emotional categories to valence and arousal scores, thereby limiting the complexity of collected emotions [15]. The acceptance and efficacy of Woebot were investigated by Frizpatrick et al. [13] with 70 participants over a two-week period. Their results suggested a good acceptance of the system. Furthermore, participants showed a significant decrease in symptoms of depression and anxiety. The acceptance of the mood journaling functionality in the application has thus far not been looked at. Moreover, the accuracy of the tracking of emotional states and ethical implications of anthropomorphism effects should be further investigated [15]. While Woebot offers the possibility to reflect on current activities, tracking of daily activities in the sense of chatbot-based journaling is not supported thus far.

The chatbot-based application *Youper*[2] follows a similar approach by mainly targeting people with depression and anxiety and by providing exercises and content based on CBT via a conversational agent. In the app, users can use a daily check-in functionality to track their moods. The mood tracking is limited to basic emotional states. While the app includes a journaling function, the isolated tracking of activities in relation to emotional states is not supported.

---

[1] Woebot Inc., https://woebothealth.com/, accessed 17.05.2023.
[2] Youper, https://www.youper.ai/, accessed 17.05.2023.

The acceptance and efficacy of the system for depression and anxiety have been investigated in a longitudinal observational study with active customers of the platform by Mehta et al. [29]. Results indicate a good acceptance and a decrease in depression and anxiety symptoms after two weeks of usage. The acceptance was, however, measured through a 5-star rating. Standardized questionnaires for determining acceptance, such as the Client Satisfaction Questionnaire for internet-based health interventions (CSQi) [8] or the Net Promoter Score (NPS) [4], were not taken into account.

The *Wysa*[3] system combines chatbot-based therapeutic exercises with one-on-one coaching through mental health professionals. Users can track their mood by choosing a predefined emotional category at the beginning of each session with the system. The application was used in multiple prospective cohort studies [20, 26] with participants with symptoms of anxiety and depression. Results indicated high patient engagement and improvements in symptoms among participants of the high-usage group when compared to the low-app-usage group. Similar to the other mentioned systems, the tracking of emotional states is not done in a dimensional approach and activities cannot be tracked with the application.

Furthermore, systems such as Moodscope[4], Daylio[5], and eMoods[6] use an app-based approach for mood tracking without the use of natural language processing. While those approaches can help users to analyze and regulate their moods [10] and can provide valid data on the emotional state of users [11], past research indicates that the use of chatbots could promote deeper self-disclosure and could improve user satisfaction and enjoyment when compared to app-based approaches [11,25].

In summary, related chatbot-based systems mainly focus on providing content and exercises based on CBT to users, without taking resource-oriented therapy approaches into account. While emotional states can be tracked in the presented cases, the collection of emotional states is based on a categorical emotional model approach with a focus on basic emotions. The chatbot-based tracking of activities in relation to emotional states in the scope of resource-oriented CBT has thus far not been investigated.

To address mentioned gaps, the following sections will present the concept and implementation of a chatbot-based system for mood and activity journaling in the scope of resource-oriented CBT.

3   Concept and Implementation

To investigate the usability and acceptance of the proposed system for chatbot-based mood and activity journaling, the concept, user interface, design of conversational flow, and implementation were based on an extensive study of related

---

[3] Wysa, https://www.wysa.com/, accessed 27.07.2023.

[4] Moodscope, https://www.moodscope.com/, accessed 30.05.2023.

[5] Daylio, https://daylio.net/, accessed 30.05.2023.

[6] eMoods, https://emoodtracker.com/, accessed 30.05.2023.

work and preliminaries. Requirements associated with the target group and general requirements for mental health applications [19] were considered in the system design.

3.1   Concept and System Design

Different actions a user can take while interacting with the system were defined as part of the design process. As shown in the use case diagram in Fig. 1, after signing in the user has the choice to launch a chat or to view previously tracked moods and activities in a calendar view.

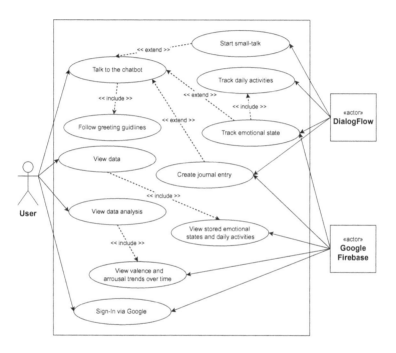

Fig. 1. Use case diagram of the proposed system

For the tracking of moods, the user is asked to define their current emotional state. Thereupon, the system asks the user to further specify their mood by presenting emotional states located most closely nearby in Russell's circumplex model as chips[7] (see Fig. 2b). Afterward, the user is asked if there was a certain activity connected to their mood entry. Consequently, the user can specify which category the activity belongs to or can choose from previously tracked activity categories to create a new entry. For each mood journal entry, the user can add multiple activities and additional journal notes.

---

[7] DialogFlow Documentation, https://developers.google.com/assistant/df-asdk/rich-responses, accessed 03.05.2023.

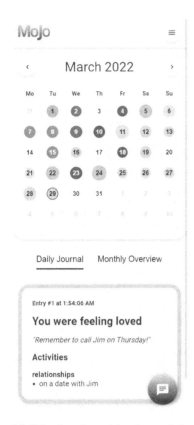

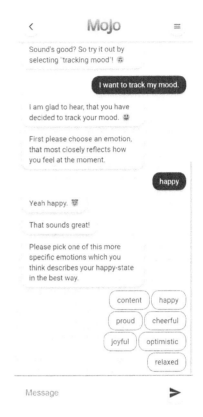

(a) Calendar view with color-coded emotional states.

(b) Chat view showcasing the mood journaling functionality.

Fig. 2. User interface of the developed system.

In the calendar view, tracked moods are displayed using a predefined color scheme for each day, thereby providing a concise overview of how the user's emotional state evolved over the month (see Fig. 2a). Therefore, the valence score is used to calculate a color value for each day whereby two colors for the valence score extrema (1;-1) were predefined based on the works of Kaya et al. [23]. By selecting an individual day in the calendar view, the user can check which activities were tracked for connected emotional states, thereby allowing the user to identify personal resources that might lead to beneficial emotional states. Additionally, the user can view the development of the tracked valence and arousal scores for a month (see Fig. 3).

3.2 Implementation

As the system strives to support the mood and activity journaling of a broad user base in a low-threshold manner, the application was developed as a pro-

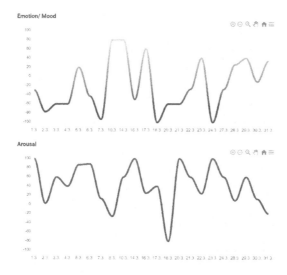

Fig. 3. Line chart showing valence and arousal trends for the selected month.

gressive web application to ensure broad platform independent access using the JavaScript framework React and the conversational agent development framework DialogFlow. As shown in Fig. 4, the front end uses static HTML components that are hosted on a web server. Collected mood and activity information is stored in a database using Firebase[8]. To provide natural, chatbot-based interaction, the system is able to handle user requests through natural language processing via the DialogFlow CX platform. A webhook hosted on Heroku[9] acts as an intermediary between the front end and the DialogFlow platform. To enable the mapping of tracked emotions by the user to a dimensional emotional model, 57 emotional states were manually mapped to different positions of four quadrants of the used dimensional model, thereby allocating each state with a valence and arousal score. Implications of this will be discussed in Sect. 5.

4 Evaluation

A single-arm online user study was conducted over a period of three days to assess user acceptance and usability of the developed system. Students were recruited as participants via social media. Participants needed to sign a privacy policy and consent form to comply with data protection provisions.

4.1 Methodology

Subjects received an introduction to the project, a description of the study procedure, a link to access a pre-test questionnaire, and access to the web application

---

[8] Firebase, https://firebase.google.com/, accessed 03.05.2023.
[9] Heroku, https://www.heroku.com/, accessed 03.05.2023.

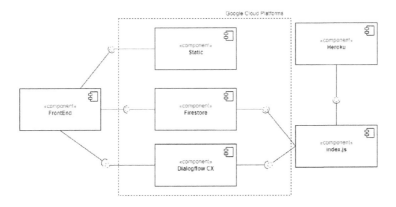

Fig. 4. Component Diagram of the proposed system

via email. Demographic information and prior knowledge of mental health and mental health apps were collected in the pre-test questionnaire. Additionally, participants were given specific tasks that had to be fulfilled while using the system for three consecutive days. Tasks included tracking their mood and at least two daily activities during the testing period. In an applied post-test questionnaire, the System Usability Scale (SUS) [9] was used to evaluate the usability of the chatbot and web application. Consumer satisfaction and acceptance in the context of digital mental health interventions were assessed using an adapted version[10] of the Client Satisfaction Questionnaire (CSQi) [3]. As a further indicator of the perceived usability and acceptance, the Net Promoter Score (NPS) [32] was applied. Additional feedback was collected in an open-question format as a formative evaluation. Collected results were anonymized to comply with data protection provisions.

4.2 Participants

9 participants, consisting of current and recent students, participated in the study (5 female, 4 male). All participants completed both the pre and post-test questionnaire and the daily tasks. The average age of participants was 24.9 years (ranging from 20 to 28). 56% of participants indicated prior experience with resource-oriented therapy techniques.

4.3 Results

SUS results overall indicated excellent usability with room for improvement for some individuals (mean (M) = 87.22, standard deviation (SD) = 18.18). CSQi results indicated a good acceptance of the system (M = 24.22, SD = 11.9). NPS results were mixed (NPS score = -11.1), indicating that not all participants

---

[10] CSQ versions, https://csqscales.com/csq-versions/, accessed 17.05.2023.

would recommend the system to others. All participants were able to fulfill all given tasks during the testing period.

In the open-question section, three participants reported technical issues with the application, as they had to reload the application on some occasions to interact with the chatbot. One participant reported being unsure if the system saved given answers. Four participants wanted to be able to access more psycho-educative content and additional methods based on ROT and CBT, such as gratefulness journaling and behavior activation, through the chatbot. An expansion of the response options of subcategories of emotional states and an increase in the number of predefined categories of activities were also desired. Furthermore, two participants indicated that they would like the chatbot to react more empathically to user inputs. Two participants emphasized how much they appreciated the concept of the application.

5   Discussion

This paper introduces the concept of resource-oriented CBT support through chatbot-based mood and activity journaling as a main contribution to the field. While some related work utilizes the tracking of categorical emotional states and the tracking of activities, thus far the tracking of emotional states in a dimensional approach combined with the tracking of mood-related activities in the scope of salutogenesis-based resource identification by means of a chatbot conversation has not been investigated.

Study results indicate excellent usability and an above-average acceptance of the system. Nevertheless, not all participants indicated that they would recommend the system to others. According to the answers to open questions, the reasons for this mainly were some technical issues that were caused, upon further investigation, by the Heroku intermediary system and can be addressed in a future version of the system. Participants, furthermore, mentioned to overall be satisfied with the system overall but expressed the wish for more input options and the possibility of having access to more therapy techniques. Some participants further missed engaging chat features such as jokes and more psycho-educational content delivered through the conversational agent. As studies on the use of chatbots in the mental health and CBT context have so far lacked standardized methods for measuring usability and acceptance, and as the related systems presented in this paper differ in terms of overall system functionalities and focus, it is difficult to compare results with related work. Nevertheless, there is limited evidence that the here presented system exceeds usability as measured through SUS in comparison to related systems (cf. [13,20,29]). This comparison must however be clearly limited by the fact that the here presented system focuses exclusively on mood and activity tracking, while analyzed related systems pursue a more holistic CBT approach. Moreover, as mentioned earlier, more elaborate studies on usability and acceptance in the field are needed in general. Even though the system uses a dimensional model of emotions instead of basic emotional categories, the mapping of 57 emotional states to valence and arousal scores was statically predefined. Therefore, while the tracking of more complex emotional states is possible in comparison to related approaches, the system is still limited to a fixed number of emotions. This could be improved in future versions by leveraging bigger word libraries of dimensional emotional models or through deep learning approaches. As there is an ongoing debate on the challenges and accuracy of mood tracking [15], the used mapping of emotions to valence and arousal scores should be validated in a follow-up study.

While results are highly promising, this study focused on the usability and acceptance of the presented concept and system for the target group of students. Effects of the system on symptoms of depression, anxiety disorders, and general well-being should be investigated in a follow-up study. Furthermore, the presented user study was conducted with a small sample size of 9 participants over a limited study period of three days in a single-arm study design to obtain first indications of the general acceptance and feasibility of the developed concept and to gather formative feedback for improving the system in future versions. Follow-up studies should therefore investigate adherence, acceptance, and efficacy of the system over a longer period with a larger sample size in a randomized controlled trial.

6   Conclusion and Future Work

This paper presented the concept and implementation of a system for chatbot-based resource-oriented CBT support through mood and activity journaling for the main target group of students. As study results regarding usability and acceptance were highly promising, the system should be improved in accordance with user feedback and used in future studies. The mapping of emotional states to valence and arousal scores should be extended either by using suitable libraries or by leveraging deep learning approaches. Furthermore, as requested by participants, the system should be extended by including more resource-oriented techniques and psycho-educational content.

Acknowledgments. Preliminary work for the presented user study was done by Tom Troschütz. Prototype development was done by Jakob Arnold, Nele Drechsler, Siqi Lan, Dominik Ziegenhagel, Philip Müller, and Timon Trettin.

References

1. Abd-Alrazaq, A.A., Alajlani, M., Alalwan, A.A., Bewick, B.M., Gardner, P., Househ, M.: An overview of the features of chatbots in mental health: a scoping review. Int. J. Med. Inform. **132**, 103978 (2019)
2. Althoff, T., Clark, K., Leskovec, J.: Large-scale analysis of counseling conversations: an application of natural language processing to mental health. Trans. Assoc. Comput. Linguist. **4**, 463–476 (2016)
3. Attkisson, C.C., Greenfield, T.K.: The client satisfaction questionnaire (CSG) scales and the service satisfaction scale-30 (sss-30). Outcomes Assess. Clin. Prac. **120**(7), 120–127 (1996)

4. Baehre, S., O'Dwyer, M., O'Malley, L., Lee, N.: The use of net promoter score (nps) to predict sales growth: insights from an empirical investigation. J. Acad. Market. Sci. 1–18 (2022)
5. Barrow, E., Thomas, G.: Exploring perceived barriers and facilitators to mental health help-seeking in adolescents: a systematic literature review. Educ. Psychol. Pract. **38**(2), 173–193 (2022)
6. Beck, A.T.: Thinking and depression: I. idiosyncratic content and cognitive distortions. Arch. General Psych. **9**(4), 324–333 (1963)
7. Borkin, S.: The healing power of writing: a therapist's guide to using journaling with clients. WW Norton & Company (2014)
8. Boß, L., et al.: Reliability and validity of assessing user satisfaction with web-based health interventions. J. Med. Internet Res. **18**(8), e5952 (2016)
9. Brooke, J., et al.: Sus-a quick and dirty usability scale. Usability Eval. Indust. **189**(194), 4–7 (1996)
10. Caldeira, C., Chen, Y., Chan, L., Pham, V., Chen, Y., Zheng, K.: Mobile apps for mood tracking: an analysis of features and user reviews. In: AMIA Annual Symposium Proceedings. vol. 2017, p. 495. American Medical Informatics Association (2017)
11. Drake, G., Csipke, E., Wykes, T.: Assessing your mood online: acceptability and use of moodscope. Psychol. Med. **43**(7), 1455–1464 (2013)
12. Fellous, J.: Models of emotion. Scholarpedia **2**(11), 1453 (2007). https://doi.org/10.4249/scholarpedia.1453, revision #140985
13. Fitzpatrick, K.K., Darcy, A., Vierhile, M.: Delivering cognitive behavior therapy to young adults with symptoms of depression and anxiety using a fully automated conversational agent (woebot): a randomized controlled trial. JMIR Mental Health **4**(2), e7785 (2017)
14. Fordham, B., et al.: Effectiveness of cognitive–behavioural therapy: a protocol for an overview of systematic reviews and meta-analyses. BMJ open **8**(12), e025761 (2018)
15. Gabriels, K.: Response to "uncertainty in emotion recognition". J. Inform., Commun. Ethics Society (2019)
16. Grobe, T.G., Steinmann, S., Szecsenyi, J.: Arztreport 2018 schriftenreihe zur gesundheitsanalyse. https://wwwbarmer.de, Access 17 July (2018)
17. Harith, S., Backhaus, I., Mohbin, N., Ngo, H.T., Khoo, S.: Effectiveness of digital mental health interventions for university students: an umbrella review. PeerJ **10**, e13111 (2022)
18. Høifødt, R.S., Strøm, C., Kolstrup, N., Eisemann, M., Waterloo, K.: Effectiveness of cognitive behavioural therapy in primary health care: a review. Fam. Pract. **28**(5), 489–504 (2011)
19. Idrees, A.R., Kraft, R., Pryss, R., Reichert, M., Baumeister, H.: Literature-based requirements analysis review of persuasive systems design for mental health applications. Proc. Comput. Sci. **191**, 143–150 (2021)
20. Inkster, B., Sarda, S., Subramanian, V., et al.: An empathy-driven, conversational artificial intelligence agent (wysa) for digital mental well-being: real-world data evaluation mixed-methods study. JMIR Mhealth Uhealth **6**(11), e12106 (2018)
21. Jonas, W.B., Chez, R.A., Smith, K., Sakallaris, B.: Salutogenesis: the defining concept for a new healthcare system. Global Adv. Health Med. **3**(3), 82–91 (2014)
22. Kawasaki, M., Yamashita, N., Lee, Y.C., Nohara, K.: Assessing users' mental status from their journaling behavior through chatbots. In: Proceedings of the 20th ACM International Conference on Intelligent Virtual Agents, pp. 1–8 (2020)

23. Kaya, N., Epps, H.H.: Relationship between color and emotion: a study of college students. Coll. Stud. J. **38**(3), 396–405 (2004)
24. Kazdin, A.E.: Addressing the treatment gap: a key challenge for extending evidence-based psychosocial interventions. Behav. Res. Ther. **88**, 7–18 (2017)
25. Lee, Y.C., Yamashita, N., Huang, Y., Fu, W.: "i hear you, i feel you": encouraging deep self-disclosure through a chatbot. In: Proceedings of the 2020 CHI Conference on Human Factors in Computing Systems, pp. 1–12 (2020)
26. Leo, A.J., et al.: A digital mental health intervention in an orthopedic setting for patients with symptoms of depression and/or anxiety: feasibility prospective cohort study. JMIR Form. Res. **6**(2), e34889 (2022)
27. Li, Z., Liu, Y., Wang, J., Liu, J., Zhang, C., Liu, Y.: Effectiveness of cognitive behavioural therapy for perinatal depression: a systematic review and meta-analysis. J. Clin. Nurs. **29**(17–18), 3170–3182 (2020)
28. Liyanage, S., et al.: Prevalence of anxiety in university students during the Covid-19 pandemic: a systematic review. Int. J. Environ. Res. Public Health **19**(1) (2022).https://doi.org/10.3390/ijerph19010062, https://www.mdpi.com/1660-4601/19/1/62
29. Mehta, A., Niles, A.N., Vargas, J.H., Marafon, T., Couto, D.D., Gross, J.J.: Acceptability and effectiveness of artificial intelligence therapy for anxiety and depression (youper): longitudinal observational study. J. Med. Internet Res. **23**(6), e26771 (2021)
30. Milne-Ives, M., et al.: The effectiveness of artificial intelligence conversational agents in health care: systematic review. J. Med. Internet Res. **22**(10), e20346 (2020)
31. Priebe, S., Omer, S., Giacco, D., Slade, M.: Resource-oriented therapeutic models in psychiatry: conceptual review. Br. J. Psych. **204**(4), 256–261 (2014). https://doi.org/10.1192/bjp.bp.113.135038
32. Reichheld, F.F.: The one number you need to grow. Harv. Bus. Rev. **81**(12), 46–55 (2003)
33. Russell, J.A.: A circumplex model of affect. J. Pers. Soc. Psychol. **39**(6), 1161 (1980)
34. Willutzki, U., Neumann, B., Haas, H., Koban, C., Schulte, D.: Zur psychotherapie sozialer ängste: Kognitive verhaltenstherapie im vergleich zu einem kombiniert ressourcenorientierten vorgehen. Z. Klin. Psychol. Psychother. **33**(1), 42–50 (2004)
35. Willutzki, U., Teismann, T., Schulte, D.: Psychotherapy for social anxiety disorder: long-term effectiveness of resource-oriented cognitive-behavioral therapy and cognitive therapy in social anxiety disorder. J. Clin. Psychol. **68**(6), 581–591 (2012)

Emotion Recognition in Dance: A Novel Approach Using Laban Movement Analysis and Artificial Intelligence

Hong Wang[1], Chenyang Zhao[1], Xu Huang[2], Yaguang Zhu[1], Chengyi Qu[3], and Wenbin Guo[4(✉)]

[1] School of Construction Machinery, Chang'an University, Xi'an 710064, China
{hong.wang,chenyang.zhao,zhuyaguang}@chd.edu.cn
[2] Department of Mechanical and Aerospace, University of Missouri, Columbia, MO 65211, USA
xuhuang@mail.missouri.edu
[3] U.A. Whitaker College of Engineering, Florida Gulf Coast University, Fort Myers, FL 33965, USA
cqu@fgcu.edu
[4] College of Medicine, University of Florida, Gainesville, FL 32611, USA
wenbin.guo@ufl.edu

Abstract. Dance, as a highly expressive form of art, conveys intense emotions through bodily movements and postures. In the field of human-computer interaction, the automated recognition of dance movements poses a significant challenge concerning artistic expression and emotional classification. Analyzing dance movements enables us to extract rich emotional information. This paper introduces a novel approach for dance emotion recognition—the Laban Movement Analysis (LMA)—which characterizes the human body based on three aspects: body distribution, body structure, and dynamic trends. Leveraging artificial intelligence-based computer vision technology, we conduct a comparative analysis and supervised learning on existing dance performance video datasets. Various machine learning algorithms are trained and compared. The results indicate that recognizing emotional information from the perspective of dance movements achieves a high level of accuracy.

Keywords: Human emotion classification · Artificial intelligence · Laban movement analysis

1 Introduction

Human emotion recognition is currently a significant research direction within the realm of human-computer interaction, with widespread applications across multiple domains such as text, audio, and video [1]. Emotion recognition is a process that utilizes computer analysis to interpret various emotional information. This involves extracting features that describe emotions and creating a correspondence between these features and different emotional states. This further includes classifying emotions to infer an individual's emotional state. This process aims to comprehensively understand and interpret human emotions through computer technology. Meanwhile, affective computing, which focuses on the development of technology and theory to promote a profound comprehension of human emotions, has sparked extensive research initiatives and garnered notable scholarly attention. Affective computing is not merely a technical task but also an interdisciplinary field that concerns human-computer interaction, artificial intelligence, and psychology. Its research aims to better perceive, understand, and respond to human emotions through computer systems, providing a more intelligent and humanized experience for human-computer interaction. Among various human behaviors, human dance exhibits a clear expression of emotions. Dance, as one of the oldest art forms of humanity, is an important branch of ancient civilization. Its origin is rooted in labor and is interpreted through human body movements. Movements in dance have a unique power to vividly convey the thoughts and emotions of the dancer [2]. This makes human dance an extremely expressive art form, providing a rich and complex data source for emotion recognition research. While exploring the field of emotion recognition, special attention to the emotional expression of human dance will provide a beneficial perspective for a deeper understanding of the complexity and diversity of emotion recognition.

The Labanotation, invented by Rudolf Laban of Hungary, is one of the most widely used notation systems for recording human dance movements in the world today [3]. This method plays a pivotal role in areas such as choreography, dance training, and the documentation and analysis of human motion, demonstrating considerable potency [4–8]. Compared to other forms of recording such as video and images, Labanotation has the advantage of being preserved in paper or digital form, characterized by small storage space, good resistance to damage, and ease of preservation and dissemination. The elements of Labanotation include the basic orientation of the body, the quality of movement, and the direction of movement in space. Professional dance performers can easily read Labanotation, which facilitates the convenient recording, learning, and dissemination of dance. Therefore, as an effective tool for recording and inheriting dance, Labanotation plays a unique role in the preservation and dissemination of dance art.

Labanotation is an intuitive, clear, and scientific system of symbols for recording human movement, far superior to ordinary text and graphics in describing dance. By observing and analyzing human movement, it provides a framework for describing and understanding actions. Currently, the Laban method, as a description method for body movement, is extensively employed in emotion recognition [9]. Based on Laban Movement Analysis (LMA), researchers have studied the correlation between human movement and emotions. The results show that there is a good correlation between LMA features and emotions. Meanwhile, research on the automatic generation of Labanotation based on human movement analysis has made significant progress. However, how to recognize emotions in dance through its features still needs further study.

In this paper, we introduce a dance emotion recognition method based on Laban features (Laban Movement Analysis, LMA). The method identifies emotions by analyzing features in dance movement data, focusing primarily on the feature expression of body distribution, body structure, and movement trends. Through this approach, we aim to capture the rich expression of emotions in dance more intricately. Simultaneously, this paper employs a multi-feature method, integrating these features into a neural network model to achieve automated emotion recognition, thereby avoiding the tedious process of manual emotion annotation. This neural network model, through learning a large amount of dance data, can abstract more complex emotional representations, improving the accuracy and universality of emotion recognition. Finally, to validate the effectiveness of our method, we not only developed a method for automatically extracting features and annotating dance emotions but also conducted comparative experiments with traditional manual emotion recognition methods. Through this series of experiments, we aim to demonstrate the superiority and feasibility of the proposed method in the field of dance emotion recognition. This has positive implications for promoting the development and application of dance emotion recognition technology.

2 Related Works

Labanotation [11], initially developed by Rudolf Laban, consists of two parts: a vertical staff and geometric symbols for dance. This Labanotation example spans three pages, read from bottom to top within a page and from left to right across pages, following the chronological order of the recorded dance movements. The body's midline divides the body into left and right sections. The staff primarily comprises nine vertical columns, each representing a part of the body. The columns on either side of the center line describe the most important parts of the body. From the center line outward, the columns sequentially represent the left and right support columns, left and right leg posture columns, torso movement column, left and right arm posture columns, and left and right hand movement columns. An additional head movement column is located on the far right.

The fundamental spatial symbols in the Labanotation system describe the horizontal and vertical directions of dance movements, which are crucial for the spatial analysis of Labanotation. The symbols for horizontal direction, with the central rectangle symbolize the "place" symbol. Centered on this symbol, other symbols represent "forward," "backward," "left," "right," "left-forward," "right-forward," "left-backward," and "right-backward," totaling nine symbols for horizontal direction. The symbols for vertical direction, sequentially from left to right as "low," "middle," and "high," represent by a different color. By combining the horizontal and vertical directions, space can be divided into 27 subspaces. Each subspace corresponds to a basic Laban symbol describing the direction of a dance movement. Therefore, there are 27 basic Laban symbols in the Labanotation system, representing 27 basic directions of dance body movements.

Aristidoue et al. [12] proposed a feature extraction framework for describing the four parameters of body, effort, shape, and space in Laban Movement Analysis (LMA). The Body component primarily involves the body structure and physical characteristics, describing the relationships, connections, and influences from other body parts or external factors in body movements. Furthermore, it reveals the sequence and relationships of body parts in motion, as well as general statements about body organization. The Effort component is dedicated to depicting the intention and dynamic characteristics of movements, including texture, sensation, and how energy is utilized in each movement. This part delves into the motivation, form, and energy distribution of movements, providing a framework for a comprehensive understanding of emotional expression in motion. The Shape component focuses on how the body shape changes in motion. It describes the shape of the body in a static state, the relationship between the body and itself and the environment, and how the body changes towards a point in space. In addition, Shape also involves how the torso changes shape to support the movements of other body parts. The Space component describes the relationship between movement and the environment, path, and spatial tension lines. It details the evolution of movement in space, including interaction with the surrounding environment, path selection, and movement characteristics related to spatial tension lines.

With the rapid development of motion capture technology, Laban Movement Analysis (LMA) has been applied in multiple aspects, such as human body movements [9] and the relationship between human movement and emotions [9]. The Microsoft Kinect sensor has been used for Laban-based motion tracking and analysis [13–15]. Although the prices of motion sensors like Kinect are becoming increasingly affordable, they have not yet become mainstream for consumers. Conversely, the widespread adoption of video sharing and streaming platforms, from teleconferencing applications to social media, has solidified traditional video recording (sans additional sensors) as the principal method for capturing and documenting human actions. In professional contexts, such as clinical environments and performances, employing a single stationary camera has emerged as the prevailing norm for monitoring and recording human motion. Therefore, to better adapt to real scenarios, it is necessary to extract skeletal keypoint information from videos. BlazePose's pose estimation method [16], launched by Google Research, is a real-time pose estimation framework suitable for mobile devices. Figure 1 shows the effect of BlazePose on dance action pose estimation. During the inference process, the BlazePose model adopts a detector-tracker design, combined with the datasets used by BlazeFace, BlazePalm, and COCO, and proposes a new topology structure with 33 key points in the human body. With the rapid development of streaming media, recording dance through video has become mainstream. However, current methods are more or less limited to dynamic trends when it comes to the relationship between human movement and the emotions it represents, with inadequate consideration for static aspects.

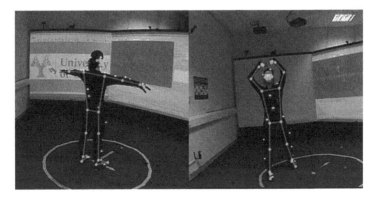

Fig. 1. BlazePose Key Points

Initially, we employ a series of artificial intelligence methods to process the original video clips of human dance movements. In the initial stage, we utilize human body detection algorithms and keypoint recognition methods to extract features of human skeletal keypoints. Subsequently, we mask redundant information to obtain keypoint distribution information and calculate feature vectors through intra-frame and inter-frame data for combination. Finally, we validate the effectiveness of this algorithm in emotion prediction through six algorithms (Decision Tree, Naïve Bayes, Support Vector Machine, Linear Model, Random Forest, Deep Neural Network). The uniqueness of this research method lies in the comprehensive application of multiple artificial intelligence technologies, from the extraction of human skeletal key points to feature vectors, and then to multi-algorithm verification, to improve the accurate prediction ability of emotions in dance movements.

3   Methods

Our methodological process aligns with most methods based on supervised learning and primarily includes the following four steps: First, we prepare and preprocess the dataset. In this stage, we are dedicated to organizing and processing data to ensure its suitability for model training. Second, we extract features related to body distribution, body structure, and dynamic trends. Through this step, we can capture key information to better describe the characteristics of the data. The third step involves training and testing the model using the processed data. In this phase, we employ supervised learning methods, allowing the model to learn the patterns in the data and evaluate its performance. The final step is to conduct experiments on entirely new data to verify the model's generalization ability on unseen data. Through these four processes, we can establish a comprehensive methodological framework to address our problem.

In our research, we utilize dance motion capture videos from the University of Cyprus [17]. This dataset consists of dance movement data from various performers. We employ the Laban Movement Analysis framework to obtain the required static and dynamic data features, necessitating the extraction of human skeletal data from the video data [12]. To identify the skeletal feature points in the video, we use MediaPipe [18], an open-source cross-platform framework based on graphic data processing, designed to build machine learning pipelines to handle streaming data, such as audio, video, and 3D point clouds. The MediaPipe skeletal keypoint detection module is an efficient and accurate human posture recognition algorithm that has been applied in fields such as human motion analysis, gesture recognition, and virtual fitting, recognizing human keypoints.

Figure 2 displays the information and total number of skeletal points extracted from the initial single frame. There are 33 points in total, including the nose, left eye (inner), left eye, left eye (outer), right eye (inner), right eye, right eye (outer), left ear, right ear, mouth (left), mouth (right), left shoulder, right shoulder, left elbow, right elbow, left wrist, right wrist, left pinky, right pinky, left index, right index, left thumb, right thumb, left hip, right hip, left knee, right knee, left ankle, right ankle, left heel, right heel, left foot index, and right foot index.

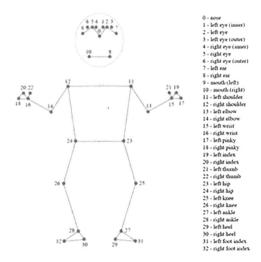

Fig. 2. MediaPipe Key Points

However, for static data, the information from 33 points is overly redundant. Therefore, we visually assess the motion trajectories of each point over a period of time based on the x and y coordinates of the video, thereby further filtering the key points to reduce subsequent computations. Ultimately, we obtain 13 points representing the body distribution of static data, as shown in Fig. 3, including the nose, left shoulder, right shoulder, left elbow, right elbow, left wrist, right wrist, left hip, right hip, left knee, right knee, left ankle, and right knee.

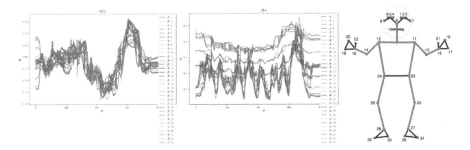

Fig. 3. Trajectory of Change

After obtaining the above data, namely the static data of body distribution, we calculate the features between frames, which include two parts: body structure and dynamic trends. The body structure includes the distance between skeleton points. In the present study, we undertake the computation of the relative distance between points on a skeleton. The feature equation, which quantifies the distance between a pair of skeleton points, is delineated in Eq. 1, where d represents the distance of the skeleton pair, and the coordinates of node i are (x_i, y_i), and the coordinates of node i's neighboring node j are denoted as (x_j, y_j).

$$d = \sqrt{(x_i - x_j)^2 - (y_i - y_j)^2} \tag{1}$$

The trend of motion is a constituent element that correlates with the fluctuations in emotional states throughout the progression of the action sequence. The influence of force is an amalgamation of four distinct components: gravity, time, smoothness, and space. We calculated the speed and acceleration of the key points. Equation 2 shows the feature equation for the speed of the bone node, where v represents the speed of the skeleton point, the coordinates of node i at the current time are (x_i, y_i), and the coordinates at the previous moment are (x_{i-1}, y_{i-1}), t is the frame time. As delineated in Eq. 3, the feature equation for the acceleration of the skeletal point is presented. In this equation, a signifies the acceleration of the skeletal node, Δv denotes the change in velocity, and t represents the time duration of the frame.

$$v = \frac{\sqrt{(x_i - x_{i-1})^2 - (y_i - y_{i-1})^2}}{t} \tag{2}$$

$$a = \frac{\Delta v}{t} \tag{3}$$

Specifically, in this paper, with respect to the aspect of limb distance, we calculate the distance between the ankle joints and hip joints on both sides of the body, the wrist joints and the nose, and the wrist joints and the hip joints, as shown in Table 1. In terms of dynamic trends, we express them from two aspects: speed and acceleration. We learn the features of the wrist joints, hip joints, and ankle joints. At the same time, in order to combine static data with dynamic data, we define a window of 10 frames in length, and with the need for 3 window lengths, we can calculate all the required features. We calculate the data of three window lengths. In terms of body structure, we analyze the minimum standard deviation, obtain the most stable part within this section as the normalization factor, and normalize other structures. In terms of dynamic trends, we calculate speed and acceleration, and finally obtain dynamic data belonging to this section. After propagating it to the static data of its belonging frame, we obtain the static distribution within a frame and the dynamic information for a subsequent period of time.

Table 1. Body structure and dynamic trends

Distance	Velocity	Acceleration
Ankle and hip	Ankle	Ankle
Wrist and nose	Hip	Hip
Wrist and hip	Wrist	Wrist

In the end, we identify changes in dance emotions by inputting video sequences into a deep neural network and five machine learning models. Our dataset uses 16 videos with 8016 frames as the training set, and 2 videos with 1002 frames as the test to verify the accuracy of the model. The distribution of the training set and the test set are shown in Table 2.

Table 2. Dataset

Emotion	Train set	Test set
Afraid	4008	501
Happy	4008	501

The five machine learning models we trained are Naïve Bayes, Support Vector Machines, Logistic regression, Decision tree and Random Forest. Naïve Bayes [19] can be applied to a range of tasks, such as classification and text classification. This algorithm has several variants, including Gaussian Naive Bayes, Bernoulli Naive Bayes, and Multinomial Naive Bayes. Support Vector Machines [20] is one of the supervised learning algorithms, which can be applied to classification, regression, and outlier detection tasks. The goal of this algorithm is to find a separable hyperplane in a high-dimensional space that can optimally divide the data into different categories or forecast the target value in a regression scenario. Logistic regression [21] is often used for binary classification tasks. It is an efficient and straightforward algorithm to execute, and it can yield successful outcomes in numerous real-world scenarios, especially when there is a roughly linear relationship between the target and independent variables. Decision tree [22] is a model that mirrors a tree-like structure and is employed for supervised learning and decision-making tasks. This algorithm divides the data into smaller, more manageable subsets according to certain criteria, with each division represented as a node in the tree. The attribute that offers the maximum information gain, quantifying the reduction in uncertainty or entropy of the target variable, is chosen for the divisions. Decision Trees can be used for both classification and regression tasks, and they are capable of handling both categorical and numerical attributes. Random forest [23] combines multiple decision trees to formulate a prediction. The algorithm is suitable for both classification and regression tasks. By combining individual trees, the model mitigates the variance and overfitting that can happen in a single decision tree, thus improving the model's stability and accuracy. Deep neural network is a type of feed forward neural network, including one input layer, one or several hidden layers, and one output layer. Information in the network travels unidirectionally, from the input to the output, without looping back. The data is processed at each layer and then sent forward to the next layer until the final output is derived. Every layer is made up of multiple neurons, with each neuron performing a fundamental computation on the weighted sum of its inputs to yield an output. The connection weights between neurons and each neuron's biases are established during the training phase using an optimization algorithm like gradient descent. In conclusion, our data feature extraction process and deep neural network model are illustrated in Fig. 4.

The evaluation of the performance was carried out using metrics such as precision, recall, accuracy, and F1 scores. Precision indicates the classifier's proficiency in correctly distinguishing negative samples, while recall reflects its capability to identify

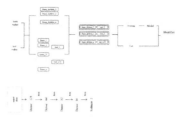

Fig. 4. Feature extraction and model structure

positive samples, with the highest possible score being 1. The F1 score, which is the harmonic mean of precision and recall, balances both metrics and ranges from 0 to 1. The corresponding formulas are as follows:

$$Precision = \frac{TP}{TP + FP} \tag{4}$$

$$Recall = \frac{TP}{TP + FN} \tag{5}$$

$$Accuracy = \frac{TP + TN}{TP + TN + FP + FN} \tag{6}$$

TP = True Positive, TN = True Negative,
FP = False Positive, FN = False Negative

$$F1\ score = 2 \times \frac{Precision \times Recall}{Precision + Recall} \tag{7}$$

4   Results

In this paper, we compare the performance of five machine learning algorithms and a deep neural network on the same features. The results show that the deep neural network outperforms the other algorithms and achieves the highest accuracy, 78.94% on this feature set. Figure 5 presents the outcomes of six machine learning algorithms: Decision Tree, Naïve Bayes, Logistics Regression, Support Vector Machines, Random Forest, and Deep Neural Network.

Figure 6 depicts the confusion matrices for each machine learning method employed in this study. The diagonal elements represent correctly classified emotions, providing a visual comparison of model accuracy. Deep neural networks demonstrate a distinct advantage in terms of true positive (TP) rates compared to traditional models (Table 3).

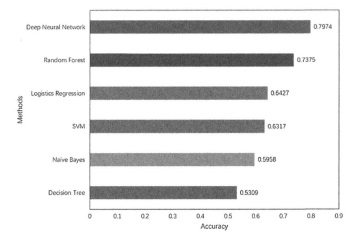

Fig. 5. Accuracy

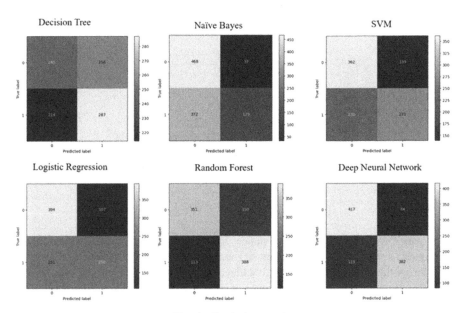

Fig. 6. Confusion matrix

Table 3. Emotion recognition using six machine learning algorithms

Algorithms	Precision	Recall	Accuracy	F1 score
Decision Tree	0.5285	0.5729	0.5309	0.5498
Naive Bayes	0.7963	0.2575	0.5958	0.3891
Support Vector Machines	0.6610	0.5409	0.6317	0.5950
Logistic Regression	0.7003	0.4990	0.6427	0.5828
Random Forest	0.7212	0.7745	0.7375	0.7469
Deep neural network	0.8197	0.7625	0.7974	0.7901

5 Discussion and Conclusion

In the present study, a novel approach was developed for the identification of emotions from video inputs, utilizing machine learning algorithms. The research encompassed the training and comparative analysis of six distinct machine learning algorithms, namely Decision Tree, Naïve Bayes, Support Vector Machines, Logistic Regression, Random Forest, and Deep Neural Network. These algorithms were trained using supervised learning techniques on pre-existing datasets of dance videos. Upon comparison of the six machine learning and deep learning methodologies, it was observed that the Deep Neural Network outperformed all other methods in terms of accuracy, achieving a rate of 79.74%. This was in contrast to the Decision Tree at 53.09%, Naïve Bayes at 59.58%, Support Vector Machines at 63.17%, Logistic Regression at 64.27%, and Random Forest at 73.75%, as depicted in Fig. 3. The findings of our study indicate that Deep Neural Networks exhibit superior performance in extracting high-level, hidden, and meaningful features from dance emotion classification.

Upon examination of the confusion matrix, it was observed that the deep neural network exhibited a total of 119 false negatives (instances where the true label was 1 but the predicted label was 0) and 84 false positives (instances where the true label was 0 but the predicted label was 1). The quantity of false negatives was found to be lower than those yielded by the other five machine learning methods under consideration. Furthermore, the Decision Tree method resulted in 214 false negatives and 256 false positives, while the Naïve Bayes method produced 372 false negatives and 33 false positives. Notably, these two methods not only had the highest rate of false classifications but also demonstrated an imbalance in their confusion matrices. The remaining three methods, namely Random Forest, Support Vector Machines, and Logistic Regression, exhibited relatively commendable performance on the confusion matrix for emotion recognition detection. Future work is warranted for a more in-depth analysis of the underlying mechanisms of these models.

Moreover, we conducted an in-depth analysis of the results. One of the primary causes of misclassification was found to be the reliance on the Mediapipe framework for keypoint extraction. In the context of video data, the capture of human keypoints may fail, leading to subsequent feature failure and erroneous emotion prediction outcomes. This suggests that the reliability of keypoint extraction poses a challenge when processing video data. Therefore, more robust and reliable handling is required in this regard to enhance the accuracy of emotion prediction.

Despite the constraints posed by the limited data, our proposed Deep Neural Network exhibits a commendable level of accuracy in the detection of human motion for the recognition of emotional patterns, leveraging AI-based techniques. The outcomes of our research suggest the feasibility of automating the analysis of human emotions through the application of machine learning algorithms. These algorithms, which function on raw video inputs, could potentially pave the way for the development of AI-driven, standardized systems for the evaluation of human motion.

Our findings further imply that such AI-driven classification of movement could facilitate the establishment of fully automated reporting mechanisms in the domain of human emotion classification.

6 Future Work

The conveyance of emotion in dance is a multifaceted process, encompassing elements such as the performer, choreography, and environment. The task of identifying emotions in dance is notably challenging. This study seeks to address this complexity by refining the extraction of pertinent features, amalgamating them with deep neural networks, and evaluating the efficacy of this methodology through comparative experimentation. The success of dance emotion recognition hinges critically upon the richness and diversity of training datasets. Consequently, urgent research priorities lie in both enhancing the resilience of models to variations and expanding the existing body of dance emotion data.

The deep neural network model architecture utilized in this study is comparatively elementary. Prospective enhancements may be achievable by implementing more intricate models and integrating the forecasting of temporal data. This insinuates that the investigation of more elaborate architectures and the contemplation of temporal dynamics may offer potential for realizing superior outcomes in the domain of dance emotion recognition.

References

1. Zeng, Z., Pantic, M., Roisman, G.I., Huang, T.S.: A survey of affect recognition methods: audio, visual, and spontaneous expressions. IEEE Trans. Pattern Anal. Mach. Intell. **31**(1), 39–58 (2009). https://doi.org/10.1109/TPAMI.2008.52
2. Shikanai, N., Hachimura, K.: Evaluation of impressions and movements related to negative emotional expressions in dance. In: Proceedings of the 15th International Conference on Control, Automation and Systems (ICCAS), Busan, South Korea, pp. 657–660 (2015). https://doi.org/10.1109/ICCAS.2015.7365000
3. Von, L.R., Ullmann, L.: The Mastery of Movement. Northcote House, London, U.K. (1988)
4. Chi, D., Costa, M., Zhao, L., Badler, N.: The EMOTE model for effort and shape. In: Proceedings of the 27th Annual Conference on Computer Graphics and Interactive Techniques, pp. 173–182 (2000)
5. Torresani, L., Hackney, P., Bregler, C.: Learning motion style synthesis from perceptual observations. In: Conference on Advances in Neural Information Processing Systems, pp. 1393–1400 (2007)

6. Aristidou, A., Charalambous, P., Chrysanthou, Y.: Emotion analysis and classification: understanding the performers' emotions using the LMA entities. Comput. Graph. Forum **34**(6), 62–276 (2015)

7. Durupinar, F., Kapadia, M., Deutsch, S., Neff, M., Badler, N.I.: Perform: perceptual approach for adding ocean personality to human motion using Laban movement analysis. ACM Trans. Graph. **36**(1), 6–7 (2017)

8. Dewan, S., Agarwal, S., Singh, N.: Spatio-temporal Laban features for dance style recognition. In: Conference on International Conference on Pattern Recognition, pp. 2911–2916 (2018)

9. Ajili, I., Mallem, M., Didier, J.-Y.: Human motions and emotions recognition inspired by LMA qualities. Vis. Comput. **35**(10), 1411–1426 (2019). https://doi.org/10.1007/s00371-018-016 19-w

10. Morita, J., Nagai, Y., Moritsu, T.: Relations between body motion and emotion: analysis based on Laban movement analysis. In: Proceedings of the Annual Meeting of the Cognitive Science Society, Berlin, Germany, pp. 1026–1031 (2013)

11. Guest, A.H.: Labanotation: The System of Analyzing and Recording Movement, 4th edn., pp. 99–110. Routledge, Evanston (2014)

12. Aristidou, A., Charalambous, P., Chrysanthou, Y.: Emotion analysis and classification: understanding the performers' emotions using the LMA entities. Comput. Graph. Forum **34**(6), 262–276 (2015). https://doi.org/10.1111/cgf.12598

13. Bernstein, R., Shafir, T., Tsachor, R., Studd, K., Schuster, A.: Laban movement analysis using kinect. Int. J. Comput. Electr. Autom. Control Inf. Eng. **9**(6), 1574–1578 (2015)

14. Ajili, I., Mallem, M., Didier, J.Y.: Robust human action recognition system using Laban movement analysis. Procedia Comput. Sci. **112**, 554–563 (2017). https://doi.org/10.1016/j. procs.2017.08.168

15. Kim, W.H., Park, J.W., Lee, W.H., Chung, M.J., Lee, H.S.: LMA based emotional motion representation using RGB-D camera. In: ACM/IEEE International Conference on Human-Robot Interaction, pp. 163–164 (2013). https://doi.org/10.1109/HRI.2013.6483552

16. Grishchenko, I., Bazarevsky, V., Zanfir, A., et al.: BlazePose GHUM holistic: real-time 3D human landmarks and pose estimation. arXiv (2022)

17. Motion Captured Performances. http://dancedb.eu/main/performances?tdsourcetag=s_pcqq. Accessed 8 July 2019

18. Lugaresi, C., et al.: MediaPipe: a framework for building perception pipelines. http://arxiv. org/abs/1906.08172 (2019)

19. Webb, G.I., Keogh, E., Miikkulainen, R.: Naïve Bayes. Encycl. Mach. Learn. **15**(1), 713–714 (2010)

20. Joachims, T.: Making large-scale SVM learning practical. Technical report, no. 1998, 28 (1998)

21. Hosmer Jr, D.W., Lemeshow, S., Sturdivant, R.X.: Applied Logistic Regression, vol. 398. Wiley, Hoboken (2013)

22. Cramer, G.M., Ford, R.A., Hall, R.L.: Estimation of toxic hazard—a decision tree approach. Food Cosmet. Toxicol. **16**(3), 255–276 (1976)

23. Breiman, L.: Random forests. Mach. Learn. **45**, 5–32 (2001)

The Effectiveness of Culinary Therapy Platform System: A Study Examining Cooking Course as a Mental Health Intervention for College Students

Xiaofeng Wu, Yijia Duan, Chengwei Kang(✉), Siu Shing Man, Xingheng Chen, and Zhiheng Zhu

School of Design, South China University of Technology, Guangzhou 510641, China
mello_21g_soul@qq.com

Abstract. The World Health Organization has pointed out that rapid environmental changes, intense competition, and the high expectations of modern society are putting immense pressure on individual psychology, leading to widespread impulsiveness and a decreased sense of security. These factors significantly impact the mental health of college students, with surveys indicating a rise in psychological disorders among them. To address this issue, colleges have introduced psychological education courses, but they often fall short in meeting students' emotional needs and practical application. To overcome these challenges, the implementation of a practical culinary therapy platform system is proposed.

Culinary therapy has been described as the therapeutic technique that uses arts, cooking, gastronomy (the art/science of good eating), plus an individual's personal, cultural, and familial relationships with food, which proves advantageous in addressing underlying emotional and psychological problems. By offering relaxed and engaging cooking classes, it aims to enhance college students' mental well-being. To evaluate the effectiveness of this approach, a structured culinary therapy platform system was developed and tested using psychometric testing and qualitative data collection. An experiment involving teaching college students to make ginger milk, a traditional Chinese dessert, showed significant improvements in positive emotions and slight reductions in negative emotions among the participants.

Building on these findings, a culinary therapy platform system was designed for use in colleges and universities, undergoing extensive testing and garnering positive feedback from users, confirming its efficacy in improving the mental health of college students.

Keywords: Culinary therapy platform system · Mental health · Qualitative approach · College students

V. G. Duffy (Ed.): HCII 2024, LNCS 14710, pp. 202–215, 2024.
https://doi.org/10.1007/978-3-031-61063-9_14

1 Introduction

1.1 Psychological Health of College Students

The issue of students' mental health has become an increasingly pressing matter within higher education (Salimi et al., 2023). Nowadays, the mental health problems of college students are becoming increasingly serious. According to surveys and statistics, about 16%–25.4% of college students in China have psychological disorders, mainly symptoms such as depression, anxiety, and neurasthenia. About 10% of them have more severe psychological disorders, and about 1% have severe psychological abnormalities. The proportion of college students with mental health problems is constantly increasing (Wu et al., 2023). Therefore, it is urgent to provide timely psychological education, intervention, and treatment for college students.

At present, many universities have established specialized psychological education courses, continuously exploring new models from scratch, continuously exploring the psychological needs of college students, and initially establishing a psychological health education system for college students, comprehensively promoting the reform of the psychological health education system. However, there are still shortcomings in the current mental health education courses for college students, such as a focus on theoretical explanations while neglecting the exploration of their true emotional needs, a classroom format that leans towards teaching rather than practice, and a lack of assessment of college students' psychological state through paper-based assessments (Li et al., 2021). It is necessary to create a more practical and experiential psychological course to address the above issues.

1.2 Cooking Practice Course

Cooking practice courses refer to educational courses that are guided by interest and experience rather than vocational training. Diet is closely related to our lives, and with the continuous improvement of people's living standards, their requirements for diet are also constantly increasing.

An increasing number of studies have found that diet is not only closely related to our physical health but also can enhance people's awareness of the benefits of health. Foreign scholars completed 30 studies through a 25-week follow-up of over 7000 patients, which showed that cooking courses were associated with improvements in attitudes, self-efficacy, and healthier dietary intake in adults and children (Hasan et al., 2019); Similarly, foreign research teams have helped participants build confidence in cooking skills and strengthen their understanding of nutritional concepts through a series of cooking courses (Marshall & Albin, 2021); According to relevant popular science papers, Australian researchers have found that having confidence in their cooking skills and good daily dietary habits is very beneficial for mental health ("Confidence in Cooking Skills Leads to Better Mental Health," 2022). Domestic scholars studying special education have also pointed out that the design and implementation of cooking courses can cultivate life skills, improve moral awareness, and so on (Fan, 2021).

Nowadays, many universities in China have offered related cooking courses, such as the cooking course offered by Northwestern Polytechnical University, which has been warmly welcomed by students; East China Normal University has also launched a pilot program for cooking courses on campus, which has also been welcomed (He, 2021). It can be seen that not only have universities gradually strengthened their emphasis on cooking courses, but students themselves are also very interested in cooking courses and willing to participate.

The benefits of cooking courses are gradually becoming apparent in daily life. More and more people are willing to actively participate in cooking courses, so cooking courses at home and abroad are gradually being welcomed by more people. Taking a domestic cooking website as an example, it offers cooking courses tailored to different cuisines, which have been highly sought after and praised by many people. The most popular cooking courses even have more than 50000 participants; The same foreign cooking course healing website also has a considerable popularity, and the courses are even subdivided into online courses, targeting different types of courses such as individuals, families, small groups, and companies.

An increasing number of studies have found that diet is not only closely related to our physical health, but people may also change their mental health during the cooking process. Therefore, it would be of positive significance to improve the mental health status of college students by offering relaxed and interesting cooking courses.

1.3 Cooking Therapy

Cooking therapy combines culinary art with medical science. The purpose is to educate on the powerful impact of food on health and disease, and to teach the skills of preparing nutritious and beneficial diets through hands-on cooking courses to prevent, manage, and reverse a range of diseases (Mauriello & Artz, 2019).

With the increasing comprehensive understanding of physical and mental health among the public, more and more research is exploring the close relationship between food and psychology. Cooking activities not only provide food that meets physiological needs but also have potential psychological health benefits. However, empirical research on the healing psychology of cooking is currently relatively limited (Farmer, Touchton-Leonard, & Ross, 2018).

A systematic review study comprehensively evaluated the impact of cooking interventions on social psychology, including 11 related studies. The results show that there is currently relatively insufficient evidence of the positive impact of cooking interventions on social psychology. However, some of these studies have also reported positive effects of cooking interventions on social and psychological outcomes. Some studies have found that participating in cooking activities can enhance an individual's self-esteem, enhance social interaction, reduce anxiety, and improve quality of life (Farmer, Touchton-Leonard, et al., 2018). These preliminary research findings suggest that culinary healing psychology may have a positive impact on social psychology, but further research is needed to confirm these findings.

Mental illness patients often face challenges such as low self-esteem, lack of self-expression, and poor social skills. In this context, food art therapy has become a highly anticipated intervention method (Kim et al., 2020). Food art therapy refers to the use of food ingredients in creative games and artistic activities to express an individual's inner world and generate positive thinking and self-discovery.

A recent study has confirmed the effectiveness of food art therapy in promoting the rehabilitation process of patients with mental illness. This study observed patients who participated in food art therapy and found significant improvements in their self-esteem, self-expression, and social skills. By participating in food art therapy, patients can build confidence, find their own voice, and engage in positive social interactions with others through interaction with ingredients and creative expression.

With the increasing attention of society to mental health issues, the development of cooking therapy for psychology has also shown some new trends. Firstly, technological advancements have provided more possibilities for cooking to heal psychology. The application of virtual reality technology and intelligent kitchen equipment makes the cooking process more convenient and innovative, providing patients with more personalized experiences and support.

Secondly, the recognition of cooking therapy psychology by communities and institutions is gradually increasing. More and more rehabilitation centers, mental health institutions, and community organizations are introducing cooking therapy as an effective intervention method for psychological recovery. These institutions provide professional guidance and support to help patients improve their mental health through cooking activities, and establish a good atmosphere of mutual assistance and support with other patients.

Although culinary therapy is still in its relatively early stages in the field of psychology, its prospects cannot be ignored. This study will help provide more specific guidance for clinical practice and bring innovation and progress to solutions in the field of mental health. By continuously developing and improving the theoretical and practical methods of cooking to heal psychology, we can provide more people with opportunities for psychological healing, and improve their quality of life and happiness.

1.4 Summary

As people's attention to cooking and mental health continues to increase, conducting psychological therapy courses with cooking therapy as the core in universities is an important direction for the development of mental health education for college students. In the future, cooking therapy courses will become an important component of the psychological education system in universities. Cooking therapy courses can not only enhance people's cooking skills but also improve their mental health to a certain extent. Therefore, it is meaningful to study and carry out good cooking courses in universities.

2 Methodology

2.1 Research Design

Pre-survey Subjects. The pre-survey targeted university students in Guangdong Province and an online survey was conducted in June 2023. To ensure the quality of the survey, each IP address could only register and respond once. A total of 82 questionnaires were collected, with 73 valid responses, resulting in an effective recovery rate of 89.02%. All respondents were either undergraduate or postgraduate students.

Experimental Subjects. Through open recruitment, students at South China University of Technology who were willing to try cooking as a way to relieve anxiety and heal psychologically were selected based on individual circumstances through surveys and interviews. The research practice was conducted in June 2023, with 4 male and 5 female students, making a total of 9 participants. This group included students with a basic understanding of cooking as well as those with no prior cooking experience. The specific experiment involved the cooking practice of a traditional Guangdong snack, ginger milk, which has a simple and easy-to-learn preparation process, while also presenting certain challenges and interesting aspects.

2.2 Research Tools

The main tools used in this experiment included a questionnaire and the Chinese version of the Positive and Negative Affect Schedule (PANAS).

The questionnaire was titled "Survey on Cooking as a Method for Culinary Therapy" and included content related to anxiety levels and the perception of food as a means of healing.

The Positive and Negative Affect Schedule (PANAS), developed by Watson and Clark in 1988 (Watson et al., 1988), is used to assess an individual's positive and negative emotions. The positive emotions factor (PA) comprises 10 adjectives describing positive emotions, while the negative emotions factor (NA) comprises 10 adjectives describing negative emotions. The entire scale uses a 5-level rating system ranging from 1 to 5 points.

2.3 Research Design and Implementation

Pre-survey. A pre-survey titled "Pre-survey Questionnaire on Cooking as a Method for Culinary Therapy" was distributed online to the university student population in Guangdong Province. A total of 82 questionnaires were collected, with 73 valid responses. The analysis of the relevant results is as follows:

1. The majority of respondents reported a moderate to high level of daily anxiety, with 92.5% of them believing that participating in experiential activities such as flower arranging, pottery making, tea tasting, and cooking could effectively alleviate stress and improve mood (Fig. 1).

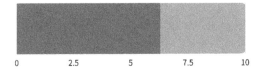

| 0 | 2.5 | 5 | 7.5 | 10 |

Fig. 1. Statistics on the stress index of university students.

2. Over 91.78% of the respondents expressed an interest in cooking (cooking, making desserts, preparing drinks, etc.), and 89.55% believed that it could help improve their mood (Figs. 2, 3 and 4).

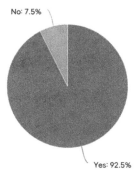

Fig. 2. Results chart on "Whether related activities can alleviate stress".

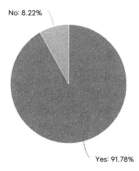

Fig. 3. Results chart on "Interest in cooking".

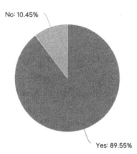

Fig. 4. Results chart on "Belief in the stress-alleviating effects of cooking".

3. The majority of people learned to cook either at home or through self-study, with only 12.33% having the opportunity to learn or experience cooking-related activities at school. However, over 90% of the respondents expressed interest in schools offering experiential cooking classes (Fig. 5).

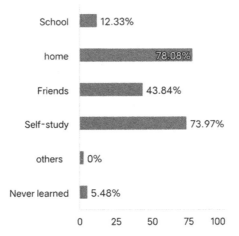

Fig. 5. Results chart on "Ways of learning to cook".

Based on the comprehensive analysis of the above and other statistical data, it can be concluded that the university student population has a high acceptance of "food as a means of healing". Therefore, it holds certain value for schools to offer cooking-related experiential activities or courses. However, further research is needed to design experiential courses for food healing that are effective and feasible.

Experiment. Based on the pre-survey, we conducted an offline experiment. Please refer to the table below for specific experimental details (Table 1).

Table 1. Specific experimental details.

Experiment name	Taking Ginger Milk as an Example to Explore the Feasibility of a Food Healing Course Design
Experimental purpose	1. Explore the feasibility of course design and find the existing problems; 2. Verify the effect of cooking on psychological healing
Experimental materials	Washed ginger (small yellow ginger), milk (buffalo milk), white granulated sugar, a grinder, filter cloth, disposable bowls, and spoons
Experimenter	9 college students
Experimental tool	Positive and Negative Emotion Scale (PANAS)

(continued)

Table 1. (*continued*)

Experimental Procedure	1. Understand the cooking basis of 9 subjects and divide them into 3 groups according to the cooking basis from high to low; 2. All subjects filled in the pre-test questionnaire "Positive and Negative Emotion Scale (PANAS) Pre-test" 3. Staff A (acting as a teacher) introduced today's dishes and test process in general; 4. Staff A demonstrated the production process of ginger milk, please taste; 5. The subject (student role) taste the teacher's work; 6. Subjects began to cook, and the specific operation was ① Grind ginger, pay attention to prevent injury; ② Wrap the ground ginger with a filter cloth and squeeze the ginger juice into a small bowl by hand; ③ Heat the milk, add an appropriate amount of white sugar, and stir constantly. Cook until there are small bubbles along the edge of the pot and a small amount of white smoke. Immediately turn off the heat, being careful not to let it boil and to prevent scalding ④ Pour the milk into the ginger juice from the height, and then let it stand for about 10 min to prevent burns; 7. Staff B, C, and D (as volunteers) shall assist the subject in the operation process and provide guidance, make records, and take photos of all the key steps in the operation process; 8. Staff E, F, and G to maintain the site order, limited tools, pay attention to arrange the order of the subjects; 9. The subjects tasted the food, shared communication, and took photos; 10. The subjects filled in the post-test questionnaire "Post-test of Positive and Negative Emotion Scale (PANAS)"; 11. Subjects fill in the questionnaire "Evaluation of this experience"

3   Results and Discussions

3.1   Comparison Analysis of the Positive and Negative Affect Schedule Pre-test and Post-test

Statistical analysis was conducted on the data of the Positive and Negative Affect Schedule (PANAS) pre-test and post-test filled out by the subjects. The average scores for each item were calculated, and bar charts were plotted as shown in the two figures below. It is visually evident that the positive emotions of the subjects significantly improved after the experiment, while the negative emotions slightly decreased. This indicates that the experiment was helpful in reducing the subjects' stress levels and improving their mood (Figs. 6 and 7).

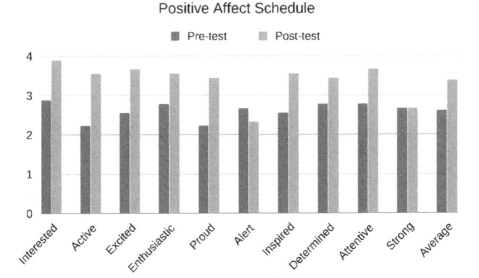

Fig. 6. Positive Affect Schedule.

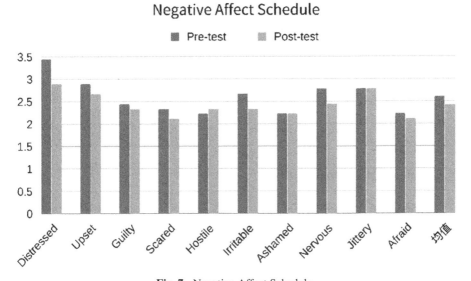

Fig. 7. Negative Affect Schedule.

3.2 Evaluation of the Experiment

The evaluation questionnaire for the experiment consists of two parts:

First, it investigates the subjects' perceived difficulty of each step during the experience. The difficulty of each step is rated on a scale of 0–10, where 0 represents very easy and 10 represents very difficult. The data is analyzed to assess the subjects' acceptance and expectations of the course difficulty, in order to optimize it. The data analysis revealed that the subjects rated the difficulty of each step below 3, indicating that they found the steps relatively simple and easy to accept. Furthermore, their expectations for difficulty were even lower, suggesting that they preferred the initial experience to be simple and easy to achieve.

Second, it evaluates the subjects' satisfaction with the end product and their overall satisfaction with the activity. Ratings are given on a scale of 0–10, where 0 represents extreme dissatisfaction and 10 represents very satisfied. The data analysis shows that the subjects expressed high levels of satisfaction with both the end product and the overall activity experience, indicating that the activity was well-received and has potential for promotion (Table 2).

Table 2. The evaluation questionnaires' results.

Problem	Mean value
The difficulty of understanding the teacher's explanation	3.00
The desired level of difficulty for the teacher's explanation	2.29
The level of difficulty in extracting ginger juice	1.86
The level of difficulty in extracting ginger juice	1.57
Desired level of difficulty for milk frothing	2.14
Satisfaction level with the finished product (ginger milk)	6.86
Satisfaction with the experience of this event	9.00

3.3 Observation Results Analysis

Conclusions were drawn from the observations and records of the subjects:

First, the presence of cooking experience has a significant impact on the cooking experience. Members of the group with strong cooking foundations were able to complete the tasks independently with higher efficiency, while the group with no cooking experience tended to have lower efficiency and encountered issues such as spilling ingredients and using inappropriate amounts. Therefore, grouping based on cooking experience from strong to weak may have issues. It is suggested to consider pairing students with and without cooking experience or allowing students to form groups freely for the experiment.

Second, the subjects experienced noticeable emotional improvements during the experiment, deriving happiness mainly from interactions among group members, successful cooking steps, and the tasting and sharing of the final product. In the process of designing and optimizing the course, it is recommended to reinforce these positive aspects, for example, by encouraging interaction among group members through a certain level of difficulty setting and implementing a feedback mechanism after each step to enhance the sense of achievement.

4   Culinary Therapy Platform System Design and Feedback

Using these experimental findings as a basis, we designed a culinary therapy platform system tailored for colleges and universities. We conducted extensive testing and implementation of the system, inviting participants to provide feedback by completing a questionnaire. We distributed 462 questionnaires, of which 458 valid questionnaires were returned. 94.52% of the participants believed that the culinary therapy platform system is effective in improving their mental state (Figs. 8 and 9).

Fig. 8. Culinary therapy platform system.

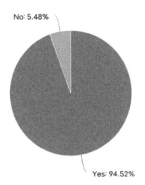

Fig. 9. Results chart on "Whether culinary therapy platform system is effective in improving their mental state".

5   Research Implications

5.1   Development of Grounded Theory

Culinary therapy is a new lifestyle intervention that differs from traditional psychotherapy. It makes full use of people's basic needs for food and aims to help people relieve stress, anxiety, depression, and other negative emotions in the form of cooking, improve people's emotional stability and happiness, and promote physical and mental health.

Studying culinary therapy can effectively explore the connection between food and psychology, and on this basis, establish a more detailed and complete treatment model with practical guidance. By accurately matching the taste and seasoning methods, patients can quickly obtain a safe and pleasant feeling, achieve the stimulation of happiness, and strengthen the cognitive factors behind positive emotional experiences, thereby realizing the complementation and promotion of people's physical health and psychological well-being.

In short, studying cooking therapy is not only an innovative psychological treatment method, but also provides theoretical support for a deeper understanding of the interaction mechanism between food nutrients and emotions, expands intervention methods in the field of psychology, and increases people's happiness and life quality.

5.2 Practical Implications

Studying culinary therapies could provide new ideas and innovations for mental health treatments and interventions. As an activity of self-expression or multi-role playing, cooking can effectively relieve negative inner emotions and enable people to improve their ability to control themselves and cope with setbacks. Introducing culinary therapy into existing mental illness intervention programs could lead to better outcomes for patients.

In addition, culinary therapy can also add new elements to social public health services. By promoting cooking therapy, we can increase opportunities for emotional resonance, promote self-popularization, and improve food safety and health knowledge. Research on culinary therapies has positive effects on scientific observations, optimizing food quality, and formulating policies related to human health.

6   Conclusions

Establishing culinary therapy courses is of great significance in colleges and universities, and it also plays a significant role in the psychological healing of college students.

First of all, through the creative method of cooking, students can effectively relieve negative emotions such as depression and anxiety. In college life, students face various challenges and pressures, and cooking can help them express and release their innermost emotions that are difficult to express through words, thereby relieving stress and anxiety.

Secondly, the healing function of food itself is conducive to promoting the development of students' physical, and mental health. The cooking process involves the selection, matching and application of techniques of ingredients, which can not only increase students' understanding of food nutrition and health, but also stimulate intelligence and creativity, and improve emotional stability and happiness.

Finally, the culinary therapy course provides a reference for future design and implementation of food therapy-related activities. Courses can be taught in the form of group work and practical exercises. At the same time, we cooperate with the guidance of professional psychologists to give full play to the effect of collective strength and mutual learning to obtain better healing effects.

All in all, offering culinary therapy courses in colleges and universities has a positive impact on students' emotional balance and physical and mental health. This provides ideas and directions for the design and implementation of cooking therapy in the future, and the above concepts can be flexibly used in practical applications to continuously innovate and develop.

Acknowledgments. Special thanks go to all the students who participated in our trials, Qingsong Liu, Yongling Huang, Zhongqing Yao, Ziyun Lin, Zhiquan Zeng, Rong Luo, Shuqing Zhuang, Kuntai Huang, Zixin Wu, Yucan Fu.

Disclosure of Interests. We confirm that there are no known conflicts of interest associated with this publica-tion and there has been no significant financial support for this work that could have influenced its outcome.

References

Confidence in Cooking Skills Leads to Better Mental Health. Home Medicine (07), 4 (2022). https://kns.cnki.net/kcms2/article/abstract?v=BS8_DD2Uwa6ULvRPXT_DHD6Wme_9 w4nbcI0a-7EY3O5x-RXMRKkeLktFB3t7898KR3yGGpDmivKhUDZgKY8uBtDONKBOt m6W7HYsJZQ_btU92OE5BwN9tsk9xCsfJZM7MRCsHMJ78k3qJL_P9hDA4A==&unipla tform=NZKPT&language=CHS

Fan, Z.: A brief analysis of the educational effect of cooking classes on students in special education schools. Writer's Paradise (22), 116–117 (2021). https://kns.cnki.net/kcms2/article/abstract?v=BS8_DD2Uwa55yl0qa7w1IK_QEQTcUAuSUdgohd9qR4tXmwwOavlBoPqo hKe2Hp_JqjOlk19c_ZEFAsGZat18ax3Q6i1NV1dgBfXaXUbmqFTY8bp9Jb5_TXqvQX nMDBTTZGOs_9gi5M5UssZkq9NiRA==&uniplatform=NZKPT&language=CHS

Farmer, N., Touchton-Leonard, K., Ross, A.: Psychosocial benefits of cooking interventions: a systematic review. Health Educ. Behav. **45**(2), 167–180 (2018). https://doi.org/10.1177/109 0198117736352

Hasan, B., et al.: The effect of culinary interventions (cooking classes) on dietary intake and behavioral change: a systematic review and evidence map. BMC Nutr. **5**, 29 (2019). https://doi.org/10.1186/s40795-019-0293-8

He, Y.: Colleges and Universities Offer "Cooking Classes" is Good to Have More of a Sense of Life. China University Students Career Guide (07), 1 (2021). https://kns.cnki.net/kcms2/article/abstract?v=BS8_DD2Uwa4PHqT9IExsw7o0hKm31MAasgB6LIdY-BZOB86glY9cf nLD93ET_36I3oLyIO37cncN8VZ3e_L8TjDk1gnT_1XXS4JzLLERsm0Ag-dNFjHFHv4 7ug2QAoliOZ-Bzb0tAVgYJZk5hyXcDw==&uniplatform=NZKPT&language=CHS

Kim, J.-H., Choe, K., Lee, K.: Effects of food art therapy on the self-esteem, self-expression, and social skills of persons with mental illness in community rehabilitation facilities. Healthcare (2020)

Li, Z., Luo, W., Hu, J.: Dilemmas and breakthroughs in the construction of mental health education courses for college students. Heilongjiang Res. High. Educ. **39**(12), 145–149 (2021). https://doi.org/10.19903/j.cnki.cn23-1074/g.2021.12.025

Marshall, H., Albin, J.: Food as medicine: a pilot nutrition and cooking curriculum for children of participants in a community-based culinary medicine class. Matern. Child Health J. **25**(1), 54–58 (2021). https://doi.org/10.1007/s10995-020-03031-0

Mauriello, L.M., Artz, K.: Culinary medicine: bringing healthcare into the kitchen. Am. J. Health Promot. **33**(5), 825–829 (2019). https://doi.org/10.1177/0890117119845711c

Salimi, N., Gere, B., Talley, W., Irioogbe, B.: College students mental health challenges: concerns and considerations in the COVID-19 pandemic. J. Coll. Stud. Psychother. **37**(1), 39–51 (2023)

Watson, D., Clark, L.A., Tellegen, A.: Development and validation of brief measures of positive and negative affect: the PANAS scales. J. Pers. Soc. Psychol. **54**(6), 1063 (1988)

Wu, Y., Zhao, A., Li, H., Zhang, Y., Hu, L., Ji, Q.: Development overview and countermeasures of mental health education for young college students. J. Qiqihar Med. Univ. **44**(10), 988–992 (2023). https://kns.cnki.net/kcms2/article/abstract?v=A4c134OkBY8xOMkJfJJOOlSHVcO chPm2wn5myPHxGgAsUvVN0W6P_lGUzk0pkW8IGDewHgqEvwtovve6xjanaBL8Xosrt 9F9pAHoMGXKglCNh-Fi_tSMKW_VqiCPN1M3mzcNbZ5rsP1AvsGWpQrPCA==&uni platform=NZKPT&language=CHS

Analysis of Proactive Health Product Design Based on the Traditional Chinese Medicine Theory

Tong Wu and Meng Li[✉]

South China University of Technology, Guangzhou 511400, China
sdwutong@mail.scut.edu.cn, mengli@scut.edu.cn

Abstract. Given the escalating global prevalence of non-communicable chronic diseases (NCDs), how to maintain health and obtain a higher quality of life has emerged as a prominent societal issue. To meet this problem, Proactive Health, regarded as the future direction of health management, was initially proposed in China. However, many people still struggle to change their detrimental lifestyle due to few daily products and services that can motivate people to act. This study aims to summarize the correlation between Proactive Health and Traditional Chinese Medicine (TCM) theory to propose design strategies for healthy products in lifestyle, such as diet, exercise, music, relaxation, digestion, and sunbathing. This research conducted comparative analyses of domestic and international products from the perspective of health factors. A questionnaire survey was also employed to understand user needs and their usage experiences. The conclusion is that the design of Proactive Health products based on TCM theory should focus on disease prevention by promoting healthy lifestyles and offering systematic and personalized health management plans after comprehensively considering various lifestyle factors. This research provides valuable guidance for the development of healthy products.

Keywords: Proactive Health · TCM Theory · Design Analysis

1 Introduction

According to the World Health Organization, non-communicable chronic diseases (NCDs) have become a significant global public health issue, accounting for 74% of the world' s deaths [1]. In China, the total mortality rate of NCDs is 88.5% [2]. The decline in national health standards has led to a substantial medical financial burden. From 2008 to 2018, the total expenses on medical and healthcare increased by as high as 362%, representing an enormous challenge for the public health security system and NCD prevention [3, 4]. Research shows that 60% of individual health factors correlate to lifestyle. In contrast, the traditional public health system focuses on disease treatment instead of prevention by promoting a healthy lifestyle [5, 6]. Therefore, Proactive Health, an emerging healthy concept, was proposed, which has been regarded as the essential component of China's health security system in the future.

V. G. Duffy (Ed.): HCII 2024, LNCS 14710, pp. 216–230, 2024.
https://doi.org/10.1007/978-3-031-61063-9_15

Proactive Health was originally proposed by experts from various fields in China's "Thirteenth Five-Year Plan" for digital healthcare and health promotion in 2015 and has been further emphasized and elucidated in the "Outline of the Healthy China 2030 Plan" [7, 8]. Proactive Health refers to a practical activities and knowledge system that focuses on thoroughly stimulating individuals' subjective initiative to conduct healthy behavior of living and carry out controllable and active interventions on human behavior by utilizing various medical methods, aiming to enhance the body's resilience ability to improve bodily functions, eradicate diseases and maintain in a healthy state [3, 9]. Its core is that the prevention and control of diseases from the source is more important than treatment.

Proactive Health is viewed as the modern inheritance and development of Traditional Chinese Medicine (TCM) theory guided by the holistic medical perspective and the TCM concept of preventive treatment of disease [10]. Additionally, TCM takes human beings as the research object and attaches great importance to the physiological and pathological responses of the body, as well as individual differences. Therefore, it aligns closely with Proactive Health, representing the disease prevention and health management model as person-centered rather than disease-centered [11]. Proactive health is an emerging concept. TCM originated more than 3000 years ago, and its theoretical system is more well-developed and proven, which can support the further development of Proactive Health.

Although Proactive Health has been widely studied at a theoretical level, the practical explorations guided by it have been relatively limited. Besides, due to the few touchpoints, such as products and services that can motivate people to live healthily, many people still struggle to change their detrimental behaviors despite the well-known fact that lifestyle significantly impacts one's health.

Therefore, this study aims to propose Health design strategies based on TCM theory by shedding light on the core characteristics of Proactive Health and TCM theory and their correlation. Moreover, this article analyzes products closely related to lifestyle factors such as diet, exercise, digestion, music relaxation, and sunbathing from the perspective of Proactive Health dimensions with the corresponding product design requirements identified through a questionnaire survey method. This research contributes to the development of TCM and Proactive Health theory, providing implications for research and actionable guidelines on healthy product and service design.

2   Related Work

2.1   Proactive Health

This study consulted literature and policies involved with the connotation of Proactive Health, summarizing the four characteristics of Proactive Health from four directions as follows. (1) "Systematic," the foundation of the Proactive Health concept, indicates that human-being is a complex biological system consisting of physical, emotional, mental, social, and other factors, with solid self-repair and self-organization abilities [3]. Therefore, the prevention measures are diverse and comprehensive, moving forward and expanding to include nutrition, exercise, sleep and other individual health management, risk factor prevention, disease screening, and so on [6]. (2) "Preventive" implies individuals should take primary responsibility for their health. Improving the body's resilience and immunity to prevent diseases by changing unhealthy lifestyles and monitoring their physical condition [3, 6, 12]. (3) "Personalized" refers to the provision of diverse, multilevel, targeted health services that are tailored to individuals' health demands [12]. (4) "Precision" means a combination of modern technology with traditional medical methods to comprehensively assess exposure to various risk factors and the health state of individuals to offer a suitable health plan after balancing multiple indicators [3, 12].

2.2 TCM Theory

TCM theory encompasses abundant content, which studies the laws of transformation between health and disease in human life activities and their prevention, diagnosis, treatment, rehabilitation, and health maintenance [13]. The four significant views of TCM theory are "holistic," "preventive," "suitable," and "harmony." "Holistic" indicates that humans keep a holistic relationship with the external environment. Climate, location, and environment have a varying impact on human physiology and pathology. Moreover, humans are treated as an organic whole, and all tissues and organs within the body interact. TCM pays more attention to disorders of overall function instead of diagnosing diseases by specific static physical data at an abnormal level. "Preventive" means preventing disease occurrence, development, and recurrence through preventive measures in lifestyle and TCM treatment, which reflects that the human body has self-repairing ability. "Suitable" means providing a suitable health management plan for individuals by considering seasons, environment, and body constitution factors. "Harmony" believes that the human body deviates from a state of harmony leading to illness. Therefore, moderate intervention to balance the Yin-Yang, Qi, and blood is necessary to maintain health.

2.3 The Correlation Between Proactive Health and TCM Theory

By studying and comparing the characteristics of Proactive Health and TCM theory, we find they coincide to some degree. Firstly, they both admit the human body is an open and complex system with the ability to self-organize and self-repair, determining that managing health needs a holistic and systematic perspective. Secondly, they greatly emphasize enhancing body function and resilience by living a healthy lifestyle to prevent diseases. Thirdly, both believe that health management should be human-centered rather than disease-centered. Therefore, it is necessary to provide a personalized health plan for each individual according to their physical condition and external factors. Fourthly, Proactive Health mentioned that measuring physical data by combining modern and traditional technology provides some moderate suggestions. Likewise, TCM needs to obtain individual conditions to offer a plan to balance the body's state. Based on the correlation between them mentioned above, undoubtedly, TCM theory can provide references for the study of Proactive Health. In particular, practical guidance for an emerging concept, Proactive Health, is scarce. TCM theory, summarized by generations of medical practitioners through their clinical practices, can provide valuable guidance for further research.

2.4 Design Strategies of Proactive Health Product Based on the TCM Theory

Proactive Health products based on TCM theory refer to products guided by the principles of TCM and aligned with the characteristics of Proactive Health, aiming to provide guidance and interventions in lifestyle, enabling users to conduct healthy behaviors easily and consistently, thereby preventing diseases and maintaining overall health. Its design strategies are summarized as follows. (1) Focus on the demands of physical and mental health and improve health systematically from diet, exercise, sleep, breathing, and other lifestyles. (2) Integrating TCM principles with modern lifestyle behaviors and user needs, promoting the active improvement of unhealthy lifestyle and behavioral habits to prevent chronic diseases. (3) Providing personalized health plans tailored to seasons, environment, body constitution, and other factors. (4) Utilize advanced measurement technology or evaluation tools to obtain the body's critical data and offer a balancing and moderate intervention. Figure 1 shows the correlation between the theories and the overall research path.

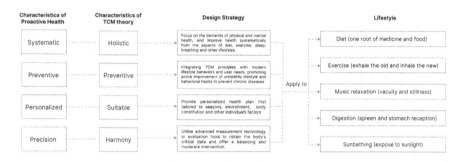

Fig. 1. Research path

3 An Analysis of Proactive Health Product Design Based on TCM Theory

3.1 Dietary Products - One Root of Medicine and Food

"One root of medicine and food" means that food has the function of treatment and healthcare as medicine [14]. Assisting users in easily choosing suitable food and cooking methods according to season, individual constitutions are a kind of dietary product design reflecting proactive health. For example, the Midea high-speed blender MJ-M4, a tool facilitating the TCM concept of "Five Grains for Nourishment," simplifies the process of cooking grains with an intelligent program, motivating users to actively engage in a healthy diet. Moreover, it provides access to user-friendly health assessments for users in the app, and personalized recommendations for a weekly nutrition menu will be presented by evaluation results (Fig. 2).

Compared with the popular high-speed mixers on the market in terms of proactive health factors, it's found that most of them consider individual differences and provide

Fig. 2. Midea high-speed blender MJ-M4

healthy diet menus with nutritional screening functions. As seen in Fig. 3. it is also equipped with functions such as regular reminders and personal preference records to encourage users to use it constantly. However, it fails to consider external factors such as seasonal and geographical influences, nor does it incorporate other lifestyles to provide comprehensive health suggestions.

Category	Item	Joyoung-L12	XiaoMi	Joyoung-Y951	Midea MJ-M4	Nutribullet	Philips-3000
Menu recommendations / Usage suggestions	Basic menu	✓	✓	✓	✓	✓	✓
	Ingredient selection		✓	✓	✓	✓	✓
	Nutrition report				✓		
Personalized recommendation	Recommendations based on seasonal changes						
	Recommendations based on individual constitution				✓		
	Recommendations based on geographical environment						
	Integrating with other products				✓		
Holistic	Exercise guidance						
	Music therapy						
	Massage recommendations						
	Sunbathing guidance						
Regular reminders		✓	✓	✓	✓		
Recording personal preferences		✓	✓	✓	✓		

Fig. 3. Competitive product analysis of blenders

To further explore the habits and needs of users using a high-speed blender, 77 valid questionnaires were gathered from individuals aged 18 to 55, and the result is shown in Fig. 4(a). For usage scenarios, people often use it for breakfast and afternoon tea. The primary purpose of using a blender is partaking of various foods (44%). 61% of users indicated that they would not continue using it, citing reasons such as high noise levels (70.13%), difficulty in cleaning (64.94%), and challenges in storage (50.65%). Besides, nearly 70% of users mentioned that systematic nutrition suggestions incorporating other lifestyles are not provided. As for using experience, most products perform well regarding ease of learning, usability, and safety. Nevertheless, they lack systematic health recommendations and real-time personalized dietary guidance (Fig. 4(b)). Dietary products in the concept of Proactive Health should cater to users' habits and demands in modern life and incorporate other lifestyles to provide personalized and comprehensive health solutions.

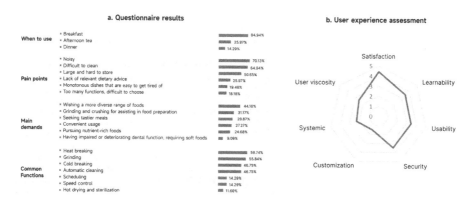

Fig. 4. User survey results on using blenders

3.2   Exercise Products—Exhale the Old and Inhale the New

TCM's concept of "exhale the old and inhale the new" indicates exhaling the turbid air from the body and breathing new air. It also reflects the relation between the intake and consumption of energy. In the Internet era, exercise products based on TCM theory and Proactive Health encourage the integration of traditional fitness practices and modern technology, presenting scientific and comprehensive health guidance tailored to each user's physical quality and living habits. For instance, Boohee Health is a mobile App that mainly helps people manage their health by calculating the calories users should intake and consume based on their age, gender, physical condition, and fitness targets (Fig. 5). In the exercise section, and it recommends suitable courses including traditional fitness techniques for users. Besides, it supports multiple device connections such as body fat scales, food scales, sports bracelets, and so on, which monitors the physical data constantly and effortlessly. It engages people to record various living habits like water drinking, menstruation, sleep, digestion, and excretion, conveying the concept of the holistic view of TCM aptly.

A comparison of domestic and international exercise apps reveals that not many apps cover traditional fitness techniques. Figure 6 shows that although some of them, such as Keep, Huawei Health, Fitcoach, and Freeletics Training, propose a personal plan based on users' exercise demands, specific recommendations on how and when to

Fig. 5. Boohee Health app

exercise are not provided. As for holistic views, most of them include dietary guidance to varying degrees without comprehensively considering other living habits, as Boohee Health does. Worth learning is that accessible principles of motion are elucidated in apps such as Keep, Intelligent Baduanjin, and Freeletics Training, helping users to work out with their minds and bodies.

Category	Item		Boohee	lifesum	Myfitnesspal	Fitbit	Keep	HUAWEI Health
Personalized recommendation	Calculate basal metabolic rate (BMR)		✓	✓	✓	✓	✓	✓
	Calculate total daily energy expenditure (TDEE)	Exercise record	✓	✓	✓	Cannot manually input other physical activities		
		Coefficient calculation						
	Calculate calorie intake budget based on target weight		✓	✓	✓		✓	
	Health assessment		✓				✓	
	Exercise recommendations		✓			✓	✓	✓
Holistic	Breathing						✓	✓
	Diet		✓	✓	✓	✓	✓	
	Sleep		✓	✓				✓
	Water drinking		✓	✓	✓	✓		
	Menstruation		✓			✓		
	Digestion		✓					
	Energy		✓	✓		✓	✓	✓
	Sunbathing		✓					
	Mindfulness		✓					
Habit formation	Regular reminders		✓				✓	✓
	Achievement badges		✓				✓	✓
	Calendar records						✓	

Fig. 6. Competitive product analysis of exercise apps

This study collected 126 valid questionnaires from individuals aged 18–50 to dig out the needs and experiences related to using exercise apps. The results are shown in Fig .7 (a). The findings suggest that 72% of users engage in physical activities primarily to maintain physical health, followed by fitness, body shaping, and social interaction. However, apps involve some pain points, which probably prevent people from continuing to use them. 62.7% of users indicated that they struggle to self-correct their movements while following exercise videos, 46.03% found it challenging to follow along due to the small screen size, and 33.33% expressed difficulty finding tutorials matching their preferences. Also, approximately 20% of users believe that the exercise app guides body shaping solely but not for maintaining health. From the user experience rating radar chart (Fig. 7(b)), it can be observed that exercise apps possess high levels of learnability and usability, whereas user retention and satisfaction levels are comparatively low. Exercise products based on Proactive Health should provide more convenient and precise guidance, including traditional fitness practices for users and motivate them to persist in acting. A general health plan should be presented with the consideration of the user's personality and other living factors.

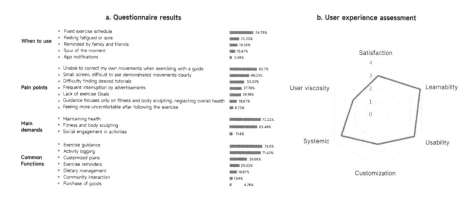

Fig. 7. User survey results on using exercise apps

3.3 Music Relaxation Products—Vacuity and Stillness

Five Element Music is an essential component of TCM theory, which has been demonstrated to have various healing indications on people when listened to at different times, bringing them vacuity and stillness [15]. Wating, an application related to Five Element music, is a typical example of music relaxation based on TCM theory and Proactive Health. It makes a suitable recommendation for users according to their constitution, mental disorder, and the external environment, such as season and time (Fig. 8).

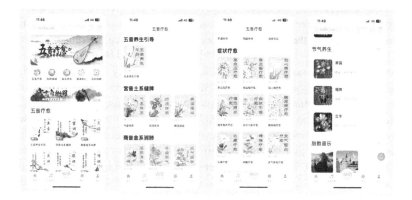

Fig. 8. Wating app

Analysis of relevant domestic and international product competition is shown in Fig. 9. It was discovered that dominant music software platforms primarily utilize white noise as a medium and classify sounds according to different users' purposes, such as sleep, focus, stress relief, and meditation. Regarding personality, Headspace and Balance customize a therapy plan for each user according to their mental health and habits of listening to music surveyed through questionnaires in the apps. Moreover, Tidal, Xinchao, and Headspace use healing videos or user-friendly animations to guide people in adjusting their breath properly, representing their proactive and systematic thinking to some degree.

Category	Item	Wating	Tidal	Xiaoshuimian	Now	Xinchao	Headspace	Balance
Personalized recommendation	Five elements music	✓						
	Music recommendations based on constitution	✓						
	Music recommendations base on season	✓						
	Listening time recommendations base on constitution							
	Music recommendations base on demand	✓	✓	✓	✓	✓	✓	✓
	Customized plan	✓	✓	✓		✓	✓	✓
Psychological assessment				✓	✓		✓	✓
Holistic	Explanation of Principle (Mind-Body Unity)							
	Diet recommendations							
	Exercise guidance							
	Massage recommendations							
	Sunbathing guidance							
Habit formation	Regular reminders		✓		✓		✓	✓
	Calendar records		✓	✓	✓			
	Visual immersion		✓			✓	✓	
	Daily schedule						✓	✓
	Achievement badges							✓

Fig. 9. Competitive product analysis of music relaxation apps

This study collected 82 valid questionnaires from users aged 18–50 regarding their usage needs and experience feedback on music relaxation apps. As Fig. 10(a) shows, we found that nearly half of the respondents choose to listen to healing music before sleep (48.78%) and while studying and working (42.68%), followed by meditation (35.37%), when they are tired and need a rest (29.27%), and when they feel anxious (26.83%). About 60% of them use apps for stress reduction and alleviating insomnia issues related to health. Users suggest that the existing apps have a limited range of sounds (51.22%), lack professional advice on adjusting personal states (47.56%), and fail to provide comprehensive recommendations that integrate other lifestyle habits (53.66%). The user rating radar chart shows that the app performs well in terms of learnability, usability, and real-time capabilities. However, the user satisfaction level is not high. Listening to music is an easily accessible means of encouraging users to actively maintain their physical and mental well-being in the long term (Fig. 10(b)). Relevant apps should be able to proactively perceive changes in user emotions and provide targeted and systematic health adjustments at physiological and psychological levels, considering other lifestyle factors.

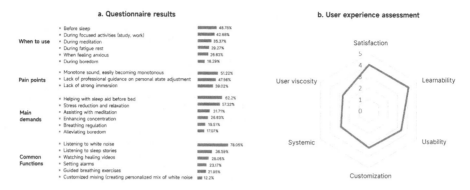

Fig. 10. User survey results on music relaxation apps

3.4   Digestive Aid Products - Spleen and Stomach Reception

In TCM theory, "spleen and stomach reception" means that the spleen and stomach work together to complete the digestion and absorption of food as well as the transportation of nutrients, thereby nourishing the whole body. The abundance or deficiency of stomach Qi is closely related to the activities and survival of humans. Due to individual variations in constitution and lifestyle habits, digestive problems can differ among people. The design of proactive health digestive products should provide multiple modes to meet users' diverse physiological and mental requirements and offer suggestions regarding the potential impact of diet, exercise, clothing choices, and other lifestyle factors on digestive functions. For instance, as seen in Fig. 11, the Hyundai abdominal massager offers three different massage modes to users and incorporates smokeless moxibustion to help users promote blood circulation, regulate Qi, and nurture the spleen and stomach.

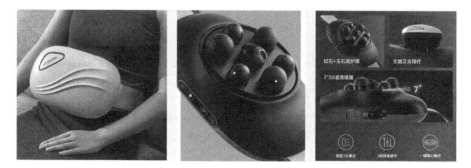

Fig. 11. Hyundai abdominal massager

Figure 12 shows the competitive product analysis of digestive aid products. It is observed that most products have similar structures and functionalities. They have not yet been able to recommend appropriate massage intensity, duration, and acupoints based on user constitution and specific digestive issues. As a result, tailored digestive rehabilitation plans cannot be formulated effectively. Moreover, the products lack guidance for users to simultaneously pay attention to other lifestyle habits, such as diet and exercise, which are crucial for comprehensive and habitual attention to spleen and stomach health.

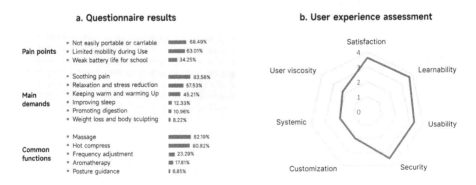

Category	Item	PGG	Medisana	Hyundai	Cellulite	Weyluk	ACK
Personalized Recommendations	Recommend modes based on physiological constitution						
	Recommend modes based on need	⊘	⊘	⊘			⊘
	Recommend intensity based on endurance		⊘	⊘			⊘
	Recommend speed based on endurance		⊘			⊘	
	Customize personal massage plan						
Holistic	Explanation of Principle (Mind-Body Unity)						
	Combine moxibustion and essential oils	⊘	⊘				
	Hand massage					⊘	
	Diet recommendations						
	Exercise guidance						
	Music therapy						
	Sunbathing						
Habit formation	Regular reminders						
	Health Tracking						

Fig. 12. Competitive product analysis of digestive aid products

To understand the usage requirements and experiences of digestive aid products, 73 valid questionnaires were collected from users between the ages of 18 and 50. Figure 13(a) visualizes the survey results. We found that approximately 77% of the respondents liked the product but did not use it frequently, which could be due to reasons such as inconvenience in storage (68.49%) and portability (63.01%), limitations in mobility during use, and weak battery life (34.25%). They often use such products to relieve pain (83.56%), reduce stress (57.53%) and keep cold and warm (45.21%). About 75% of the users suggest that the products fail to provide personalized guidance and lack a comprehensive approach to offer systematic health management plans. Based on user feedback, this type of product performs well regarding learnability, usability, safety, and satisfaction. However, it lacks systematic, real-time, customized functionalities (Fig. 13(b)).

a. Questionnaire results

Pain points	Not easily portable or carriable	68.49%
	Limited mobility during Use	63.01%
	Weak battery life for school	34.25%
Main demands	Soothing pain	83.56%
	Relaxation and stress reduction	57.53%
	Keeping warm and warming Up	45.21%
	Improving sleep	12.33%
	Promoting digestion	10.96%
	Weight loss and body sculpting	8.22%
Common functions	Massage	82.19%
	Hot compress	80.82%
	Frequency adjustment	23.29%
	Aromatherapy	17.81%
	Posture guidance	6.85%

b. User experience assessment

(Radar chart with axes: Satisfaction, Learnability, Usability, Security, Customization, Systemic, User viscosity; scale 0 to 4)

Fig. 13. User survey results on digestive aid products

3.5   Lighting Products - Exposed to Sunlight

Sunlight has been regarded as an essential nutrient, assisting people in maintaining normal physiological functions and regulating emotions [16, 17]. Most people spend most of their time indoors in modern life, exposed to artificial light sources such as incandescent bulbs that emit an uneven spectrum of light. Insufficient sunlight is detrimental to their physical and mental health. Therefore, the design of lighting products based on TCM theory and proactive health encompasses two aspects: firstly, creating sensory experiences that mimic sunlight and its diurnal variations to regulate hormones through retinal ganglion cells and stabilize emotions. For example, Aquara Skylight supports the adaptive lighting feature of Apple HomeKit, automatically adjusting the color temperature of the light based on different periods, actively creating a realistic natural light environment. Secondly, addressing the problem of uneven spectrum in artificial light sources and providing user guidance for healthy behaviors based on specific usage scenarios (Fig. 14). Eye protection lamp Opple 2Pro is a typical example (Fig. 15). It utilizes LED beads that simulate the spectrum of sunlight and incorporates intelligent features such as automatic adjustment of brightness based on ambient light changes and timed reminders for rest. This reduces the potential harm caused by excessive blue light from artificial sources and helps users develop healthy eye protection habits.

Fig. 14. Aquara skylight

Figure 16 depicts the competitive product analysis of lighting products. It is found that no products can construct targeted lighting plans based on users' constitution and mental needs currently. Moreover, there is a lack of comprehensive and systematic health recommendations that integrate aspects such as diet and exercise for users.

To further gather design requirements for lighting products, desktop research was conducted to summarize user usage needs and feedback. As Fig. 17(a) shows, many users believed that the product achieved the effect of replicating natural light but lacked sufficient brightness. Additionally, they complain that the current interaction is cumbersome. From the user experience assessment, as seen in Fig. 17(b), most products had limited functionality and performed poorly in systematization and customization. Proactive health lighting products expand the opportunity for urban residents to access natural light exposure, helping them regulate circadian rhythms and alleviate mood disorders.

Fig. 15. Opple 2Pro

Category	Item	Yeelight	Pak	Aquara	Coelux	Honeywell	Opple 2Pro
Basic Performance	No Blue Light Hazard (RG0)		⊘	⊘		⊘	⊘
	Slight warm sensation, promotes vitamin absorption		⊘				
Personalized Recommendations	Regular reminders						⊘
	Adjusting according to time			⊘	⊘		
	Adjusting based on environmental conditions						⊘
	Adapting based on physiological consitution						
	Adjusting according to usage needs	⊘		⊘	⊘		
	Integrating with Other Smart Products			⊘	⊘		⊘
Holistic	Diet recommendations						
	Exercise guidance						
	Music therapy						
	Massage guidance						

Fig. 16. Competitive product analysis of lighting products

Also, it is important to promote health by considering users' conditions, physical and mental needs, and lifestyle habits.

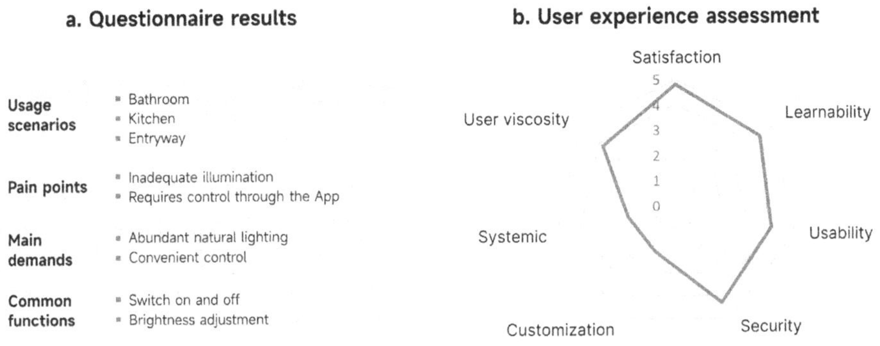

a. Questionnaire results

Usage scenarios	▪ Bathroom ▪ Kitchen ▪ Entryway
Pain points	▪ Inadequate illumination ▪ Requires control through the App
Main demands	▪ Abundant natural lighting ▪ Convenient control
Common functions	▪ Switch on and off ▪ Brightness adjustment

b. User experience assessment

Satisfaction, Learnability, Usability, Security, Customization, Systemic, User viscosity

Fig. 17. User survey results on lighting products

4 Conclusion

With the gradual increase in chronic diseases worldwide, maintaining health and obtaining a higher quality of life have become a social focus. The core concepts of Proactive Health, such as "prevention is better than cure," "holistic view," and the emphasis on improving adverse lifestyle factors to restore physical resilience, share many similarities with TCM theory. Therefore, this research aims to integrate the TCM theory with the Proactive Health concept, guiding modern people to maintain health. Corresponding design strategies are proposed from the perspectives of systematicity, preventiveness, personality, and harmony. Comparative research and analysis are conducted on relevant products in the market in five aspects: diet, exercise, music relaxation, digestion, and sunbathing. Based on TCM theory, proactive health products must consider users' modern lifestyle habits and physical constitution. Comprehensive and systematical health solutions that encompass various lifestyle factors should be proposed, aiming to assist individuals in maintaining physical resilience and adaptability. This research is a practical supplement to the theory of proactive health, exploring access to enhance the health level of the population and providing valuable insights for the development of lifestyle-oriented health products.

References

1. Noncommunicable diseases. https://www.who.int/news-room/fact-sheets/detail/noncommun icable-diseases
2. The Information Office of the State Council held a press conference on the Report on the Status of Nutrition and Chronic Diseases of Chinese Residents. https://www.gov.cn/xinwen/2020-12/24/content_5572983.htm
3. Li, X.C., Yu, M.S.: Proactive health: from idea to model. China Sport Sci. **40**(2), 83–89 (2020)
4. Gao, X., Li, X.G., Liang, Z., et al.: Reflection and exploration of digital chronic disease management based on the proactive health index. J. Shanghai Jiao Tong Univ. (Med. Sci.) **43**(2), 131–142 (2023)
5. Ziglio, E., Currie, C., Rasmussen, Rasmussen, V.B.: The WHO cross-national study of health behavior in school-aged children from 35 countries: findings from 2001–2002. J. School Health **74**(6), 204–206 (2004)
6. Sun, C., Tang, S., Chen, C., et al.: Connotation of active health: a literature analysis. Chin. J. Public Health **39**(1), 68–72 (2023)
7. Rodriguez, J.A., Shachar, C., Bates, D.: Digital inclusion as health care: supporting health care equity with digital-infrastructure initiatives. N. Engl. J. Med. **386**(12), 1101–1103 (2022)
8. "Healthy China 2030" Planning Outline. https://www.gov.cn/zhengce/2016-10/25/content_5 124174.htm?eqid=9d4da6bb000833c0000000046496f297. Accessed 15 Nov 2023
9. Zhang, Q., Jin, H., Shi X., et al.: Proactive care in china: implementation status and recommendation strategies for various undertaking bodies. Chin. Gen. Pract. **25**(31), 3923–3927, 3932 (2022)
10. Zhang, Z., Ma, L., Ma, L., et al.: The value and application prospect of transcutaneous electrical acupoint stimulation to regulate blood pressure from the perspective of proactive healthcare. Acupunct. Res. 1–15 (2023)
11. Chen, L., Li, F., Wang, Q., et al.: Discussion on proactive health based on the traditional Chinese medicine constitution theory. China J. Tradit. Chin. Med. Pharm. **37**(08), 4315–4318 (2022)

12. Liu, J., Li, W., Yao, H., Liu, J.: Proactive health: an imperative to achieve the goal of healthy China. China CDC Weekly **4**(36), 799–801 (2022)
13. Zhang, Z.: The influence of the theory of yin-yang and the five elements on the development of traditional Chinese medicine theory. Stud. Philos. Sci. Technol. **1**, 76–79, 83 (2004)
14. Shan, F., Huang, L., Guo, J., Chen, M.: History and development of "one root of medicine and food." Chin Bull Life Sci. **27**(8), 106–1069 (2015)
15. Zhang, Z., Cai, Z., Yu, Y., Wu, L., Zhang, Y.: Effect of Lixujieyu recipe in combination with five elements music therapy on chronic fatigue syndrome. J. Tradit. Chin. Med. **35**(6), 637–641 (2015)
16. Bao, Z., Tian, Q., Gao, X.: Exploring the correlation between depression and deficiency of Yang Qi. Jiangxi J. Tradit. Chin. Med. **40**(6), 9–10 (2009)
17. Cui, Y., Gong, Q., Huang, C., et al.: The relationship between sunlight exposure duration and depressive symptoms: a cross-sectional study on elderly Chinese women. PLoS One **16**(7) (2021)

Artificial Intelligence and Health Applications

A Machine Learning Model for Predicting the Risk of Perinatal Mortality in Low-and-Middle-Income Countries: A Case Study

Sebastian Arias-Fonseca[1], Miguel Ortiz-Barrios[1(✉)], Alexandros Konios[2],
Martha Gutierrez de Piñeres-Jalile[3], María Montero-Estrada[4],
Carlos Hernández-Lalinde[4], Eliecer Medina-Pacheco[3], Fanny Lambraño-Coronado[3],
Ibett Figueroa-Salazar[5], Jesús Araujo-Torres[6], and Richard Prasca-de la Hoz[7]

[1] Department of Productivity and Innovation, Universidad de La Costa CUC,
080002 Barranquilla, Colombia
{sarias9,mortiz1}@cuc.edu.co
[2] Department of Computer Science, Nottingham Trent University, Nottingham 4081112, UK
alexandros.konios@ntu.ac.uk
[3] Medical Management, Previsalud, 080020 Barranquilla, Colombia
{marta.gutierrez,eliecer.medina,
fanny.lambrano}@previsalud.com.co
[4] Quality Department, Previsalud, 080020 Barranquilla, Colombia
{maria.montero,carlos.hernandez}@previsalud.com.co
[5] Medical Audit, Previsalud, 080020 Barranquilla, Colombia
ibett.figueroa@previsalud.com.co
[6] Obstetric Risk Program, Calidad Médica IPS, 200001 Valledupar, Colombia
Jesuobstetra@gmail.com
[7] Maternal Perinatal Risk Program, Salud Social IPS, 080005 Barranquilla, Colombia

Abstract. Perinatal mortality is the death that happens between 22 weeks of gestation and the first seven days of birth. This has become an essential indicator for measuring the quality of maternal and childcare in Low-and-Middle-Income Countries (LMICs). Tools based on Artificial Intelligence (AI) have emerged with immediate relevance in medical contexts, more precisely with Machine Learning (ML) tools due to the ability to learn from past and present observations and be able to generate future predictions, promising positive results in maternal and childcare processes. This paper presents a Random Forest (RF) model for predicting the risk of perinatal mortality in LMICs. We initially characterized the prenatal control process in LMICs. Second, potentially predictive features of perinatal mortality were identified considering the literature review and medical expertise. Subsequently, a data pre-processing procedure was executed to improve the data quality. The RF algorithm was employed to model the risk of perinatal mortality based on social and clinical variables. A case study in a Colombian healthcare institution was used to validate the proposed approach. The results show an RF model with an accuracy of 99.16%, sensibility = 87.50%, and specificity = 100%.

© The Author(s), under exclusive license to Springer Nature Switzerland AG 2024
V. G. Duffy (Ed.): HCII 2024, LNCS 14710, pp. 233–250, 2024.
https://doi.org/10.1007/978-3-031-61063-9_16

234   S. Arias-Fonseca et al.

Keywords: Artificial Intelligence (AI) · Random Forest (RF) · Perinatal
Mortality · Low-and-Middle-Income Countries (LMICs) · Healthcare

1 Introduction

Perinatal mortality, defined as fetal death after twenty-two weeks of gestation or neonatal death within the first four weeks after birth, remains a significant public health concern globally, with profound implications for maternal and child health outcomes. The World Health Organization (WHO) reports that approximately 2.4 million perinatal deaths occur annually worldwide, with the majority transpiring in low- and middle-income countries, where access to quality healthcare services may be limited [24]. These statistics underscore the urgent need for comprehensive strategies to address the underlying determinants of perinatal mortality, including socioeconomic disparities, inadequate prenatal care, maternal health conditions, and obstetric complications. Despite advancements in healthcare and prenatal interventions, perinatal mortality rates vary widely across regions and socioeconomic strata, indicating persistent challenges in addressing this complex issue.

Recent studies have elucidated emerging trends and risk factors associated with perinatal mortality. For instance, the research in [20] identified maternal age, pre-existing medical conditions, and gestational age at delivery as significant predictors of perinatal mortality in high-income settings. Additionally, findings from a systematic review by researchers [15] emphasized the impact of environmental factors, such as air pollution and maternal exposure to toxins, on fetal development and perinatal outcomes.

The impact of perinatal mortality extends beyond immediate health outcomes, affecting families emotionally, socially, and economically [4]. Understanding the underlying causes and risk factors associated with perinatal mortality is crucial for developing effective interventions and policies to mitigate its occurrence. Recent literature underscores the multifactorial nature of perinatal mortality, with factors such as maternal age, socioeconomic status, access to healthcare, maternal nutrition, maternal comorbidities, obstetric complications, and quality of perinatal care playing pivotal roles [7, 10], and [28].

Moreover, disparities in perinatal mortality persist among different racial and ethnic groups, highlighting the importance of addressing structural inequalities in healthcare delivery and access [16]. Evidence suggests that interventions targeting modifiable risk factors, such as improving antenatal care, promoting skilled birth attendance, enhancing emergency obstetric care, and strengthening health systems, can significantly reduce perinatal mortality rates [3, 10], and [68].

Perinatal mortality, encompassing stillbirths and early neonatal deaths, represents a formidable challenge to maternal and child health in Low-and-Middle-Income Countries (LMICs). Despite global efforts to improve healthcare infrastructure and access to essential maternal and neonatal services, LMICs continue to bear a disproportionate burden of perinatal mortality. The World Health Organization (WHO) estimates that approximately 98% of the 2.4 million annual perinatal deaths occur in LMICs, reflecting stark disparities in healthcare access and quality [23]. Understanding the epidemiology and determinants of perinatal mortality in LMICs is paramount for designing targeted interventions to address this critical public health issue.

A complex interplay of socioeconomic, cultural, and healthcare-related factors shapes the burden of perinatal mortality in LMICs. Limited access to prenatal care, skilled birth attendance, emergency obstetric services, and postnatal care exacerbate the risk of adverse perinatal outcomes [10]. Moreover, inadequate nutrition, infectious diseases, such as malaria and HIV/AIDS, and suboptimal maternal health contribute to the high incidence of stillbirths and neonatal deaths in LMICs [3].

Maternal education, household income, and geographical remoteness are significant determinants of perinatal mortality in LMICs, underscoring the importance of addressing socioeconomic disparities in healthcare access and utilization [21]. Ethnic minorities and marginalized populations are particularly vulnerable to adverse perinatal outcomes due to systemic barriers to healthcare access and discrimination [16].

Efforts to reduce perinatal mortality in LMICs necessitate a multifaceted approach, including strengthening healthcare infrastructure, enhancing antenatal and obstetric care, promoting maternal nutrition and hygiene, and addressing social determinants of health [3, 10], and [69]. Evidence-based interventions tailored to the specific contexts and needs of LMICs have the potential to significantly reduce perinatal mortality rates and improve maternal and child health outcomes.

Perinatal mortality, encompassing stillbirths and early neonatal deaths within the first four weeks of life, remains a significant public health concern in Colombia, reflecting both the quality of maternal and newborn healthcare and the broader social determinants of health. Understanding the prevalence, trends, and determinants of perinatal mortality in Colombia is crucial for designing targeted interventions to reduce its burden and improve maternal and child health outcomes in the country.

Recent literature underscores the complex interplay of factors contributing to perinatal mortality in Colombia, including healthcare access, quality of care, and socioeconomic disparities. According to data from the Colombian Ministry of Health, approximately 10 out of every 1,000 pregnancies end in perinatal death, with disparities observed across regions and socio-economic strata [12]. These statistics highlight the need for tailored interventions to address the underlying drivers of perinatal mortality and reduce disparities in access to maternal and neonatal healthcare services.

Other recent studies have shed light on specific risk factors associated with perinatal mortality in Colombia. For instance, research in [9] identified inadequate prenatal care, maternal malnutrition, and limited access to skilled birth attendance as key contributors to perinatal deaths in marginalized communities. Additionally, findings from a study [8] emphasized the impact of maternal health conditions, such as hypertensive disorders and gestational diabetes, on perinatal outcomes in Colombia.

The advancement of technology, and particularly of Artificial Intelligence, would be useful in effectively reducing the perinatal death rate by accurately predicting tools based on Artificial Intelligence (AI) have emerged with immediate relevance in medical contexts, more precisely with Machine Learning (ML) tools due to the ability to learn from past and present observations and be able to generate future predictions, promising positive results in maternal and childcare processes. This research aims to develop an

AI model using the Random Forest (RF) technique for predicting and preventing perinatal mortality in pregnant mothers in Colombia. Initially, the study cohort is developed
considering pregnant women served between January 2021 and August 2023.

The remainder of this paper is organized as follows: Section 2 provides an overview
of related work in the realms of artificial intelligence and machine learning techniques
used in associated issues. Section 3 details the methodology used for conducting the
research and presents the respective approach. Section 4 presents the data analysis and
results obtained, while Sect. 5 discusses the result evaluation. Finally, Sect. 5 concludes
the paper, summarizing key findings and suggesting directions for future research.

2 Literature Review

Despite advances in medical science and healthcare delivery, perinatal mortality rates
persist, especially in low-resource settings. According to the World Health Organization
(WHO), 75% of neonatal deaths (deaths during the first month of life) take place within
the first week. Despite the efforts and goals set to reduce perinatal death indicators, in
countries such as Colombia, the perinatal mortality rate has increased from 14.5 (2016)
to 16 (2021). Artificial Intelligence (AI) offers innovative solutions for predicting and
preventing perinatal deaths by analysing complex data patterns and providing actionable
insights for healthcare providers.

Artificial Intelligence, particularly Machine Learning (ML) algorithms, has demonstrated remarkable capabilities in various healthcare domains, including diagnostics,
treatment optimization, and predictive analytics [6]. By analysing large datasets comprising clinical, genetic, and environmental factors, AI-powered models can identify
subtle patterns and accurately predict health outcomes [17]. In perinatal health, AI is
promising to enhance risk stratification, guide clinical decision-making, and ultimately
improve outcomes for pregnant mothers and newborns.

Machine learning techniques, such as neural networks, support vector machines,
decision trees, and ensemble methods like Random Forest and gradient boosting, have
been employed to develop predictive models for perinatal mortality. These algorithms
utilize diverse data sources, including maternal demographics, medical history, prenatal
care records, ultrasound findings, and fetal monitoring parameters, to generate individualized risk assessments [14]. By leveraging large datasets and advanced analytical
techniques, machine learning models can identify complex patterns and predict perinatal
outcomes with high accuracy.

The study in [13] explores the application of machine learning techniques to predict perinatal mortality using data from a birth registry in northern Tanzania. It aims
to develop models that can accurately predict perinatal deaths, subsequently informing
interventions to reduce perinatal mortality rates in the region. The primary goal of this
work was to develop machine-learning models capable of predicting perinatal deaths
using data available in a birth registry in northern Tanzania. For that reason, it is based
on a birth registry-based cohort design. Data were collected from the Kilimanjaro Chris-
tian Medical Centre (KCMC) Birth Registry, which captures information on all births
and perinatal deaths in the catchment area. Various demographic, clinical, and obstetric variables were collected for each birth, including maternal age, gestational age, birth

weight, mode of delivery, and others. The researchers employed several machine learning algorithms to develop prediction models for perinatal death. These algorithms include logistic regression, decision trees, random forests, support vector machines, and artificial neural networks. The models were trained and tested using the available data, with performance metrics such as accuracy, sensitivity, specificity, and area under the receiver operating characteristic curve (AUC-ROC) used to evaluate their predictive capabilities. The study found that the random forest algorithm yielded the highest predictive performance for perinatal death, with an AUC-ROC of 0.848. Other machine learning models also demonstrated reasonably good predictive accuracy, with AUC-ROC values ranging from 0.780 to 0.828. Including various demographic and clinical variables in the models contributed to their predictive power. Furthermore, the authors acknowledge several limitations, including the reliance on data from a single birth registry, which may limit the generalizability of the findings. Additionally, they focused on a specific geographical area, and results may only be applicable to other regions with validation.

The authors in [5] investigate the use of machine learning techniques to predict perinatal mortality rates based on maternal health status and health insurance coverage in Ethiopia. The study aims to develop predictive models that can assist healthcare providers and policymakers in identifying high-risk pregnancies and implementing targeted interventions to reduce perinatal mortality rates. This research focuses on developing predictive models for perinatal mortality using maternal health status and health insurance service data in Ethiopia. Data were collected from the Ethiopian Demographic and Health Survey (EDHS) and the Ethiopian National Health Insurance Agency (ENHIA) database considering various factors such as demographic, clinical, and insurance-related variables were considered as potential predictors of perinatal mortality. The study found that the developed machine learning models achieved good predictive performance for perinatal mortality based on maternal health status and health insurance service data. Specifically, they demonstrated high accuracy, sensitivity, specificity, and AUC-ROC values, indicating their ability to identify high-risk pregnancies accurately. Moreover, health insurance service data used in the models improves their results, highlighting the importance of access to healthcare services in reducing perinatal mortality rates. Finally, this work's limitations relate to the potential biases in the data sources and the absence of certain important variables that could influence perinatal mortality rates.

A population-based retrospective approach is presented in [26]. This work developed predictive models that can assist in identifying infants at high risk of mortality, thereby enabling early interventions and improved healthcare planning. Notably, the authors developed machine learning models that predict infant mortality based on population-level data. In this study, infant mortality refers to deaths that occur within the first year of life (including perinatal deaths). This work involves the employment of a range of machine learning algorithms, e.g., decision trees, random forests, and others, which are trained and tested using historical data on infant deaths and related predictors, with performance metrics such as accuracy, sensitivity, specificity, and area under the receiver operating characteristic curve (AUC-ROC) used to evaluate their effectiveness. The results demonstrate high accuracy, sensitivity, specificity, and AUC-ROC values (over 90% in most cases), indicating their ability to identify infants at high risk of mortality effectively.

The study presented in [11] explores the utilization of machine learning techniques to predict the risk of stillbirth in a large dataset covering births in Western Australia over 35 years. Specifically, the study considers a large cohort of births from 1980 to 2015 in Western Australia. This extensive dataset provides a rich source of information regarding various maternal and fetal factors, enabling a thorough analysis of stillbirth risk factors. The researchers considered several different potential predictors for stillbirth risk, including maternal age, parity, gestational age, birth weight, maternal smoking status, socioeconomic status, and maternal health conditions such as diabetes and hypertension. The machine learning algorithms used in this work include decision trees, random forest, extreme gradient boosting (XGBoost), and a multilayer perceptron neural network. The findings indicate that the best-performing classifier (XGBoost) predicted 45% (95% CI: 43%, 46%) of stillbirths for all women and 45% (95% CI: 43%, 47%) of stillbirths after the inclusion of previous pregnancy history.

Another study carried out in Brazil assesses the performance of machine learning models in predicting neonatal mortality risk in the country, considering the period from 2000 to 2016 [1]. The researchers used various machine learning algorithms to construct predictive models for neonatal mortality risk. The performance of the machine learning models is assessed using standard metrics such as sensitivity, specificity, accuracy, area under the receiver operating characteristic curve (AUC-ROC), and precision-recall curves. The performance and accuracy results were relatively high, achieving values over 85%. This work highlights that this kind of method can help health experts make decisions whether more intensive care is necessary for newborns in Brazil.

AlShwaish et al. [2] conducted research using six supervised machine learning models (i.e., Support Vector Machine (SVM), Logistic Regression (LR), Gradient Boosting (GB), Random Forest (RF), Deep Learning (DL), and the Ensemble Model) to predict the mortality risk in newborns and during the perinatal period using imbalanced data. Imbalanced data refers to datasets where the number of instances belonging to one class (e.g., surviving newborns) is significantly higher than the other (e.g., deceased newborns). The study analyses a dataset comprising information on newborns and perinatal outcomes. This dataset considers factors such as maternal health status, prenatal care, birth complications, gestational age, birth weight, and neonatal outcomes (survival or mortality). The data were collected from hospitals, healthcare registries, and medical records from New York from 2012 to 2016. The performance of the predictive models was tested using standard evaluation metrics such as sensitivity, specificity, accuracy, precision, recall, F1-score, and area under the receiver operating characteristic curve (AUC-ROC). The results obtained were quite encouraging for both types of datasets, with the best-performing model being the Ensemble Model, which had 97.44% and 80.65% accuracy for the Imbalanced and Balanced datasets, respectively. The authors stress the importance of accurately predicting mortality risk as this could help healthcare professionals implement timely interventions, improve prenatal and neonatal care practices, and reduce mortality rates among newborns and during the perinatal period.

In [19], the authors developed machine learning models to predict infant mortality, covering different mortality classes such as perinatal, early neonatal, late neonatal, and post-neonatal. In this approach, the researchers investigated how effective the proposed models were in predicting deaths that fall under different mortality classes and causes.

For that purpose, they used external features attached to the birth certificates to build models for slices of the population examined, e.g., different races, to evaluate their accuracy. The dataset utilised contained a total of 12 million birth certificates in the United States of America from 2000 to 2002, out of which 83 thousand were related to infants who did not survive until their first birthday. The predicted models were created using machine learning methods like Gaussian Naïve Bayes, One-class SVMs, Boosted trees, and Neural Networks. According to the evaluation of the results obtained, the best score was achieved using all the features in the 1:10 training set with the Boosted Trees model, with Accuracy being approximately 0.92. Finally, the findings of this work demonstrate that half of the birth certificate features per race are not related directly to the fetus or newborn but to the mother.

The emerging field of artificial intelligence (AI) and machine learning (ML) offers promising strategies for enhancing predicting and managing perinatal health outcomes, including neonatal mortality and preterm birth. Yasrebinia and Rezaei [25] conducted a systematic review focusing on using artificial intelligence to predict neonatal mortality post-pregnancy. Their work meticulously evaluates various AI models, underscoring their potential to improve predictive accuracy and, thus, potentially save lives. Moreover, Ramakrishnan et al. [18] provide a comprehensive review of the application of artificial intelligence in predicting perinatal health outcomes. Their article delves into how AI can be leveraged to identify key predictors of perinatal health, offering a glimpse into the future of personalized and pre-emptive healthcare strategies. This review illuminates the path forward for integrating AI into maternal and child healthcare, highlighting its role in enhancing decision-making processes and improving health outcomes. Finally, Włodarczyk et al. [22] explore the application of machine learning methods specifically for the predicting preterm birth, a critical factor in perinatal health. Their review systematically analyses various ML algorithms and their effectiveness in early detection and prevention strategies. By focusing on the technological advancements in ML, the authors emphasize the potential of these tools in revolutionizing the approach to managing pre-term births, thereby reducing associated risks and improving neonatal care.

All the aforementioned research works highlight the necessity of using artificial intelligence (AI) in predicting perinatal deaths lies in its potential to significantly improve maternal and neonatal health outcomes through early identification and intervention. Traditional methods of predicting perinatal deaths often rely on standard clinical parameters and historical data, which may not capture the complex, multifactorial nature of perinatal health risks. AI and machine learning models can analyse vast amounts of data, including demographic, socioeconomic, environmental, and clinical variables, to uncover subtle patterns and risk factors that may not be apparent to humans. This capability allows for the development of predictive models that can provide personalized risk assessments, enabling healthcare providers to tailor interventions to each patient's specific needs. Furthermore, AI can facilitate continuous learning and improvement of prediction models as more data becomes available, ensuring that predictive capabilities evolve with emerging health trends and evidence. Ultimately, the use of AI in predicting perinatal deaths represents a transformative approach to perinatal care, promising to reduce mortality rates through more accurate predictions, timely interventions, and enhanced understanding of the underlying causes of adverse outcomes.

In this research, we develop a Random Forest (RF) technique for predicting and preventing perinatal mortality in pregnant mothers in Colombia, considering pregnant women served between January 2021 and August 2023. According to the best of our knowledge, this field is not widely explored, and we introduce an approach that would lead to further research and exploration of the different features that could be included in future experiments to improve the perinatal death rates in a Low-and-Middle-Income Country like Colombia.

3 Methodology

Figure 1 presents the proposed 4-phase methodology. The description of each step is shown below:

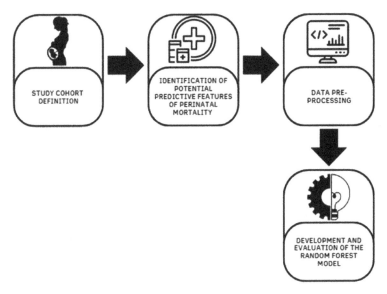

Fig. 1. The proposed methodology for predicting the risk of perinatal mortality

Study Cohort Definition. We considered pregnant women served between January 2021 and August 2023 in a clinical center in Colombia. The pregnant women's data was extracted using the individualized medical records of each pregnancy care appointment.

Identification of Potential Predictive Features of Perinatal Mortality. A list of potential perinatal mortality features is established, taking into account the literature review and medical experience. The list includes the gynecobstetric history, sociodemographic, and clinical features.

Data Pre-processing. Data pre-processing was executed to improve the quality of the data. It is known that healthcare databases have incomplete and missing data, which can lead to medical errors and difficulty in research analysis [27]. For this reason, incomplete data will be imputed using the median of each variable.

Development and Evaluation of the Random Forest Model. The significance of features is appraised through the Mean Decrease in Gini Coefficient (MDGC). On the other hand, given the still-existing imbalance between classes, undersampling and oversampling procedures are widely recommended [29, 30], and [31]. The final feature vector is randomly divided into training and test subsets. Finally, the RF model is derived to predict the probability of perinatal mortality. The model is later evaluated using performance metrics such as Accuracy, Sensitivity, Specificity, Positive Predictive Value, Negative Predictive Value, McNemar's Test P-Value, and The Area Under Curve (AUC).

4 Results

The increase in perinatal mortality rates is one of the main problems in healthcare worldwide. This problem may be partially explained by non-adherence to pre-natal control and low-quality healthcare monitoring [32–34], and [35]. These mortality rates can be affected by the ignorance or omission of warning signs during a high-risk pregnancy by medical personnel. Knowing this, a clinical center in Colombia deployed a study with more than 5,000 pregnant women aiming to develop a decision-making tool for predicting perinatal mortality likelihood. The following subsections illustrate this application and the main findings.

4.1 Study Cohort

The initial dataset contains 5,022 records of pregnant patients between January 2021 and August 2023. The individual patient data includes information regarding gynecobstetric history, pregnancy data, vital signs, laboratory results, and the pregnancy outcome. Databases originating from gynecological consultations and medical records were taken into account. The use of this data was approved by the ethical committee of the medical center, which also provided informed consent on the project deployment.

4.2 Potential Predictive Features of Perinatal Mortality

The perinatal mortality is given by a set of features from different domains. The list of possible predictors (Table 1) emerges from the reported literature and the medical experience of experts.

Within the variables that were studied, their importance was evaluated with the MDGC, in which variables such as BMI (MDGC > 2.1172), mother's age (MDGC = 1.375), gestational age (MDGC > 0.8946), hemoglobin (MDGC > 1.0471), and blood glucose (MDGC > 0.6637) presented a higher MDGC per month of consultation.

Table 1. List of potential predictors of perinatal mortality.

Predictor name	Description	Literature reference
Age	Pregnant woman's age at the time of first gynecological appointment	Geiger et al. [36], Saccone et al. [37]
Obstetric gynecological history: "pregnancies", "deliveries", "abortions", "cesarean sections"	Description of gynecological history: Number of "pregnancies", "deliveries", "abortions", "cesarean sections"	Abdelmageed et al. [38], Tadese et al. [39]
Gestational age	Pregnant woman's gestational age at first gynecological appointment and each follow-up visit	Murray et al. [40], Manjavidze et al. [41]
Body Max Index (BMI)	BMI at each gynecological appointment	Vats et al. [42], Simko et al. [43]
Systolic blood pressure	Systolic Blood Pressure (Mm/Hg) at each gynecological appointment	Garanet et al. [44], Grover et al. [45]
Diastolic blood pressure	Diastolic Blood Pressure (Mm/Hg) at each gynecological appointment	
Hemoglobin	Hemoglobin level (g/dL) calculated by the lab	Young et al. [46], Jung et al. [47]
Asymptomatic bacteriuria	A significant amount of bacteria in the urine of a pregnant woman (urine test) "1": Normal, "2": Abnormal	Neelima et al. [48], Wingert et al. [49]
Presence of Bacteria in Urine	Evaluates whether there is a concentration of bacteria in the urine of the pregnant woman (Urine culture test) "1": Normal, "2": Abnormal	Naamany et al. [50], Cohen et al. [51]
Blood glucose	Glucose level (Mg/dL) calculated by the lab	Lepercq et al. [52], Rasheed et al. [53]
Glucose tolerance	Glucose Tolerance (Mg/dL) calculated by the lab	Yokomichi et al. [54], Kung et al. [55]
Hepatitis B	Hepatitis test result "1": Reactive, "2" Not reactive	Wu et al. [56], Sirilert et al. [57]
Toxoplasma IgG	Toxoplasma IgG test result "1": Reactive, "2" Not reactive	Ahmed et al. [58], Martinez et al. [59]

(continued)

Table 1. (*continued*)

Predictor name	Description	Literature reference
Toxoplasma IgM	Toxoplasma IgM test result "1": Reactive, "2" Not reactive	
Cervical Infection or Cervical Cancer	Presence of cervical infection or cervical cancer by cytology "1": Normal, "2": Abnormal	Mailhot et al. [60], Jar-Allah et al. [61]
Bacterial vaginosis	Presence of bacterial vaginosis (Vaginal smear test) "1": Normal, "2": Abnormal	Shaffi et al. [62], Mohanty et al. [63]
Syphilis	Syphilis in the first, second, or third trimester "1": Positive, "2": Negative	Eppes et al. [64], Thornton et al. [65]
Group B Streptococcus	Group B Streptococcus result at the end of pregnancy "1": Normal, "2": Abnormal	Steer et al. [66], Gonçalves et al. [67]

4.3 Dataset Pre-processing

A dataset was constructed using the information of 5,022 pregnant patients. In this case, "1" was assigned to the pregnant women who suffered perinatal mortality; otherwise, "0". Twenty-seven patients were discarded due to inconsistent information (incoherent and missing) from the pregnant women. Finally, those pregnant women with incomplete information were imputed using the mean value of the response levels [70]. More details on the data management procedure employed in this model can be noted in Fig. 2.

4.4 Random Forest Model

The cohort was split 60/40 for the training and test sets, respectively. Due to the apparent imbalance between positive and negative classes, as seen in Fig. 2, oversampling was performed to generate new synthetic data from positive data in the training and test sets. The oversampling was performed using the Synthetic Minority Oversampling Technique (SMOTE), which has been reported in different AI applications in healthcare [71–73]. The random forest model was developed in R (v. 4.3.2) and RStudio (v. 2023.09.1 + 494).

Finally, the model was evaluated through six performance metrics, as shown in Table 2. In addition, McNemar's Test p-value (0.1336 indicated homogeneity among the proportion of mischaracterized pregnant women.

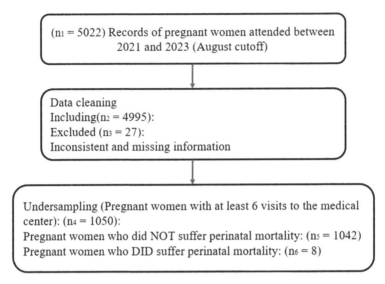

Fig. 2. Data management procedure in the AI model.

Table 2. RF model performance metrics

% Accuracy	% Sensitivity
99.16	87.50
% Specificity	% Positive predictive value
100.00	100.00
% Negative predictive value	% AUC-ROC
99.10	99.91

The model can predict whether a pregnancy may end in perinatal mortality, considering all performance metrics above 90%. The sensitivity shows that the model is capable of predicting well between eight and nine out of every ten patients who will suffer perinatal mortality, while the specificity indicates that the model can perfectly predict that a pregnant woman will not suffer perinatal mortality.

Finally, the predictive behavior of the model is confirmed by the AUC, which shows good discrimination between patients who would suffer perinatal mortality and those who would not (Fig. 3).

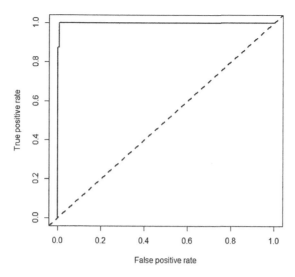

Fig. 3. Resulting ROC Curve corresponding to the derived RF model.

5 Conclusions

The growth of perinatal mortality rates and the development of new agile and reliable tools allow medical centers to have early warnings that can reduce the risk of perinatal mortality. In this study, an AI model was proposed for perinatal mortality prediction. The design of this tool is helpful for frontline medical staff caring for pregnant women since it provides support to determine the possibility of suffering perinatal mortality considering the characteristics of each patient [74].

The use of these tools is still in its initial stages, and the support of experts will be necessary for effective adoption in the wild. For future work, it is suggested to link the model outcomes with a risk categorization level and intervention routes coherent with the likelihood of perinatal mortality. Also, it is advised to test other AI methods to perform comparative analysis and use technology adoption models to predict model implementation effectiveness in similar healthcare institutions.

Acknowledgments. Authors thank the support of Adriana Quintero Linero and Yina Urueta Vasquez during this project.

Funding. This work was supported by the Ministerio de Ciencia, Tecnología e Innovación under the framework of the call 932 of 2022 - Convocatoria "Estancias con propósito empresarial. Fortalecimiento de la relación entre el sector académico, actores del Sistema Nacional de Ciencia, Tecnología e Innovación (SNCTI) y empresas colom-bianas".

Disclosure of Interests. The authors declare no competing interests regarding this manuscript.

References

1. Alves, L.C., Beluzo, C.E., Arruda, N.M., Bresan, R.C., Carvalho, T.: Assessing the Performance of Machine Learning Models to Predict Neonatal Mortality Risk in Brazil, 2000–2016. medRxiv (2020). https://doi.org/10.1101/2020.05.22.20109165
2. Alshwaish, W.M., Alabdulhafith, M.I.: Mortality prediction based on imbalanced new born and perinatal period data. IJACSA Int. J. Adv. Comput. Sci. Appl. **10**(8) (2019). https://doi.org/10.14569/IJACSA.2019.0100808
3. Bhutta, Z.A., et al.: Can available interventions end preventable deaths in mothers, newborn babies, and stillbirths, and at what cost? Lancet **384**(9940), 347–370 (2014). https://doi.org/10.1016/s0140-6736(14)60792-3
4. Blencowe, H., et al.: National, regional, and worldwide estimates of stillbirth rates in 2015, with trends from 2000: a systematic analysis. Lancet Glob. Health **4**(2), e98–e108 (2016). https://doi.org/10.1016/S2214-109X(15)00275-2
5. Bogale, D.S., Abuhay, T.M., Dejene, B.E.: Predicting perinatal mortality based on maternal health status and health insurance service using homogeneous ensemble machine learning methods. BMC Med. Inform. Decis. Mak. **22**(1), 341 (2022). https://doi.org/10.1186/s12911-022-02084-1
6. Esteva, A., et al.: A guide to deep learning in healthcare. Nat. Med. **25**(1), 24–29 (2019). https://doi.org/10.1038/s41591-018-0316-z
7. Flenady, V., et al.: Stillbirths: the way forward in high-income countries. Lancet **377**(9778), 1703–1717 (2011). https://doi.org/10.1016/s0140-6736(11)60064-0
8. García, G.A., Prada, G.E., Baracaldo, M.J., Jaimes, A.P.: Perinatal mortality in a high-complexity hospital in Colombia: an analysis of causes and associated factors. Revista de Salud Pública **22**(2), 1–7 (2020)
9. Gaviria, A., Guzman, J.M., Uribe, L.F.: Factors associated with perinatal mortality in women treated at a teaching hospital in Quibdó, Chocó, Colombia. Biomedica: Revista del Instituto Nacional de Salud **38**(3), 344–353 (2018)
10. Lawn, J.E., et al.: Stillbirths: rates, risk factors, and acceleration towards 2030. Lancet **387**(10018), 587–603 (2016). https://doi.org/10.1016/s0140-6736(15)00837-5
11. Malacova, E., et al.: Stillbirth risk prediction using machine learning for a large cohort of births from Western Australia, 1980–2015. Sci. Rep. **10**(1), 5354 (2020). https://doi.org/10.1038/s41598-020-62210-9
12. Ministerio de Salud y Protección Social de Colombia: Indicadores Básicos de Salud Colombia (2021). https://www.minsalud.gov.co/salud/publica/epidemiologia/Paginas/BoletinesEpidemiologicos.aspx
13. Mboya, I.B., Mahande, M.J., Mohammed, M., Obure, J., Mwambi, H.G.: Prediction of perinatal death using machine learning models: a birth registry-based cohort study in northern Tanzania. BMJ Open **10**(10), e040132 (2020). https://doi.org/10.1136/bmjopen-2020-040132
14. Miotto, R., Wang, F., Wang, S., Jiang, X., Dudley, J.T.: Deep learning for healthcare: review, opportunities and challenges. Brief. Bioinform. **19**(6), 1236–1246 (2017). https://doi.org/10.1093/bib/bbx044
15. Padula, A.M., et al.: A review of maternal prenatal exposures to environmental chemicals and psychosocial stressors—implications for research on perinatal outcomes in the ECHO program. J. Perinatol. **40**(1), 10–24 (2020). https://doi.org/10.1038/s41372-019-0510-y
16. Petersen, E.E., et al.: MMWR - racial/ethnic disparities in pregnancy-related deaths — United States, 2007–2016. MMWR Morb. Mortal. Wkly Rep. **68**(35), 762–765 (2019). https://doi.org/10.15585/mmwr.mm6835a3
17. Rajkomar, A., Dean, J., Kohane, I.: Machine learning in medicine. N. Engl. J. Med. **380**(14), 1347–1358 (2019). https://doi.org/10.1056/nejmra1814259

18. Ramakrishnan, R., Rao, S., He, J.R.: Perinatal health predictors using artificial intelligence: a review. Women's Health **17** (2021). https://doi.org/10.1177/17455065211046132

19. Saravanou, A., Noelke, C., Huntington, N., Acevedo-Garcia, D., Gunopulos, D.: Predictive modeling of infant mortality. Data Min. Knowl. Discov. **35**(4), 1785–1807 (2021). https://doi.org/10.1007/s10618-020-00728-2

20. Smith, L.K., et al.: Quantifying the burden of stillbirths before 28 weeks of completed gestational age in high-income countries: a population-based study of 19 European countries. Lancet **392**(10158), 1639–1646 (2018). https://doi.org/10.1016/S0140-6736(18)31651-9

21. Victora, C.G., et al.: Breastfeeding in the 21st century: epidemiology, mechanisms, and lifelong effect. Lancet **387**(10017), 475–490 (2016). https://doi.org/10.1016/S0140-6736(15)01024-7

22. Włodarczyk, T., et al.: Machine learning methods for preterm birth prediction: a review. Electronics **10**(5), 1–24 (2021). https://doi.org/10.3390/electronics10050586

23. World Health Organization: Maternal mortality (2019). https://www.who.int/news-room/fact-sheets/detail/maternal-mortality

24. World Health Organization: Maternal, newborn, child and adolescent health: New-borns: Reducing mortality (2021). https://www.who.int/news-room/fact-sheets/detail/newborns-reducing-mortality

25. Yasrebinia, S., Rezaei, M.: Artificial intelligence for predicting neonatal mortality in post-pregnancy: a systematic review. EJCMPR **3**(1), 81–87 (2024). https://doi.org/10.5281/zenodo.20231109

26. Zhang, Z., Xiao, Q., Luo, J.: Infant death prediction using machine learning: a population-based retrospective study. Comput. Biol. Med. **165**(107423) (2023). https://doi.org/10.1016/j.compbiomed.2023.107423

27. Liu, C., Talaei-Khoei, A., Zowghi, D., Daniel, J.: Data completeness in healthcare: a literature survey. Pac. Asia J. Assoc. Inf. Syst. 75–100 (2017). https://doi.org/10.17705/1pais.09204

28. Ortiz-Barrios, M., Lopez-Meza, P., McClean, S., Polifroni-Avendaño, G.: Discrete-event simulation for performance evaluation and improvement of gynecology outpatient departments: a case study in the public sector. In: Duffy, V.G. (ed.) HCII 2019. LNCS, vol. 11582, pp. 101–112. Springer, Cham (2019). https://doi.org/10.1007/978-3-030-22219-2_8

29. Fujiwara, K., et al.: Over- and under-sampling approach for extremely imbalanced and small minority data problem in health record analysis. Front. Public Health **8** (2020). https://doi.org/10.3389/fpubh.2020.00178

30. Ortiz-Barrios, M., Arias-Fonseca, S., Ishizaka, A., Barbati, M., Avendaño-Collante, B., Navarro-Jiménez, E.: Artificial intelligence and discrete-event simulation for capacity management of intensive care units during the Covid-19 pandemic: A case study. J. Bus. Res. **160**, 113806 (2023). https://doi.org/10.1016/j.jbusres.2023.113806

31. Sowjanya, A.M., Mrudula, O.: Effective treatment of imbalanced datasets in health care using modified SMOTE coupled with stacked deep learning algorithms. Appl. Nanosci. **13**(3), 1829–1840 (2023). https://doi.org/10.1007/s13204-021-02063-4

32. Ortiz Barrios, M.A., Felizzola Jiménez, H.: Use of six sigma methodology to reduce appointment lead-time in obstetrics outpatient department. J. Med. Syst. **40**(10) (2016). https://doi.org/10.1007/s10916-016-0577-3

33. Grand-Guillaume-Perrenoud, J.A., Origlia, P., Cignacco, E.: Barriers and facilitators of maternal healthcare utilisation in the perinatal period among women with social disadvantage: a theory-guided systematic review. Midwifery **105**, 103237 (2022). https://doi.org/10.1016/j.midw.2021.103237

34. Ortiz, M.A., McClean, S., Nugent, C.D., Castillo, A.: Reducing appointment lead-time in an outpatient department of gynecology and obstetrics through discrete-event simulation: a case study. In: García, C.R., Caballero-Gil, P., Burmester, M., Quesada-Arencibia, A. (eds.) UCAmI 2016. LNCS, vol. 10069, pp. 274–285. Springer, Cham (2016). https://doi.org/10.1007/978-3-319-48746-5_28

35. Ortíz-Barrios, M., McClean, S., Jiménez-Delgado, G., Martínez-Sierra, D.E.: Integrating lean six sigma and discrete-event simulation for shortening the appointment lead-time in gynecobstetrics departments: a case study. In: Duffy, V.G. (ed.) HCII 2020. LNCS, vol. 12199, pp. 378–389. Springer, Cham (2020). https://doi.org/10.1007/978-3-030-49907-5_27

36. Geiger, C.K., Clapp, M.A., Cohen, J.L.: Association of prenatal care services, maternal morbidity, and perinatal mortality with the advanced maternal age cutoff of 35 years. JAMA Health Forum 2(12), E214044 (2021). https://doi.org/10.1001/jamahealthforum.2021.4044

37. Saccone, G., et al.: Maternal and perinatal complications according to maternal age: a systematic review and meta-analysis. Int. J. Gynecol. Obstet. (2022). https://doi.org/10.1002/ijgo.14100

38. Abdelmageed, E., Bahaeldin, H., Nadiah, A., Abdelbagi, A., Duria, R., Ishag, A.: Maternal and neonatal outcomes of grand multiparity in Khartoum, Sudan. Afr. Health Sci. 22, 164–171 (2022). https://doi.org/10.4314/ahs.v22i1.21

39. Tadese, M., Tessema, S.D., Taye, B.T.: Adverse perinatal outcomes among grand multiparous and low multiparous women and its associated factors in north shewa zone public hospitals: the role of parity. Int. J. Gen. Med. 14, 6539–6548 (2021). https://doi.org/10.2147/IJGM.S333033

40. Murray, S., Mackay, D., Stock, S., Pell, J., Norman, J.: Association of gestational age at birth with risk of perinatal mortality and special educational need among twins. JAMA Pediatr. 174(5), 437–445 (2020). https://doi.org/10.1001/jamapediatrics.2019.6317

41. Manjavidze, T., Rylander, C., Skjeldestad, F.E., Kazakhashvili, N., Anda, E.E.: Incidence and causes of perinatal mortality in Georgia. J. Epidemiol. Glob. Health 9(3), 163–168 (2019). https://doi.org/10.2991/jegh.k.190818.001

42. Vats, H., Saxena, R., Sachdeva, M.P., Walia, G.K., Gupta, V.: Impact of maternal pre-pregnancy body mass index on maternal, fetal and neonatal adverse outcomes in the worldwide populations: a systematic review and meta-analysis. Obes. Res. Clin. Pract. 15(6), 536–545 (2021). https://doi.org/10.1016/j.orcp.2021.10.005

43. Simko, M., et al.: Maternal body mass index and gestational weight gain and their association with pregnancy complications and perinatal conditions. Int. J. Environ. Res. Public Health 16(10) (2019). https://doi.org/10.3390/ijerph16101751

44. Garanet, F., et al.: Perinatal outcomes in women with lower-range elevated blood pressure and stage 1 hypertension: insights from the Kaya health and demographic surveillance system, Burkina Faso. BMC Public Health 23(1), 2539 (2023). https://doi.org/10.1186/s12889-023-17424-7

45. Grover, S., Brandt, J.S., Reddy, U.M., Ananth, C.V.: Chronic hypertension, perinatal mortality and the impact of preterm delivery: a population-based study. BJOG 129(4), 572–579 (2022). https://doi.org/10.1111/1471-0528.16932

46. Young, M.F., Oaks, B.M., Tandon, S., Martorell, R., Dewey, K.G., Wendt, A.S.: Maternal hemoglobin concentrations across pregnancy and maternal and child health: a systematic review and meta-analysis. Ann. New York Acad. Sci. 1450(1), 47–68 (2019). https://doi.org/10.1111/nyas.14093

47. Jung, J., et al.: Effects of hemoglobin levels during pregnancy on adverse maternal and infant outcomes: a systematic review and meta-analysis. Ann. New York Acad. Sci. 1450(1), 69–82 (2019). https://doi.org/10.1111/nyas.14112

48. Neelima, N., Gopalan, U., Jayakumar, K.: Asymptomatic bacteriuria in South Indian pregnant women and treatment effect on outcome of pregnancy. Indian J. Obstet. Gynecol. Res. **8**(3), 314–322 (2021). https://doi.org/10.18231/j.ijogr.2021.067

49. Wingert, A., et al.: Asymptomatic bacteriuria in pregnancy: systematic reviews of screening and treatment effectiveness and patient preferences. BMJ Open **9**(3) (2019). https://doi.org/10.1136/bmjopen-2017-021347

50. Naamany, E., Ayalon-Dangur, I., Hadar, E., Sagy, I., Yahav, D., Shiber, S.: Pregnancy outcome following bacteriuria in pregnancy and the significance of nitrites in urinalysis-a retrospective cohort study. J. Perinat. Med. **47**(6), 611–618 (2019). https://doi.org/10.1515/jpm-2018-0428

51. Cohen, R., Gutvirtz, G., Wainstock, T., Sheiner, E.: Maternal urinary tract infection during pregnancy and long-term infectious morbidity of the offspring. Early Hum. Dev. **136**, 54–59 (2019). https://doi.org/10.1016/j.earlhumdev.2019.07.002

52. Lepercq, J., Le Ray, C., Godefroy, C., Pelage, L., Dubois-Laforgue, D., Timsit, J.: Determinants of a good perinatal outcome in 588 pregnancies in women with type 1 diabetes. Diabetes Metab. **45**(2), 191–196 (2019). https://doi.org/10.1016/j.diabet.2018.04.007

53. Rasheed, J., Isa, S., Rasheed, F., Siddiq, K., Saqlain, Z., Nasir, Z.: Perinatal outcome in diabetic mothers with relation to glycemic control during pregnancy. Prof. Med. J. **28**(03), 382–386 (2021). https://doi.org/10.29309/tpmj/2021.28.03.4084

54. Yokomichi, H., et al.: Gestational age, birth weight, and perinatal complications in mothers with diabetes and impaired glucose tolerance: Japan environment and children's study cohort. PLoS One **17**(6) (2022). https://doi.org/10.1371/journal.pone.0269610

55. Kung, W.J., et al.: Association between gestational abnormal glucose tolerance and maternal-fetal outcomes. J. Obstet. Gynaecol. Res. **48**(10), 2505–2513 (2022). https://doi.org/10.1111/jog.15350

56. Wu, K., Wang, H., Li, S., Zhang, H., Zhu, B.: Maternal hepatitis B infection status and adverse pregnancy outcomes: a retrospective cohort analysis. Arch. Gynecol. Obstet. **302**(3), 595–602 (2020). https://doi.org/10.1007/s00404-020-05630-2

57. Sirilert, S., Tongsong, T.: Hepatitis b virus infection in pregnancy: immunological response, natural course and pregnancy outcomes. J. Clin. Med. **10**(13), 2926 (2021). https://doi.org/10.3390/jcm10132926

58. Ahmed, M., Sood, A., Gupta, J.: Toxoplasmosis in pregnancy. Eur. J. Obstet. Gynecol. Reprod. Biol. **255**, 44–50 (2020). https://doi.org/10.1016/j.ejogrb.2020.10.003

59. Martinez, V.O., dos Santos, N.R., Bah, H.A.F., Junior, E.A.G., Costa, D.O., Menezes-Filho, J.A.: Impact of chronic toxoplasmosis in pregnancy: association between maternal seropositivity for Toxoplasma gondii IgG antibodies and fetal growth restriction. Parasitol. Res. **123**(1), 25 (2024). https://doi.org/10.1007/s00436-023-08068-y

60. Mailhot Vega, R.B., Balogun, O.D., Ishaq, O.F., Bray, F., Ginsburg, O., Formenti, S.C.: Estimating child mortality associated with maternal mortality from breast and cervical cancer. Cancer **125**(1), 109–117 (2019). https://doi.org/10.1002/cncr.31780

61. Jar-Allah, T., et al.: Abnormal cervical cytology is associated with preterm delivery: a population based study. Acta Obstet. Gynecol. Scand. **98**(6), 777–786 (2019). https://doi.org/10.1111/aogs.13543

62. Shaffi, A.F., Balandya, B., Majigo, M., Aboud, S.: Predictors of bacterial vaginosis among pregnant women attending antenatal clinic at tertiary care hospital in tanzania: a cross sectional study. East Afr. Health Res. J. **5**(1), 59 (2021). https://doi.org/10.24248/eahrj.v5i1.652

63. Mohanty, T., Doke, P.P., Khuroo, S.R.: Effect of bacterial vaginosis on preterm birth: a meta-analysis. Arch. Gynecol. Obstet. **308**, 1247–1255 (2023). https://doi.org/10.24248/eahrj.v5i1.652

64. Eppes, C.S., Stafford, I., Rac, M.: Syphilis in pregnancy: an ongoing public health threat. Am. J. Obstet. Gynecol. **227**(6), 822–838 (2022). https://doi.org/10.1016/j.ajog.2022.07.041

65. Thornton, C., Chaisson, L.H., Bleasdale, S.C.: Characteristics of pregnant women with syphilis and factors associated with congenital syphilis at a chicago hospital. Open Forum Infect. Dis. **9**(5) (2022). https://doi.org/10.1093/ofid/ofac169

66. Steer, P.J., Russell, A.B., Kochhar, S., Cox, P., Plumb, J., Gopal Rao, G.: Group B streptococcal disease in the mother and newborn—a review. Eur. J. Obstet. Gynecol. Reprod. Biol. **252**, 526–533 (2020). https://doi.org/10.1016/j.ejogrb.2020.06.024

67. Gonçalves, B.P., et al.: Group B streptococcus infection during pregnancy and infancy: estimates of regional and global burden. Lancet Glob. Health **10**(6), e807–e819 (2022). https://doi.org/10.1016/S2214-109X(22)00093-6

68. Ortíz-Barrios, M., Jimenez-Delgado, G., De Avila-Villalobos, J.: A computer simulation approach to reduce appointment lead-time in outpatient perinatology departments: a case study in a maternal-child hospital. In: Siuly, S., et al. (eds.) HIS 2017. LNCS, vol. 10594, pp. 32–39. Springer, Cham (2017). https://doi.org/10.1007/978-3-319-69182-4_4

69. Ortíz-Barrios, M., et al.: A multicriteria decision-making framework for assessing the performance of gynecobstetrics departments: a case study. Int. Trans. Oper. Res. **30**(1), 328–368 (2023). https://doi.org/10.1111/itor.12946

70. Kabir, G., Tesfamariam, S., Hemsing, J., Sadiq, R.: Handling incomplete and missing data in water network database using imputation methods. Sustain. Resilient. Infrastruct. **5**(6), 365–377 (2020). https://doi.org/10.1080/23789689.2019.1600960

71. Hassanzadeh, R., Farhadian, M., Rafieemehr, H.: Hospital mortality prediction in traumatic injuries patients: comparing different SMOTE-based machine learning algorithms. BMC Med. Res. Methodol. **23**(1), 101 (2023). https://doi.org/10.1186/s12874-023-01920-w

72. Alghamdi, M., Al-Mallah, M., Keteyian, S., Brawner, C., Ehrman, J., Sakr, S.: Predicting diabetes mellitus using SMOTE and ensemble machine learning approach: the henry ford exercise testing (FIT) project. PLoS One **12**(7) (2017). https://doi.org/10.1371/journal.pone.0179805

73. Elreedy, D., Atiya, A.F.: A comprehensive analysis of synthetic minority oversampling technique (SMOTE) for handling class imbalance. Inf. Sci. **505**, 32–64 (2019). https://doi.org/10.1016/j.ins.2019.07.070

74. Flórez, E.R.N., Ortiz, R.V., García, J.J.B.: Sistema experto basado en lógica difusa tipo 1 para determinar el grado de riesgo de preeclampsia. INGE CUC **10**(1), 43–50 (2014)

AI in Healthcare and Medicine: A Systematic Literature Review and Reappraisal

Heidi B. Clark[✉], James Egger, and Vincent G. Duffy

Purdue University, West Lafayette, IN 47907, USA
{htheisen,egger,duffy}@purdue.edu

Abstract. Healthcare and medicine are on the verge of undergoing an artificial intelligence-powered transformation. The expected benefits range from improved patient safety, new treatment options, precise medical diagnoses, personalized health monitoring, and a reduction in healthcare costs. With large amounts of existing data stored in electronic health records (EHRs) and advanced multi-sensor health tracking devices generating new data, artificial intelligence (AI) will be able to generate insights that aid physicians in providing high-quality medical care. Due to AI becoming a recent mainstream topic, which is advancing rapidly, understanding the potential positive impacts, negative impacts, and current research landscape is important in guiding available resources. This document is a systematic literature review of our topic choice using current literature and emergent trends. The review was conducted using several tools like VOSviewer, Harzing's Publish or Perish, CiteSpace, and NVivo, as well as multiple databases like Scite.ai, Scopus, Web of Science, Google Scholar, Dimensions.ai, and Springer. Bibliometric, co-citation, citation burst, and content analyses conducted with use of these databases and tools to demonstrate the connections among AI and healthcare and medicine. The results of the analyses indicate that *AI in healthcare and medicine* is an emerging topic of interest and aided in the identification of articles revealing five key subtopics including disease diagnosis using medical imaging, drug discovery and re-purposing, wearable devices, sensors, and edge computing. Overall, the results of this study indicate that the ethical and responsible implementation of AI in healthcare will transform the delivery of patient care.

Keywords: Artificial Intelligence · Healthcare · Wearables · Diagnostic Imaging · Drug Discovery · Drug Repurposing · Deep Learning

1 Introduction and Background

Artificial Intelligence (AI) has the potential to revolutionize healthcare and modernize medicine. If AI is implemented effectively and ethically, it will benefit individuals by improving patient safety, offering new treatment options, offering precise medical diagnoses, offering personalized health monitoring devices, and potentially reducing the cost of healthcare. AI is of particular importance now that there is a large, increasing amount of data stored in electronic health records (EHRs) and personal health monitoring applications, and it is important to consider patient safety and privacy. AI can leverage this

V. G. Duffy (Ed.): HCII 2024, LNCS 14710, pp. 251–270, 2024.
https://doi.org/10.1007/978-3-031-61063-9_17

big data to aid physicians in providing high-quality medical care while ensuring patient confidentiality. The role of AI in healthcare is also important to the field of industrial engineering (IE). An industrial engineer in the healthcare industry is "responsible for optimizing the efficiency and productivity of healthcare systems, eliminating waste and saving money by adjusting and organizing healthcare operations" (Indeed, 2022). Thus, the topic of *AI in healthcare and medicine* is particularly important to IE since AI has the computational power to make a significant improvement in the efficiency of various sectors of the medical industry.

Outside of industrial engineering, advancements in artificial intelligence algorithms and data science techniques are being developed. With the potential to improve the usefulness and accuracy of the systems they are integrated with. Breakthrough innovations in bioengineered devices that offer human-integrated monitoring of vitals while being minimally invasive are in development, alongside new forms of wearable devices. These devices will offer a new level of persistent and data-rich monitoring for enhanced healthcare outcomes. AI has become a mainstream topic of interest in society, with vast amounts of private and public funding flowing into the many potential use cases. A need for regulatory frameworks is of pressing concern, to ensure patient safety, privacy, and security within the healthcare system. Doing so will lead to wider adoption of AI technologies through the reduction of perceived danger by patients, thus generating more data to be leveraged, and increasing positive healthcare outcomes for all. Currently, many different efforts have been made by those within the human factors engineering (HFE), human-computer interaction (HCI), and safety-related communities. These include usability studies to verify that interfaces, devices, and new systems involving AI are designed with the end user in mind for better safety and fewer errors. Simulation and training programs are being developed and improved to familiarize healthcare workers with these complex systems. An expanding effort is taking place to develop standardizations and guidelines to ensure these new technologies have strict adherence to established safety processes.

2 Problem Statement

The objective of this study is to perform a bibliometric analysis and systematic literature review of data and articles related to the topic of *AI in healthcare and medicine*. There is a significant opportunity for AI to advance the medical field and provide benefits to all. In the following sections, this topic will be investigated by conducting searches in various databases, performing a trend analysis, and connecting the topic to fundamental topics of human factors and ergonomics. Subsequently, co-citation and content analyses will be performed, and relevant subtopics will be explored.

3 Procedure and Results

3.1 Database Searches

An analysis of the literature related to our topic was conducted through a multi-site keyword search to gather articles/data of interest. We used a combination of several databases to form a holistic and complete picture of the available research. We performed this keyword search using Scite.ai, Scopus, Web of Science, Google Scholar, Dimensions.ai, and Springer. Comparable search terms were used across all sites, broader terms were used if results lacked relevant articles. Shown in Table 1 are the databases, search terms, and results used for our research. Some of the databases provided significantly more results, such as Scite.ai and Springer. These increased results can be attributed to larger databases, and/or how their search engine determines if documents are relevant. In the case of Scopus, search results were very conservative and returned highly relevant results to our topic using the search terms in the table below (Table 1).

Table 1. Database search results with topic-relevant search terms

Database	Search Term	Results
Scopus	"AI in Healthcare and Medicine" OR "AI in Healthcare" OR "AI in Medicine" OR "Artificial Intelligence in Medical Field"	784
Web of Science	"AI in Healthcare and Medicine"	7,277
Google Scholar	"AI in Healthcare and Medicine" OR "AI in Healthcare" OR "AI in Medicine" OR "Artificial Intelligence in Medical Field"	16,300
Springer	"AI in Healthcare and Medicine"	35,546
Dimensions.ai	"AI in Healthcare and Medicine" OR "AI in Healthcare" OR "AI in Medicine" OR "Artificial Intelligence in Medical Field"	11,323
Scite.ai	"AI in Healthcare and Medicine" OR "AI in Healthcare" OR "AI in Medicine" OR "Artificial Intelligence in Medical Field"	18,036

3.2 Trend Analysis

The trend analysis for the literature review was completed with two online tools, Google Ngram and Web of Science. To begin our trend analysis, we first used Google Ngram shown in Fig. 1 by inputting related topic queries "AI in healthcare" and "AI in medicine" along with two additional more ambiguous topic terms "healthcare automation" and "AI in industry" provided from class. Google Ngram determines the amount of usage of each term within literature over time (Google, n.d.). All years up to 2019 were analyzed for these terms. Before 1950, no usage of these terms was detected, so we updated the graph to begin around that date. The results show an increase in usage during the '80s and '90s for "AI in medicine" and then a large increase in usage occurred around 2015 for "AI in healthcare" and "AI in medicine". This graph indicates that a recent and rather significant trend upward has occurred, likely due to the exponential advancements in technology that are driving AI progress.

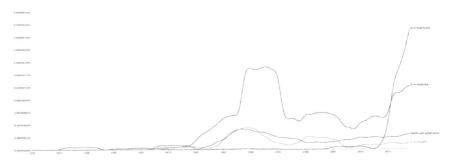

Fig. 1. Google Ngram showing our intended topics of "AI in healthcare" and "AI in medicine" with two additional topics "healthcare automation" and "AI in industry" from the example topic list.

We continued the analysis using the initial search results returned from the Web of Science database on "AI in healthcare and medicine." Shown in Fig. 2, these results are displayed in a bar graph that represents the number of topic-related articles published for a particular year starting in 2014 and continuing to 2023. A continuing trend upward in articles published per year starting in 2015 to 2023 is noticeable within the graph. The year 2014 had roughly 200 new articles published, while the year 2023 had over 1,300 related articles published in that year alone. This is nearly a 7-fold increase in yearly publication output within a decade. This graph also supports the notion our topic is experiencing a surge in popularity in recent years, and that "AI in healthcare and medicine" is of timely relevance.

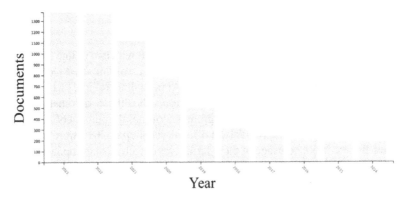

Fig. 2. Trend diagram based on Web of Science data using a search of the topic "AI in healthcare and medicine" demonstrating an increase in topic-relevant research over time.

3.3 Emergence Indicator

A clear emergence indicator for the topic is shown in Table 2 using the results from a Web of Science search on the topic "AI in healthcare and medicine." Of the 7,277 articles found, from 2011 to 2019 the overall percentage of publications were within the single digits, with 2011 having a total of 120 related articles that year. Comparatively, the year 2022 had 1,364 articles published and 2023 has 1,380 articles published thus far. A nearly 10-fold increase in about a decade for yearly publications on our topic.

Table 2. Database search results from Web of Science with articles published over time.

Field: Publication Years	Record Count	% of 7,277
2023	1,380	18.964%
2022	1,364	18.744%
2021	1,117	15.350%
2020	781	10.732%
2019	498	6.843%
2018	308	4.233%
2017	243	3.339%
2016	201	2.762%
2015	182	2.501%
2014	180	2.474%
2013	167	2.295%
2012	154	2.116%
2011	120	1.649%

The topic of "AI in healthcare and medicine" is distinct from the topics presented in the Handbook of Human Factors and Ergonomics (Salvendy & Karwowski, 2021). The chapter that most closely relates to this topic is Chapter 53, Human Factors and Ergonomics in Health Care, which only briefly mentions the topic in 5.1 Emerging Issues of Health IT and the Role of HFE (Carayon, Wust, Hose, & Salwei, 2021). This signifies the importance of further and upcoming research in this area and indicates the uniqueness of AI in healthcare and medicine. The emergence of this topic is also evident by observing the trend diagram shown in Fig. 3, which shows an increasing number of publications per year from a search of the topic in Scopus (Scopus, n.d.).

3.4 Applications Justification

AI has various potential applications in the medical field. Two possible applications are AI-powered medical diagnostic systems and drug discovery tools. The motivation for implementing AI in these areas is to improve the efficiency and accuracy of medical diagnoses and advance available treatment options by discovering and re-purposing drugs. Figure 4 shows the number of documents per year between 1964 and 2022 from searching for "AI medical diagnosis" in Scopus. The year 2023 was not included in this analysis since 2023 has not yet ended. Observing Fig. 4, between the years 1964–2017, there was little discussion surrounding the use of AI in these areas. However, beginning in 2017 and through 2022, there is an increasing amount of research regarding the use of AI in medicine. This indicates that this topic is an emerging application of AI in healthcare.

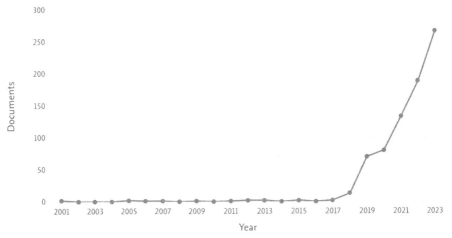

Fig. 3. Trend diagram of publications per year related to "AI in healthcare and medicine" demonstrating a recent increase in interest surrounding the topic (Scopus, n.d.)

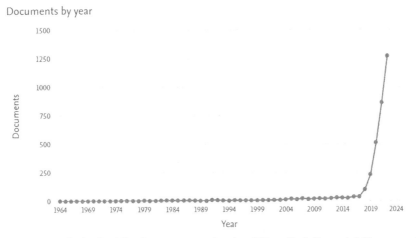

Fig. 4. Trend analysis of publications per year related to "AI medical diagnosis" (Scopus, n.d.)

3.5 Relationship to Fundamental Human Factors and Ergonomics Topics

The topic of *AI in healthcare and medicine* is closely connected to Chapters 5, *Information Process*ing, and 53, *Human Factors and Ergonomics in Healthcare*, in the Handbook of Human Factors and Ergonomics (Salvendy & Karwowski, 2021). Medical professionals make decisions to diagnose patients daily. The decision a physician makes to diagnose a patient with a particular condition or malady can be correlated with Wicken's model of human information processing (Wickens & Carswell, 2021, 116). A medical diagnosis is influenced by the physician's medical knowledge in their long-term memory, observable patient symptoms they perceive or are told, the physician's level of experience, and the physician's attentional resources directed towards the patient. Wicken's model shows a closed-loop system where an event or stimuli is first perceived, then received by a central processor where a decision and response selection are made, and finally, a response execution is made (Wickens & Carswell, 2021, 116). An individual's attentional resources and long-term and working memory also have an impact on information processing.

A significant number of patient deaths and injuries occur due to medical errors (Carayon, Wust, Hose, & Salwei, 2021, 1421). The goal of utilizing AI in healthcare would be to reduce the cognitive burden placed on medical professionals, mitigate misdiagnoses to improve patient safety, and assist in recommending treatment options. "The emergence of artificial intelligence (AI) in health care is bringing a new set of challenges as well as opportunities to improve care quality and safety" (Carayon, Wust, Hose, & Salwei, 2021, 1425). AI has already been utilized to improve the time to diagnose a variety of conditions including intercranial hemorrhage on CT scans (Carayon, Wust, Hose, & Salwei, 2021, 1425), diabetic retinopathy and macular edema in fundus photographs (Carayon, Wust, Hose, & Salwei, 2021, 1425), COVID-19 pneumonia and viral pneumonia in chest X-rays (Chowdhury, et al., 2020), rheumatoid arthritis (Wang, et al., 2021), and various types of cancer (Wang, et al. 2021, 2–3). Additionally, AI has grown in the "discovery, optimization and verification of drug target and lead compounds in drug discovery" (Wang, et al. 2021, 2–3).

3.6 Foremost Authors, Institutions, and Articles

To explore the topic of AI in healthcare and medicine, various searches were performed utilizing Scopus, Web of Science, and Harzing's Publish or Perish. Three tables were created based on the search results to identify leading authors, leading institutions, and leading articles relevant to the topic. Table 3 shows a list of leading authors and Table 4 shows a list of leading institutions, both of which are from a search in Scopus using the search phrase "artificial intelligence in medical field." This search phrase was selected after closely examining the results of various searches and refining the search phrase to ensure that the results closely matched the topic of interest.

In Table 3, the years of each author's publications relevant to the topic, leading keywords from each author's publications, and the number of publications for each leading author were recorded. The results from this analysis further support the emergence of this topic as indicated in the trend diagrams shown in Fig. 3 and Fig. 4 since the leading authors' publications are from 2016 to 2023. In Table 4, the country associated with each leading institution, leading keywords from each institution's related publications, and the number of publications associated with each institution were recorded. Given that this search was general to the topic of AI in healthcare and medicine, it is notable that the keywords shown in Table 3 and Table 4 frequently include "diagnosis," "medical imaging," "deep learning," "machine learning," and "automated pattern recognition," all of which correlate with the use of AI for diagnosing medical conditions. This inspired further investigation on the subtopic of AI for disease diagnosis, which will be addressed in Sect. 4.

Table 5 shows a list of leading articles identified from a series of searches in Scopus, Web of Science, and Google Scholar using Harzing's Publish or Perish. In each database, the search phrase was varied slightly to optimize the results relevant to the topic of interest. Five leading articles are identified in Table 5 from these searches which were selected based on a combination of the number of times the article had been cited by other articles as well as the relevancy of the article to the topic of interest.

Additionally, a PivotChart was created as shown in Fig. 5 using the data extracted from performing a Google Scholar search in Harzing's Publish or Perish with the search phrase "AI in healthcare and medicine" (Harzing's Publish or Perish).

Table 3. Leading authors identified from Scopus search (Scopus, n.d.)

Author	Years	Leading Keywords	Publication Count
Shen, D.	2017-2018, 2021-2022	Artificial Intelligence, Medical Imaging, Automated Pattern Recognition, Computer Assisted Diagnosis	17
Holzinger, A.	2020, 2022-2023	Artificial Intelligence, Machine Learning, Medical Informatics, Learning Systems, Digital Pathology, Diagnosis, Decision Making	12
Ting, D.S.W.	2019, 2021-2023	Artificial Intelligence, Deep Learning, Ophthalmology, Diabetic Retinopathy, Glaucoma, Medical Imaging, Machine Learning	11
Acharya, U.R.	2021-2023	Artificial Intelligence, Human, Deep Learning, Machine Learning, Diagnosis, Medical Imaging, Learning Models, Diagnostic Imaging	10
Navab, N.	2016, 2020-2021, 2023	Artificial Intelligence, Medical Imaging, Humans, Computer Assisted Diagnosis, Algorithms, Automated Pattern Recognition, Computer-Assisted Image Interpretation	10

Table 4. Leading institutions identified from Scopus search (Scopus, n.d.)

Institution	Country	Leading Keywords	Publication Count
Harvard Medical School	USA	Artificial Intelligence, Human, Machine Learning, Algorithm, Deep Learning, Diagnostic Imaging	88
Inserm	France	Artificial Intelligence, Human, Machine Learning, Deep Learning, Radiomics, Diagnostic Imaging, Algorithms, Natural Language Processing	78
Stanford University	USA	Artificial Intelligence, Human, Machine Learning, Priority Journal, Deep Learning, Medical Imaging, Procedures	56
Chinese Academy of Sciences	China	Artificial Intelligence, Medical Imaging, Deep Learning, Human, Diagnosis, Image Segmentation	56
Ministry of Education of the People's Republic of China	China	Artificial Intelligence, Human, Deep Learning, Diagnosis, Medical Imaging, Machine Learning, Convolutional Neural Network	48

Table 5. Leading articles identified from Scopus (Scopus, n.d.), Web of Science (Web of Science, n.d.), and Google Scholar (Harzing's Publish or Perish) searches

Article Title	Author(s)	Leading Keywords	Year	Citations	Database article located in
Artificial intelligence in healthcare: Past, present and future	Jiang, F.; Jiang, Y.; Zhi, H.; Dong, Y.; Li, H.; Ma, S.; Wang, Y.; Dong, Q.; Shen, H.; Wang, Y.	Artificial Intelligence; Data Mining; Delivery of Health Care; Computer-Assisted Diagnosis; Diffusion of Innovation; Early Diagnosis; Computer Assisted Therapy	2017	2,713 (Google Scholar/Harzing) 1,127 (Web of Science) 1,581 (Scopus)	Google Scholar/Harzing; Web of Science; Scite.ai; Scopus
Artificial intelligence in healthcare	Kun-Hsing, Y.; Beam, A.L.; Kohane, I.S.	Artificial Intelligence; Biomarkers; Delivery of Health Care; Humans; Image Processing, Computer-Assisted (Computer); Neural Networks (Computer); Robotic Surgical Procedures; Wearable Electronic Devices	2018	1,705 (Google Scholar/Harzing) 1,110 (Scopus)	Google Scholar/Harzing; Scopus
Identifying Medical Diagnoses and Treatable Diseases by Image-Based Deep Learning	Kermany, D.S.; Goldbaum, M.; Cai, W.; Valentim, C.C.S.; Liang, H.; Baxter, S.L.; McKeown, A.; Yang, G.; Wu, X.; Yan, F.; Dong, J.; Prasadha, M.K.	Age-related Macular Degeneration; Artificial Intelligence; Choroidal Neovascularization; Deep Learning; Diabetic Macular Edema; Diabetic Retinopathy; Pneumonia	2018	2,486	Scopus
Artificial intelligence in radiology	Hosny, A.; Parmar, C.; Quackenbush, J.; Schwartz, L.H.; Aerts, H.J.W.L.	Algorithms; Artificial Intelligence; Deep Learning; Humans; Image Processing, Computer-Assisted	2018	1,544	Scopus
Can AI Help in Screening Viral and COVID-19 Pneumonia?	Chowdhury, M.E.H.; Rahman, T.; Khandakar, A.; Mazhar, R.; Kadir, M.A.; Mahbub, Z.B.; Islam, K.R.; Khan, M.S.; Iqbal, A.; Emadi, N.A.; Reaz, M.B.I.; Islam, M.T.	Artificial intelligence; computer-aided diagnostic tool; COVID-19 pneumonia; machine learning; transfer learning; viral pneumonia	2020	852	Scopus

3.7 Co-citation Analysis

According to Fahimnia, Sarkis, and Davarzani, "Publications are co-cited if they appear together in the reference lists of other documents" (Fahimnia, Sarkis, & Davarzani, 2015). A co-citation analysis provides insight into the coupling of references and can indicate a pair of articles' influences in a particular topic area. For this study, a cited sources co-citation analysis was performed on a search from Scopus using VOSviewer which has been previously used by other researchers including Taylor Duffy (Duffy & Duffy, 2022). The results of this analysis are shown Fig. 6 and Fig. 7. The search phrase "artificial intelligence in healthcare" was used to collect data for this analysis which resulted in a total of 13,048 documents (Scopus, n.d.). In VOSviewer, the minimum number of citations of a source was set to seven, and of the 67,181 cited references, 29 met the threshold and were selected for analysis (VOSviewer). Figure 6 shows a list of cited references with the number of citations associated with each reference as well as the strength of the citation. Figure 7 shows the network diagram created in VOSviewer which includes the largest set of connected items for a total of five primary clusters.

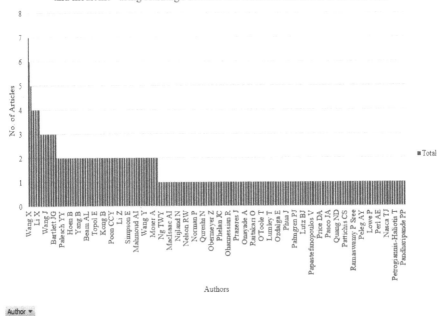

Fig. 5. Excel PivotChart of articles per author related to "AI in healthcare and medicine" (Harzing's Publish or Perish)

3.8   Citation Burst Analysis

Researchers often use visualization analysis tools that help make sense of data, one such tool is called CiteSpace. We used this tool to conduct a burst analysis (citation burst) of data we collected from searching Web of Science for articles related to "AI in healthcare and medicine" and then exported these results into CiteSpace. A burst in bibliometric-related data happens when a surge of use occurs for a certain subject or keyword. This often happens when a domain of research abruptly becomes popular, resulting in a "citation burst" within that research domain. Most of the settings were kept at default except for the "scale factor K" which was lowered to 5 for the program to run properly, essentially reducing the overall size of the resultant network to meet our needs. A total of 7,277 articles were analyzed to generate the figure shown below based on our topic of interest. The figure contains the top 25 references with the strongest citation bursts (Fig. 8).

Create Map   ✕

Verify selected cited references

Selected	Cited reference	Citations ✔	Total link strength
☑	lecun y., bengio y., hinton g., deep learning, nature, 521, pp. 436-444, (2...	40	49
☑	esteva a., et al., dermatologist-level classification of skin cancer with de...	14	27
☑	topol e.j., high-performance medicine: the convergence of human and...	14	16
☑	topol e.j., high-performance medicine: the convergence of human and...	14	10
☑	lecun y., bengio y., hinton g., deep learning, nature, 521, 7553, pp. 436-...	14	5
☑	goodfellow i., bengio y., courville a., deep learning, (2016)	12	10
☑	lakhani p., sundaram b., deep learning at chest radiography: automate...	11	21
☑	bishop c.m., pattern recognition and machine learning, (2006)	11	7
☑	gulshan v., et al., development and validation of a deep learning algorit...	10	22
☑	krizhevsky a., sutskever i., hinton g.e., imagenet classification with deep...	10	10
☑	adadi a., berrada m., peeking inside the black-box: a survey on explaina...	10	8
☑	hamet p., tremblay j., artificial intelligence in medicine, metabolism, 69...	10	5
☑	deo r.c., machine learning in medicine, circulation, 132, pp. 1920-1930, ...	9	15
☑	simonyan k., zisserman a., very deep convolutional networks for large-s...	9	13
☑	esteva a., kuprel b., novoa r.a., et al., dermatologist-level classification ...	9	9
☑	obermeyer z., powers b., vogeli c., mullainathan s., dissecting racial bia...	9	8
☑	doshi-velez f., kim b., towards a rigorous science of interpretable machi...	8	11
☑	chen m., hao y., hwang k., wang l., wang l., disease prediction by mach...	8	7
☑	jordan m.i., mitchell t.m., machine learning: trends, perspectives, and p...	7	11

     < Back   Next >   Finish   Cancel

Fig. 6. VOSviewer cited references list from a Scopus search (Scopus, n.d.) (VOSviewer)

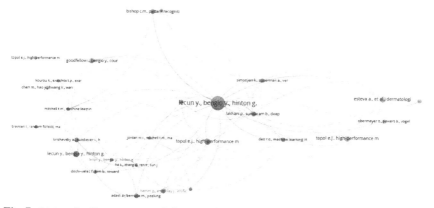

Fig. 7. Network diagram created from a Scopus search (Scopus, n.d.) using VOSviewer (VOSviewer)

3.9 Content Analyses

Word Cloud. A collection of fifteen articles, including those listed in Table 5 as well as two other relevant articles, were chosen from sites such as Scite.ai, Scopus, and Google Scholar and selected for further evaluation. These articles were further analyzed to

Top 25 References with the Strongest Citation Bursts

References	Year	Strength	Begin	End	2015 - 2023
Gulshan V, 2016, JAMA-J AM MED ASSOC, V316, P2402, DOI 10.1001/jama.2016.17216, DOI	2016	25.06	**2018**	2021	
LeCun Y, 2015, NATURE, V521, P436, DOI 10.1038/nature14539, DOI	2015	14.42	**2018**	2020	
Esteva A, 2017, NATURE, V542, P115, DOI 10.1038/nature21056, DOI	2017	14.3	**2018**	2020	
Obermeyer Z, 2016, NEW ENGL J MED, V375, P1216, DOI 10.1056/NEJMp1606181, DOI	2016	9.88	**2018**	2021	
Cabitza F, 2017, JAMA-J AM MED ASSOC, V318, P517, DOI 10.1001/jama.2017.7797, DOI	2017	8.14	**2018**	2020	
Chen JH, 2017, NEW ENGL J MED, V376, P2507, DOI 10.1056/NEJMp1702071, DOI	2017	7.18	**2018**	2020	
Bejnordi BE, 2017, JAMA-J AM MED ASSOC, V318, P2199, DOI 10.1001/jama.2017.14585, DOI	2017	7.13	**2018**	2019	
Beam AL, 2018, JAMA-J AM MED ASSOC, V319, P1317, DOI 10.1001/jama.2017.18391, DOI	2018	5.74	**2018**	2021	
Dicker D, 2018, LANCET, V392, P1684, DOI 10.1016/s0140-6736(18)31891-9, DOI	2018	5.5	**2018**	2019	
Abràmoff MD, 2016, INVEST OPHTH VIS SCI, V57, P5200, DOI 10.1167/iovs.16-19964, DOI	2016	5.46	**2018**	2021	
Rusk N, 2016, NAT METHODS, V13, P35, DOI 10.1038/nmeth.3707, DOI	2016	9.97	**2019**	2021	
Ronneberger O, 2015, LECT NOTES COMPUT SC, V9351, P234, DOI 10.1007/978-3-319-24574-4, 28, DOI	2015	8.46	**2019**	2020	
Zhang J, 2018, CIRCULATION, V138, P1623, DOI 10.1161/CIRCULATIONAHA.118.034338, DOI	2018	6.46	**2019**	2020	
Jiang F, 2017, STROKE VASC NEUROL, V2, P230, DOI 10.1136/svn-2017-000101, DOI	2017	6.38	**2019**	2021	
He KM, 2016, PROC CVPR IEEE, V0, PP770, DOI 10.1109/CVPR.2016.90, DOI	2016	11.11	**2020**	2021	
Chen JH, 2016, MEDICINE, V95, P0, DOI 10.1097/MD.0000000000003268, DOI	2016	9.66	**2020**	2021	
Yen YC, 2017, CANCER-AM CANCER SOC, V123, P2043, DOI 10.1002/cncr.30565, DOI	2017	8.22	**2020**	2021	
Gillies RJ, 2016, RADIOLOGY, V278, P563, DOI 10.1148/radiol.2015151169, DOI	2016	7.14	**2020**	2021	
Krizhevsky Alex, 2017, COMMUNICATIONS OF THE ACM, V60, P84, DOI 10.1145/3065386, DOI	2017	6.88	**2020**	2021	
Zech JR, 2018, PLOS MED, V15, P0, DOI 10.1371/journal.pmed.1002683, DOI	2018	6.79	**2020**	2021	
Nagendran M, 2020, BMJ-BRIT MED J, V368, P0, DOI 10.1136/bmj.m689, DOI	2020	7.17	**2021**	2023	
Wynants L, 2020, BMJ-BRIT MED J, V369, P0, DOI 10.1136/bmj.m1328, DOI	2020	6.49	**2021**	2023	
Collins GS, 2019, LANCET, V393, P1577, DOI 10.1016/S0140-6736(19)30037-6, DOI	2019	5.36	**2021**	2023	
Ai T, 2020, RADIOLOGY, V296, PE32, DOI 10.1148/radiol.2020200642, DOI	2020	5.14	**2021**	2023	
Paszke A, 2019, ADV NEUR IN, V32, P0	2019	5.14	**2021**	2023	

Fig. 8. Citation burst analysis produced from CiteSpace using exported Web of Science data on the topic of "AI in healthcare and medicine" (CiteSpace).

generate a list of the most relevant key terms. A word cloud was created from the sixteen articles selected using NVivo as shown in Fig. 9. The most frequently occurring words are "data," "COVID," "learning," "industry," "healthcare," and "medical." However, these words did not give much additional insight into the topic of *AI in healthcare and medicine*. By more closely evaluating the word cloud, other words began to stand out. Some commonly occurring words in this word cloud include "devices," "diagnosis," "images," "disease," "computing," and "sensors." These relatively frequent words were utilized to identify subtopics related to *AI in healthcare and medicine* which will be discussed in Sect. 4.

Lexical Search Terms. Utilizing the keywords identified in the leading tables and the word cloud, lexical searches were performed within the selected articles to gain additional insight into the selected subtopics, identify key information, and drive further discussion. Lexical searches were performed directly in the downloaded articles using the Query function in NVivo as well as CTRL + F in individually downloaded files. Examples of search terms used include "diagnosis," "drug," "discovery," "device," "computation," "measure," "technology," and "IOT" (internet of things), some of which appear as high-frequency words from the selected articles as shown in Fig. 10. These search terms fostered a deeper analysis of the relevant key subtopics within the selected articles.

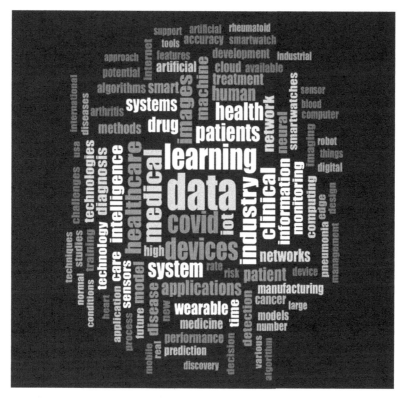

Fig. 9. Word cloud from selected articles using NVivo (NVivo)

4   Discussion

Medical-Imaging Disease Diagnosis. As shown in the word cloud in Fig. 9, "diagnosis," "images," "imaging," and "disease" are words that occur with a relatively high frequency across the selected articles. Artificial intelligence is used to diagnose multiple types of diseases using a variety of different methods. Emphasis is placed on implementing AI for the diagnosis of diseases that are treatable or require early diagnosis to provide the most successful outcome for the patient (Jiang, et al., 2017). Cancer, nervous system disease, and cardiovascular disease are the primary areas of focus for AI in healthcare, and AI can leverage clinical notes from physical examinations and laboratory results to aid in the diagnosis of such diseases (Jiang, et al., 2017). Specifically, "image, genetic, and electrophysiological (EP) data" is converted "to machine-understandable electronic medical record (EMR)" for analysis (Jiang, et al., 2017).

Diagnostic imaging was a commonly occurring leading keyword phrase used in lexical searches in multiple articles. Yu, Beam, and Kohane argue that image-based diagnosis is "the most successful domain of medical AI applications," and discuss medical-image diagnosis in the fields of radiology, dermatology, ophthalmology, and pathology (Yu, Beam, & Kohane, 2018). Additionally, medical imaging can also be used for the diagnosis of retinal diseases with optical coherence tomography (OCT) images as well

Word	Length	Count	Weighted Percentage ∨
data	4	965	0.78%
learning	8	626	0.51%
covid	5	519	0.42%
medical	7	516	0.42%
devices	7	515	0.42%
industry	8	459	0.37%
healthcare	10	446	0.36%
clinical	8	404	0.33%
patients	8	403	0.33%
images	6	394	0.32%
system	6	394	0.32%
health	6	389	0.31%
iot	3	326	0.26%
drug	4	319	0.26%
intelligence	12	318	0.26%
applications	12	304	0.25%
human	5	303	0.24%
systems	7	284	0.23%
information	11	277	0.22%
machine	7	276	0.22%
patient	7	273	0.22%
wearable	8	260	0.21%
network	7	253	0.20%
diagnosis	9	250	0.20%
model	5	243	0.20%

Fig. 10. Word frequencies from selected articles evaluated using NVivo (NVivo)

as pediatric pneumonia using chest X-ray images (Kermany, et al., 2018). This was demonstrated by Kermany, et al. via the development of an applied AI diagnostic tool for clinical-decision support which uses convolutional neural network (CNN) based deep learning (Kermany, et al., 2018). Similarly, CNN-based deep learning was used by Chowdhury, et al. in the development of a diagnostic tool capable of improving the speed and accuracy of diagnosing viral pneumonia and COVID-19 pneumonia, which provided a more efficient screening method for the virus amidst the pandemic when resources for diagnosis were limited (Chowdhury, et al., 2020).

In the field of radiology, Yu, Beam, and Kohane discuss the "expert-level diagnostic accuracies" of AI in the diagnosis of lung diseases and identification of breast-mass, and mention a clinical application of AI for the diagnosis of cardiovascular diseases that received FDA approval in 2018 (Yu, Beam, & Kohane, 2018). Hosny, et al. also discuss AI in radiology, specifically its impact in oncology related to detecting abnormalities, characterizing them for diagnosis, and monitoring diseases identified to ensure a proper treatment response (Hosny, Parmar, Quackenbush, Schwartz, & Aerts, 2018). Furthermore, they attribute the "emergence of AI in medical imaging" to the overarching "desire for greater efficacy and efficiency in clinical care," (Hosny, Parmar, Quackenbush, Schwartz, & Aerts, 2018) which calls to attention the focus on minimizing the cognitive workload of medical staff discussed earlier. However, since a "comprehensive AI system able to detect multiple abnormalities within the entire human body is yet to be developed," (Hosny, Parmar, Quackenbush, Schwartz, & Aerts, 2018) much progress is still needed before clinicians can rely solely on diagnoses made by medical-imaging diagnostic AI systems.

Drug Discovery and Repurposing. In the medical field, AI can also be applied to the translational research of drug discovery and drug repurposing (Yu, Beam, & Kohane, 2018). The drug development process is "time-consuming and expensive," and despite the dedication of an average of US$2.8 billion and over a decade for each drug, "nine out of ten therapeutic molecules fail Phase II clinical trials and regulatory approval" (Paul, et al., 2021). However, AI can reduce the cost and time of this process by aiding in the "identification of repurposable drug candidates" (Arora, et al., 2021). AI can also assist in both the design and screening process of drug development (Paul, et al., 2021). In particular, AI can be used to predict the bioactivity, toxicity, and physicochemical properties of drug candidates, and can also be used to predict the protein structure of target molecules and drug-protein interactions in drug design (Paul, et al., 2021). Further, it is important to assess the "toxicity, efficacy and response, interaction with other biomolecules, bioavailability, and metabolism" when drug screening (Arora, et al., 2021). Failure to properly assess the properties of drug candidates is often the cause of failed clinical trials (Arora, et al., 2021). Arora, et. al discuss the promise of utilizing AI to repurpose drugs for COVID-19 treatments and to aid in successful clinical trials (Arora, et al., 2021).

Wearable Devices. From our co-citation analysis, a new article was discovered that perfectly describes how the data from wearable devices provides two avenues of direct benefit. One to the patient through personalized recommendations, and one that helps improve overall healthcare design (Hamet & Tremblay, 2017). One of these devices is the smartwatch, which has become increasingly popular in recent years and can track many health indicators like sleep patterns, physical movement, heart rate, and blood oxygen levels (Hosseini, Hosseini, Qayumi, Hosseinzadeh, & Tabar, 2023). Many types of other emerging wearables exist, like smart textiles, face masks, smart rings, electronic tattoos, microneedle patches, teeth sensors, smart lenses, smart necklaces, and smartphones, that are continually being developed and entering the market (Al-kahtani, Khan, & Taekeun, 2022). Certain discrepancies between different wearable device hardware and their algorithms can also be problematic in a healthcare setting. The accuracy and reliability of these devices are crucial (Hosseini, Hosseini, Qayumi, Hosseinzadeh, & Tabar, 2023).

Beyond the importance of accuracy and reliability of the devices being used by a user, is what the user thinks of the devices. If the device is cumbersome, non-user-friendly, or imposes some other kind of physical, cognitive, or emotional burden on the user, the ongoing usage of such a device could be hindered, and potential medical benefits for their health will be lost. Because the real-world benefit of these devices depends on their uptake, a study was conducted to understand the user's perspectives on wearable biometric monitoring devices, mainly what they believed to be the benefits and dangers (Tran, Riveros, & Ravaud, 2019). Of some potential use cases presented, some covered distant monitoring to foresee exacerbations of enduring conditions, electronic-integrated clothes for physical therapy, chatbots, and AI screening of skin cancer (Tran, Riveros, & Ravaud, 2019). Of the 1183 patients enrolled, only 20% believed that the advantages of improving responsiveness in care and decreasing the burden of care offset the risks, 35% intended to refuse "at least one existing or soon-to-be" treatment-based mediation that leveraged biometric monitoring devices and AI, and 3% said the negative aspects greatly outweighed the benefits (Tran, Riveros, & Ravaud, 2019). Some potential negative aspects could include things like hacking, wrongful use of private data, and AI not being up to the same standard as human-based intelligence. These concerns are of high importance when trying to implement such technology for the benefit of healthcare.

The current list of approved devices is also of interest and ties back to the idea of wanting some accuracy, reliability, and safety to be represented in AI-powered medical devices. As of 2021, only 222 devices have been permitted in the United States, while 240 devices have been approved in Europe (Muehlematter, Daniore, & Vokinger, 2021). A substantial number of approved devices already in the market as of 2021 demonstrates a need for more regulation as there is no specific regulatory pathway for AI/ML devices. It is recommended in the literature that more transparency needs to be provided on how devices are regulated and approved to ensure public trust and quality, amongst other measures are upheld (Muehlematter, Daniore, & Vokinger, 2021).

Sensors. The ability to collect data in the physical world is often thanks to sensors, "the important objectives of the sensors are to regulate, monitor, control, warn, and track the activities of the patient" (Al-kahtani, Khan, & Taekeun, 2022). Sensors are used to examine and assess users in a noninvasive manner which helps our healthcare system be more independent, reducing provider involvement (Al-kahtani, Khan, & Taekeun, 2022). Many sensor types have been developed and implemented, ranging from complex to simple that can be applied in healthcare, such as the EEG (electroencephalogram), temperature monitor, blood pressure monitor, ECG (echocardiogram), EMG (electromyography), motion monitor (consisting of accelerometers and gyroscopes), heart rate monitor, and glucose monitors (Al-kahtani, Khan, & Taekeun, 2022). Depending on the application, sensors can be used alone, or in combination to enhance their effectiveness. Some sensors need specific placement, like being clamped onto fingers, put onto the scalp, worn like jewelry, or adhesively attached for optimal accuracy (Nandi, Mishra, & Majumder, 2022). From the co-citation analysis, a new related article was discovered that discusses how even ambient sensors can be integrated into safety forward procedures that detect and monitor staff handwashing (Topol, 2019).

Edge Computing. The latency that exists between IOT-based devices and their Internet-connected cloud-based computer systems can be problematic, with the potential safety and privacy issues demonstrating serious matters that stop the "Internet of Medical Things (IoMT) and architectures from being a reliable and effective solution" (Greco, Percannella, Ritrovato, Tortorella, & Vento, 2020). Due to these inherent issues with using the cloud, and ever-growing use cases for AI-based technology within healthcare, a reliable and effective solution is needed which can ensure privacy and trust for users while lowering the overall risk of the technology. This is where edge computing can potentially help alleviate existing pain points. This would allow the offloading of delay-sensitive and communicating-intensive tasks locally to improve services and benefit the user (Wan, Gu, & Ni, 2020). Preprocessing as much data as possible locally enables faster response times, helps build trust, and ensures privacy for the users while reducing the severity of an event where an internet connection is disrupted. Additionally, because IOT technologies are getting wide acceptance and have a growing adoption in healthcare, reducing the need for constant internet connectivity can save money and prevent potential network congestion (from the 1000s of additional devices being brought online) which could cause potential disruptions in other services (Wan, Gu, & Ni, 2020).

Edge computing has the unique ability to reduce communication overhead while allowing applications to perform "useful operations such as data processing, cache coherency, computing offloading, transferring, and delivering requests" even in desolate locations (Maddikunta, et al., 2022). By bringing localized processing farther away from the network, in some cases right to the sensor being used, a near-perfect integration of computation processes with the data source can be achieved (Wan, Gu, & Ni, 2020). Each device or sensor can act as its dispatcher, either sending information to another edge device or a centralized server if additional specialized processing is required, allowing each device to individually contribute to processing. Because of this network spreading, organizations also gain another way of enhancing their productivity, "by concentrating resources on certain tasks and making health IT systems more efficient by decentralizing IT infrastructure" (Wan, Gu, & Ni, 2020). It seems likely that more devices with onboard processing, or gateway devices with sensors nearby will continue to aid the growth of edge computing within healthcare, in the form of wearable devices such as smartphones, smartwatches, embedded systems, and potentially new forms that haven't been conceived (Greco, Percannella, Ritrovato, Tortorella, & Vento, 2020).

5   Conclusions

This review demonstrates that AI in healthcare and medicine is a rapidly growing topic that is gaining high levels of interest due to recent technological breakthroughs and a myriad of potential benefits. The literary usage and related articles being published have increased year over year during the last decade with a continued projected upward trajectory. Researchers will continue to work on privacy and safety concerns, through techniques such as edge computing to help people become more trusting of AI technology within healthcare. The advance of new sensors, sophisticated ergonomic wearable devices, and powerful AI models will continue to bring to light new insights that can improve the health outcomes of all people. Additionally, the rapid development of diagnostic and drug development AI tools will enhance the delivery of high-quality healthcare by reducing the cognitive workload of medical professionals, minimizing human error in disease diagnosis, and providing a variety of effective treatment options. Overall, the results of this study indicate that the ethical and responsible implementation of AI will transform patient care.

6   Future Work

Despite the early success of AI in healthcare and medicine, additional research is needed to guarantee the effectiveness and principled use of AI. The National Science Foundation (NSF) is a key agency in fueling the advancement of knowledge in areas of science and engineering through research grant awards. These awards indicate the upcoming and future work in a given field, so a search was performed using the NSF award search tool (National Science Foundation, n.d.). In the area of medical diagnosis, a grant of $150,000 was awarded to Principal Investigator Roger Azevedo starting in January 2022 with an estimated end date of December 2024 titled "Augmenting Healthcare Professionals?

Training, Expertise Development, and Diagnostic Reasoning with AI-based Immersive Technologies in Telehealth." According to Azevedo et al. (2021), a primary focus is "to design an intelligent collaborative virtual telehealth system prototype that supports healthcare professionals' diagnostic reasoning, expertise development, and training that can be used in various healthcare scenarios." The overarching focus of this research is to "enhance medical education and training to accelerate expertise development, minimize medical errors, and deliver high-quality medical care" (Azevedo, Gurupur, Neider, Shoss, & Torre, 2021).

The NSF also awarded a grant to Principal Investigator Swaroop Ghosh starting in July 2022 in the amount of $1,200,000 to create a toolset utilizing quantum AI to explore the area of drug discovery (Gosh & Dokholyan, 2022). Assuming the project's success, this research will unveil "new computational capabilities in discovery applications, e.g., by selecting novel lead chemical compounds versus important target proteins to treat diseases, such as cancer, by converging multiple disciplines" (Gosh & Dokholyan, 2022). The emergence of AI in healthcare applications is bolstered by the distribution of these grants and indicates a few of many areas where research in this area should continue to promote patient safety.

AI in healthcare is a rapidly advancing area with many complexities. Cutting-edge technologies are being leveraged which include software, network architectures, and physical hardware. The adoption of such technologies in healthcare also depends on the acceptance by users, which requires ensured security, trust, and usability. Another NSF award was given in August 2023 for $200,000.00 to Christopher Yang from the University of South Carolina to explore "Knowledge-guided neurosymbolic AI with guardrails for safe virtual health assistants" (Yang, 2023). The main innovation in this research lies in "leveraging Knowledge Graphs (KGs) to construct guardrails that help ensure the safety of AI systems" (Yang, 2023). It will be made in collaboration with healthcare experts to integrate medical terminology and procedure/process knowledge to "uphold high safety standards in clinical settings" (Yang, 2023).

An NSF award issued in August 2023 for $50,000.00 to Jamie A. Camelio from the University of Texas at Austin is intended to explore "Contextualization of Explainable Artificial Intelligence (AI) for Better Health" (Camelio, 2023). The broader impact of this research is "the development of the explainable Artificial Intelligence (XAI) methods for healthcare data," the healthcare industry is extremely regulated, and explainability for black-box AI models is increasingly critical for any AI application (Camelio, 2023). This relates to the idea that "users need to comprehend and trust the results and output created by machine learning algorithms," so this future research is highly relevant from a human factors and ergonomics perspective to ensure uptake of the technology for healthcare usage (Camelio, 2023).

References

Al-Kahtani, M.S., Khan, F., Taekeun, W.: Application of internet of things and sensors in healthcare. Sensors **22**(15), 5738 (2022). https://doi.org/10.3390/s22155738

Arora, G., Joshi, J., Mandal, R.S., Shrivastava, N., Virmani, R., Sethi, T.: Artificial intelligence in surveillance, diagnosis, drug discovery and vaccine development against COVID-19. Pathogens **10**(8), 1–21 (2021). https://doi.org/10.3390/pathogens10081048

Azevedo, R., Gurupur, V., Neider, M., Shoss, M., Torre, D.: Award Abstract # 2128684 FW-HTF-P: Augmenting Healthcare Professionals? Training, Expertise Development, and Diagnostic Reasoning with AI-based Immersive Technologies in Telehealth. National Science Foundation (2021). https://www.nsf.gov/awardsearch/showAward?AWD_ID=2128684&HistoricalAwards=false. Accessed Nov 2023

Camelio, J.A.: NSF Award Search: Award #2331366-I-Corps: Contextualization of Explainable Artificial Intelligence (AI) for Better Health (2023). https://www.nsf.gov/awardsearch/showAward?AWD_ID=2331366&HistoricalAwards=false. Accessed 26 Nov 2023

Carayon, P., Wust, K., Hose, B.-Z., Salwei, M.E.: Human factors and ergonomics in health care. In: Salvendy, G., Karwowski, W. (eds.) Handbook of Human Factors and Ergonomics, 5th edn., pp. 1417–1437. Wiley, Hoboken (2021)

Chen, M., Hao, Y., Hwang, K., Wang, L., Wang, L.: Disease prediction by machine learning over big data from healthcare communities. IEEE Access **5**, 8869–8879 (2017)

Chowdhury, M.E., et al.: Can AI help in screening viral and COVID-19 pneumonia? IEEE Access **8**, 132665–132676 (2020). https://doi.org/10.1109/ACCESS.2020.3010287

CiteSpace (n.d.). Accessed Nov 2023

Deo, R.C.: Machine Learning in Medicine. American Heart Association, 1920–30 (2015)

Duffy, T., Duffy, V.G.: Moderating stress in task design and motivation: a systematic review. In: Duffy, V.G., Ziefle, M., Rau, P.L.P., Tseng, M.M. (eds.) Human-Automation Interaction: Mobile Computing, pp. 415–430. Springer, Cham (2022). https://doi.org/10.1007/978-3-031-10788-7_25

Esteva, A., et al.: Dermatologist-level classification of skin cancer with deep neural networks. Nature **542**, 115–118 (2017)

Fahimnia, B., Sarkis, J., Davarzani, H.: Green supply chain management: a review and bibliometric analysis. Int. J. Prod. Econ. **162**, 101–114 (2015). https://doi.org/10.1016/j.ijpe.2015.01.003

Google. Google Books Ngram Viewer (n.d.). https://books.google.com/ngrams/. Accessed 21 Nov 2023

Gosh, S., Dokholyan, N.: Award Abstract # 2210963 FET:Medium: Drug discovery using quantum machine learning (2022). National Science Foundation. https://www.nsf.gov/awardsearch/showAward?AWD_ID=2210963&HistoricalAwards=false. Accessed 27 Nov 2023

Greco, L., Percannella, G., Ritrovato, P., Tortorella, F., Vento, M.: Trends in IOT based solutions for health care: moving AI to the edge. Pattern Recogn. Lett. **135**, 346–353 (2020). https://doi.org/10.1016/j.patrec.2020.05.016

Gulshan, V., Peng, L., Coram, M., &, et al.: Development and validation of a deep learning algorithm for detection of diabetic retinopathy in retinal fundus photographs. JAMA **316**, 2402–2410 (2016)

Hamet, P., Tremblay, J.: Artificial intelligence in medicine. Metabolism **69**, S36–S40 (2017)

Harzing's Publish or Perish. Tarma Software Research Ltd (n.d.). Accessed Nov 2023

Hosny, A., Parmar, C., Quackenbush, J., Schwartz, L.H., Aerts, H.J.: Artificial intelligence in radiology. Nat. Rev. Cancer **18**(8), 500–510 (2018). https://doi.org/10.1038/s41568-018-0016-5

Hosseini, M.M., Hosseini, S.T., Qayumi, K., Hosseinzadeh, S., Tabar, S.S.: Smartwatches in healthcare medicine: assistance and monitoring; a scoping review. BMC Med. Inform. Decis. Mak. **23**(1), 248 (2023). https://doi.org/10.1186/s12911-023-02350-w

Indeed. What Is the Role of Industrial Engineering in Healthcare? (2022). Indeed. https://www.indeed.com/career-advice/finding-a-job/industrial-engineering-in-healthcare. Accessed 29 Nov 2023

Jiang, F., et al.: Artificial intelligence in healthcare: past, present and future. Stroke Vasc. Neurol. **2**(4), 230–243 (2017). https://doi.org/10.1136/svn-2017-000101

Kermany, D.S., Goldbaum, M., Cai, W., Lewis, M., Xia, H., Zhang, K.: Identifying medical diagnoses and treatable diseases by image-based deep learning. Cell **172**(5), 1122–1131.E9 (2018). https://doi.org/10.1016/j.cell.2018.02.010

Lakhani, P., Sundaram, B.: Deep learning at chest radiography: automated classification of pulmonary tuberculosis by using convolutional neural networks. Radiology **284**, 574–582 (2017)

Maddikunta, P.K., et al.: Industry 5.0: A survey on enabling technologies and potential applications. J. Ind. Inf. Integr. **26**, 100257 (2022). https://doi.org/10.1016/j.jii.2021.100257

Muehlematter, U.J., Daniore, P., Vokinger, K.N.: Approval of artificial intelligence and machine learning-based medical devices in the USA and Europe (2015–20): a comparative analysis. Lancet Digit. Health **3**(3), e195–203 (2021). https://doi.org/10.1016/S2589-7500(20)30292-2

Nandi, S., Mishra, M., Majumder, S.: Usage of AI and wearable IoT devices for healthcare data: a study. Mach. Learn. Algorithms Signal Image Process. 315–337 (2022). https://doi.org/10.1002/9781119861850.ch18

National Science Foundation. Awards Simple Search. National Science Foundation (n.d.). https://www.nsf.gov/awardsearch

NVivo. QSR International (n.d.). Accessed Nov 2023

Obermeyer, Z., Powers, B., Vogeli, C., Mullainathan, S.: Dissecting racial bias in an algorithm used to manage the health of populations. Science **366**, 447–453 (2019)

Paul, D., Sanap, G., Shenoy, S., Kalyane, D., Kalia, K., Tekade, R.K.: Artificial intelligence in drug discovery and development. Drug Discov. Today **26**(1), 80–93 (2021). https://doi.org/10.1016/j.drudis.2020.10.010

Salvendy, G., Karwowski, W.: Handbook of Human Factors and Ergonomics, 5th edn. Wiley, Hoboken (2021)

Scopus. Scopus Homepage (n.d.). Scopus. https://www.scopus.com/search/form.uri?display=basic#basic

Topol, E.J.: High-performance medicine: the convergence of human and artificial intelligence. Nat. Med. **25**, 44–56 (2019)

Tran, V.-T., Riveros, C., Ravaud, P.: Patients' views of wearable devices and AI in healthcare: findings from the compare E-cohort. NPJ Digit. Med. **2**(1), 53 (2019). https://doi.org/10.1038/s41746-019-0132-y

VOSviewer (n.d.). Accessed Nov 2023

Wan, S., Gu, Z., Ni, Q.: Cognitive computing and wireless communications on the edge for healthcare service robots. Comput. Commun. **149**, 99–106 (2020). https://doi.org/10.1016/j.comcom.2019.10.012

Wang, S., Hou, Y., Li, X., Meng, X., Zhang, Y., Wang, X.: Practical implementation of artificial intelligence-based deep learning and cloud computing on the application of traditional medicine and western medicine in the diagnosis and treatment of rheumatoid arthritis. Front. Pharmacol. **12**, 1–18 (2021). https://doi.org/10.3389/fphar.2021.765435

Web of Science. Web of Science Core Collection (n.d.). Clarivate. https://www.webofscience.com/wos/woscc/basic-search

Wickens, C.D., Carswell, C.M.: Information processing. In: Salvendy, G., Karwowski, W. (eds.) Handbook of Human Factors and Ergonomics, 5th edn., pp. 114–158. Wiley, Hoboken (2021)

Yang, C.: NSF Award Search: Award # 2335967 - EAGER: Knowledge-guided neurosymbolic AI with guardrails for safe virtual health assistants (2023). https://www.nsf.gov/awardsearch/showAward?AWD_ID=2335967&HistoricalAwards=false. Accessed 26 Nov 2023

Yu, K.-H., Beam, A.L., Kohane, I.S.: Artificial intelligence in healthcare. Nat. Biomed. Eng. **2**, 719–731 (2018). https://doi.org/10.1038/s41551-018-0305-z

Development and Application of a Machine Learning-Based Prediction Model for 6-Month Unplanned Readmission in Heart Failure Patients

Juncheng Hu[1] and Chunbao Mo[2(✉)]

[1] School of Intelligent Medicine and Biotechnology,
Guilin Medical University, Guilin 541199, China
[2] Zhonglin Sci-Tech Development Group Co., Ltd., Nanning 530201, China
molipol@163.com

Abstract. Accurately predicting the risk of readmission for patients with heart failure is of utmost importance for their prognostic management. In this study, prediction models for 6-month unplanned readmission in heart failure patients were developed using a cohort of 1888 individuals. The cohort was divided into training and testing sets in an 8:2 ratio. Variable selection was performed using Lasso regression, and the prediction models were trained using logistic regression, random forest, decision tree, Bayesian classifier, and support vector machines algorithms. A set of 17 predictive indicators were identified, including age, gender, basophil ratio, monocyte count, neutrophil count, calcium, sodium, glomerular filtration rate, uric acid, prothrombin activity, dementia, type of heart failure, consciousness, cardiac function classification, diabetes, chronic kidney disease and length of hospital stay. Among the models tested, the Bayesian classifier model exhibited a relatively stronger predictive performance (Area under the curve: 0.60, sensitivity: 0.81, specificity: 0.38). Additionally, a user-friendly software application based on the R Shiny package was developed to facilitate the practical implementation of the prediction models.

Keywords: Heart Failure · Readmission · Prediction Model · Application

1 Introduction

Heart failure (HF) is a clinical syndrome that has been conventionally described as a condition where the heart's pumping ability and/or filling capacity are reduced, leading to insufficient cardiac output. This insufficiency can arise from structural or functional abnormalities of the heart, which are often accompanied by compensatory neurohormonal activation and elevated left ventricular filling pressures. According to the Global Burden of Disease Study in 2017, there were approximately 64.3 million HF patients worldwide [1]. Similarly, estimates by Hu et al. indicate that the number of heart failure (HF) patients in China was approximately 8.9 million in 2019 [2]. Furthermore,

V. G. Duffy (Ed.): HCII 2024, LNCS 14710, pp. 271–279, 2024.
https://doi.org/10.1007/978-3-031-61063-9_18

The China Hypertension Survey showed that the prevalence of HF among hypertensive individuals in China was approximately 1.3%, with an in-hospital crude mortality rate of about 4.1%. [3] Therefore, both globally and in China, HF has become a significant public health issue, imposing a substantial disease burden [4]. HF patients face the challenges of long-term treatment and a high risk of recurrence. Interventions targeting the control of risk factors such as smoking cessation, alcohol restriction, blood pressure management, blood glucose control, and lipid-lowering measures are effective strategies for reducing HF recurrence, improving prognosis, and lowering mortality rates.

With the development of artificial intelligence technology, machine learning algorithms were being increasingly applied in the research of clinical prediction models. Similarly, some researchers had started exploring and developing models that could accurately predict the prognosis of heart failure patients. Such as Tian et al. [5] constructed a prediction model for all-cause mortality in heart failure patients based on 941 patients with chronic heart failure. Li et al. [6] utilized an extreme gradient boosting model to develop an interpretable machine learning model for predicting the risk of mortality in heart failure patients. Zheng et al. [7] utilized a Cox proportional hazards model to predict the risk of readmission in heart failure patients. Although a significant number of prognostic models for heart failure had been published at the theoretical research level, there were relatively few studies that had developed these prediction models into products that could be implemented in clinical practice. Therefore, this study aimed to build a predictive model for the risk of unplanned readmission within six months for heart failure patients and integrated this model into a practical application software, bridging the gap between theory and application. Specifically, we would use the dataset from the Heart Failure Patients Study in Zigong. And we employed the Lasso regression to select factors highly associated with unplanned readmission within six months as prediction indicators. Subsequently, five machine learning algorithms would be used to construct prediction models, and their performance would be individually validated. Finally, the best-performing model would be selected for the development of a clinical prediction application software.

2   Method

2.1   Study Participants

We utilized an online open-source database from a study conducted on heart failure patients in Zigong, a city located in Sichuan province, China [8]. This research was conducted by Zigong Fourth People's Hospital and focused on investigating the prognosis of heart failure patients. The study included heart failure patients admitted to the hospital between December 2016 and June 2019. Comprehensive information, including demographic data, physiological measurements, biochemical indicators, and medical history, was collected for these patients. Follow-up was conducted to track outcomes, including death and readmission. The raw data collected were then aggregated, resulting in a dataset consisting of 2008 study subjects and 166 attributes. This study was approved by ethics committee of Zigong Fourth People's Hospital (Approval Number: 2020–010). In present study, 1888 eligible participants were included after excluding the patients with missing value (N = 122, Fig. 1).

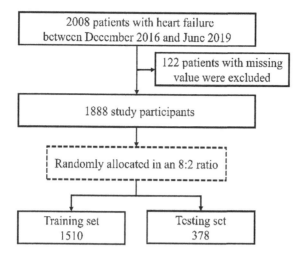

Fig. 1. The flowchart of the participants selection.

2.2 Prediction Indicators and Outcomes

We initially chose 80 variables from the dataset as potential predictors. These variables encompass various aspects, including demographic characteristics (e.g., age, gender, occupation), clinical indicators (e.g., blood pressure, pulse rate, BMI, type of heart failure, NYHA cardiac function classification), diagnostic indicators (e.g., blood glucose, lipid profile), medical history (e.g., diabetes, hypertension), and length of hospital stay. The primary outcome of this study was to determine the occurrence of unplanned readmissions within 6 months following patient discharge.

2.3 Selection of Predictors and Construction of Prediction Models

The original dataset will be randomly divided into training and testing sets in an 8:2 ratios. The training set will be used to train the prediction models, while the testing set will be used to evaluate the performance of these prediction models. When constructing the prediction models, it is not necessary to include all candidate predictors. Instead, we would utilize the Lasso regression method to select the most valuable predictors that contribute to the prediction outcome. These selected predictors would be used as the formal predictive indicators for training the final prediction models. The machine learning algorithms employed for training the prediction models comprised Logistic regression (LR), Random forest (RF), Decision tree (DT), Bayesian classifier (BC), and Support vector machines (SVM). Once the prediction models had been trained, their performance would be assessed using the testing set. Models exhibiting good prediction performance would be selected for further development as an application software. Evaluation indicators, such as area under the curve (AUC), accuracy, sensitivity, and specificity, would be employed to assess the prediction performance of the models. These metrics provided valuable insights into the effectiveness and reliability of the models in making accurate predictions. The strategy for constructing the prediction models was illustrated in Fig. 2.

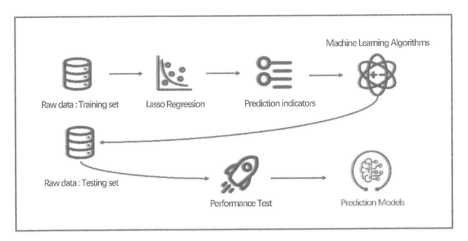

Fig. 2. Strategies for constructing prediction models.

2.4 Developing an Application Software

To develop an application software for a prediction model, two R scripts were necessary: ui.R and server.R. The ui.R script was responsible for creating the user-facing graphical interfaces, while the server.R script served as the server-side script for executing commands and performing computations. The application was designed using a dashboard approach, which aimed to enhance man-machine interaction and include functions such as predicting the risk of unplanned readmission and visualization. The primary goal of the application was to enable seamless interaction between users and the system, allowing them to input relevant data and obtain visual predictions regarding the risk of unplanned readmission.

2.5 Statistical Analysis

Continuous variables were summarized using measures such as mean and standard deviation, while categorical variables were described using the count of cases and composition ratio. To compare the baseline characteristics between the readmission and non-readmission groups, t-tests and chi-square tests were performed. All the above-mentioned analyses and the development of the application software were conducted using R software (version 4.1.3) and its packages, including "Shiny," "shinyWidgets," "Tidyverse," "HighCharter," and "ShinyDashboard."

3   Results

3.1 Predictors Selection

Based on the analysis using lasso regression and considering clinical expertise, a total of 17 predictive indicators were selected for inclusion in this study. These indicators include Age, Gender, Basophil ratio, and others (Table 1).

Table 1. Prediction Indicators and Corresponding Data Formats in the Present Study.

Prediction indicators	Data formats
Age	Multiple categories
Gender	Binary categories
Basophil ratio	Continuous variables
Monocyte count	Continuous variables
Neutrophil count	Continuous variables
Calcium	Continuous variables
Sodium	Continuous variables
Glomerular filtration rate	Continuous variables
Uric acid	Continuous variables
Prothrombin activity	Continuous variables
Type of heart failure	Multiple categories
NYHA cardiac function classification	Multiple categories
Consciousness	Multiple categories
Dementia	Binary categories
Diabetes	Binary categories
Chronic kidney disease	Binary categories
Length of hospital stay	Continuous variables

3.2   Baseline Characteristics of Study Participants

The baseline characteristics of the study subjects were presented in Table 2. Among all the study subjects, there were 732 individuals who experienced readmission within 6 months and 1156 individuals who did not. The age distribution was predominantly in the 70~ age range, accounting for 75.0% and 71.3% in the readmission and non-readmission groups, respectively. The gender distribution was predominantly female, comprising 56.6% in the readmission group and 58.5% in the non-readmission group. In comparison to the non-readmission group, the readmission group exhibited higher values for basophil ratio, uric acid, and length of hospital stay. Furthermore, the readmission group had a higher proportion of individuals with type of heart failure classified as "both", NYHA cardiac function classification of IV, dementia, diabetes, and chronic kidney disease. However, the readmission group had lower values for neutrophil count, calcium, sodium, and prothrombin activity.

3.3   Performance of Prediction Models

Logistic regression, random forest, decision tree, Bayesian classifier and support vector machines (SVM) algorithms were utilized to train the prediction models. Among

Table 2. Baseline Characteristics of Study Participants.

		6-Month Unplanned Readmission		
		Yes (N = 732)	No (N = 1156)	*P value*
Age, years old	21~39	3 (0.4)	10 (0.9)	0.135
	40~69	180 (24.6)	322 (27.9)	
	70~	549 (75.0)	824 (71.3)	
Gender	Female	414 (56.6)	676 (58.5)	0.438
	Male	318 (43.4)	480 (41.5)	
Basophil ratio, %		0.005 (0.004)	0.004(0.004)	<0.001**
Monocyte count, 10^9/L		0.5 (0.2)	0.5 (0.3)	0.250
Neutrophil count, 10^9/L		5.5 (3.0)	5.8 (3.4)	0.049*
Calcium, mmol/L		2.3 (0.2)	2.3 (0.2)	0.001*
Sodium, mmol/L		137.9 (4.8)	138.5 (4.9)	0.011*
Glomerular filtration rate, mL/min/1.73 m^2		64.2 (34.8)	71.6 (36.9)	<0.001**
Uric acid, umol/L		503.8 (171.6)	470.3 (166.3)	<0.001**
Prothrombin activity, %		64.8 (18.8)	67.1 (18.0)	0.008*
Type of heart failure	Both	596 (81.4)	801 (69.3)	<0.001**
	Left	119 (16.3)	322 (27.9)	
	Right	17 (2.3)	33 (2.9)	
NYHA cardiac function classification	II	95 (13.0)	225 (19.5)	<0.001**
	III	375 (51.2)	610 (52.8)	
	IV	262 (35.8)	321 (27.8)	
Consciousness	Clear	725 (99.0)	1130 (97.8)	0.068
	Nonresponsive	0 (0.0)	10 (0.9)	
	Responsive to pain	1 (0.1)	3 (0.3)	
	Responsive to sound	6 (0.8)	13 (1.1)	
Dementia	Yes	55 (7.5)	56 (4.8)	0.021*
	No	677 (92.5)	1100 (95.2)	
Diabetes	Yes	206 (28.1)	238 (20.6)	<0.001**
	No	526 (71.9)	918 (79.4)	

(continued)

Table 2. (*continued*)

		6-Month Unplanned Readmission		
		Yes (N = 732)	No (N = 1156)	*P value*
Chronic kidney disease	Yes	207 (28.3)	238 (20.6)	<0.001**
	No	525 (71.7)	918 (79.4)	
Length of hospital stay, days		10.3 (9.4)	8.7 (6.7)	<0.001**

Footnotes: Continuous variables were represented as mean (± standard deviation), and categorical variables were represented as counts (percentages); *P < 0.05* or **P < 0.01* was considered statistically significant.

the models tested, the Bayesian classifier model exhibited a relatively stronger predictive performance (Area under the curve: 0.60 (95% Confidence interval: 0.55–0.64), sensitivity: 0.81, specificity: 0.38, Table 3).

Table 3. Performance of Prediction Models.

Models	AUC (95% CI)	Accuracy (%)	Sensitivity (%)	Specificity (%)
Logistic regression	0.53 (0.50–0.56)	0.61	0.93	0.12
Random forest	0.56 (0.51–0.60)	0.61	0.83	0.28
Decision tree	0.52 (0.47–0.57)	0.54	0.63	0.40
Bayesian classifier	0.60 (0.55–0.64)	0.64	0.81	0.38
Support vector machines	0.55(0.51–0.59)	0.62	0.90	0.20

Footnotes: AUC, area under the curve; 95% CI, 95% confidence interval.

3.4   The Application Software of Prediction Model

An application software was designed and developed to apply the theoretical model to clinical practice. This software utilizes the Bayesian classifier model trained in the present study as the prediction model. The design of the application was illustrated in Fig. 3. It is capable of receiving raw input data from the healthcare system, which undergoes data preprocessing before being transmitted to the prediction model (Bayesian classifier model). Subsequently, the prediction model outputs the predicted risk values for readmission within 6 months. The application software could be integrated into healthcare professionals' patient management systems, offering them scientific and rational guidance in managing and treating heart failure patients. Furthermore, it could also function as a standalone mobile application, providing patients with alert information regarding their own risk of readmission.

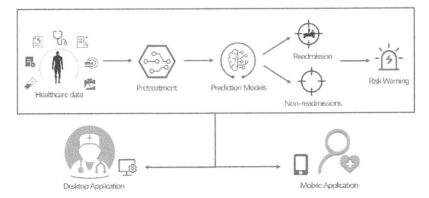

Fig. 3. Practical Design of Prediction Model.

The software interface was shown in Fig. 4, which was a user-friendly and visually streamlined application. It could accept data from the electronic medical record system in hospital or user input, automatically calculating the patient's risk of readmission. As depicted in the figure, the left side of the interface consists of input fields for prediction indicators, while the right side displays the output of the results.

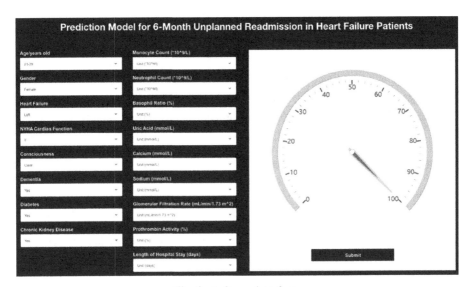

Fig. 4. Software interface.

4 Conclusion

The primary objective of in present study was to create a robust prediction model that could assess the risk of unplanned readmissions within a 6-month period for patients with heart failure. The prediction model would be integrated into a practical software application. Specifically, a cohort contained 1888 heart failure patients was study, and a careful selection of 17 prediction indicators was performed using the Lasso regression. Initially, five machine learning algorithms were utilized to construct the prediction models. Ultimately, the Bayesian classifier model, which demonstrated exceptional performance, was selected for integration and further development into the application software. The resultant software could provide healthcare professionals and patients with an intuitive platform for accessing clinical prediction services, thereby serving as a valuable tool for guiding clinical treatment decisions and prognosis management.

Acknowledgments. The work of this paper is supported by Acute Myocardial Infarction Electrocardiogram Intelligent Pre-Hospital Monitoring and Early Warning, Guangdong and Guangxi Cooperation R&D Talent Introduction (No. AC22035089) and Research and Application Demonstration of Medical Image-Assisted Disease Diagnosis Based on Artificial Intelligence Technology, Training Plan for Thousands of Young and Middle-Aged Backbone Teachers in Colleges and Universities in Guangxi (The Fifth Phase).

References

1. Global, regional, and national incidence, prevalence, and years lived with disability for 354 diseases and injuries for 195 countries and territories, 1990–2017: a systematic analysis for the Global Burden of Disease Study 2017. Lancet **392**, 1789–1858 (2018)
2. In, C.T., Hu, S.S.: Report on cardiovascular health and diseases in China 2021: an updated summary. J. Geriatr. Cardiol. **20**, 399–430 (2023)
3. Al-Omary, A.M.S., et al.: Mortality and readmission following hospitalisation for heart failure in Australia: a systematic review and meta-analysis. Heart Lung Circ. **27**, 917–927 (2018)
4. Savarese, G., Becher, P.M., Lund, L.H., Seferovic, P., Rosano, G., Coats, A.: Global burden of heart failure: a comprehensive and updated review of epidemiology. Cardiovasc. Res. **118**, 3272–3287 (2023)
5. Tian, J., et al.: Machine learning prognosis model based on patient-reported outcomes for chronic heart failure patients after discharge. Health Qual. Life Outcomes **21**, 31 (2023)
6. Li, J., Liu, S., Hu, Y., Zhu, L., Mao, Y., Liu, J.: Predicting mortality in intensive care unit patients with heart failure using an interpretable machine learning model: retrospective cohort study. J. Med. Internet Res. **24**, e38082 (2022)
7. Zheng, L., Smith, N.J., Teng, B.Q., Szabo, A., Joyce, D.L.: Predictive model for heart failure readmission using nationwide readmissions database. Mayo Clin. Proc. Innov. Qual Outcomes **6**, 228–238 (2022)
8. Zhang, Z., Cao, L., Chen, R., Zhao, Y., Lv, L., Xu, Z., et al.: Electronic healthcare records and external outcome data for hospitalized patients with heart failure. Sci. Data **8**, 46 (2021)

Design and Optimization Strategy of a CNN Aided Pre-hospital Diagnosis System for Myocardial Infarction

Juncheng Hu[1(✉)], Youtian Zhou[2], and Chunbao Mo[3]

[1] Intelligent Medicine and Biotechnology, Guilin Medical University, Guilin 541199, China
jc.hu@glmc.edu.cn
[2] School of Design, Guangxi Normal University, Guilin 541004, China
[3] Zhonglin Sci-Tech Development Group Co., Ltd., Nanning 530201, China

Abstract. Myocardial Infarction (MI), commonly known as a heart attack, is a prevalent acute cardiovascular disease and one of the deadliest types of cardiovascular diseases in China. Electrocardiogram (ECG) serves as the primary tool for analysis and diagnosis, recording the heart's electrical activity to detect abnormal patterns. ECG exhibits nonlinear and unstable characteristics, with its noise being random. Therefore, the extraction and identification of ECG features related to MI are crucial for intelligent assisted diagnosis of heart attacks. In this paper, a MI assisted pre-hospital diagnosis system based on CNN (Convolution Neural Network, CNN) is designed, to assist healthcare professionals in improving the accuracy and efficiency of MI diagnosis. The MI assisted diagnosis system, based on the CNN MI intelligent diagnostic model, is established with the goal of intelligent identification of MI in the context of computer-aided diagnosis systems. It aims to address key issues such as automatic feature extraction and analysis diagnosis, focusing on ECG research and exploring MI intelligent identification methods based on CNN. This system is dedicated to providing assistance and support for clinical diagnosis by healthcare professionals, enhancing diagnostic accuracy and efficiency to ensure early diagnosis and timely treatment of MI. Additionally, in cases of sudden cardiac emergencies among ECG users, the system is capable of providing timely assistance and treatment plans, offering critical support to ECG users in need.

Keywords: Artificial Intelligence & Smart Services · Myocardial Infarction · Healthcare · Diagnosis System · CNN

1 Introduction

Cardiovascular disease is the leading cause of death for both urban and rural residents. According to the "2022 Report on Cardiovascular Health and Diseases in China" released in 2023 [1], two out of every five deaths are due to cardiovascular disease, and the number of people with vascular diseases in China is increasing year by year. Acute cardiovascular diseases, such as heart attacks, pose a significant threat to patients' lives. ECG is currently

© The Author(s), under exclusive license to Springer Nature Switzerland AG 2024
V. G. Duffy (Ed.): HCII 2024, LNCS 14710, pp. 280–299, 2024.
https://doi.org/10.1007/978-3-031-61063-9_19

an important basis for diagnosing heart attacks [2]. However, clinical judgment of heart attacks still relies on doctors observing morphological changes in various waves and segments of the ECG, leading to issues such as time consumption, labor intensiveness, missed diagnoses, or misdiagnoses. Computer-aided diagnosis systems can overcome the limitations of manual ECG detection and effectively address the subjective uncertainty in the diagnostic process.

With the advancement of artificial intelligence technology, deep learning has been widely applied in the field of medical image processing [3]. CNNs, as a new generation of artificial intelligence technology, have made significant breakthroughs in computer vision [4–6]. CNN network models are mainly applied in cardiovascular diseases for disease prediction, disease management, and assisting diagnosis based on ECG signals. As a data-driven end-to-end neural network learning model, CNN is suitable for nonlinear ECG signals. It automatically extracts features from input ECG signals and integrates and clusters these features for identification and classification purposes.

This study adopts a deep learning approach, designing a CNN network based on residual learning for clinical ECG and combining it with a pooling strategy incorporating attention mechanisms to comprehensively explore the features of clinical ECG in China. By utilizing signal processing and deep learning techniques to process ECG signals, extract ECG feature information, and establish a smart diagnosis model for heart attacks, a system for assisting in diagnosing heart attacks has been designed and implemented.

By leveraging the advantages of CNN network models in ECG feature detection and classification, they are applied to the classification and identification of heart attacks, providing timely assistance and support to doctors in clinical diagnosis. This not only improves the efficiency of diagnosis but also significantly increases the accuracy of diagnosis by reducing human errors. The software can quickly push emergency treatment plans for these patients, striving for the best treatment time and reducing the mortality rate of heart attack patients. Through an intelligent process, it improves the inconvenience of previous processes requiring hospital registration and consultation for ECG examination. Patients can detect and obtain their own electrocardiographic information anytime and anywhere, helping them better manage their health. At the same time, it provides a platform for communication between patients and doctors, enabling patients to communicate with doctors in a timely manner. This greatly improves the patient's medical experience and has significant research significance and application value.

2 Datasets and Data Preprocessing

2.1 Dataset Introduction

The Chinese Cardiovascular Disease Database (CCDD) is a clinical multi-lead ECG dataset specifically designed for the Chinese population [7]. All ECG data in the CCDD dataset are clinically collected and manually annotated by multiple authoritative cardiovascular disease experts. The CCDD dataset consists of 12-lead ECG data, totaling over 170,000 ECG data records, with each record lasting approximately 10–18 s. Each ECG data record comes from different patients and is labeled with an annotation in Extensible Markup Language (.xml) format, which can be converted to.mat format for easier reading.

The PTB ECG Database mainly includes data on MI, healthy control group data, heart failure, atrioventricular block, rhythm disorders, myocardial hypertrophy, heart valve disease, myocarditis, and other types of cardiovascular disease data. These ECG data can be obtained from the PhysioNet website. In this study, ECG data were selected from 148 cases of MI and 52 cases of healthy control groups. The ECG sampling frequency in this dataset is 1000 Hz with a resolution of 16 bits, and the duration of each ECG data record is mostly 2 min.

2.2 Data Preprocessing

Data Filtering. The CCDD ECG dataset contains multiple types of cardiovascular disease ECG data. From the CCDD dataset, 612 sets of MI ECG data were selected. To maintain the balance of the experimental dataset and prevent overfitting, 980 sets were randomly selected from over 20,000 sets of normal ECG data. This resulted in a total of 1592 sets of 12-lead ECG data. Considering the relationship between ECG leads and the correlation among the 12 leads, 8-lead ECG data were extracted for MI disease identification diagnosis in practical applications. The selected 8 ECG leads are: II, III, V1, V2, V3, V4, V5, and V6 leads. The sampling rate of the 8-lead ECG data was downsampled from 500 Hz to 200 Hz, and each set of ECG data records was truncated to 1900 sampling points.

Data Denoising. The importance of ECG noise recognition lies in two main aspects. Firstly, it prevents mistaking changes in electrical potential not generated by myocardial excitation for changes caused by myocardial excitation, thus avoiding errors in ECG diagnosis. Secondly, certain noises can mask abnormal conditions in the ECG itself, making disease diagnosis challenging.

Based on the characteristics of ECG, it is known that noise interference comes from various sources, mainly including baseline drift, electromyographic interference, and power line interference. Figure 1 shows an ECG affected by baseline drift, mainly caused by human respiration or electrode movement, resulting in significant interference in the ST segment of the ECG waveform. The ST segment is an important parameter for diagnosing whether a patient has a MI. ECG affected by electromyographic interference, as shown in Fig. 2, is generally caused by muscle contractions and tremors in the human body. It is a high-frequency noise with small interference amplitude and high frequency. As seen in the figure, small ripples are superimposed on the original ECG, obscuring the original waveform and causing distortion in the ECG waveform.

Fig. 1. ECG Affected by Baseline Drift Interference.

Data Augmentation. When selecting ECG data, the number of normal samples is often greater than the number of MI samples. To increase the sample size, data augmentation

Fig. 2. ECG Affected by Electromyographic Interference.

methods are commonly employed. Due to the temporal and cyclical nature of ECG data, we choose to shift the starting point of the ECG to increase the sample count. During ECG data collection, the starting point's position is uncertain, so shifting the starting point each time results in a new ECG sequence. This method not only increases the volume of sample data but also improves the robustness and fault tolerance of the MI classification algorithm. For example, for ECG data with 1900 points downsampled to 200 Hz, we can take 1800 points and shift by 20 points each time (equivalent to 0.1 s of data), thereby obtaining six times the number of ECG data in the end.

3   Model Building, Training and Prediction

3.1   Res-CNN Based Classification Model for MI

Res-CNN. In CNNs, as the network depth increases, its ability to extract ECG features improves. However, in the actual training process, when the network depth increases to a certain extent, the model becomes increasingly difficult to train. Simply increasing the model depth may lead to the problem of network degradation. Therefore, the deep residual CNN (Res-CNN) model is used for MI classification diagnosis.

The Res-CNN network introduces residual blocks, the basic idea of which is to skip one or more network layers by stacking models, instead of simply stacking network layers with "shortcut connections". The stacked model of residual learning is illustrated in Fig. 3: where x is the input of the residual structure, H(x) represents the optimal solution mapping, and F(x) is the mapping of identity residuals. By letting the stacked nonlinear layers fit another mapping $F(x) = H(x) - x$, the original optimal solution mapping H(x) can be rewritten as $F(x) + x$. The residual mapping is easier to optimize compared to the original mapping. Under extreme conditions, if the mapping is optimized, it is easier to approximate the residuals to zero than to approximate the mapping to another nonlinear layer. The expression $F(x) + x$ can be implemented using a feedforward neural network with "shortcut connections".

After learning the identity mapping, the residual network achieves a deeper network structure, integrating low-level features and high-level features of MI ECG data to improve the performance of the Res-CNN network architecture, achieve higher training and testing accuracy rates, and the entire network can still be trained end-to-end.

Attention Mechanism. In ECG, different morphological waveforms contain varying degrees of inherent feature information, with more essential features carrying greater influence weights. In order to effectively extract the most important feature information from MI (MI) ECG and utilize these extracted features for MI classification diagnosis, the attention mechanism, a widely discussed technique in current deep learning, is introduced. In the convolutional layers, feature matrices are obtained, v_i representing

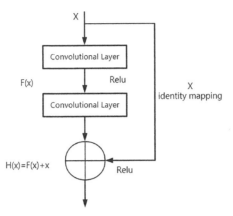

Fig. 3. Residual Learning: Stacking Model.

the features extracted by all convolutional kernels at a certain position of the ECG data matrix. Initially, cosine similarity is calculated among local convolutional features e_i (Eq. 1), followed by e_i obtaining attention weight values a_i (Eq. 2):

$$e_i = \cos sim(v_i) \tag{1}$$

$$a_i = \frac{\exp(e_i)}{\sum_{j}^{n} \exp(e_i)} \tag{2}$$

After calculating the attention weights for all local convolutional features, an attention weight matrix is obtained. Then, each local convolutional feature v_i is weighted by its corresponding attention weight value a_i. . Finally, the weighted local convolutional features are accumulated, resulting in the final representation of the ECG data denoted as R (Eq. 3):

$$R = \sum_{i=1}^{n} a_i v_i \tag{3}$$

Attention-based pooling calculates the influence weight of local features on the entire ECG to measure the importance of local convolutional features. This approach retains more ECG information, reduces information loss in the pooling layer, learns effective ECG features, and selectively allocates computational resources to reduce the computational complexity of ECG feature extraction. This enhances experimental effectiveness and optimizes MI classification models.

Implementation of Res-CNN Network Model Based on Attention Mechanism. The Res-CNN network structure based on the attention mechanism is illustrated in Fig. 4:

The network framework mainly consists of an input stem, 4 residual blocks, two fully connected layers, and an output layer. Each residual block has 4 or more layers of convolutional layers, followed by batch normalization layers and a Dropout layer.

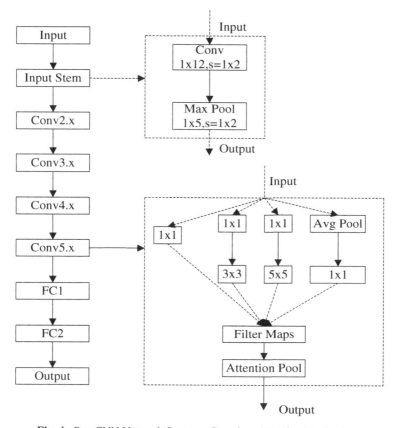

Fig. 4. Res-CNN Network Structure Based on Attention Mechanism.

LeakyReLU is used as the activation function for the convolutional layers, and Softmax is used as the classifier in the output layer with cross-entropy loss function.

The experimental study employed the improved function of ReLU, known as LeakyReLU [9]. Its functional form is given by Eq. (5). Its graphical representation, as shown in Fig. 5(B), introduces a parameter ∂ on the negative axis of x. This ensures that the derivative of the function is non-zero in the x < 0 region, correcting the ECG data and retaining values when x < 0. This prevents the loss of ECG information and results in better training outcomes.

$$f(x) = \begin{cases} x, x \geq 0 \\ 0, x < 0 \end{cases} \tag{4}$$

$$f(x) = \begin{cases} x, x \geq 0 \\ \partial x, x < 0 \end{cases} \tag{5}$$

In the MI classification model based on Res-CNN, Adam is employed as the optimization algorithm instead of stochastic gradient descent (SGD). Adam iteratively updates the weights of the neural network based on training data and offers several advantages: Efficiency in computation and requiring less memory. Invariance to diagonal rescaling of gradients. Applicability to non-stationary objectives. Relatively simple

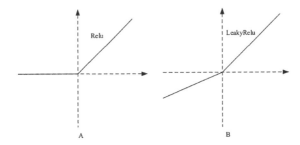

Fig. 5. Activation Function Image.

parameter tuning process. Overall, Adam demonstrates good performance in terms of its working efficiency.

3.2 Classification Model of MI Based on Res-CNN-SVM

Res-CNN-SVM Network Analysis. The attention mechanism-based Res-CNN network automatically extracts features from ECG data, avoiding errors introduced by manual feature selection, reducing the complexity of ECG feature extraction, and enhancing the stability of MI classification results. However, Res-CNN, as a neural network algorithm, utilizes error backpropagation and is based on the principle of empirical minimization for training, often requiring a large amount of training data and susceptible to overfitting.

In this study, an ensemble modeling approach is adopted. The Res-CNN network is utilized as one method for ECG feature extraction, and it is integrated with an SVM standard classifier. Combining the advantages of both approaches, a hybrid Res-CNN-SVM model based on the attention mechanism is constructed. This model leverages the automatic extraction of effective ECG features by the attention mechanism-based Res-CNN network while utilizing SVM to enhance the classification performance of the MI model.

The attention mechanism-based Res-CNN network has been analyzed previously, and SVM is a supervised learning classifier. By adjusting different kernel functions k(x,y) in SVM, both linear classification and non-linear separable problem can be addressed.

For a binary classification problem, the data is denoted as $(x_i\ y_i)$, where i is a continuous positive integer, x belongs to the real number domain, y is a category symbol with only two values. The classification discriminant function is denoted as $g(x) = w*x+b$, and the SVM classification hyperplane can be represented as $w*x+b = 0$. The above formula is normalized to ensure that the absolute value of g(x) for each data sample is not less than 1. If the absolute value of g(x) for the sample closest to the classification hyperplane is 1, then the maximum margin at this point is $2/\|w\|$. The classification hyperplane satisfies Eq. (6).

$$y_i = [(w*x_i + b)] - 1 \geq 0, i = 1, 2, \ldots, n \tag{6}$$

If there exists a hyperplane that satisfies condition (Eq. 6) among different hyperplanes and minimizes $\|w\|$, then that hyperplane is considered the optimal solution. By utilizing optimization algorithms, the problem-solving process can be transformed into a maximization problem, specifically, maximizing Eq. (7) over α_i under the constraint.

$$\sum_{i=1}^{n} y_i \alpha_i = 0, \alpha_i \geq 0 \ i = 1, 2, \ldots n$$

$$Q(\alpha) = \sum_{i=1}^{n} \alpha_i - \frac{1}{2} \sum_{i,j=1}^{n} \alpha_i \alpha_j y_i y_j (x_i \cdot y_j) \tag{7}$$

where α_i represents the Lagrange multipliers corresponding to the original problem and Eq. (6). If α_i is the optimal solution, then $w^* = \sum_{i=1}^{n} y_i \alpha_i^* x_i$, derived from the linear combination of all inputs, forms the weight vector of the optimal hyperplane. Only a small portion of α_i in the solution is nonzero, and these samples where α_i becomes zero are called support vectors. Finally, the classification function of the optimal hyperplane obtained from the solution is given by Eq. (8):

$$f(x) = \text{sgn}\{(w^* \cdot x) + b^*\} = \text{sgn} \sum_{i=1}^{n} \alpha_i^* y_j (x_i \cdot x) + b^* \tag{8}$$

Using a nonlinear transformation $\emptyset$, the ECG training data is mapped to a higher-dimensional space. In this new high-dimensional space, the optimal classification hyperplane is sought using the dot product operation, denoted as $\emptyset(x_i)\emptyset(x_j)$. In the high-dimensional space, a nonlinear kernel function S is found such that $S(x_i, x_j) = \emptyset(x_i)\emptyset(x_j)$ and only dot product operations are used, while functions in the original space can accomplish this inner product operation. By finding an appropriate inner product function and applying it to the optimal classification hyperplane, the problem of linear inseparability in low-dimensional space is addressed. The objective function Eq. (7) is transformed into Eq. (9):

$$Q(\alpha) = \sum_{i=1}^{n} \alpha_i - \frac{1}{2} \sum_{i,j=1}^{n} \alpha_i \alpha_j y_i y_j k(x_i \cdot y_j) \tag{9}$$

The corresponding classification function becomes Eq. (10):

$$f(x) = \text{sgn}\left\{\sum_{i=1}^{n} \alpha_i^* y_i k(x_i \cdot x) + b^*\right\} \tag{10}$$

Res-CNN-SVM Network Model Implementation. The Res-CNN-SVM hybrid network model employed in the ECG feature extraction process utilizes the architecture of Res-CNN based on attention mechanism. The detailed information of the network structure parameters is presented in Table 1.

Figure 6 illustrates the training process of the Res-CNN-SVM hybrid network model. The ECG data is randomly shuffled and divided into training and testing sets according to a certain ratio, with 70% of the ECG data used for training and 30% for testing. The training set data is input into the Res-CNN network for feature extraction, and then the automatically extracted ECG features are input into the SVM classifier for training. Finally, the classification results of heart attacks are output. The testing set ECG data is used for model testing and analysis.

In the training of the Res-CNN-SVM hybrid network model, the choice of kernel function directly affects the classification performance and complexity of the SVM. In

Table 1. Network Structure Parameters of Res-CNN-SVM.

NAME	OUTPUT	Res CNN network structure
Input	8×1900	
Conv1	8×945	1×12, stride: 1×2
Conv2.x	8×471	$\begin{Bmatrix} 3 \times 3,128 \\ 3 \times 3,128 \end{Bmatrix}_{\times 3}$
Conv3.x	8×118	$\begin{Bmatrix} 3 \times 3,128 \\ 3 \times 3,128 \end{Bmatrix}_{\times 4}$
Conv4.x	8×30	$\begin{Bmatrix} 3 \times 3,512 \\ 3 \times 3,512 \end{Bmatrix}_{\times 6}$
Conv5.x	8×8	$\begin{Bmatrix} 3 \times 3,512 \\ 3 \times 3,512 \end{Bmatrix}_{\times 2}$ $1 \times 1, 3 \times 3, 5 \times 5$, AvgPool, Stride: 1×1, Attention Pool
Fc 1	1×1	2048-d Fc
Fc 2	1×1	2-d Fc Softmax

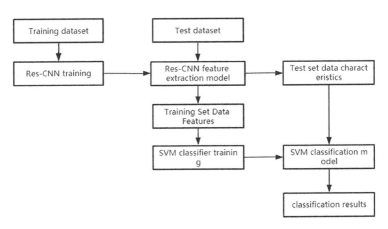

Fig. 6. Implementation Process of Res-CNN-SVM Hybrid Network Model.

order to achieve better heart attack classification results, two different kernel functions were tested in the SVM: linear kernel and Gaussian kernel. The test results indicate that using the Gaussian kernel function improves the accuracy of heart attack classification by 3.1% compared to the linear kernel function. Therefore, the Gaussian kernel function was adopted in the training and testing of the Res-CNN-SVM hybrid network model.

During the experimental research process, we conducted quantitative tests to optimize parameters such as learning rate, momentum coefficient, regularization parameter, and variance for the Res-CNN-based heart attack classification model. The optimal performance of the classification model was achieved when the values were set to 0.09, 0.9, 7, and 2.85, respectively.

3.3 Analysis of Experimental Results

Model Evaluation Indicators. The intelligent diagnosis model for heart attacks belongs to binary classification learning, typically represented by a confusion matrix [8]. When evaluating the intelligent diagnosis model for heart attacks, the specific meanings are as follows:

TP (True Positive): Samples with the true class label of heart attack that are correctly predicted as heart attack samples.
FP (False Positive): Samples with the true class label of normal that are incorrectly predicted as heart attack samples.
TN (True Negative): Samples with the true class label of normal that are correctly predicted as normal samples.
FN (False Negative): Samples with the true class label of heart attack that are incorrectly predicted as normal samples.

In this study, the classification performance of the intelligent diagnosis model for heart attacks is evaluated using several metrics from the classification algorithm model evaluation, including accuracy (Acc), sensitivity (Sen), specificity (Spe), and the area under the ROC curve (AUC).

The higher the accuracy, the better the predictive performance of the heart attack model.

$$Accurary = \frac{TP + YN}{TP + TN + FP + FN} \tag{11}$$

Sensitivity, also known as recall of positive cases, represents the proportion of heart attack data samples that are identified.

$$Sensitivity = \frac{TP}{TP + FN} \tag{12}$$

Specificity, also known as recall of negative cases, represents the proportion of normal data samples that are identified.

$$Specificity = \frac{TN}{FP + TN} \tag{13}$$

In addition, the Receiver Operating Characteristic (ROC) curve is a powerful tool for studying the generalization performance of classifiers. According to the definition, the Area Under the Curve (AUC) can be obtained by summing the areas under different parts of the ROC curve. Assuming the ROC curve is formed by connecting points $\{(x_1, y_1), (x_2, y_2), \ldots, (x_m, y_m)\}$ in sequence to form $(x_1 = 0, x_m = 1)$, the calculation of the AUC value is shown in Eq. (14). From the formula for calculating the AUC value, it is known that its range is generally between 0.5 and 1. The larger the AUC value, the better the classification performance. If the AUC value is between 0.50–0.60, the classification model is basically ineffective; between 0.60–0.70, the classification performance is poor; between 0.70–0.80, the classification performance is fair; between

0.80–0.90, the classification performance is good; between 0.90–1.00, the classification performance is very good.

$$AUC = \frac{1}{2} \sum_{i=1}^{m+1} ((x_{i+1} - x_i) \cdot (y_i + y_{i+1})) \tag{14}$$

Analysis of Experimental Results. The CNN-based MI intelligent diagnosis model serves two objectives: feature extraction and classification recognition. Initially, the Residual Network (ResNet) within the CNN framework is employed as the experimental network model. Combining the attention mechanism to incorporate influential weighting information into local convolution features, a MI classification model based on Res-CNN is established. Subsequently, an ensemble model approach is utilized, integrating the feature learning model of Res-CNN with the SVM classifier to construct the MI classification model based on Res-CNN-SVM. Figures 7 and 8 illustrate the experimental results of these two classification models on the CCDD dataset.

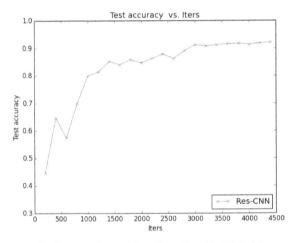

Fig. 7. Experimental Results of Res CNN Model.

The analysis mainly focuses on four metrics for MI classification of two different models: accuracy, sensitivity, specificity, and AUC. For the Res-CNN network model, the classification accuracy is 0.9183, sensitivity is 0.87562, specificity is 0.9241, and the AUC value is 0.8926. As for the Res-CNN-SVM hybrid network model, the classification accuracy is 0.9796, sensitivity is 0.9675, specificity is 0.9867, and the AUC value is 0.9748 (Table 2).

Based on the comparative analysis of various indicators from the experimental results, we can draw the following conclusions: The Res-CNN-SVM classification model outperforms the Res-CNN classification model with a 6.14% increase in classification accuracy. This indicates that the performance of the hybrid network model is superior to that of a single-structure neural network. Additionally, it suggests that the Res-CNN network based on the attention mechanism is more suitable for feature learning rather

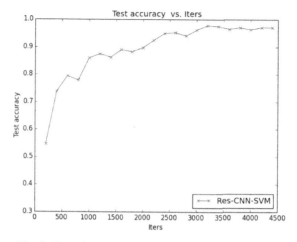

Fig. 8. Experimental Results of Res-CNN-SVM Model.

Table 2. Comparison of MI Classification Results for Different Models.

Classification Method	Precision	Sensitivity	Specificity	AUC value
Res-CNN	0.9183	0.8752	0.9241	0.8926
Res-CNN-SVM	0.9796	0.9675	0.9867	0.9748

than serving as a classifier, and combining its automatic feature learning mechanism with other appropriate standard classifiers can lead to better classification performance.

The CCDD clinical multi-lead ECG data used in this study are real ECG data from different patients, which effectively addresses the problem of unstable classification results caused by significant differences in ECGs among different MI patients. It also avoids the issue of poor identification performance due to potential differences in ECGs from the same patient at different times of the day. Furthermore, traditional automatic ECG classification methods require manual selection of ECG features. However, selecting the optimal feature set for classifying normal and MI ECGs can be challenging and requires multiple tests and selections. The hybrid network model based on the attention mechanism of Res-CNN-SVM used in this study for training clinical multi-lead ECG data to identify MI eliminates the need for manual ECG feature extraction and selection, automatically extracts ECG features, simplifies the feature extraction process, effectively avoids errors caused by manual selection of ECG features, improves the performance of MI classification algorithms, and reduces the complexity of MI classification.

In the experiment, we also utilized the PTB ECG dataset. The ECG dimensions in the two datasets differ, requiring fine-tuning of the network structure during the training of the Res-CNN and Res-CNN-SVM models. When using the Res-CNN model for MI classification, the accuracy achieved was 94.16%, whereas the Res-CNN-SVM hybrid model achieved an impressive accuracy of 98.91%, demonstrating the superiority of the hybrid network classification model.

In summary, the MI intelligent diagnosis model used in this study automatically extracts ECG features from ECGs to achieve MI classification and identification. The primary goal is to diagnose and detect the risk of MI in individuals, thus providing reference assistance for clinical diagnosis by doctors. This approach has implications for the diagnosis of other types of cardiovascular diseases.

4 System Structure Design and Implementation

4.1 Overall System Design

The ECG monitoring system employs Internet of Things (IoT) technology to monitor the ECG data of users in real-time. Machine learning algorithms are utilized to determine whether a MI has occurred based on the real-time collected ECG data. Simultaneously, modern communication technology is used to transmit the ECG data collected by the monitoring system to a monitoring center. In cases of sudden cardiac emergencies, timely assistance measures and treatment plans are provided to patients, serving as a platform for communication between patients and doctors.

Figure 9 depicts the Big Data Platform for ECGs, which collects patient ECG data via wearable devices and transmits it to the cloud through the internet. The big data of ECGs are analyzed using artificial intelligence systems, complemented by diagnoses from top-tier hospital specialists, to provide timely and accurate remote diagnostic services for grassroots cardiac patients.

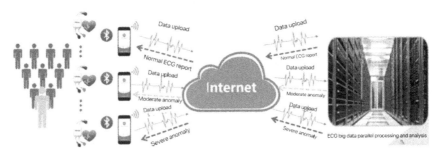

Fig. 9. ECG Big Data Platform.

The MI auxiliary diagnostic system facilitates the collection and uploading of user ECG data, ECG data preprocessing, analysis and diagnosis using intelligent algorithms, user management, and other functions. Based on its basic functionalities, the system is divided into three layers: the collection end, the server end, and the user end. The system's functional structure diagram is depicted in Fig. 10 above.

At the collection end, wearable ECG monitoring devices are worn by users to achieve real-time ECG data collection and uploading functionality. The server end realizes ECG data preprocessing and analysis-diagnosis functions by first storing the data, applying signal processing algorithms for ECG data filtering, and utilizing deep learning intelligent diagnostic algorithms for MI disease identification and diagnosis.

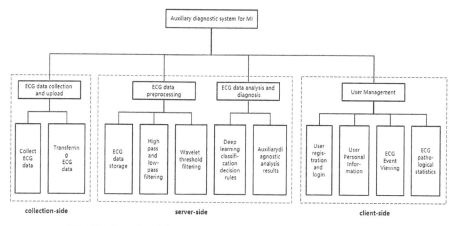

Fig. 10. Functional Structure of Auxiliary Diagnosis System for MI.

The user end provides visual operation functionalities for user management, including user registration, login, and personal information management. It sends requests to the server end to obtain ECG analysis-diagnosis results, allowing users to view personal ECG events and pathological statistics. In the event of a sudden cardiac incident, the system provides timely assistance and treatment options for users. The flowchart of the MI auxiliary diagnostic system is illustrated in Fig. 11 below.

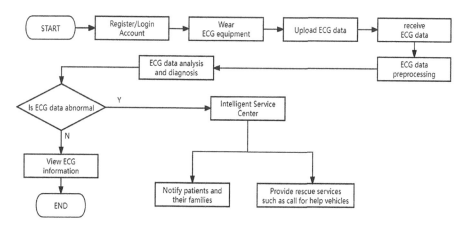

Fig. 11. Flow of Auxiliary Diagnosis System for MI.

4.2 System Function Realization

Collection-Side. ECG, a weak physiological electrical signal, typically ranges from 10 μV to 5 mV, with the majority of its energy spectrum distributed between 0.05 to 40 Hz, demonstrating characteristics of low amplitude and low frequency. During

ECG acquisition, it is essential to ensure low noise, portability, and safety. This system utilizes the ADS1293 module and MCU (Micro Control Unit) microprocessor unit to collect ECG data from users, transmitted via BLE (Bluetooth Low Energy).

The ADS1293 module encompasses features necessary for ECG applications, including portability, low power consumption, and three high-resolution ECG channels with synchronous sampling rates up to 25.6 ksps, consuming only 0.3 mW per channel. Additionally, the ADS1293 integrates right-leg drive amplifiers, oscillators, and references, along with flexible power-down and standby modes. BLE technology offers 37 data channels and 3 broadcast channels, with a 2 MHz spacing accommodating up to 40 channels. Its key attributes include low power consumption, low latency, and low throughput, making it increasingly adopted in mobile devices with stringent real-time requirements. However, due to its limitations in data transmission speed, BLE is primarily utilized in products with lower data rates. Given the staged nature of ECG data acquisition, resulting in lower data transfer rates, BLE is employed for data transmission. The structural diagram of the collection-end module is depicted in Fig. 12 below.

Fig. 12. Structure Diagram of Collection-Side Module.

Server-Side. The server-side functionalities include ECG data storage and processing, ECG data analysis and diagnosis, and responding to user-side requests. The software architecture diagram of the server-side is illustrated in Fig. 13 below. This architecture is based on the principles of microservices and RPC, comprising 9 core servers.

The ECG filtering process in ECG Analyze employs wavelet thresholding to remove high-frequency noise and high-pass filtering to eliminate baseline drift low-frequency noise. The deep learning ECG classification algorithm in ECG Analyze involves studying the intelligent diagnosis model for heart attacks, establishing two types of intelligent heart attack classification models (Res-CNN and Res-CNN-SVM). Through comparative analysis of the experimental results of different classification algorithms, the ensemble model approach demonstrates better performance in classification. The attention-based Res-CNN-SVM hybrid classification model utilizes residual networks to automatically learn feature mechanisms as ECG feature extractors and utilizes SVM classifiers for classifying and identifying automatically extracted features, simplifying the feature extraction process, avoiding manual selection and extraction of features, and improving existing heart attack classification algorithms.

Client-Side. The user-side functionalities primarily involve retrieving ECG data from the server-side, displaying ECG analysis results, and managing user information through

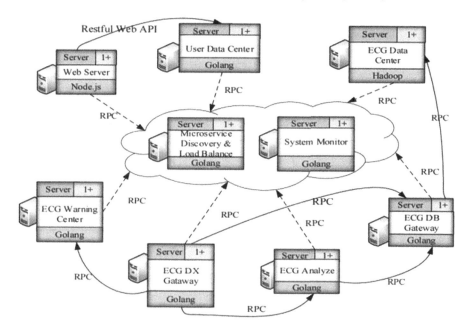

Fig. 13. Software Architecture Diagram of Server-side.

visual interaction. The implementation of the user-side should emphasize compatibility, with interface design principles focusing on simplicity and ease of operation to enhance user experience. The system employs HTML, CSS, and JavaScript to implement the user-side web pages, where HTML and CSS are used for interface design, and JavaScript is used for dynamic page updates and data transmission.

The functional structure diagram of the user-side is illustrated in Fig. 14 below, with key functionalities including user registration and login, user profile management, ECG event viewing, and ECG pathology statistics. It allows new users to register and existing users to log in. After logging in, users can view and modify their respective personal information, access ECG data reports, heart rate trend graphs, etc.

4.3 System Test

Classification Algorithm Performance Test

ECG Data Set Test. The test results for randomly selected 30 sets of ECG data records from the CCDD and PTB ECG datasets are shown in Table 3. Among the 30 sets of ECG data analyzed, there were 2 instances of misdiagnosis. Therefore, the testing accuracy of the classification diagnostic algorithm is 93.33%.

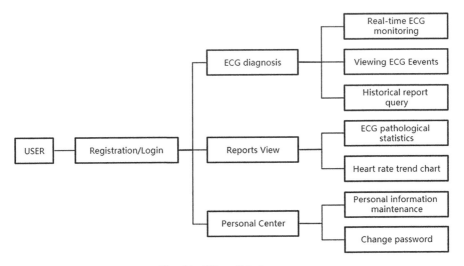

Fig. 14. Client-Side Structure.

Additionally, we randomly selected 50 sets, 100 sets, and 150 sets of ECG data for further testing, resulting in testing accuracies of 96.00%, 96.00%, and 96.67%, respectively.

Table 3. ECG Data Analysis Diagnosis Test Results.

S/N	ECG data results	System results	Correct(Y/N)
1	normal	normal	Y
2	AMI	AMI	Y
……	……	……	……
28	AMI	AMI	Y
29	normal	AMI	N
30	AMI	AMI	Y

Online Monitoring of ECG Data. The test involved 6 volunteers for the evaluation of the ECG classification algorithm. Initially, users registered and logged into the system, wore the ECG monitoring device, collected and uploaded their ECG data to the server. The server received the ECG data and performed the analysis. The user interface then sent requests to the server to obtain the corresponding analysis results, allowing users to interactively view their ECG situation.

The ECG patches collected the human body's ECG, which was then transmitted to the ECG monitoring system. Deep learning algorithms were utilized for intelligent ECG diagnostic analysis. Table 4 presents the ECG test results of the participants, while Fig. 15 displays the test results of the ECG classification algorithm, showing the ECG waveforms of the participants alongside the diagnostic results (Table 5).

Table 4. ECG Classification Algorithm Test Process.

NAME	Online testing of ECG classification algorithm
Illustration	Test the ECG acquisition, analysis and diagnosis function of the system of MI
Procedure	1 The tester first registers to log in to the system
	2 Testers wear ECG equipment and upload ECG data
	3 Open the real-time monitoring web interface of the system and select the monitoring object
	4 Check the tester's ECG
	5 Observe whether there is abnormal ECG data and deal with the abnormal situation
	6 Whether feedback can be received after abnormal signal output

Table 5. ECG Test Results.

S/N	AGE	SEX	Auxiliary Diagnostic Results		NOTE
			AvgHR	Disease Type	
1	22	M	73/min	normal	Healthy, enjoy sports
2	25	F	112/min	Suspected tachycardia	Healthy, detection after intense exercise
3	27	M	56/min	Suspected bradycardia	Healthy, rarely exercising
4	27	F	69/min	normal	Healthy
5	48	M	59/min	Suspected irregular heart rate	Existence of CVD
6	42	F	80/min	normal	Healthy

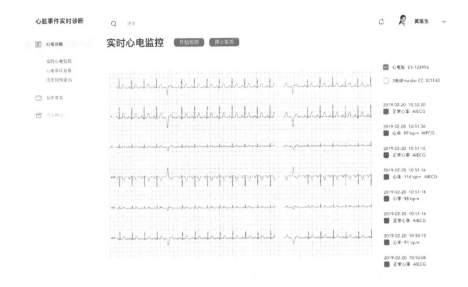

Fig. 15. System ECG Classification Algorithm Test Interface.

5   Conclusion

This study focuses on the research of MI auxiliary pre-hospital diagnosis technology based on CNN, establishing a mixed Res-CNN-SVM network model based on attention mechanism to recognize MI, achieving good classification results. Moreover, a MI auxiliary diagnosis system is designed, which preprocesses ECG data through data transformation, wavelet denoising, and other processes, conducts diagnostic analysis of ECG data using deep residual CNN algorithms, and returns diagnostic results to the user end. By leveraging the advantages of CNN network models in ECG feature detection and classification applications, this research applies them to MI classification and recognition, providing assistance and support for clinical diagnosis by doctors, improving diagnosis efficiency and accuracy, and holding significant research and application value for early diagnosis and timely treatment of MI diseases.

Acknowledgments. The work of this paper is supported by Acute Myocardial Infarction Electrocardiogram Intelligent Pre-Hospital Monitoring and Early Warning, Guangdong and Guangxi Cooperation R&D Talent Introduction (No. AC22035089) and the South China University of Technology - Guilin Medical University 5G Intelligent Medical Platform and Demonstration Base Construction (No. AD21075054), Special Program of Base Construction and Outstanding Scholarship for Science and Technology Department of Guangxi Province.

References

1. National Center for Cardiovascular Diseases. Annual Report on Cardiovascular Health and Diseases in China. Peking Union Medical College Press, Beijing (2023)

2. Xin, C., Wan, H.: Clinical ECG, pp. 42–52. People's Medical Publishing House, Beijing (2009)
3. Razzak, M.I., Naz, S., Zaib, A.: Deep learning for medical image processing: overview, challenges and the future. Classification BioApps Autom. Decis. Mak. 323–350 (2018)
4. Gu, J., Wang, Z., Kuen, J., et al.: Recent advances in convolutional neural networks. Pattern Recogn. **77**, 354–377 (2018)
5. Ajit, A., Acharya, K., Samanta, A.: A review of convolutional neural networks. In: 2020 International Conference on Emerging Trends in Information Technology and Engineering (ic-ETITE), pp. 1–5. IEEE (2020)
6. Aketkar, N., Moolayil, J., Ketkar, N., et al.: Convolutional neural networks. Deep Learning with Python: Learn Best Practices of Deep Learning Models with PyTorch, pp. 197–242 (2021)
7. Zhang, J.W., Liu, X., Dong, J.: CCDD: an enhanced standard ECG database with its management and annotation tools. Int. J. Artif. Intell. Tools **21**(05), 1240020 (2012)
8. Ohsaki, M., Wang, P., Matsuda, K., et al.: Confusion-matrix-based kernel logistic regression for imbalanced data classification. IEEE Trans. Knowl. Data Eng. 1 (2017)
9. Wixted, J.T., Mickes, L., Wetmore, S.A., et al.: ROC analysis in theory and practice. J. Appl. Res. Mem. Cogn. **6**(3), 343–351 (2017)

CardioRisk: Predictive Application for Myocardial Infarction Incident Risk Assessment Based on Blood Pressure-Glucose-Lipid Patterns

Xin Shu[1], Xin Sun[1], Juncheng Hu[1(✉)], and Chunbao Mo[2]

[1] School of Intelligent Medicine and Biotechnology, Guilin Medical University, Guilin 541199, China
jc.hu@glmc.edu.cn
[2] Zhonglin Sci-Tech Development Group Co., Ltd, Nanning 530201, China

Abstract. Background: Myocardial Infarction (MI) is a severe cardiovascular disease, typically characterized by ischemic necrosis of myocardial tissue due to sudden occlusion of coronary arteries. MI has a high incidence worldwide, and there is abundant evidence showing a close correlation between MI and factors such as Blood Pressure, Blood Glucose, and Blood Lipid. There is still insufficient in-depth research on the relationship between the Blood Pressure-Glucose-Lipid Patterns and MI. This study aims to explore the association between the Blood Pressure-Glucose-Lipid Patterns and MI, and to establish a corresponding warning model. Develop an application software to provide effective support for the early warning and prevention of MI.

Methods: A case-control design was used to study 901 valid samples from a hospital in Sichuan. Principal Component Analysis (PCA) was used to identify Blood Pressure-Glucose-Lipid Patterns in each study subject. Logistic regression models were used to evaluate the association between different patterns and MI. The optimal prediction model was used to develop an application software.

Results: Through PCA, three patterns of Blood Pressure-Glucose-Lipid were identified. Results from the logistic regression indicated that the association between the patterns and MI was statistically significant. After evaluation by the test set, the accuracy of the prediction model is 0.821 (95% CI: 0.748–0.866), and the area under the curve is 0.710 (0.606−0.814).

Conclusion: Different Blood Pressure-Glucose-Lipid Patterns may associate with the risk of MI. A user-friendly and easy-to-use predictive application: CardioRisk, specifically designed and developed to enhance the efficiency of detecting the incidence risk of MI.

Keywords: Artificial Intelligence & Smart Servicers · Patients and Healthcare · Predictive Application · Myocardial Infarction · Logistic Regression

© The Author(s), under exclusive license to Springer Nature Switzerland AG 2024
V. G. Duffy (Ed.): HCII 2024, LNCS 14710, pp. 300–312, 2024.
https://doi.org/10.1007/978-3-031-61063-9_20

1   Introduction

Myocardial Infarction (MI) is a serious cardiovascular disease, usually referring to ischemic necrosis of myocardial tissue caused by sudden blockage of the coronary artery. Most patients have emotional abnormalities, chest and heart discomfort before the onset of the disease, and often have oppressive pain in the precordial area or chest tightness for more than 20 min when the disease occurs [1].

Existing research indicates that, globally, MI is a significant cause of decreased life expectancy [2], becoming a serious public health issue. According to the "China Cardiovascular Health and Disease Report 2022", it is estimated that there are about 330 million cardiovascular patients in China, among which, the number of patients of MI is about 2.6 million, the incidence rate of MI is still on the rise, and MI have become one of the major causes of death among the population [3]. Data from the American Heart Association shows that the overall incidence rate of MI in American adults over 20 years old is 3.1% [4]. At the same time, MI is also one of the most common causes of death among people under 75 years old in Europe [5].

Due to the characteristics of MI, such as sudden onset and poor prognosis, early identification and warning of MI are particularly important. "Three highs" refers to Hypertension, Hyperglycemia and Hyperlipidemia, which are important risk factors for MI. Previous research on the relationship between Blood Pressure, Blood Glucose, Blood Lipid and MI mostly analyzed these factors as single risk factors [6], which may overlook the potential interrelationships among them. Therefore, this study will start from an overall perspective, use principal component analysis to identify different Blood Pressure-Glucose-Lipid Patterns, and construct a preliminary MI prediction model, in order to provide a basis for MI and prevention of MI.

Firstly, this study uses a case-control design to study 901 valid samples from a hospital in Sichuan. Secondly, Principal Component Analysis (PCA) is used to identify the Blood Pressure-Glucose-Lipid Patterns of each research subject. Thirdly, a logistic regression model is used to evaluate the association between different patterns and MI. Finally, sensitivity analysis and subgroup analysis are used to assess the robustness of the main results. After stepwise regression analysis, Gender, Age, BMI, History of COPD, and Blood Pressure-Glucose-Lipid Patterns are selected as the main prediction indicators. These indicators are used to establish a model and develop prediction application.

2   Objects and Methods

2.1   Source of Information

The research data comes from the public research dataset of Zhongheng and others [7]. This dataset collects relevant data from heart failure patients in a hospital in Sichuan Province, China from 2016 to 2019. The total sample size is 2008, including 168 variables such as population characteristics, disease status, and biochemical tests. This study selects MI, Blood Pressure (Systolic, Diastolic), Fasting Blood Glucose, Blood Lipid (Total Cholesterol, Triglycerides, High/Low-Density Lipoprotein), and some disease states as research variables from this dataset. After excluding research subjects with missing records of Blood Pressure, Blood Glucose, and Blood Lipid, a total of 901 research samples were included. This study follows "the Helsinki Declaration" and has been approved by the hospital's ethics committee (approval number: 2020–010).

2.2 Principal Component Analysis (PCA)

PCA aims to achieve dimensionality reduction of data by retaining the main variability in the dataset [8], thus effectively simplifying high-dimensional datasets. It is commonly used for summarizing and exploring patterns. The main steps of the PCA method are as follows:

Assume there are n original data samples, each with m observation indicators, then there is a data table as shown in Table 1. The mathematical expression is as shown in Eq. 1.

$$X_i = (X_{i1}, X_{i2}, \cdots, X_{in}), \ I = 1, 2, 3, \ldots, m. \tag{1}$$

Table 1. Original Data Table for PCA

Sample Number	Observation Indicators			
	X_1	X_2	...	X_m
1	X_{11}	X_{12}	...	X_{1m}
2	X_{21}	X_{22}	...	X_{2m}
.	.	.	.	.
.	.	.	.	.
.	.	.	.	.
n	X_{n1}	X_{n2}	...	X_{nm}

1. The original data is standardized using Eq. 3 to obtain the standardized observation indicators, denoted as Z_{ij}. The matrix of the standardized data is denoted as:

$$Z_i = (Z_{i1}, Z_{i2}, \cdots, Z_{in}), \ a = 1, 2, 3, \ldots, m. \tag{2}$$

$$Z_{ij} = \frac{X_{ij} - \overline{X}_j}{S_j} \tag{3}$$

$\overline{X}_j$ is the mean of the jth original observation indicator, and S_j is the standard deviation of the jth original observation indicator.

2. By constructing the standardized matrix Z_i, the correlation coefficient matrix R is constructed through Eq. 4:

$$R = [r_{ij}]_n x_n = \frac{Z_i^T Z_i}{m - 1} \tag{4}$$

3. By constructing the correlation coefficient matrix R, the eigenvalues and eigenvectors of R are obtained by solving the characteristic equation constructed by Eq. 5.

$$|R - \lambda I_n| = 0 \tag{5}$$

The m non-negative eigenvalues obtained are arranged in descending order, denoted as:

$$\lambda_1 \geq \lambda_2 \geq \cdots \geq \lambda_m \geq 0$$

According to Eq. 6, the eigenvectors $\alpha_i = (\alpha_{i1}, \alpha_{i2}, \cdots, \alpha_{im})'$ corresponding to each eigenvalue are determined.

$$\begin{cases} (R - \lambda_i I)\alpha i = 0 \\ \alpha_i' \alpha_i = 1 \end{cases} \tag{6}$$

Based on the obtained eigenvector $\alpha_i = (\alpha_{i1}, \alpha_{i2}, \cdots, \alpha_{im})'$, substitute it into equation five to calculate the principal component A_i.

$$A_i = \alpha_i' Z_i = \alpha_{i1} Z_1 + \alpha_{i2} Z_2 + \cdots + \alpha_{i3} Z_m, \; I = 1, 2, 3, \ldots, m. \tag{7}$$

This study will identify the patterns of Blood Pressure-Glucose-Lipid in the subjects. The number of patterns is determined by the cumulative contribution rate of each component. It is generally believed that when the cumulative contribution rate $\geq 85\%$, the selected components have a good explanatory power for the total. This study will use a case-control analysis method to compare the association between different Blood Pressure-Glucose-Lipid Patterns and MI. Therefore, the exposure in this study is defined as the different Blood Pressure-Glucose-Lipid Patterns identified by PCA analysis. The outcome is defined as MI. In addition, Age, Gender, Body Mass Index (BMI), Diabetes, Chronic Obstructive Pulmonary Disease (COPD), Cerebrovascular Disease, and Dementia are used as covariates.

2.3 Statistical Methods

The statistical methods and basic procedures used in this study are shown in Fig. 1. Continuous variables and categorical variables are statistically described using means (standard deviations) and numbers (proportions), respectively. Chi-square tests and variance analysis are used to compare the differences between different types of variables in each pattern. Logistic regression is used to analyze the association between different patterns and MI and estimate the Odds Ratio (OR) and 95% Confidence Interval (CI). The model includes a crude model and an adjusted model. In the sensitivity analysis, this study will also use the Bootstrap method, repeating self-sampling 1000, 10000, 100000 times, to estimate robust confidence intervals and P values. In addition, this study will also conduct subgroup analysis to evaluate the differences in the main results in each subgroup. The test level $\alpha = 0.05$. To construct a MI prediction model, this study will randomly split the dataset into a training set (720 cases) and a test set (181 cases) at a ratio of 8:2, use stepwise logistic regression to screen prediction variables, and use logistic regression to construct a prediction model in the training set. Finally, the predictive performance of the model is evaluated through the test set, and the receiver operating characteristic curve (ROC) is drawn and the area under the curve (AUC) and accuracy are calculated. All the above analyses are implemented through R (version 4.2.3).

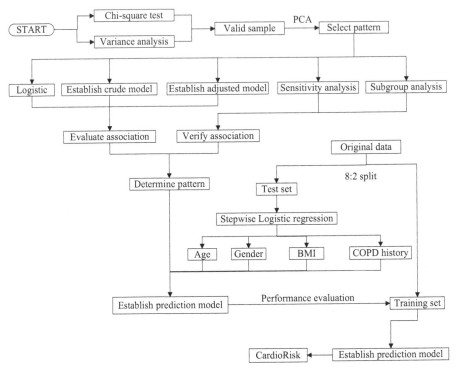

Fig. 1. Basic Flowchart of Statistical Methods

2.4 The Development of the Prediction Model: CardioRisk

In order to implement a prediction model application with excellent user experience, efficient operation performance, friendly interaction, and a sense of pleasure, two R scripts were necessary: ui.R and server.R. The ui.R script is responsible for creating a user-oriented graphical interface, while the server.R script serves as a server-side script for executing commands and performing calculations. The application adopts a dashboard design method, aiming to enhance human-computer interaction, and includes functions such as predicting the risk of unplanned readmission and visualization. The main goal of the application is to make the interaction between users and the system seamless, allowing them to input relevant data and obtain visual predictions about the risk of unplanned readmission.

3   Results

3.1 Blood Pressure-Glucose-Lipid Patterns

The results of the PCA analysis show that when the first three patterns are adopted, the cumulative contribution rate has reached 90.7%, so this study only uses the following three Blood Pressure-Glucose-Lipid Patterns. As shown in Table 2, the factor loads of each variable vary greatly in each mode, and we summarize the characteristics of each pattern based on the size of the factor load. Pattern 1 is mainly based on SBP (load factor: 0.529), DBP(0.469), LDL-C(0.416); Pattern 2 is mainly based on FBG(0.520), LDL-C(0.469), HDL-C(0.415); Pattern 3 is mainly based on HDL-C(0.628), TG (0.413), DBP(0.413).

Table 2. Blood Pressure-Glucose-Lipid Patterns and factor load

Variable	Pattern1	Pattern2	Pattern3
SBP	0.529	0.141	0.239
DBP	0.469	0.168	0.413
FBG	0.157	0.520	0.302
TC	0.377	0.482	0.049
TG	0.381	0.239	0.493
LDL-C	0.416	0.469	0.203
HDL-C	0.122	0.415	0.628
Cumulative Contribution Rate	40.9%	72.4%	90.7%

Notes: SBP/DBP: Systolic/ Diastolic Blood Pressure;
FBG: Fasting Blood-Glucose; TC: Total Cholesterol;
TG: Triglyceride; LDL-C/HDL-C: Low/High-Density Lipoprotein Cholesterol.

3.2 Characteristics of the Subjects Under Different Patterns

As shown in Table 3, the distribution of each research factor is relatively uniform under the three patterns, but the distribution differences of SBP, DBP, FBG, TG, LDL-C, HDL-C between the three patterns are significant ($P < 0.05$). In Pattern 1, the average values of SBP, BDP, and LDL-C are significantly higher than other patterns; in Pattern 2, except for the higher FBG, the rest of LDL-C and HDL-C are significantly lower than other patterns. Finally, in Pattern 3, besides the higher HDL-C, DBP is at a medium level in other patterns.

Table 3. Distribution of subject characteristics under different patterns

Project	Pattern1 (n = 337)	Pattern2 (n = 355)	Pattern3 (n = 209)	P value
Gender				
female	193 (57.3)	197 (55.5)	110 (52.6)	0.570
male	144 (42.7)	158 (44.5)	99 (47,4)	

(continued)

Table 3. (*continued*)

Project	Pattern1 (n = 337)	Pattern2 (n = 355)	Pattern3 (n = 209)	P value
Age				
<60	28 (8.3)	27 (7.6)	13 (6.2)	0.667
>= 60	309 (91.7)	328 (92.4)	196 (93.8)	
BMI	21.38 (4.26)	21.61 (3.95)	21.00 (4.10)	0.236
SBP	138.70 (28.16)	128.04 (22.33)	129.89 (23.82)	<0.001*
DBP	81.07 (16.15)	74.66 (12.53)	74.91 (14.41)	<0.001*
FBG	7.51 (3.32)	8.45 (5.03)	7.52 (3.30)	0.004*
TC	3.97 (1.11)	3.48 (1.26)	3.95 (0.82)	<0.001*
TG	1.18 (0.87)	1.06 (0.58)	1.17 (1.65)	0.282
LDL-C	2.04 (0.82)	1.76 (0.83)	1.83 (0.59)	<0.001*
HDL-C	1.13 (0.28)	1.00 (0.38)	1.32 (0.36)	<0.001*
Diabetes				
No	256 (76.0)	253 (71.3)	160 (76.6)	0.253
Yes	81 (24.0)	102 (28.7)	49 (23.4)	
COPD				
No	279 (82.8)	310 (87.3)	169 (80.9)	0.089
Yes	58 (17.2)	45 (12.7)	40 (19.1)	
Cerebrovascular Disease				
No	309 (91.7)	323 (91.0)	194 (92.8)	0.748
Yes	28 (8.3)	32 (9.0)	15 (7.2)	
Dementia				
No	309 (91.7)	333 (93.8)	191 (91.4)	0.461
Yes	28 (8.3)	22 (6.2)	18 (8.6)	
MI				
No	301 (89.3)	334 (94.1)	192 (91.9)	0.074
Yes	36 (10.7)	21 (5.9)	17 (8.1)	

Note: BMI: Body Mass Index; SBP/DBP: Systolic/Diastolic Blood Pressure;
FBG: Fasting Blood-Glucose; TC: Total Cholesterol; TG: Triglyceride;
LDL-C/HDL-C: Low/High-Density Lipoprotein Cholesterol;
COPD: Chronic Obstructive Pulmonary Disease

3.3 The Association Between Different Patterns and MI

The results of the correlation analysis show that there is a correlation between different Blood Pressure-Glucose-Lipid Patterns and MI. Specifically, compared to pattern 1, the risk of MI in pattern 2 is 50% lower (Adjusted OR:0.50, 95%CI:0.28−0.87). However, for pattern 3 (0.73, 0.39−1.32), a similar protective effect was not observed (Table 4). Sensitivity analysis suggests that after performing 1000, 10000, and 100000 times of self-sampling respectively, the association between pattern 2 and the low risk of MI remains very stable (Table 4). In addition, the results of the subgroup analysis show that this correlation is also significant in the population aged ≥60 years, females, non-diabetics, non-COPD, non-cerebrovascular disease, and non-dementia (Fig. 2).

Table 4. Correlation analysis between each mode and MI

Pattern	Crude model			Adjusted model		
	Crude OR	95%CI	P	Adjusted OR	95%CI	P
Pattern1	1.00(Ref.)			1.00(Ref.)		
Pattern2	0.53	(0.30−0.91)	0.024*	0.50	(0.28−0.87)	0.016*
Pattern3	0.74	(0.40−1.34)	0.330	0.73	(0.39−1.32)	0.311
Bootstrapped Estimation (n = 1000)						
Pattern2		(0.30−0.90)	0.021*		(0.27−0.90)	0.014*
Pattern3		(0.39−1.38)	0.338		(0.36−1.33)	0.285
Bootstrapped Estimation (n = 10000)						
Pattern2		(0.29−0.91)	0.024*		(0.27−0.87)	0.016*
Pattern3		(0.37−1.33)	0.318		(0.37−1.31)	0.289
Bootstrapped Estimation (n = 100000)						
Pattern2		(0.29−0.91)	0.022*		(0.27−0.86)	0.013*
Pattern3		(0.38−1.33)	0.313		(0.37−1.32)	0.299

Note: OR: odds ratio; 95%CI: 95 % confidence interval
Adjusted: The model has adjusted for age, gender, BMI, diabetes, chronic obstructive pulmonary disease, cerebrovascular disease, and dementia; * P < 0.05;

Bootstrap is used for sensitivity analysis, repeating self-sampling 1000, 10000, 100000 times to estimate robust confidence intervals and P values

Subgroup	Patterns	Adjusted OR (95% CI)	Adjusted P
Age>=60	Pattern 2	0.53 (0.30~0.94)	0.031*
	Pattern 3	0.77 (0.41~1.41)	0.411
Gender=male	Pattern 2	0.78 (0.33~1.79)	0.553
	Pattern 3	1.08 (0.44~2.59)	0.856
Gender=female	Pattern 2	0.35 (0.15~0.76)	0.010*
	Pattern 3	0.49 (0.19~1.14)	0.118
Diabetes=No	Pattern 2	0.35 (0.16~0.71)	0.005*
	Pattern 3	0.71 (0.34~1.39)	0.326
Diabetes=Yes	Pattern 2	0.97 (0.36~2.69)	0.949
	Pattern 3	0.81 (0.20~2.83)	0.751
COPD=No	Pattern 2	0.52 (0.28~0.94)	0.032*
	Pattern 3	0.80 (0.41~1.52)	0.506
Cerebrovascular Disease=No	Pattern 2	0.55 (0.30~0.97)	0.043*
	Pattern 3	0.76 (0.40~1.42)	0.405
Cerebrovascular Disease=Yes	Pattern 2	0.17 (0.01~1.38)	0.142
	Pattern 3	0.55 (0.02~5.42)	0.641
Dementia=No	Pattern 2	0.45 (0.25~0.80)	0.008*
	Pattern 3	0.65 (0.34~1.22)	0.193

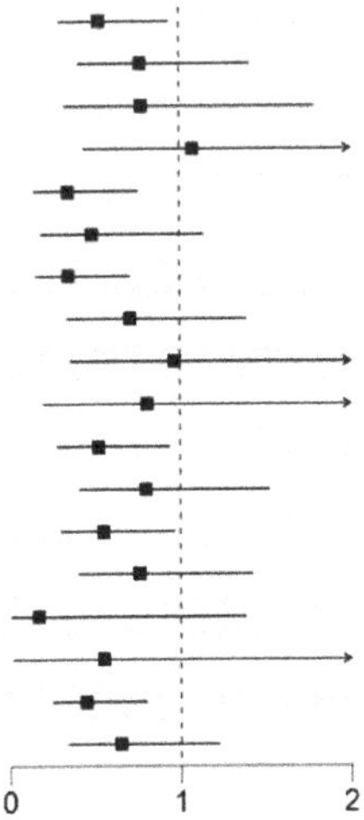

Note: Pattern 1 is used as a reference; OR: odds ratio; 95%CI: 95% confidence interval;
* P < 0.05;
Adjusted: The model has adjusted for Age, Gender, BMI, Diabetes, COPD, Cerebrovascular Disease, and Dementia;
COPD: chronic obstructive pulmonary disease;
Due to the limitation of sample size, the effect value (OR) of the subgroup with Age<60, COPD=Yes, Dementia=Yes cannot be estimated.

Fig. 2. Analysis of the association between different patterns and MI in each subgroup.

3.4 MI Prediction Model

After stepwise regression analysis, Gender, Age, BMI, History of COPD, and Blood Pressure-Glucose-Lipid Patterns were selected as the main predictive indicators. When building the model, considering the possible outliers and interactions between variables, to improve the predictive performance of the model, this study will perform natural logarithm(ln) transformation on some indicators and add interaction terms (*). The final model is: Age + Gender + ln (BMI) + COPD + (Blood Pressure-Glucose-Lipid Patterns) + Age*Gender + Age*COPD + Age* (Blood Pressure-Glucose-Lipid Patterns) + Gender*(Blood Pressure-Glucose-Lipid Patterns). The results on the test set are shown in Fig. 3, the prediction accuracy of this model is 0.821 (95%CI: 0.748–0.866), and the AUC is 0.710 (0.606–0.814).

3.5 CardioRisk

The system interface of the CardioRisk is shown in Fig. 4. The main function of the software is to provide prediction results based on the information provided by the user.

ROC curve:

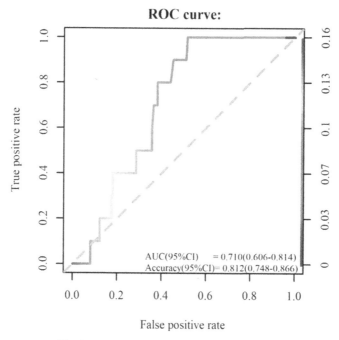

Fig. 3. ROC Curve of the MI Prediction Model

In use, users only need to input a few basic pieces of information such as Age, Gender, History of COPD, BMI, Blood Pressure, Blood Glucose, and Blood Lipid to easily and conveniently obtain the risk prediction results for MI.

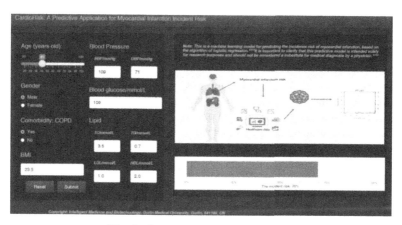

Fig. 4. System Interface of CardioRisk

4 Consultation

This study is based on the relevant data of heart failure patients in a hospital in Sichuan Province, China from 2016 to 2019, and analyzes the association between different Blood Pressure-Glucose-Lipid Patterns and MI. This study summarizes three Blood Pressure-Glucose-Lipid Patterns, including Pattern 1 dominated by increased SBP, DBP, LDL-C, Pattern 2 dominated by decreased LDL-C and HDL-C, and Pattern 3 at intermediate levels. The correlation analysis found that there is a significant correlation between different Blood Pressure-Glucose-Lipid Patterns and MI. The results of sensitivity analysis and subgroup analysis are basically consistent with the main results. In addition, the performance of the MI risk prediction model constructed in this study is acceptable, with an accuracy of 0.821 and an AUC of 0.710.

Blood Pressure, Blood Glucose, and Blood Lipid have been widely studied and confirmed as important risk factors for MI. However, there are few reports on the study of the association between Blood Pressure-Glucose-Lipid Patterns and MI from an overall perspective. Most of the studies on the association between these risk factors and MI analyze them as single factors. For example, Lee et al.'s research showed that the higher the blood pressure classification, the higher the incidence of MI [9]. Mata et al.'s study demonstrated a strong association between abnormal blood glucose levels and MI [10]. Zhang et al.'s study indicated that patients under the age of 35 with MI have higher levels of LDL-C, and LDL-C is positively correlated with the degree of coronary artery stenosis in these patients [11].

As is well known, there is a close intrinsic relationship between Blood Pressure, Blood Glucose, and Blood Lipid. Hyperglycemia and abnormal Blood Lipid have a certain correlation with hypertension and are risk factors for hypertension Hypertensive patients are more likely to have abnormal blood lipid compared to non-hypertensive patients [12]. Similarly, Hyperglycemia is very likely to cause abnormal Blood Lipid, and abnormal Blood Lipid will exacerbate Blood Glucose disorders. Therefore, with our deepening understanding of Blood Pressure, Blood Lipid, and Blood Glucose, the comprehensive management of Hyperglycemia-Hypertension-Hyperlipidemia has become an important preventive measure to prevent and improve the prognosis of cardiovascular disease patients [13]. Therefore, in the context of emphasizing the co-management of the "three highs", exploring the association between Blood Pressure, Blood Glucose, and Blood Lipid patterns and MI risk is a meaningful attempt.

This study found that compared with pattern 1, the risk of MI in pattern 2 is lower, while there is no significant difference in the risk of MI between pattern 3 and pattern 1. Existing evidence shows that abnormal Blood Lipid are the most common independent risk factor for AMI patients, and high-density lipoprotein cholesterol is a protective factor [14]. At the same time, an increase in systolic or diastolic Blood Pressure levels will also increase the risk of MI [15]. Another study pointed out that the level of LDL-C is positively correlated with the degree of coronary heart disease, while the level of HDL-C is negatively correlated with the degree of the disease [16]. In this study, pattern 1 is mainly characterized by increased SBP, DBP, and LDL-C, while pattern 2 is mainly characterized by decreased Blood Pressure and LDL-C. This suggests that the simultaneous increase in Blood Pressure and LDL-C may be a sign of a significant increase in the risk of MI, and a lower LDL-C may be key to reducing the risk of

MI. Therefore, this study emphasizes the positive significance of low Blood Lipid in preventing and reducing the risk of AMI. In preventing the risk of MI, in addition to the reasonable control of Blood Pressure and Blood Glucose, we should pay more attention to the management of Blood Lipid.

In this study, we constructed a MI risk prediction model with Blood Pressure-Glucose-Lipid Patterns, Gender, Age, BMI, etc. as the main prediction indicators, and incorporated logarithmic transformation and interaction terms into the model. On the one hand, the indicators after logarithmic transformation can reduce the impact of extreme values on the prediction results. On the other hand, interaction terms can consider the potential interaction between variables based on the full use of data information. In general, the performance of the MI risk prediction model constructed in this study is acceptable, with an AUC value of 0.710 (0.606–0.814) and an accuracy of 0.821 (95%CI: 0.748–0.866).

In our application, we place special emphasis on user experience. Our application is designed to be simple, with a user-friendly interface that allows users to easily operate and interact. Our ui.R script is responsible for creating an intuitive user interface, while the server.R script is responsible for performing backend calculations. The combination of these two makes our application run smoothly and provides an excellent user experience. Our application uses a dashboard design method, which is designed to enhance human-computer interaction and allow users to easily input data and obtain prediction results. In addition, our application also includes functions such as predicting the risk of unplanned readmission and visualization, which are all to meet the needs and expectations of users.

Compared with other studies, this study has several advantages. First, compared with previous studies that explored the relationship between single influencing factors and MI, this study starts from an overall perspective and explores the association between each pattern and the risk of MI based on the perspective of Blood Pressure-Glucose-Lipid Patterns, considering more comprehensively. Second, in statistical analysis, by designing sensitivity analysis and subgroup analysis, the robustness of the results is verified.

In summary, this study summarizes three Blood Pressure-Glucose-Lipid Patterns, verifies the robustness of the results through sensitivity analysis and subgroup analysis. Based on the summary of the three Blood Pressure-Glucose-Lipid Patterns, a MI risk prediction model is constructed by combining with four prediction factors: Gender, Age, BMI, and History of COPD. On this basis, the application is completed using the R.

Acknowledgments. The work of this paper is supported by Acute Myocardial Infarction Electrocardiogram Intelligent Pre-Hospital Monitoring and Early Warning, Guangdong and Guangxi Cooperation R&D Talent Introduction (No. AC22035089) and the South China University of Technology - Guilin Medical University 5G Intelligent Medical Platform and Demonstration Base Construction (No. AD21075054), Special Program of Base Construction and Outstanding Scholarship for Science and Technology Department of Guangxi Province.

References

1. Schmitz, T., et al.: Association between acute myocardial infarction symptoms and short-and long-term mortality after the event. Can. J. Cardiol. (2024)

2. Oliveira, G.B., Avezum, A., Roever, L.:Cardiovascular disease burden: evolving knowledge of risk factors in myocardial infarction and stroke through population-based research and perspectives in global prevention. Front. Cardiovasc. Med. **2**(32) (2015)
3. The writing committee of the report on cardiovascular health and diseases in China. Chin. Circ. J. **38**(06), 583–612 (2023)
4. Connie, W.T., Aaron, W.A., Zaid, I.A., et al.: Heart disease and stroke statistics—2022 update: a report from the American heart association. Circulation, CIR0000000000001052-CIR0000000000001052 (2022)
5. Lisowska, A., Makarewicz-Wujec, M., Filipiak, K.J.:Risk factors, prognosis, and secondary prevention of myocardial infarction in young adults in Poland. Kardiologia Polska **74**(10), 1148–1153 (2016)
6. Teo, K.K., Rafiq, T.: Cardiovascular risk factors and prevention: a perspective from developing countries. Can. J. Cardiol. **37**(5), 733–743 (2021)
7. Zhang, Z., Cao, L., Zhao, Y., et al.: Hospitalized Patients with Heart Failure: Integrating Electronic Healthcare Records and External Outcome Data (version 1.2). PhysioNet (2020). https://doi.org/10.13026/8a9e-w734
8. Meeusen, W., Broeckj, V.D.: Efficiency estimation from cobb-douglas production functions with composed error. Int. Econ. Rev. 435–444 (1977)
9. Hokyou, L., Yui chiro, Y., Jemma, M.S.C., et al.: Cardiovascular risk of isolated systolic or diastolic hypertension in young adults. Cirulation, **141**(22), 1778–1786 (2020)
10. Alberto, L.M.M., Johannes, S., Andreas, F., et al.: Prevalence and Clinical characteristics of prediabetes and diabetes mellitus in young patients with ST-segment elevation myocardial infarction. Clin. Res. Cardiol. Offic. J. German Card. Soc. **110**(10), 1–12 (2021)
11. Min, Z., Hui Juan, Z., Hong Xia, Y., et al.: Trends in low-density lipoprotein cholesterol level among Chinese young adults hospitalized with first acute myocardial infarction. Ann. Transl. Med. **9**(20), 1536–1536 (2021)
12. Justyna, W., Edyta, Ł., Grzegorz, S., et al.: Association and risk factors for hypertension and dyslipidemia in young adults from poland. Int. J. Environ. Res. Public Health **20**(2), 982–982 (2023)
13. Fai, Y.E.W., Cheung, S.C.F., Tak, Y.E.Y., et al.: Effect of multifactorial treatment targets and relative importance of hemoglobin A1c, blood pressure, and low-density lipoprotein-cholesterol on cardiovascular diseases in Chinese primary care patients with type 2 diabetes mellitus: a population-based retrospective cohort study. J. Am. Heart Assoc. **6**(8), e006400–e006400 (2017)
14. Burke, P.A., Virmani, R.: Pathophysiology of acute myocardial infarction. Med. Clin. North Am. **91**(4), 553–572 (2007)
15. Qiang, Z.Y., Ting, T.F., Zheng, W., et al.: Causal associations between blood pressure and the risk of myocardial infarction: a bidirectional mendelian randomization study. Front. Cardiovasc. Med. (2022)
16. Martin, S.S., et al.:HDL cholesterol subclasses, myocardial infarction, and mortality in secondary prevention: the lipoprotein investigators collaborative. Eur. Heart J. **36**(1), 22–30 (2015)

5G MEC+AI Pathology "Anti-Cancer Guardian": Design of Intelligent Gastric Cancer Auxiliary Diagnosis and Warning Platform for Smart Hospital System

Xin Sun[1], Xin Shu[1], Juncheng Hu[1(✉)], and Chunbao Mo[2]

[1] Guilin Medical University, Guilin 541199, China
jc.hu@glmc.edu.cn
[2] Zhonglin Sci-Tech Development Group Co., Ltd., Nanning 530201, China

Abstract. Purpose: Investigate the technical means of intelligent Gastric Cancer (GC) auxiliary diagnosis and warning, providing treatment guidance for physicians. Methods: The product is developed from a technical perspective, involving algorithm design, software development, and application design. Based on the UNet3+ digital pathology slices auxiliary diagnosis method, it enables precise segmentation of breast cancer pathology slices across the entire field of view, addressing issues such as excessive network complexity, high false positives, and inadequate capture of multi-scale information in existing algorithms. Additionally, utilizing a convolutional neural network-based cancer cell image classification algorithm enables rapid generation of predictive results for pathology slices. Key algorithms in 5G Mobile Edge Computing (MEC) for smart healthcare applications facilitate specific applications of 5G technology in integrated data exchange and device integration within medical consortia, achieving offloading of computational tasks and storage content to MEC nodes. This implementation includes patient physiological indicator warning mechanisms and device management techniques based on MEC nodes. The platform assists physicians in diagnosing more efficiently, aiding patients in earlier recovery, and providing robust support for treatment. Results: The new algorithm accurately segments and predicts entire cancer pathology slices, identifying cancerous regions. Conclusion: The "AI Pathology Anti-Cancer Guardian" intelligent GC auxiliary diagnosis and warning platform can analyze gastroscopy results more quickly and accurately, aiding physicians in diagnosis and treatment.

Keywords: Gastric Cancer · Auxiliary Diagnosis · Early Warning · Deep Learning Algorithms

1 Introduction

Gastric cancer (GC) is a serious illness that can cause patients discomfort symptoms such as stomach pain, bloating, nausea, and vomiting, as well as affect their digestion and absorption abilities, leading to malnutrition and weight loss. Once GC is not detected

V. G. Duffy (Ed.): HCII 2024, LNCS 14710, pp. 313–327, 2024.
https://doi.org/10.1007/978-3-031-61063-9_21

in a timely manner, it often leads to the worsening of the condition, even progressing to advanced stages [1]. Early screening for GC enables timely treatment measures, which can increase the cure rate and survival rate, as well as help patients avoid unnecessary surgeries and chemotherapy, reducing the pain and cost of treatment. Therefore, early detection, diagnosis, and treatment are particularly important for the prevention and control of GC.

Known as the "gold standard" of pathological diagnosis, the diagnostic accuracy for cancer can exceed 95%, with a relatively low misdiagnosis rate. In traditional methods [2], if abnormalities are detected during gastroscopy, a biopsy is conducted, and pathology slides are prepared. Microscopic analysis is then performed to meticulously examine the morphology, distribution, and size of glands, glandular lumens, and cell nuclei to determine malignancy, staging, and classification. However, there are several drawbacks to this approach: Firstly, the preparation of slides is time-consuming, taking from several tens of minutes to several hours per slide. Secondly, according to statistics, the number of licensed pathologists in China is less than ten thousand, resulting in a shortfall of tens of thousands. Thirdly, there is a highly uneven distribution of pathologists across different hospital tiers. Lastly, the diagnostic accuracy can be influenced by the pathologist's experience in reviewing slides.

There is a significant disparity in the pathology departments across various levels of healthcare institutions. Most grassroots healthcare institutions lack the capability to analyze pathology slides, often having to send specimens to larger hospitals. This situation can lead to treatment delays, with consequences that are difficult to rectify.

As the connection between artificial intelligence and healthcare becomes increasingly tight, the importance of medical artificial intelligence is also growing [3]. Currently, medical artificial intelligence in China is in its growth stage, with numerous policies driving its rapid development. In the future, AI will assist in the management and research and development of hospitals and pharmaceutical companies, enhancing the level of grassroots medical institutions [4].

This project, based on artificial intelligence, analyzes GC pathology slides, reducing the diagnostic time from several days to just a few minutes. This enables faster and more accurate diagnosis, while also saving transportation costs and reducing transportation risks.

The "AI Pathology Anti-Cancer Guardian" intelligent GC auxiliary diagnosis and warning system, based on a modular approach in pathology, integrates early cancer screening warnings and auxiliary diagnosis. It assists doctors in teaching and clinical judgment of disease types and severity, facilitating a streamlined process and supporting a more efficient and secure 5G remote real-time consultation comprehensive medical collaborative service platform. Utilizing deep learning algorithms and image recognition [5], it analyzes gastroscopy results, automatically identifying and marking areas potentially affected by disease, aiding doctors in diagnosing more efficiently and assisting patients in earlier recovery [6].

The product starts from a technological standpoint, involving algorithm design, software development, and application design. It adopts the following key technologies: the UNet3+ -based digital pathology slice auxiliary diagnosis method, the convolutional neural network-based cancer cell image classification algorithm, and the key algorithms of 5G mobile edge computing (MEC) tailored for smart healthcare. These technologies assist doctors in diagnosing and treating patients more quickly and accurately, providing robust support for the medical industry.

2   Platform Introduction

2.1   Technology Roadmap

This platform focuses on key technologies of the GC pathology slice screening system, conducting research and development on whole-slide preprocessing technology, neural network design, neural network optimization, and intelligent visualization platform development. Research efforts are aimed at developing a GC pathology slice screening system based on deep learning, with a focus on overcoming challenges such as insufficient datasets, low accuracy, and poor real-time performance.

As shown in Fig. 1, the development of this system can be broadly divided into four stages: dataset creation and processing, algorithm design, software development, and clinical testing. Each stage must pass testing before proceeding to the next phase of development. In the event of test failure, debugging is required, with errors located and corrected based on identified reasons.

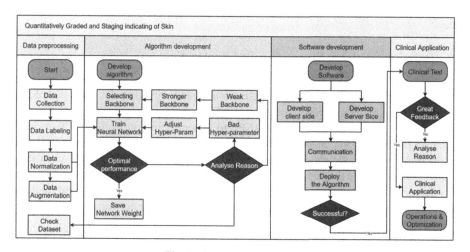

Fig. 1. Technology Roadmap.

Key points in pathology AI diagnosis include standardized slide preparation, digital processing, sufficient foundational data for algorithm training, and control of false negative rates in AI algorithms (misidentification of lesion cells as normal cells) [7]. For example, in the diagnosis of GC, the intelligent diagnosis distinguishes between "benign" and "malignant" for GC and precancerous lesions. It covers various types of adenocarcinomas, including well-differentiated, moderately differentiated, and poorly differentiated adenocarcinomas, while also studying precancerous lesions. The algorithm can also provide intelligent guidance for immunohistochemistry. The product is segmented into different modules for breast cancer, cervical cancer, etc., assisting doctors in issuing accurate diagnostic reports.

This technology can also be utilized for rapid frozen section diagnosis, offering unparalleled advantages in quantitative analysis of statistical areas, volumes, cell counts, etc. (Fig. 2)

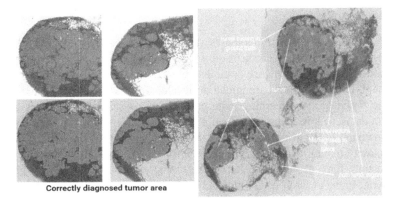

Fig. 2. Predictive heatmaps for precise identification of cancer cells.

2.2 Technical Roadmap Process Detailed Explanation

Dataset Creation and Preprocessing. First, scan the pathology slide specimens using a scanner and store the digital pathology slides on a computer. Second, use the pathology slide annotation software ASAP to annotate and export the annotations in XML format. Third, utilize the Python interface of ASPP to generate ground truth for GC lesions based on the coordinates in the XML files, and utilize Openslide (a Python package for handling pathology slides) to segment the pathology slides and ground truth into patches or tiles. Create the dataset in VOC format using PIL and OpenCV. Fourth, apply data augmentation techniques such as random flipping, random cropping, and random Gaussian blur to the dataset to enhance the effectiveness of the network.

Algorithm Design. For the identification of cancer cells, our approach mainly consists of two self-developed high-performance optimization algorithms: "One based on UNet3+ digital pathology slices auxiliary diagnosis method" and "One based on convolutional neural network for cancer cell image classification algorithm." Regarding the establishment of the 5G platform, it is based on our company's independently developed "Key technology of 5G MEC for smart healthcare."

Software Development. Firstly, frontend development based on Vue.js and Node-Webkit. Vue.js is a progressive framework for building user interfaces. When combined with Node-Webkit, it efficiently develops lightweight application software with front-end and back-end separation. Secondly, backend development based on Node.js. Node.js is a JavaScript runtime environment based on the Chrome V8 engine. It utilizes an event-driven, non-blocking I/O model for scripting, making it easy to build fast and scalable network applications. It is particularly suitable for data-intensive real-time applications running on distributed devices.

Clinical Testing. According to the requirements of "Key Points for the Evaluation of Medical Device Software Assisted by Deep Learning", AI software should submit clinical evaluation data based on clinical trials. From the perspective of clinical trials, clinical trials for AI software are essentially diagnostic trials. Therefore, in the design of trials, they share similar characteristics with traditional diagnostic trials. For example, if a certain AI software has been approved for the diagnosis of diabetic retinopathy, its main indicators are sensitivity and specificity, and the evaluation result is a simple binary variable, i.e., "diseased" or "not diseased" The trial design features are basically consistent with traditional diagnostic trials.

3 Innovative Algorithms

3.1 The Digital Pathology Slices Auxiliary Diagnosis Method Based on UNet3+

This algorithm, based on UNet3+, achieves precise segmentation of GC whole-slide pathology images. It addresses issues found in existing algorithms such as excessive network complexity, high false positive rates, and insufficient capture of multiscale information (Fig. 3).

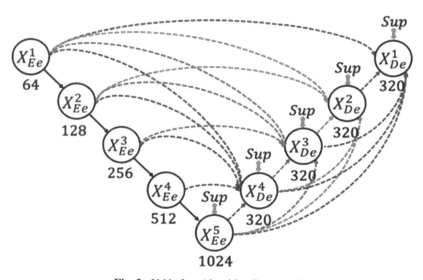

Fig. 3. U-Net3 + Algorithm Framework.

STEP 1: Generate real labels, equivalent in size to the pathology slides, excluding cavities, based on the Otsu algorithm. This step involves sequentially generating positive mask images from annotation files, extracting foreground regions using the Otsu algorithm, and finally performing an "AND" operation on the two mask images.

STEP 2: Data preprocessing algorithm, primarily based on the concept of sliding windows, ensuring that the shape of the sliding window is suitable for neural network processing.

STEP 3: Build the encoder for UNet3+ using SeResNext. Replace the convolutional layers of ResNet with grouped convolutions and add squeeze-and-excitation modules to complete the construction of the SeResNext network, preserving feature maps before each downsampling operation.

STEP 4: Design the fully concatenated U-Net3 + decoder. Adjust the shape of the encoder's output feature maps using 3×3 convolutional layers. Construct the decoder layers sequentially from the fourth to the first by concatenating feature maps. Then, perform upsampling to adjust the segmentation map to the same shape as the input image.

STEP 5: Design binary cross-entropy loss function and Dice loss function separately. Combine the two loss functions to obtain the BCE-Dice loss function. Instantiate the Adam optimizer.

STEP 6: Complete the training of UNet3+ using random negative sample sampling. Before starting, generate file collections for positive and negative samples. Randomly select the same number of samples from negative samples as positive samples to form the initial training set. Repeat the sampling process after each epoch.

STEP 7: Implement neural network prediction on whole-slide pathology images based on the tiled overlapping algorithm. Initialize two matrices of zeros, both equal in size to the original slide. One matrix stores the network's prediction results, while the other records the number of times each pixel has been predicted by the network. Utilize a sliding window with a certain stride to generate the test set for network prediction in the form of a coordinate set. The matrix recording the number of predictions for each pixel is continuously updated. Once the neural network is trained, it will predict the dataset with a certain batch size. The predicted results will be accumulated according to coordinates into the first matrix defined earlier. The final result is obtained by dividing the result matrix by the map matrix and taking the integer value (Figs. 4 and 5).

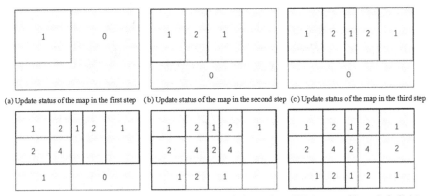

(a) Update status of the map in the first step   (b) Update status of the map in the second step   (c) Update status of the map in the third step

(d) Update status of the map in the first step   (e) Update status of the map in the second step   (f) Update status of the map in the third step

Fig. 4. Tiled Overlapping Algorithm Illustration.

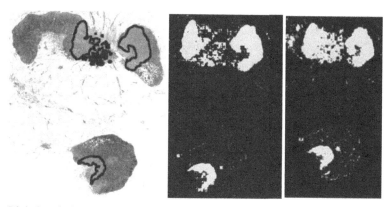

Fig. 5. Digital pathology slides and annotations, UNet3+ prediction results, UNet prediction results.

Innovation Point 1: Random Negative Sample Sampling. Target regions in medical images are often sparse, resulting in negative samples covering a much larger area than positive samples. This imbalance causes the model to be biased towards negative sample features. The most common approach is to randomly sample the same number of negative samples as positive samples, or sample negative samples at a certain ratio. Although morphologically, normal cell morphology is limited while cancer cell morphology is diverse, the features in negative samples are much fewer than those in positive samples. However, sampling negative samples only once may neglect some features in the negative samples during training, leading to severe overfitting of the model. Therefore, during training, random negative sample sampling is performed, meaning the same number of negative samples are sampled as positive samples for each epoch, and they are combined with positive samples to form the dataset.

Innovation Point 2: Using ASPP to Connect the Encoder and Decoder. In many cases, the output of a UNet-like network encoder is directly fed into the decoder. If we reduce the number of channels entering the decoder, we can cascade a 3x3 convolutional layer at the output of the encoder to reduce the dimensionality of the output channels. The innovation here is to use ASPP to connect the encoder and decoder of UNet3+. Although ASPP is originally designed to fully extract multi-scale features, UNet3+ itself already integrates multi-scale features adequately through its dense skip connections. However, introducing innovations from Deeplab, such as dilated convolutions and spatial pyramid pooling, into UNet-like networks can still leverage the advantages of Deeplab networks in U-Net3+ (Fig. 6).

Innovation Point 3: Implementing Skip Connections in UNet3+ using Depthwise Separable Convolutions. Replace conventional convolutional layers with depthwise separable convolutions to reduce the computational and parameter burden of the neural network. Since feature maps from different levels have different dimensions, the skip connections in UNet3+ are not a direct concatenation of feature maps. In the implementation of UNet3+, two 3×3 convolutional layers are concatenated for the feature maps to be joined. Each layer of the UNet3+ decoder requires concatenating five feature maps.

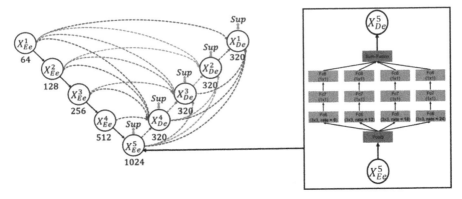

Fig. 6. Connecting the encoder and decoder using ASPP.

Consequently, before concatenation, each feature map in the decoder requires ten 3×3 convolutional layers. In order to reduce the deployment cost of the model, lightweight models have been popular in recent years. Replacing the decoder of UNet3+ with depthwise separable convolutions, by substituting depthwise separable convolutional layers for the regular convolutional layers in the UNet3+ decoder, can significantly reduce the model's parameter count and computational burden, achieving lightweight UNet3+ models (Fig. 7).

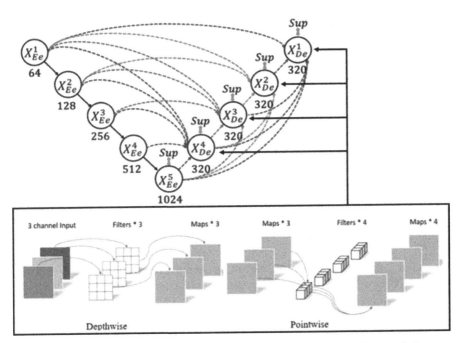

Fig. 7. Implementing the decoder of U-Net3 + using depthwise separable convolutions.

3.2 Cancer Cell Image Classification Algorithm Based on Convolutional Neural Networks

STEP1: Utilize the Otsu algorithm and color space conversion to extract tissue regions from pathological slices, eliminating blank backgrounds. In certain types of cancers, there may be empty cavity areas within glandular tissues. If these cavities are not filtered out before generating the ground truth, many of them may be annotated as positive, leading to unstable training or even non-convergence. A data preprocessing algorithm developed based on the Otsu algorithm can filter out these cavities (Fig. 8).

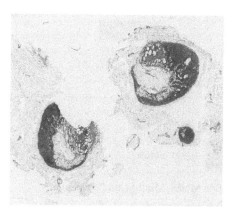

Fig. 8. Effectiveness of Tissue Region Generation Based on the Otsu Algorithm.

STEP2: Combine the extracted tissue region with the annotated cancerous regions in the pathological slides and perform overlapped sampling of the whole-slide pathological sections, ensuring overlapping segments to obtain more diverse sample data. Simultaneously, leverage the contextual information of the pathological slides to prevent disruption of certain specific structures due to segmentation.

STEP3: Employ specific image augmentation techniques tailored to the characteristics of the training samples to augment the dataset, supplementing samples with poorer recognition performance to enhance the model's generalization ability.

STEP4: Considering the diagnostic characteristics of pathologists observing pathological slides at different magnification levels, introduce multi-scale inputs into the original classification network during training and fine-tuning. This involves incorporating images of different resolutions at various stages of the original network and modifying the network's convolutional layers to adequately extract multi-scale information. Additionally, the choice of backbone network in the model can be flexibly adjusted based on the trade-off between accuracy and efficiency (Fig. 9).

STEP5: Utilize the trained model and the Overlapping Tiles algorithm to predict the entire pathology slide and identify cancerous regions. However, unlike Algorithm One, the tiling algorithm does not adopt overlapping patterns, ensuring that the cancerous areas of the pathology slide are delineated without distortion of the results 错误!未找到引用源。(Fig. 10).

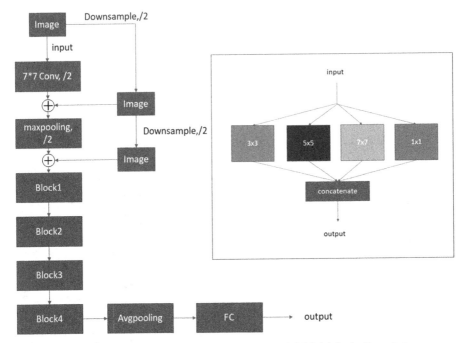

Fig. 9. Multi-Scale Cancer Cell Classification Model, Multi-Scale Convolution.

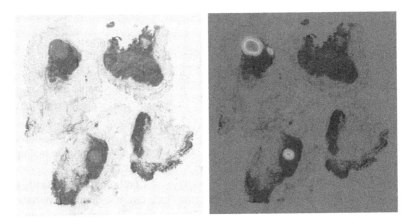

Fig. 10. Original slide, Cancer heatmap.

Innovation Point One: Introduction of Multiscale. This algorithm introduces two different types of multiscale information from the perspectives of image input and network structure. It leverages both the multiscale information presented in the original image and the combination of high-level semantic information from feature extraction at different scales.

Innovation Point Two: High Flexibility. This algorithm does not fix the backbone structure of the network and allows for flexibility to change according to practical needs. Additionally, the two modules introducing multiscale information from different perspectives are relatively independent, allowing for plug-and-play functionality. This enables coordination based on specific circumstances to balance diagnostic accuracy and speed.

3.3 Key Technologies for 5G MEC in Smart Healthcare

The specific applications of 5G technology in medical consortia include integrated data exchange and device access. Additionally, MEC nodes are utilized for offloading computing tasks and storage content. Furthermore, technologies based on MEC nodes are employed for patient physiological warning mechanisms and device management mechanisms.

In 5G data transmission, Massive MIMO significantly enhances system capacity and spectrum efficiency. For inter-hospital integrated data transmission, large-scale antenna array beamforming technology is employed to achieve precise transmission of narrow beams, enabling high-quality inter-hospital data transmission. Within hospitals, MEC nodes can also utilize Massive MIMO to form multiple spatially independent narrow beams for device connectivity, allowing for simultaneous access of multiple devices and greatly increasing device connectivity.

Within hospital-based MEC, individual edge nodes may experience overload due to local congestion caused by heavy human traffic. In such cases, a decision to offload tasks and data is made using Deep Q-Network (DQN) reinforcement learning. This method leverages idle edge node resources, such as computing power and storage, to alleviate the overload. DQN interacts with the environment to optimize and update the algorithm autonomously, allowing for adaptive adjustments based on external conditions.

Based on MEC nodes, the indicator data detected by hospital equipment will be directly analyzed at the edge nodes, requiring the edge nodes to have the capability of handling multiple data formats. Deploying deep neural networks such as CNN to standardize various data formats, using decision tree algorithms to judge patients' various indicators, and automatically alerting abnormal data. MEC nodes can also utilize their advantages of discrete distribution and location awareness to track equipment within the hospital, monitor devices by interacting with them, and achieve standardization and informatization of hospital equipment.

4 Application Design

The "AI Pathology Anti-Cancer Guardian" intelligent GC auxiliary diagnostic warning system is an advanced tool capable of automatically detecting cancerous regions in medical images. This system comprises a digital pathology slice-assisted diagnostic method based on UNet3+, a convolutional neural network-based cancer cell image classification algorithm, and advanced algorithms for 5G mobile edge computing critical technologies aimed at smart healthcare. It enables faster and more accurate identification of cancer locations, effectively reducing the risk of misdiagnosis, allowing doctors to obtain diagnostic results in a short time, and enhancing speed and quality.

In practical applications, the "AI Pathology Anti-Cancer Guardian" intelligent GC auxiliary diagnostic warning system has demonstrated high effectiveness, aiding doctors in diagnosis and assisting patients in treatment, achieving satisfactory results. The system is primarily divided into order management, user management, doctor management, and statistical management.

First, Order Management. Order Management serves as the main interface of the system and is also the most frequently used interface. On the left side of the Order Management interface are four main function switch entrances. In the middle of the order interface, there is an entrance to upload patient sample images. In the top right corner of the order interface, doctors can view the progress of diagnosis to determine if there are any incomplete diagnostic reports. In the bottom right corner of the order interface, users can view sample results to see reports that have been completed by AI diagnosis. To begin, log in to the system. If the patient is a new user, please proceed to the User Management interface to enter the new patient's information. If the patient is an existing user, the system will match the user, and the doctor will input the pathology slices. Typically, four slices are required to ensure accuracy (Fig. 11).

After AI-assisted diagnosis, preliminary diagnostic results are obtained. These results can be found for the corresponding patient in the "View Sample Results" section at the bottom right corner of the main interface. In the report details interface, AI will highlight risky areas in red. Doctors can click on the image to zoom in on the AI-identified areas or click the "Switch Original Image" button to toggle between the original and annotated images. Finally, based on the prompts provided by AI, the report will be generated (Fig. 12).

Second, User Management. In the center of the User Management interface, you can see relevant information of the entered patients. You can perform three operations by using the buttons at the bottom: Previous Page, Next Page, and Batch Export. On the right side of the interface, you can also filter by conditions. Currently supported filtering modes include Filter by grading, Filter by case library, Filter by printing status, Filter by reporting doctor, Filter by received date, Filter by report date, and Filter by hospital number.

Third, Doctor Management. In the center of the Doctor Management interface, you can see relevant information of the doctors. On the right side of the interface, you can filter by conditions. Currently supported filtering modes include Filter by grading, Filter by doctor's name, Filter by primary diagnosis doctor, Filter by reporting doctor, Filter by received date, and Filter by report date.

Fourth, Statistical Management. In the Statistical Management interface, you will see the age distribution, gender distribution, geographic distribution, early and late stage distribution, histological classification (AJCC, TNM staging), and lymph node metastasis status of the patients entered into this system.

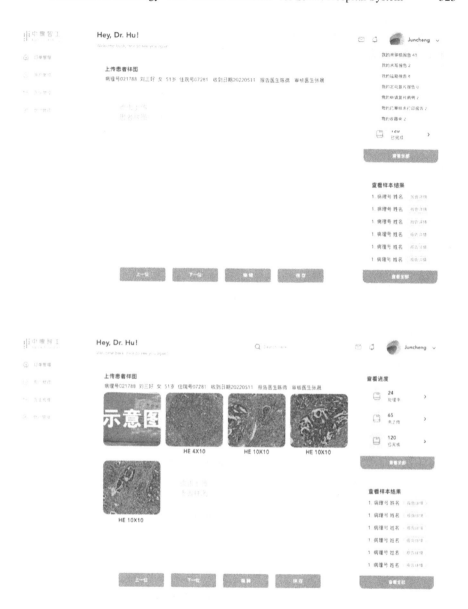

Fig. 11. Basic interface layout, uploading patient sample images.

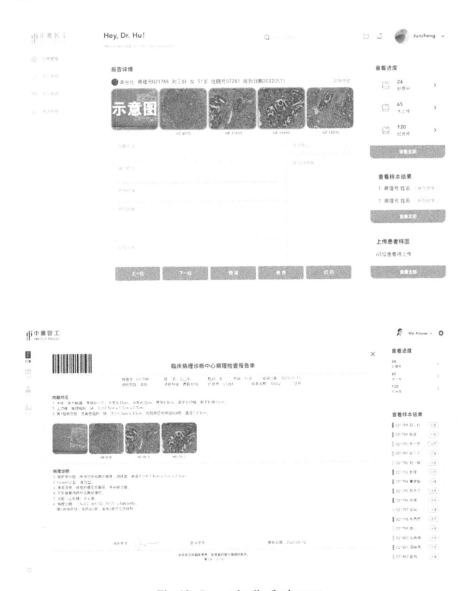

Fig. 12. Report details, final report.

5   Conclusion

The 5G MEC + AI Pathology "Anti-Cancer Guardian" intelligent GC auxiliary diagnostic warning system is an innovative technology that combines computer science and medical fields to assist doctors in analyzing and processing large amounts of medical data, providing more accurate auxiliary diagnosis and treatment recommendations. The platform not only implements intelligent GC screening and warning functions but also helps optimize the allocation of medical resources, improving the efficiency of medical services. This platform has the following advantages: Firstly, accuracy - it can utilize a large amount of medical data for training to enhance the accuracy of auxiliary diagnosis and treatment recommendations; Secondly, high efficiency - it can rapidly process large amounts of medical data; Thirdly, personalization - it can provide personalized services based on individual patient differences; Fourthly, wide applicability - it can be applied to various medical fields such as radiology and pathology. This technology has enormous potential, and it is believed that in the future, advanced artificial intelligence recognition and classification technologies based on the 5G MEC + AI Pathology "Anti-Cancer Guardian" intelligent GC auxiliary diagnostic warning platform will be more widely applied, serving the healthcare industry and human well-being.

Acknowledgments. The work of this paper is supported by Research on Smart Medical Demonstration Application System of Affiliated Hospital of Guilin Medical University Based on 5G+MEC Technology (No. AD21220072), Science and Technology Base and Talent Project of Guangxi Province, and the South China University of Technology - Guilin Medical University 5G Intelligent Medical Platform and Demonstration Base Construction (No. AD21075054), Special Program of Base Construction and Outstanding Scholarship for Science and Technology Department of Guangxi Province.

References

1. Xia, J.Y., Aadam, A.A.: Advances in screening and detection of gastric cancer. J. Surg. Oncol. **125**(7), 1104–1109 (2022). https://doi.org/10.1002/jso.26844.PMID:35481909;PMCID:PMC 9322671
2. Niu, P.H., Zhao, L.L., Wu, H.L., Zhao, D.B., Chen, Y.T.: Artificial intelligence in gastric cancer: application and future perspectives. World J. Gastroenterol. **26**(36), 5408–5419 (2020). https://doi.org/10.3748/wjg.v26.i36.5408.PMID:33024393;PMCID:PMC7520602
3. Oikawa, K., Saito, A., Kiyuna, T., Graf, H.P., Cosatto, E., Kuroda, M.: Pathological diagnosis of gastric cancers with a novel computerized analysis system. J. Pathol. Inform. **28**(8), 5 (2017). https://doi.org/10.4103/2153-3539.201114.PMID:28400994;PMCID:PMC5359998
4. Qin, Y., Deng, Y., Jiang, H., Hu, N., Song, B.: Artificial intelligence in the imaging of gastric cancer: current applications and future direction. Front. Oncol. **21**(11), 631–686 (2021). https://doi.org/10.3389/fonc.2021.631686.PMID:34367946;PMCID:PMC8335156
5. Huang, B., et al.: Accurate diagnosis and prognosis prediction of gastric cancer using deep learning on digital pathological images: a retrospective multicentre study. EBioMedicine. **73**, 103631 (2021). https://doi.org/10.1016/j.ebiom.2021.103631. Epub 2021 Oct 19. PMID: 34678610; PMCID: PMC8529077
6. Acs, B., Rantalainen, M., Hartman, J.: Artificial intelligence as the next step towards precision pathology. J. Intern. Med. **288**(1), 62–81 (2020). https://doi.org/10.1111/joim.13030. Epub 2020 Mar 3 PMID: 32128929
7. Ba, W., et al.: Assessment of deep learning assistance for the pathological diagnosis of gastric cancer. Mod Pathol. **35**(9), 1262–1268 (2022). https://doi.org/10.1038/s41379-022-01073-z. Epub 2022 PMID: 35396459; PMCID: PMC9424110
8. Noda, H., et al.: Convolutional neural network-based system for endocytoscopic diagnosis of early gastric cancer. BMC Gastroenterol.Gastroenterol. **22**(1), 237 (2022). https://doi.org/10.1186/s12876-022-02312-y.PMID:35549679;PMCID:PMC9102244

Study and Validation Protocol of Risk Prediction Model for Deep Venous Thrombosis After Severe Traumatic Brain Injury Based on Machine Learning Algorithms

Yongping Wei[1], Qin Lin[2], and Juncheng Hu[3(✉)]

[1] Neurosurgery, Guangxi International Zhuang Medicine Hospital, Nanning 530001, China
[2] Nursing Department, Guangxi International Zhuang Medicine Hospital, Nanning 530001, China
[3] School of Intelligent Medicine and Biotechnology, Guilin Medical University, Guilin 541199, China
jc.hu@glmc.edu.cn

Abstract. Traumatic Brain Injury (TBI) is a severe traumatic disease, mostly caused by external forces such as traffic accidents, collisions, falls from heights, compression, and head trauma, leading to organic damage to brain tissue. Postoperatively, patients are at risk of Deep Vein Thrombosis (DVT), directly impacting their postoperative quality of life. This paper designs observational clinical studies and validation schemes related to interdisciplinary research on this matter, aiming to study the risk prediction model of DVT in patients with severe TBI postoperatively using machine learning algorithms. It aims to grasp the risk factors for DVT in patients with severe TBI postoperatively and thoroughly analyze the relationship between these risk factors. Using a risk prediction model for DVT in patients with severe TBI postoperatively as guidance, this research constructs a model based on risk prediction line charts and conducts empirical studies to validate the application effect of the model, enabling early identification and accurate prediction of the occurrence of DVT in patients with severe TBI postoperatively. Guided by the risk prediction model for DVT in patients with severe TBI postoperatively, it provides medical personnel with effective reference for identifying and preventing DVT in patients with severe TBI postoperatively, and provides nursing reference basis for individualized prediction of DVT occurrence risk in clinical practice, thereby significantly improving the nursing experience of patients in the hospital.

Keywords: Severe Traumatic Brain Injury · Deep Vein Thrombosis Risk Prediction · Machine Learning

1 Research Background

TBI is a severe traumatic condition, often caused by external forces such as traffic accidents, impact injuries, falls from heights, compression, and head trauma, resulting in organic damage to brain tissue. It can lead to impairments in sensory, motor, cognitive, behavioral, and psychological functions. With economic development, the incidence of accidents such as traffic accidents has significantly increased. Data shows that approximately 600,000 people suffer from TBI annually in China, with 100,000 deaths attributed to it [1]. According to statistics from the Beijing Neurosurgical Institute, the incidence of TBI in China is 55.4 per 100,000 population per year, with a prevalence of 783.3 per 100,000 population, more common in males than females, and more prevalent among young adults. Regarding age distribution, some statistics from the United States indicate that the highest incidence is in the age group of 10 to 29 years, accounting for 62%; followed by the age group of 30 to 39 years, accounting for 12%; and 40 to 49 years, accounting for 8%. Clinical symptoms of TBI vary depending on the location of the injury, often presenting with symptoms such as impaired consciousness, neurological dysfunction, increased intracranial pressure, and headache, accompanied by significant positive neurological signs. The severity of TBI and the duration of coma are inversely related to prognosis [2]. Patients with TBI undergo a series of stressors such as trauma and shock, followed by intracranial hematoma clearance surgery, which aims to relieve symptoms by reducing intracranial pressure, bone flap removal, and drainage. Patients with severe conditions often require prolonged bed rest, treatment for systemic infections and dehydration, and central venous catheterization. As cerebral venous sinuses serve as capacitance vessels with slow blood flow and poor elasticity, and cortical veins enter the sinuses at varying angles, if the flow direction opposes the sinus flow, it can reduce flow velocity and lead to turbulence formation, resulting in uneven sinus surfaces and promoting thrombus formation. Prolonged bed rest, inability to move limbs voluntarily, and disturbances in coagulation mechanisms in patients after TBI predispose them to venous thromboembolism [3].

Venous Thromboembolism (VTE) has a significant impact on the incidence and mortality rates of neurosurgical patients. Identifying useful risk factors in practice is a challenge. In non-Asian patients, those lacking postoperative ambulation, and patients with complications of septic shock, the incidence of VTE is also high. This approach helps predict thromboembolism in neurosurgical patients [4].

The incidence of lower limb deep vein thrombosis (DVT) after cranial surgery is very high. Independent risk factors for lower limb DVT occurrence were determined through univariate and multivariate analysis. A nomogram was created to predict independent risk factors for lower limb DVT occurrence in patients undergoing cranial surgery. 47.7% of patients experienced lower limb DVT after cranial surgery. Patients with longer surgical duration are at higher risk of postoperative DVT, while patients undergoing intraoperative intermittent pneumatic compression have a lower likelihood of postoperative DVT [5].

84% of DVT cases occur within one week after neurosurgical procedures, with 92% occurring within two weeks. There is a linear correlation between the duration of surgery and the occurrence of DVT. Subcutaneous injection of heparin within 24 or 48 h postoperatively can reduce the incidence of DVT from 16% to 9%, without increasing bleeding complications. Although drug intervention reduces the occurrence of lower limb DVT by 43%, there is no correlation between the use of prophylactic medication at any time point and the occurrence of PE, and it does not increase bleeding at the surgical site [6].

For most ICU patients, VTE risk prediction models demonstrate good predictive performance. VTE history, mechanical ventilation, BMI > 30, and immobility are high-risk factors for VTE occurrence in ICU patients. Healthcare providers can select appropriate models based on clinical circumstances and implement personalized and precise preventive measures for patients [7].

GCS score, age, gender, intubation, ICU admission, blood transfusion, central venous catheterization, pelvic fracture, lower limb fracture, age at major surgery, obesity, injury due to motorcycle accidents, arrival at the hospital by ambulance or helicopter, pulse at emergency admission, injured body parts (including chest, abdomen, and lower limbs), and admission to the ICU are factors that improve the quality of research on VTE risk prediction in hospitalized trauma patients [8].

Female gender, history of hypertension, history of ischemic stroke, and Grade 2 collateral compensation factors may increase the risk of Intracerebral Hemorrhage (ICH) after Carotid Artery Stenting (CAS) in patients with carotid artery stenosis. A nomogram model constructed based on the above risk factors predicts CAS-related ICH with high calibration and discrimination [9].

According to multifactorial logistic Regression (LR) analysis, age, white blood cell count, neutrophil count, platelet count, admission GCS $\leq$ 8, lower limb immobilization are associated with VTE occurrence in TBI patients. Advanced age, lower limb immobilization, and admission GCS $\leq$ 8 are independent risk factors for VTE in TBI patients. A risk assessment model for predicting VTE in TBI patients is constructed based on independent risk factors for VTE in TBI, with a maximum Youden index of 0.417, sensitivity of 69.8%, specificity of 71.9%, and a predictive accuracy of 71.5%. This model demonstrates good risk prediction capabilities [10].

Surgery is the main treatment for severe TBI, with a postoperative incidence of VTE ranging from 30% to 50% [11]. Preventing postoperative venous thrombosis in patients with severe TBI is crucial for promoting patient recovery and avoiding mortality and disability. Effectively identifying the occurrence of DVT in patients after severe TBI surgery is a pressing issue that needs to be addressed.

Machine Learning (ML) is a multidisciplinary field involving probability theory, statistics, approximation theory, convex analysis, algorithm complexity theory, and other disciplines. There are many ML algorithms, including classification, regression, clustering, recommendation systems, image recognition, and more. Specific algorithms include linear regression, LR, naive Bayes, Random Forests (RF), Support Vector Machines (SVM), and neural networks. In this study, LR, Classification and Regression Trees (CART), RF, and SVM are employed to establish a risk prediction model for DVT in patients with severe TBI postoperatively. A risk prediction model utilizes principles of data mining to quantitatively predict the risk of future events [12]. LR, Cox regression, and linear regression can all be used to construct risk prediction models, with LR being the most commonly used modeling method [13]. Nomograms, as visual tools for regression models, replace complex mathematical equations with images, offering strong operability advantages, while also maintaining the precision of LR predictions [1]. Decision trees, as one of the ML methods, offer the advantage of rapid prediction [1]. The models are comprehensively evaluated from the perspectives of discrimination

(ROC curve), calibration (calibration curve), and clinical utility (decision curve analysis, DCA). All data analysis is performed using the R programming language.

As nurses are the primary operators of postoperative VTE prevention care for severe TBI patients, they need to assess postoperative complications such as DVT, improve operational readiness, implement procedural steps, and conduct overall evaluations during routine care [14]. A rapid and accurate postoperative DVT risk prediction model can help healthcare professionals reduce their workload, implement quality management for preventing DVT, and ensure patient safety.

1.1 Scientific Rationale Opinion

The project intends to use four ML algorithms: LR, CART, RF, and SVM to establish a risk prediction model for DVT in patients with severe TBI postoperatively. The model will be validated from three perspectives: discrimination (ROC curve), calibration (calibration curve), and clinical utility (decision analysis curve DCA). By establishing a risk prediction model for DVT in patients with severe TBI postoperatively, it can rapidly and accurately determine the relevant factors, influencing factors, and protective factors for patients at high risk of DVT after severe TBI surgery. This will provide healthcare professionals with more intuitive and rational reference information for making decisions regarding diagnosis, treatment, and nursing care for patients. Targeted intervention measures can be implemented during the perioperative and rehabilitation periods to prevent DVT. The research plan is scientifically designed, with reasonable statistical calculations, high feasibility, and possesses a certain level of innovation and research significance.

1.2 Engineering Methodology

This study employs four machine learning algorithms, to establish a predictive model for postoperative deep vein thrombosis risk in patients with severe TBI, LR is an efficient method and can be chosen as an example to explained.

LR is a widely used machine learning algorithm that falls under the category of classification algorithms. Its primary objective is to predict the probability of a sample belonging to a certain class. The fundamental idea is that for binary classification problems, it can directly predict the probability of a sample belonging to the positive class.

To achieve this objective, LR utilizes a special function called the Sigmoid function. This function maps any real number to the (0,1) interval, allowing us to interpret it as a probability. The expression of the Sigmoid function is shown in Eq. 1, and its function graph is depicted in Fig. 1.

$$\sigma(x) = \frac{1}{1 + e^{-x}} \tag{1}$$

In LR, we first map the feature vectors of the samples to a linear model through linear transformation (i.e., weighted sum). The function expression of this linear model, denoted as g(x), is shown in Eq. 2.

$$g(x) = w^T x = w_0 + w_1 x_1 + w_2 x_2 + w_3 x_3 + \ldots + w_n x_n \tag{2}$$

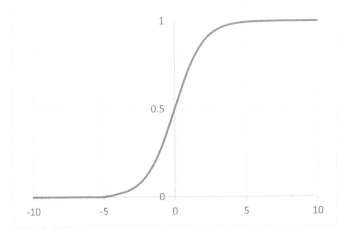

Fig. 1. Graph of the Sigmoid Function

The parameter w, which is to be determined, is often estimated using the maximum likelihood estimation method. The basic idea is to find a set of parameters that maximize the probability (likelihood) of observing the actual data under these parameters.

Then, the linear model is mapped to the (0,1) interval using the Sigmoid function to obtain the LR model. The function expression of the LR model, denoted as h(x), is shown in Eq. 3.

$$h(x) = \sigma g((x)) = \sigma\left(w^T x\right) = \frac{1}{1 + e^{-w^T x}} \tag{3}$$

To better determine the classification of our samples, we also need to plot a decision boundary, which helps us predict the type of a sample directly based on its position in the feature space. The decision boundary is depicted in Fig. 2.

Additionally, we will evaluate the model performance by plotting the ROC curve (Receiver Operating Characteristic Curve). It illustrates the true positive rate (TPR) and false positive rate (FPR) of the model at different thresholds.

In LR, we typically choose a threshold. If the predicted probability exceeds this threshold, we classify the sample as a positive instance; otherwise, we classify it as a negative instance. Different thresholds yield different TPR and FPR values. Plotting these points on a Two-Dimensional Coordinate System result in the ROC curve.

The area under the ROC curve (AUC) is used to evaluate the overall performance of a model. AUC values range between 0 and 1, where higher values indicate better model performance.

Thus, we can use the LR model to compute the probability of a sample, and based on this calculated probability, we can classify the sample. If the probability is greater than 0.5, we classify the sample as a positive instance; otherwise, we classify it as a negative instance.

LR is a simple and powerful classification algorithm that can handle both linearly separable data and linearly indivisible data by introducing techniques such as regularization. LR has a wide range of applications in many practical problems. LR also has

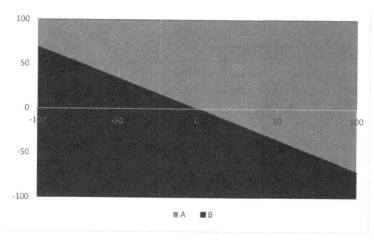

Fig. 2. Decision Boundary of LR

the following advantages: the implementation process of LR is relatively simple, the computational complexity is small, the storage occupation is low, and it can be used in big data scenarios. Online learning can be used to easily update parameters without the need to retrain the entire model. The interpretability of the model is very good, and the influence of different features on the final result can be seen from the weight of the features. LR is suitable for handling binary classification problems without the need to scale input features. Just store the feature values of each dimension. No need to assume data distribution in advance, avoiding the problems caused by inaccurate assumed distribution. It is useful for many tasks that utilize probability to assist decision-making, rather than directly judging whether it is 0 or 1 through knowledge.

2   Research Objectives

This research has three objectives, and the detailed content is as follows.

1. By studying the risk prediction model for DVT in patients with severe TBI postoperatively using ML algorithms, we aim to understand the risk factors for DVT in these patients and thoroughly analyze the relationships between these risk factors.
2. Utilizing risk prediction nomograms for DVT in patients with severe TBI postoperatively to construct models, we conduct empirical studies to validate the application effectiveness of the model. This helps in early identification and precise prediction of the occurrence of DVT in patients after severe TBI surgery.
3. With the risk prediction model for DVT in patients with severe TBI postoperatively as guidance, we aim to provide healthcare professionals with references for effectively identifying and preventing DVT in these patients. This model also serves as a nursing reference basis for clinically individualized prediction of the risk of DVT occurrence in patients after severe TBI surgery.

3 Research Design

3.1 Study Site and Study Population

Clinical Data. This study will include 509 critically ill patients undergoing neurosurgery at the Guangxi International Zhuang Medicine Hospital.

Cohort Study

Inclusion Criteria for Case Selection. Patients who meet the following conditions will be included in the study population.

1. Patients with a history of TBI, confirmed by clinical presentation and cranial CT or MRI showing skull fractures, severe brain edema, or intracranial hematoma larger than 30ml, with unstable vital signs, especially unstable blood pressure and oxygen saturation.
2. Time from injury to admission <24 h, Glasgow Coma Scale (GCS) score between 3 and 8, undergoing craniotomy for intracranial hematoma evacuation under general anesthesia, with an expected survival of more than 1 month; Caprini thrombosis risk assessment score ≥5.
3. Patients aged 18–60, of any gender, who are informed about the study and provide signed informed consent.

Exclusion Criteria for Case Selection. Patients who meet the following conditions will be excluded from the study population.

1. Patients with impaired cardiac, liver, kidney function, or diabetes.
2. Patients with a history of severe gastrointestinal injury.
3. Patients with severe coagulation disorders.

Eliminate Criteria for Case Selection. Patients who meet the following conditions will be eliminated from the study population.

1. Patients transferred or deceased during the study period.
2. Patients with missing follow-up data or unable to be followed up during the study period.
3. Patients discharged, transferred, or transferred to another department during the study, or cases unable to continue participating in the study due to serious illness during the study period.

Study Procedure. A total of 509 patients admitted to our hospital's neurosurgery department from January 2022 to June 2026, and assessed as high-risk for DVT post severe TBI surgery, were selected as the study subjects. The surgical conditions included TBI, cerebral hemorrhage, cranial tumors, vascular diseases, spinal cord diseases, intracranial infections, and functional neurological disorders.

Among them, 356 patients hospitalized from January 2022 to January 2024 were selected as the modeling group. Based on whether thrombosis occurred, they were divided into thrombus and non-thrombus groups. LR analyses were conducted on the modeling dataset to identify the correlation and influencing factors of DVT in patients post severe TBI surgery. A prediction model was established using predictive factors, and further, a prediction nomogram and CART decision tree model were constructed to observe the repeatability of the prediction model. Internal validation was conducted using Bootstrap resampling, and the risk threshold of the prediction model was determined based on the maximum Youden index principle. A calculator for predicting the risk of DVT in patients post severe TBI surgery was built using programming.

Additionally, data from 153 patients hospitalized from February 2024 to June 2026 were selected as the validation group. A ML algorithm was used to construct a risk prediction model for DVT in patients post severe TBI surgery. The DVT risk was calculated, and receiver operating characteristic curves were plotted to evaluate the model's performance. Data analysis was completed using the R programming language.

Source of Cases of Case Selection. All patients are post severe TBI surgery patients from the neurosurgery department. After review by the hospital's ethics committee, patients and their families voluntarily participated and were informed about the research content.

Sample Size of Case Selection. A total of 509 cases.

Case Groups of Case Selection. There are 356 cases in the modeling group and 153 cases in the validation group.

3.2 Methodology for Determining Sample

The determination of sample size utilizes a sample size calculation formula, where $\alpha = 0.05$, and 1.96 represents the test power. The sample size depends on the number of candidate predictor variables and the total number of participants, ensuring that each predictor variable has at least 10 outcome events (event per variable $= 10$). It is planned to select 509 patients and divide them into modeling and validation groups in a 7:3 ratio.

3.3 Technical Approach

A total of 509 patients will be selected and divided into modeling and validation groups in a 7:3 ratio. Relevant factors and influencing factors will be analyzed, and the model's effectiveness will be verified. The Model construction and validation process is illustrated in Fig. 3.

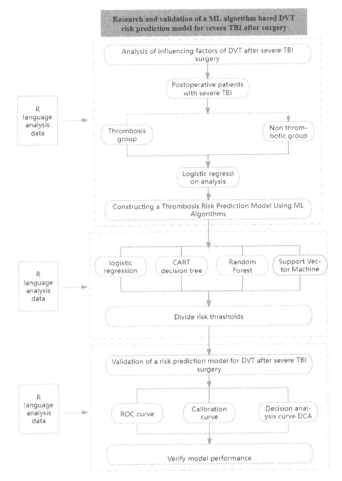

Fig. 3. Model Construction and Validation Process.

3.4 Survey Content (CRF Form)

The collection of patient demographic data and other relevant information (as outlined in the tables below) will be conducted to analyze the correlation and influencing factors contributing to the occurrence of DVT in patients post severe TBI surgery (Tables 3 and 4).

Table 1. Retrospective Research Process Table.

Research Stage		Screening Period	Data Collection Period		
		Visit 1 (V1)	Data Collection 2 (V2)	Data Collection 3 (V3)	Data Collection 4 (V4)
Activities		Days -3 to 0	Week 1	Week 2	Week 6
General Conditions	Enrollment/Exclusion Criteria	▲			
	Medical History Record 2	▲			
	Vital Signs 3	▲	▲	▲	▲
	Physical Examination	▲	▲	▲	▲
	Glasgow Coma Scale Evaluation	▲	▲	▲	▲
	Caprini Thrombosis Assessment	▲	▲	▲	▲
Physical and chemical examination	Coagulation Function Test	▲	▲	▲	▲
	Blood Routine Test	▲	▲	▲	▲
	MRI Examination	▲		▲	
	Doppler Ultrasound of Lower Limbs	▲		▲	▲
	CT Head and Chest CT	▲	▲	▲	
Efficacy Indicators	Coagulation Function Test	▲	▲	▲	▲
	Doppler Ultrasound of Lower Limbs	▲	▲	▲	▲
	Caprini Thrombosis Assessment	▲	▲	▲	▲
Others	Record Adverse Events		▲	▲	▲
	Record Concomitant Medications	▲	▲	▲	▲

Note: The flowchart and Table 1 above represent the case data required for retrospective research

Table 2. Prospective Study Process Table.

Research Stage		Screening Period	Observation Period		
		Visit 1 (V1)	Observation 2 (V2)	Observation 3 (V3)	Observation 4 (V4)
Activities		Days -3 to 0	Week 1	Week 2	Week 6
General Conditions	Enrollment/Exclusion Criteria	▲			
	Informed Consent	▲			
	Demographic Data 2	▲			
	Medical History Record 3	▲			
	Vital Signs 4	▲	▲	▲	▲
	Physical Examination	▲	▲	▲	▲
	Glasgow Coma Scale Evaluation	▲	▲	▲	▲
	Caprini Thrombosis Assessment	▲	▲	▲	▲
Physical and chemical examination	Coagulation Function Test	▲	▲	▲	▲
	Blood Routine Test	▲	▲	▲	▲
	MRI Examination	▲		▲	
	Doppler Ultrasound of Lower Limbs	▲		▲	▲
	CT Head and Chest CT	▲	▲	▲	
Efficacy Indicators	Coagulation Function Test	▲	▲	▲	▲
	Doppler Ultrasound of Lower Limbs	▲	▲	▲	▲
	Caprini Thrombosis Assessment	▲	▲	▲	▲
Others	Record Adverse Events		▲	▲	▲
	Record Concomitant Medications	▲	▲	▲	▲

Note: The flowchart and Table 2 above represent the case data required for prospective research. Demographic information (age, gender, ethnicity, marital status, occupation, education level, etc.), vital signs (temperature, heart rate, respiratory rate, blood pressure, height, weight, body position), physical examination (skin and mucous membranes, head, neck, eyes, ears, nose, throat, respiratory system, cardiovascular system, abdomen, musculoskeletal system, nervous system), laboratory tests (red blood cells (RBC), hemoglobin (HGB), white blood cells (WBC), platelets (PLT), D-dimer, prothrombin time (PT), activated partial thromboplastin time (APTT), thrombin time (TT), fibrinogen (FIB)), and auxiliary examinations (magnetic resonance imaging, CT of the head and chest, Doppler ultrasound of the lower extremities) will be collected

Table 3. Surgical VTE Risk Factor Assessment Form (Caprini).

Scoring Criteria	Risk Factors	Scoring Criteria	Risk Factors
5 points/item	□ Stroke (within 1 month) □ Selective joint replacement surgery □ Hip, pelvis, or leg fracture □ Acute spinal cord injury (paralysis) (within 1 month)	3 points/item	□ Age ≥ 75 years □ History of VTE □ Family history of VTE □ Factor V Leiden mutation □ Prothrombin G20210A mutation □ Positive lupus anticoagulant □ Positive anticardiolipin antibodies □ Elevated serum homocysteine □ Heparin-induced thrombocytopenia □ Other congenital or acquired predisposition to thrombosis
2 points/item	□ Age 61-74 (years) □ Planned arthroscopic surgery >45 min □ Planned open surgery (>45 min) □ Planned laparoscopic surgery (>45 min)	2 points/item	□ Restricted bed rest (>72h) □ Plaster immobilization □ Malignancy □ Central venous catheterization
1 point/item	□ Age 41-60 (years) □ Minor surgery □ BMI > 25 kg/m2 □ Lower limb edema □ Varicose veins □ Sepsis (within 1 month) □ Acute myocardial infarction □ Congestive heart failure (within 1 month) □ Activity restriction <72 hours □ Inflammatory bowel disease	1 point/item	□ Severe pulmonary disease (including pneumonia) (within 1 month) □ Abnormal lung function □ Oral contraceptive or hormone replacement therapy □ Pregnancy or within 1 month postpartum □ Unexplained or recurrent spontaneous abortion history
0 points	□ No above risk factors		

Import the case data dataset, read the dataset, and examine variable information. The dataset comprises 11 variables for 509 patients. V1 represents patient ID, V2-V10 denote 9 variable features calculated based on images of DVT after severe TBI, and V11 represents diagnosis. Rename variables according to their meanings. Use the sample ()

Table 4. Glasgow coma scale, GCS.

Examination Item	Patient Response	Points
Eye Opening (E)	Spontaneously	4
	To Verbal Command	3
	To Painful Stimulus	2
	No Eye Opening	1
Verbal Response (V)	Oriented and coherent	5
	Confused conversation	4
	Inappropriate words	3
	Incomprehensible sounds	2
	No verbal response	1
Motor Response (M)	Obeys commands	6
	Localizes to pain	5
	Withdraws from pain	4
	Flexion to pain	3
	Extension to pain	2
	No motor response	1

function to split the dataset into modeling and validation groups at a ratio of 7:3. Utilize the Caret package to establish four ML models: LR, CART, RF, and SVM. V2-V10 serve as predictor variables, while V11 acts as the outcome variable. Convert the Class variable into a binary classification variable for modeling convenience. Input the functions for the four ML models to obtain the risk probabilities. Assess discrimination using the plotROC package and ggtplot2 input functions library (plotROC) and library(ggplot2) to plot ROC curves. Calculate the Area Under the Curve (AUC) using the roc () and auc () functions from the pROC package to determine discrimination. Use the calibration () function from the rms package and ggplot2 package to plot calibration curves for the LR and RF models. Employ the dca () function to generate Decision Curve Analysis (DCA) curves to evaluate the clinical utility of the four models, i.e., the clinical net benefit. The research and validation of the risk prediction model for DVT after severe TBI are based on individual characteristics to statistically assess the probability of thrombosis occurrence. This assists nurses in stratifying the severity of DVT during the perioperative and postoperative periods, reveals risk features for prognosis, and provides valuable guidance and reference for nurses to implement preventive measures for patients.

3.5 Data Management and Statistical Analysis Plan

The collected research data, original electronic data forms, and optimized forms are collected, organized, and securely stored by a research team consisting of two individuals. Statistical analysis will be conducted using SPSS 23.0 statistical analysis software. For baseline data, statistical analysis will utilize one-way analysis of variance (ANOVA) for grouped data (if normally distributed and homoscedasticity is met) or the Kruskal-Wallis test for grouped data (if not normally distributed or if homoscedasticity is not met). Rank-sum tests will be used for ordinal data, frequency counts will represent categorical data, and the chi-square test will be employed. Continuous data will be presented as "n, mean $\pm$ standard deviation" (n, $\pm$ s) and analyzed using the t-test. The significance level will be set at 0.05.

4   Conclusion

From the perspective of the interdisciplinary field of medical engineering, this paper has designed a series of observational clinical studies and validation protocols. The aim is to establish a predictive model for the risk of DVT after severe TBI, rapidly and accurately identifying the correlation factors, influential factors, and protective factors for high-risk DVT patients after severe TBI. This will provide medical staff with more intuitive and rational reference information for devising diagnosis, treatment, and nursing measures for patients during the perioperative and recovery periods, enabling targeted interventions to prevent DVT. The research plan is scientifically designed, statistically reasonable, highly feasible, and has a certain level of innovation and research significance, playing a positive role in improving hospital experiences and postoperative recovery.

Acknowledgments. The work of this paper is supported by Clinical Study on Prevention of Deep Vein Thrombosis after Severe Craniocerebral Injury by Living Leech Therapy, 2022 Self-funded Research Project of Traditional Chinese Medicine Administration of Guangxi Zhuang Autonomous Region (GXZYA20220169) and the South China University of Technology - Guilin Medical University 5G Intelligent Medical Platform and Demonstration Base Construction (No. AD21075054), Special Program of Base Construction and Outstanding Scholarship for Science and Technology Department of Guangxi Province.

References

1. Emami, P., Czorlich, P., Fritzsche, F., et al.: Impact of Glasgow Coma Scale score and pupil parameters on mortality rate and outcome in pediatric and adult severe traumatic brain injury: a retrospective multicenter cohort study. J. Neurosurg. **126**(3), >60->67 (2017). 10.3171/2016. 1. JNS152385
2. Ren, C., Wang, L., Xu, Y.: Influence of early nursing intervention combined with traditional Chinese medicine treatment on rehabilitation of severe traumatic brain injury neurological function. Chin. J. Hosp. Pharm. Eval. Analy. **16**(SI), 42–43 (2016)
3. Yang, L., Huang, X., Zuo, J.: Application of OEC management mode in preventing postoperative deep vein thrombosis in patients with severe traumatic brain injury. Chin. Clin. Nurs. **13**(04) (2021)
4. Parmontree, P., Ketprathum, P., Ladnok, T., Meeaium, S., Thanaratsiriworakul, T., Sonhoim, U.: Predictive risk factors for venous thromboembolism in neurosurgical patients: a retrospective analysis single center cohort study. Ann Med Surg (Lond). **14**(77), 103628 (2022). https://doi.org/10.1016/j.amsu.2022.103628.PMID:35638055;PMCID:PMC9142669

5. Su, Z.J., Wang, H.R., Liu, L.Q., Li, N., Hong, X.Y.: Analysis of risk factors for postoperative deep vein thrombosis after craniotomy and nomogram model construction. World J. Clin. Cases. **11**(31), 7543–7552 (2023). https://doi.org/10.12998/wjcc.v11.i31.7543.PMID: 38078121;PMCID:PMC10698453

6. Khaldi, A., Helo, N., Schneck, M.J., Origitano, T.C.: Venous thromboembolism: deep venous thrombosis and pulmonary embolism in a neurosurgical population. J. Neurosurg. **114**(1), 40–46 (2011). https://doi.org/10.3171/2010.8.JNS10332. Epub 2010 Sep 3 PMID: 20815694

7. Yang, X., Ma, S.S., Xu, H.M., et al.: Systematic evaluation of risk prediction models for venous thromboembolism in ICU patients. J. Qilu Nurs. **28**(24), 24–30 (2022)

8. Fang, Q.Y., Dou, X.F., He, Q., et al.: Systematic evaluation of risk prediction models for venous thromboembolism in hospitalized trauma patients. Gen. Med. Clin. Educ. **20**(08), 750–754 (2022). https://doi.org/10.13558/j.cnki.issn1672-3686.2022.008.023

9. Zhang, M.Y., Teng, W.H., Zhang, X.J., et al.: Analysis of risk factors for intracerebral hemorrhage in CAS and construction of risk prediction model. J. Qingdao Univ. (Med. Ed.) **59**(06), 835–839 (2023). https://doi.org/10.11712/jms.2096-5532.2023.59.178

10. Li, F.X.: Analysis of risk factors for venous thromboembolism and construction of prediction model in traumatic brain injury. Shanxi Medical University (2023).https://doi.org/10.27288/d.cnki.gsxyu.2023.001088

11. Zhang, Y.: Influence of targeted nursing based on goal strategy on lower limb blood flow and deep vein thrombosis in patients with severe craniocerebral injury after surgery. Med. Res. Henan **29**(29), 5527–5529 (2020)

12. Zhang, L.Q.: Value and diagnosis of thromboelastography combined with D-dimer dynamic monitoring in the formation of deep venous thrombosis after severe craniocerebral injury. J. Brain Nervous Dis. **25**(9), 542–546 (2017)

13. Zhang, L.Q.: Application value of thromboelastography in evaluating deep venous thrombosis after severe craniocerebral injury. J. Hebei Med. Univ. **38**(10), 1148–1152 (2017)

14. Gao, Y., Qin, H., Fan, G.F., et al.: Research progress on venous thromboembolism after severe craniocerebral injury. Chin. J. Clin. Neurosurg. **23**(8), 60–62 (2018)

Author Index

V. G. Duffy (Ed.): HCII 2024, LNCS 14710, pp. 343–346, 2024.
https://doi.org/10.1007/978-3-031-61063-9